S0-BAT-559

THE USE AND ABUSE OF SOCIAL SCIENCE

TRANSACTION STUDIES IN SOCIAL POLICY

SP1 *People and Politics in the Middle East*
SP2 *The Use and Abuse of Social Science*

THE USE
AND ABUSE
OF
SOCIAL
SCIENCE

EDITED BY
IRVING LOUIS HOROWITZ

*trans*action*books*

New Brunswick, New Jersey
Distributed by E.P. Dutton & Co.

Copyright © 1971 by Transaction, Inc.
All rights reserved including the right of reproduction
in whole or in part in any form or by any means.
Printed in the United States of America
Library of Congress Catalog Number 79-140616
ISBN number: 0-87855-00101 casebound/0-87855-501-3 paperback

*tran*saction *books*
Rutgers University, New Brunswick, N.J. 08904

Preface

The essays contained in *The Use and Abuse of Social Science* are drawn from papers originally presented at a conference on the theme of social science and national policy, held in November 1969 at Rutgers University. Basically, I wanted to gather a group of people who not only write about how social science and public policy relate to each other; but more important, how social scientists working in public policy agencies perceive that relationship. In my introduction, this aspect of the conference is detailed. Suffice to say that, while every participant did not live up to the charge of the conference, most did; and even those that did not contributed new perspectives of the problem of policy-making. This they did by a mutually shared confidence in the moral nature of the process of policy-making.

The volume therefore is the rational synthesis of what transpired at the conference. And if as many problems are raised by the volume as are resolved by it, that too, is an accurate reflection of the conference proceedings. This is not said either as apologia or in resignation. Rather, the novelty of the conference, and the excitement involved, was in the general discovery that volition and choice are so much of the social world, and that therefore so much is determined by people. This shift from a deterministic to a stochastic model in appraising human events itself makes for a certain open ended quality to many of these studies.

My indebtedness is on two functional levels, separated in time by nearly a year: my appreciation for the people who funded and supported the conference and my equal sense of obligation to the people who helped me assemble this volume as a permanent record. What connects the conference to the volume is, of course, each contributor. And it is to them that I offer my sincerest thanks. I know how difficult I can be to work with at times, and their perseverance in producing these papers is at least as much a tribute to the partipant-authors, as to this participant-editor.

Heading the list of folks to whom I am obligated is S. Michael Miller of New York University. At the time, Mike was working with the Ford Foundation, and with his guidance and support, I managed to prepare a proposal that was found meaningful and meritorious enough to earn support from the National Affairs division of the Ford Foundation, in its special programs on the research and training of people working in public policy. In this connection, I must also express my appreciation to Lee Rainwater of Harvard University, who while unable to participate in the conference itself, did a tremendous amount to make sure that the initial proposal was intellectually sound and operationally feasible. David J. Pittman, head of the Social Science Institute at Washington University also gave of his time and energy to make sure that my proposal for a policy conference would not falter prematurely. Thus to Mike, Lee and Dave go my deepest thanks.

The actual details of the conference were beautifully handled by a number of people, including J. Dudley Hill, director of the Center for Continuing Education at Rutgers—which undoubtedly has some of the finest conference facilities I have ever seen. Margaret May, who was in charge of details, handled them with the mastery of an aristocratic grande dame (which she is not) and with the ebullience of a teen-ager (which she is). The staff at *trans*action, particularly Mary S. Strong, Nelson W. Aldrich, Joshua Feigenbaum, and Mary E. Curtis, saw to it that every detail from transporting the participants to recording their commentaries was taken care of. With such excellent groundwork, the preparation of the book became a matter of routine. Mary Curtis did the sort of editing that made my own work move along without trial or tribulation; and in this effort, she was greatly helped by the sensitive support of Nelson Aldrich.

In short, the organizational cooperation of the Ford Foundation, Rutgers University, and Transaction Inc. worked in concert to make this conference possible; while the human cooperation of people at each of these institutions made this conference and this volume a notable experience. But when all is written in appreciation and acknowledgement, the book remains—and it is the final product, not the pleasure and pain that went into its manufacture—that remains decisive. As a book it is for its readers to determine its worth.

Irving Louis Horowitz

Rutgers University
New Brunswick, N.J.
February 12, 1971

Contents

Preface   v

Introduction   1
    Irving Louis Horowitz

Part I
THE THEORY OF SOCIAL POLICY

Social Science for Social Policy   13
    Herbert J. Gans

The Misallocation
of Intellectual Resources in Economics   34
    Kenneth E. Boulding

Public Policy and the White Working Class   52
    John Howard

The Management of Federal Expenditures
for Research on Social Problems   71
    Benjamin Chinitz

Changing Priorities
in Government Investment in Technology   86
    Murray L. Weidenbaum

Fascist Social Policy   90
    Michael A. Ledeen

Applied Social Science and Systems Analysis   109
    Yehezkel Dror

The Social Science Study Groups   133
    Gene M. Lyons

Part II
THE PRACTICE OF SOCIAL POLICY

Public Policy and Private Interest   155
    Alvin L. Schorr

Tax-Exempt Foundations:
Their Effects on National Policy   170
    Irving Louis Horowitz and Ruth Leonora Horowitz

The Policy Researcher:
His Habitat, Care and Feeding   196
    Adam Yarmolinsky

Pitfalls and Politics in Commissioned Policy Research   212
    Kurt Lang

The Violence Commission:
Internal Politics and Public Policy   234
    Jerome H. Skolnick

Television Comes to the People of the Book   249
    Elihu Katz

Policy Scientists and Nuclear Weapons   272
    Roy E. Licklider

Policy Initiation in the American Political System   296
    Nelson W. Polsby

The Prince's Counselors:
Notes on Government Sponsored Research
on International and Foreign Affairs   309
    Pio D. Uliassi

Name and Title Index   345

Contributors   348

Introduction

IRVING LOUIS HOROWITZ

The history of social science, like most other history, tends to be carved up into decades, with each decade tidily labelled according to its dominant principle. In the 1950s we had functionalism; and developmentalism in the 1960s. For the 1970s the dominant organizing principle seems to be policy making. In the last year alone, eleven books on policy making by distinguished social scientists have crossed my desk, and there are doubtless others.[1] Even basic economic documents are being phrased in policy terms rather than strictly fiscal terms. It was once the case that economic issues were posed in terms of past performance; now they are presented in terms of "setting national priorities."[2]

There are many indications that the next few years will see a growing institutionalization of social science research and expertise as part of the policy-making process. The recent application of the program planning budget system (PPBS) to all federal government activities, the interest stimulated by work in the area of social indicators and future planning, and the ramifications of these interests throughout the executive and legislative branches of the federal government—all point to a growing use of social science in formulating and executing public

1

policy. It can be surmised that the demand for policy-related activity on the part of social scientists will increase sharply over the next decade—regardless of differences in political party "styles." In a sense, then, we are at a turning point: The question in an age of social science affluence is not the *scientific status* of the social sciences, but the *social and political uses* of these "soft" sciences.

Four areas subsume most of the specific issues that might be raised about the social science/public policy relationship. These areas are over and above the particular substantive issues of exactly what social science has to say about particular public policy issues, and whether particular public policies are or are not desirable or effective. (These substantive issues, I believe, are most appropriately dealt with in conferences devoted to particular public policy problems, such as poverty, race relations, economic policy and so forth.) The key issues that crosscut all of these substantive problems seem to be the following ones.

First, there is the issue of the autonomy of social science versus its utility, relevance, and the commitment of social scientists to do policy-relevant work. Many social scientists are concerned, both in their own work and in their evaluation of what is done by others in the field, with the problem of preserving the autonomy of social science while at the same time performing socially constructive and useful work in connection with the public policy issues that confront the nation. One discovers in the recent literature a healthy amount of polemic, but little in the way of considered, systematic analysis of this issue. (There is also, of course, a wide range in the degree to which these issues have been historically relevant to the different social sciences; economists have lived with it longer than sociologists, for example.)

Second, there is the question of the availability of social science to all parties in the formulation of public policy. The appetite of the federal government for social science consultation and research increased rapidly during the 1960s, and many social scientists are concerned about the possible weakening of pluralistic policy debate and formulation due to the competitive disadvantage of private and local governmental groups vis-a-vis federal government-al agencies because of their relative lack of access to social science knowledge, research and expertise. Recently, individual social scientists and some foundations have taken a few steps to redress

IRVING LOUIS HOROWITZ

the balance between the "knowledge resources" of government and those of private organizations involved in policy formulation.

Third, there is the question of the relationship between the design of social systems and the analysis of such systems. Increasingly, the social sciences have come to perform a role in the technological change of forms traditional to modern ways of living. This design of the future has raised a host of new issues: What is the relationship between social design and personal autonomy and choice? How does designing reflect utopian as well as ideological elements in the present state of social science information? What is the relationship between long-range planning based on generic design and short-range planning based on continuance of the status quo?

These questions have thus far not been raised in any concerted way and deserve a wide consideration in any examination of the present state of the relationship between social science and public policy.

Finally, there is the question of the readiness of the social sciences to meet the growing demand for policy-relevant knowledge and research. The traditional training of social scientists within the separate disciplines seems to set up many barriers to policy-relevant work (of course there is a range here; economics and political science have been more concerned to provide such training than have sociology, anthropology and psychology). It seems clear that policy problems do not come in neat, discipline-defined packages, but rather require the simultaneous consideration of issues that traditionally have been regarded as the province of several social science disciplines. Therefore, it seems likely that training social scientists to do policy-relevant work requires a much higher level of disciplinary pluralism than has been traditional. At the same time, however, the historical experience in training interdisciplinary applied specialists (in urban planning, housing, social welfare, international relations and so forth) is generally considered not to have been very successful.

Ever since the collapse of the "policy-science" approach in the early fifties—a collapse made inevitable by the conflicting drives of professionalism within the social sciences on one hand and conceptual fuzziness within government on the other—there has been a constant undercurrent of concern and confusion over the secular status of the social sciences; that is, the worldly use of the social sciences. This problem finally becomes dominant with the flowering of formal social science disciplines. The great shock of such things as the so-called Moynihan Report on black family life in America and Project Camelot—among others—is due at least as much to the recognition that social science is indeed capable of rendering accurate predictions and judgments, as it is to any newfound moral revulsion for functionalism in the social sciences.

The fact is, too, that we have come to a much broader and deeper realization that social science does much more (or less, as the case may be) than study strictly human interaction. In part, decisions are made and actions taken on the scantiest warranties. Stated another way, social science may in part—a large part—serve as a legitimizing mechanism for enacting or originating policy at least as often as it serves empirically to explain the world.[3]

Thus the study of policy-making has become central as we come to realize the teleological, and not just the empirical aspects of our work. There is little point in bemoaning this condition, or in stating that causality is more scientific than teleology—God knows whether this is even so; and in any event God is not around to guide the advocates of policy-making roles for social scientists, or for that matter to bail them out lest they make fools of themselves.

Since policy making is concerned with many things—some pleasant, like setting up foreign and domestic policy; and some unpleasant, like the amount of coercion and deceit that may be necessary to implement such policy—the first need is for a social science of policy making: what is studied, how, and toward what ends.

The conference from which this volume emerged dealt with the natural history of social science products: how does a piece of research get commented upon; how does a piece of research get implemented; how does it get discarded; who makes use of any research? Then there are the institutional and informational factors involved: the biases of the investigators, the stipulated and real needs of the purchasers of information; the selective use of researchers in order to screen out undesirable elements, or overrepresent others.

There are two strategies for such a conference—design it in modest terms, reach the intended goals and have the whole business ignored; or design an immodest conference, have only a

IRVING LOUIS HOROWITZ

part of the aims realized and get taken seriously. Obviously the latter technique is infinitely to be preferred.

More than that we wanted to convert the moral propositions into empirical propositions: that is, change the current currency of younger social scientists in particular from problems about the value of social science into problems about social science values. How in fact have social science findings and personnel been used in the Vietnam War or in the War on Poverty? It may turn out that we have a pseudo-problem, that is, there may not be any real utilization of social science to begin with; only rationalization.

However, once the legitimizing services of policy-oriented social science research were fully exploited, the same problems which existed at the end of World War II reappeared a quarter of a century later—cutting a deeper swath in the American fabric and in a social milieu seemingly less subject to human control and planning. The problem of converting a wartime economy to a peacetime economy is amazingly still on the agenda. The problem of mass housing for the poor and slum clearance has become accentuated over the years by engineering concepts of crash housing for mass needs. The problem of overall planning itself seems more distant of solution than in the past. Thus the enormous increase in appropriations for such research agencies as the National Institute of Mental Health and the National Aeronautics Space Agency had the effect of creating a powerful inner group of social scientists, limited in number and restricted in intellectual horizons, but it failed to crack the hard crust of longstanding social ills that led to the veritable blank check federal appropriations to begin with. Under such circumstances, the necessity for some sort of non-cliche ridden "agonizing appraisal" became apparent. And this conference can be viewed as precisely one large-scale series of reevaluations, the consequence of which is a clearer idea of the scope and limits of social science intervention into the policy processes.

At first there was a concern for bringing in recent representative styles of policy making in foreign and domestic contexts, in public as well as private settings. While this original ambition is in part realized in the composition of the conference, it is far less important than the substantive issues we took up—for they have little to do with conventional barriers, boundaries or disciplinary affiliations.

This conference was designed without the usual panoply of panelists, moderators, discussants and so forth—the assumption being that it was to be a working conference in which each major participant not only delivered a paper, but also served to inform and enlighten the works of others. The conference was a success—in the sense that it helped to move both the social scientific and policy-making communities one step closer toward the truth of this relationship and toward the good for which such enormous expenditures of energy and funds have been made.

While these essays must each be considered individually, they do, interestingly enough, seem to fall into various and sundry categories. When the questions are raised from a microscopic viewpoint, a kind of "how to do it" level, what emerges are intensely autobiographical summaries. The role of personality and idiosyncracy looms extremely large in decision making—and this holds for organizing a task force for a federal presidential commission to setting up a national television system. When the questions of policy are raised from a macroscopic viewpoint, then autobiographical concerns tend to evaporate. Instead, functional and systemic considerations seem to predominate. And whether the concerns are these same commissions, or the effort to explain all of the paradigms and vectors that enter into policy-making activities, the world created is of order and reason. It might well be that the sort of decision-making theory and game theory ostensibly used to settle policy disputes come upon the irrationalities exposed by psychoanalytic and personality models. Just how rational and therapeutic models intersect, and with what effect, remains a task better raised than answered in these exploratory papers. But at least they have the merit of being acutely raised. And this will perhaps provide a more adequate social science for handling policy questions than the "game of chicken" approach that only elevates irrationality to the level of a system.

These essays also forcefully draw to our attention the different ways in which policy-related matters can be treated. Modestly, policy serves as a handmaiden for politics. Realistically, policy provides an independent input that can be estimated along with other considerations—such as evaluations in terms of constituencies and constitutionalities. Immodestly, policy lives independent of politics. The policy sector is a world of unlisted and unredeemed experts; while politics is a world of inexperts linked to electoral processes. It is the failure to resolve these sorts of conceptual problems that made the birth of the policy sciences abortive 20 years ago when it was first announced. Where does one go to find the policy scientist? No single branch of the behavioral sciences has been willing to house the policy sciences, yet none have been quite willing to discard the possibilities in this approach. Here too, the essays reveal an acute sensitivity as to the current status of policy making *as* a science, no less than the relationship between policy making and social science.

The conference provided an opportunity for renewed attention to the problem of disciplinary excellence versus disciplinary pluralism. (The inevitability of disciplinary pluralism in the application of social science perspectives to policy is apparent in the staffing of many government agencies. It has been common for high-level government executives who are concerned with program planning budget systems, social indicators and the like, to be economists, yet the variables by which they assess policy goals are very often "sociological" ones. Similarly, in private policy-oriented organizations the responsible executives are often trained in law, yet the variables they must assess in coming to policy positions may be economic or sociological or psychological.)

Finally, a question that gets raised with a unique urgency in these essays is the relationship between the actual conduct of policy and the indirect as well as direct social science inputs. For example, Lord Keynes' economics provide the underpinning for all economic decisions made by both Democratic and Republican administrations—yet the work of John Maynard Keynes was certainly not devised with the future of American society in mind. And while there is little comparable to the impact of Keynes on economics, there have in fact been many social science researchers that are hostile to, much less uninvolved with, the efforts of federal policy making. The Millsian notion of "military-industrial complex" and the Galbraithian notion of "techno-structure" both are firmly fixed in the parlance, if not the behavior of federal political officials, yet they were not done in connection with direct policy goals. Other levels of analysis, such as studies of national development, have served as basic policy briefings for State Department and Defense Department officials; yet these too, were unsponsored and unconnected to government. Finally, there are the works that are produced in connection with policy inputs per se. But this volume raises the interesting possibility that we are spending a much larger amount for direct policy research bearing a lower payoff than is warranted. That in fact, indirect support and greater cultivation of the policy-making sector may actually be a wiser course of action than the expenditure of greater amounts of money. In short, policy making may prove to be less dependent upon policy makers than upon the general intellectual productions of a given epoch.

It is important simply to note that these essays should be judged for their individual merits. It should surprise no one that in my opinion any conglomeration of 20 brilliant minds will produce a major intellectual event. And it can be demonstrated that the problems of the seventies for the social sciences will be different, but not any less demanding than those issues that came before.

Although I have purposely exchewed any mention of the moral dimension of policy making, an avoidance made necessary by how little we know about the ways in which things work, and how much we presume to know about the ways in which things ought to work, when push turns to shove, the ethical issue of detachment or involvement—an issue that can be and has been framed in many ways and in many social science languages—remains central to our concerns. And although it may be an example of my ex cathedra ministerial commitment, I nonetheless must believe that what brought these writers all together was not so much the struggle between detachment and involvement, as the agonies of involvement as such. In this connection, it is well to listen to the words of that fine good mind of the world of Canadian letters and politics, James Eayrs. "It is the intellect of commitment which in spite of all my cautionary tales I must finally commend to you. Not just because it is in short supply. But rather because it alone enables the intellectual to do his job. A detached mind may keep watch upon itself, but it watches over wasteland. Only a mind ethically anaesthetized, morally lobotomized, remains detached from what statesmen are doing to our world."[4] If anything, the problems that link social science to public policy have grown more severe during the past few years.

NOTES

[1] Raymond A. Bauer, and Kenneth J. Gergen (editors) *The Study of Policy Formation.* New York: The Free Press—Macmillan Co., 1968; Ralph L. Beals, *Politics of Social Research: An Inquiry into the Ethics and Responsibilities of*

Social Scientists. Chicago: Aldine Publishing Co., 1969; Gunnar Boalt, *The Sociology of Research*. Carbondale and Edwardsville: Southern Illinois University Press, 1969; Lars Dencik, (editor) *Scientific Research and Politics*. Lund, Sweden: Student Literature, 1969; Yehezkel Dror, *Public Policymaking Reexamined*. San Francisco: Chandler Publishing Co., 1968; Howard E. Freeman, (General Editor) *Social Research and Social Policy*. Englewood Cliffs, N.J.: Prentice-Hall, Inc., 1969; Charles E. Lindblom, *The Policy-Making Process* Englewood Cliffs, N.J.: Prentice-Hall, Inc., 1968; Gene M. Lyons, *The Uneasy Partnership: Social Science and the Federal Government in the Twentieth Century*. New York: Russell-Sage Foundation, 1969; S.M. Miller, and Frank Reissman *Social Class and Social Policy?* New York and London: Basic Books, Inc., 1968; Michael D. Reagan, *Social Science and the Federal Patron*. New York: Oxford University Press, 1969; Richard Rose, (editor) *Policy-Making in Britain*. New York: The Free Press, 1969.

[2] Charles Schultze, (with Edward K. Hamilton and Allen Schick) *Setting National Priorities: The 1971 Budget*. Washington, D.C.: The Brookings Institution, 1970.

[3] Irving Louis Horowitz, (editor) *The Rise and Fall of Project Camelot: Studies in the Relationship Between Social Sciences and Practical Politics*. Cambridge, Mass.: M.I.T. Press, 1967.

[4] James Eayrs, *Right and Wrong in Foreign Policy*. Toronto, Canada: University of Toronto Press, 1966.

Part I
THE THEORY OF SOCIAL POLICY

Social Science
for Social Policy

HERBERT J. GANS

In recent years, planners, systems analysts, policy specialists and others at work on the formulation or design of public policy have begun to develop a niche for themselves in government, particularly in Washington and in the larger American cities. At the same time, social scientists have become interested again in policy research, partly to train the policy designers but also to conduct studies that support, broaden and criticize government policies. Much of this research has itself originated or taken place in government agencies, but it is now also emerging in the universities, so much so that institutes of policy studies may soon complement or even replace institutes of urban studies on the campus.

Intellectually speaking, policy research is still in its infancy, deriving its theory and concepts largely from the existing academic social sciences. However, since policy researchers are concerned with changing society rather than understanding it, they must have—and create—a policy-oriented social science, independent of but related to and not estranged from the academic disciplines.

I want here to describe some of the characteristics of a policy-oriented social science. My analysis begins by considering the nature of social policy and policy design, and then suggests some conceptual and theoretical requirements of a policy-oriented social science through a discussion of the shortcomings of academic social science for policy research. A final section lists these requirements in summary form. The analysis of both types of social science will draw largely on my own discipline of sociology.

THE NATURE OF SOCIAL POLICY AND POLICY DESIGN

By social policy, I mean any proposal for deliberate activity to affect the workings of society or any of its parts. Properly speaking, the prefix social is superfluous, because all policies that affect more than one person are social. However, the prefix is often used to distinguish some types of policy from others, for example, economic or environmental policy. I shall use the term social policy in its broadest meaning, to include economic, environmental and other policies, because they too are intrinsically social. Some semantic confusion might be alleviated by the term societal policy, except that it connotes deliberate activities to affect the society in toto, and I could use the term public policy, since most policy is designed for and by public agencies, except that I do not wish to exclude consideration of "private policy," designed by and for non-public agencies.

As I understand it, social policy differs from planning or social planning only in scale; a plan is nothing more than a set of interrelated social policies.[1] Similarly, social policy differs from politics largely in degree; politicians also engage in deliberate activities to affect society. They tend, however, to choose activities which can be implemented through the political institutions, whereas the designers of social policy are less limited in their choice of activities or institutions. (Of course, policy design cannot take place without attention to political considerations, and policy implementation must normally take place with the help of politicians.)

The distinctive quality of social policy is its aim for what might be called programmatic rationality; it seeks to achieve substantive goals through instrumental action programs that can be proven, logically or empirically, to achieve these goals. Political activity, on the other hand, must by its very nature emphasize the

HERBERT J. GANS

politically rational, which places greater priority on political goals such as keeping the party in office than on substantive ones, and is as likely to stress expressive programs as instrumental ones.[2] For example, politicians may well resort to symbolic appeals for "law and order" when faced with a public demand for crime reduction, even if these appeals do not achieve the substantive goal. The designer of social policy, however, will be concerned first and foremost with programs that actually lead to a reduction in crime. (Even so, he will also and inevitably pursue his own political goals, and work to expand his own agency's budget.)

A Model for Social Policy Design

Inherent in these observations is a model of social policy design, which not only describes the components of the social policy process but also spells out the kinds of social science data needed by the policy designer. As I conceive it, social policy design has three major components: goals, programs and consequences, and the policy-designer works toward the achievement of a (social) goal by the development of programs that can reasonably be predicted to achieve that goal, accompanied by an optimal set of consequences.[3] By programs, I mean simply the specific activities required for goal-achievement; by consequences, the by-products, effects or externalities of a given program. Consequences may also be understood as the benefits and costs of a program for the various sectors of society affected by it, and an optimal set of consequences is that array of maximal benefits and minimal costs which will be most effective in achieving the goal. (Obviously, there can be no single optimum here, for not only do different programs have different benefits and costs, but alternative programs which may achieve a given goal differ widely as to which sectors of society obtain benefits and which must endure costs. Indeed, the major value question the policy designer must answer is, as Harold Lasswell put it over a generation ago, who gets what.)

The determination of consequences is a vital part of social policy design, for all programs have costs and benefits, and these must be determined or at least estimated before the final draft of the policy design so that the program can be revised to eliminate costs which would prevent it from being carried out, or which would be less desirable than the goal being sought. For example, a program which is so costly that funds for it cannot be obtained obviously needs revision; similarly, a delinquency prevention program that helps to make delinquents into heroin users should be revised, for the individual and social costs of delinquency are undoubtedly less than the costs of drug addiction.

The policy designer is typically most active in three stages of the policy design process: goal-operationalizing, determining goal-program relationships and dealing with program-consequences relationships. Although he may play a role in deciding what goal is to be achieved in the first place, in most instances his employer or sponsor, whether a public agency or a ghetto protest group, will make the final decision about the goal for which policy is to be designed.[4] The designer's role, then, is to operationalize that goal, reformulating it so that he can design programs which will achieve it, estimate their consequences, and undertake the program revision to make sure that the array of consequences is optimal.[5] In this process, he must pay particular attention to assuring that the program and its consequences are beneficial to the intended clients.[6]

The Role of the Policy Researcher

So far, I have limited the discussion to policy design, as carried out by policy designers (and, of course, implementers). The policy researcher's role in this process is to provide conceptual and theoretical inputs, the necessary empirical data, the empirical "guesstimates" when data are unavailable, and a critical analysis of the policy design when it is completed.[7]

In the model I have presented, the policy researcher participates in the same three stages of the process as the designer. At the goal-operationalizing stage, the researcher may have to do some intensive interviewing in the sponsoring agency, for sponsors are often vague about the goals they seek, and when the sponsor is an agency, there is likely to be disagreement about goals as well. Without knowing how different parts of an agency feel, the policy designer may find that he has designed a program that will not engender the participation or allegiance of the total agency, for example, the lower bureaucracy of a public agency, or the less active members of a ghetto protest group. And if the goal requires participation or allegiance from clients outside the sponsoring agency, information will be required on how they feel about the goal. For example, if a sponsor seeks to improve the quality of

HERBERT J. GANS

housing among poor people, he ought to know what kind of housing these clients want and will accept: whether they will live in public housing or would prefer rent subsidies to help them compete in the private housing market. If more than one goal is being sought by the various participants in the policy design, as is often the case, the researcher can also help the designer in determining which goals are most important, if all cannot be incorporated into a single policy design.

The policy researcher must also make the designer aware of latent goals, particularly institutional maintenance or growth, for sponsoring agencies rarely pursue a policy which does not at least maintain its present level of resources or power.

The major need for policy research is, however, in the other two stages of the policy design process. First, the policy-designer needs information about which programs will achieve his goal, and wherever possible, empirical evidence to this effect. Ideally, the policy researcher should be able to provide what I have elsewhere called a policy-catalog, that is, a list of programs relevant to all possible conceivable goals from crime reduction to economic equality that have been proven, by empirical research, to achieve these goals.[8] Since both goals and programs are nearly infinite, putting together such a catalog would require an immense amount of action research, social experimentation and evaluation studies. The policy catalog would allow a policy researcher to supply a policy designer with generalized programmatic statements, based on as many cases and studies as possible, which the designer can then apply to the specific situation or community in which he is working. In this application, he may require some bridging research to move from the generalized statement to a specific program.

When the goal in question is the elimination of a social problem the policy researcher must provide findings on the major causes, those explaining most of the variance, and on the immediate causes, for the most rational programs are those that eliminate the major causes, while the most easily implemented programs are usually those that get at immediate causes.

Moreover, policy research ought to provide the policy designer with a model, as empirically based as possible, of all the components and stages of the social-political process by which a social problem is eliminated or a goal achieved. This model should include all of the *activities* involved in the process, the *agents* (institutional and other) whose normal social role is to bring these activities into being or who can be recruited to do so, and the *levers* (incentives and sanctions) needed to activate these agents. Needless to say, activities, agents and levers must all be spelled out in highly specific terms, the ideal being a step-by-step model of the process by which a present state is transformed into an end-state.

Finally,the policy researcher must provide information, or at least estimates, of the consequences of a given program, from first order to nth order effects, preferably in terms of benefits and costs of all participants, direct and indirect, in both the program and its implementation. (By indirect participants, I mean especially the bystanders of a process, who may not be directly involved but who always play a role in the political climate that can spell success or failure to a program.) Ideally, the previously described policy catalog should also provide information on the various consequences of each program, and here the research task is even more massive, for effects research is difficult to do, at best, and many of the important consequences of any program cannot be isolated empirically. Thus policy designers may have to be satisfied with informed guesses on the part of policy researchers.

The major types of research needed are about financial and political consequences. The policy designer must have data to help him determine the money costs of a program, but he must also have some estimate of indirect costs paid by various participants, as well as financial benefits that might accrue to others. Data are also needed to estimate political consequences for direct and indirect participants, that is, for whom will a given program result in increases or decreases of political power. Political must be defined broadly, however, for data are also needed on the status consequences of a policy, for any program which results in a loss of status to some indirect participants in the process will inevitably result in political opposition to the policy.

In addition, the policy researcher needs to trace all other possible consequences of a program. Ideally, he should know how the beneficiaries and all other participants will be affected by it, that is, to what extent their own behavior and important attitudes may change as a result, if only to assure the political survival of his policy. He must also have such data to make sure that programs do not cause unintended harm to intended clients or other participants in the social process being generated. For example, the policy researcher must know that a birth control program will not wreak havoc with other aspects of the conjugal relationship among the intended beneficiaries; that the cooling of interethnic or interracial conflicts among teenage gangs in a mixed neighborhood does not just transfer such conflicts to the adults; or that a racial integration program on the job or in the community does not result in a white exodus. Such data are needed, as noted before, to revise programs so that optimal consequences result, or to encourage the design of additional programs to deal with unintended but harmful consequences.

Needless to say, most of the policy research I have suggested here will never be done, and in most policy design situations, a policy researcher can draw only on his understanding of society, the social process, and the effects of deliberate intervention in the process to offer help to the designer. But even this modest role cannot be carried out properly until we begin to develop policy-oriented social science.

THE UNSUITABILITIES OF ACADEMIC SOCIAL SCIENCE

One way of thinking about the characteristics and requirements of policy-oriented social science is to look at the unsuitabilities of academic social science for policy research. That such unsuitabilities exist is obvious; academic social science seeks to understand society, not to intervene in it, resulting in many organizational, theoretical and methodological features that cannot be applied to policy research.[9] This is not a criticism of academic social science, for understanding society is a prerequisite to intervening as well as a useful task per se, and besides, policy-oriented social science needs its academic peer.

It is of course impossible to generalize about as large and variegated a phenomenon as academic social science, but it is possible to identify some prevailing theoretical and conceptual features that make it unsuitable for policy purposes. These are: its detachment, "impersonal universalism," high levels of generality and abstractness, and last but not least, its metaphysical perspectives. Moreover, as noted earlier, I will limit my analysis to one social science, sociology.

Detachment

Academic sociology, like most academic social science, views itself as detached from society. For example, academic sociologists rarely make studies to affect the workings of society; instead, they are more likely to study the people who do so. By detachment, I do not refer here to the illusory attempt at objective or value-free research, but rather to a general perspective: that of the outside observer who is examining a society in which he is not involved, at least as researcher.

The detached perspective is not helpful in policy-oriented research, for it generates theories and concepts more suitable for the bystander to the social process than the participant. Although participants must sometimes take the bystander role to be able to evaluate their participation, the policy researcher must provide dynamic theories of the social process to the policy designer so that he can find footholds from which to intervene. Parsonian theory may be useful in understanding how society as such is put together, but it does not, despite its concern with "action", supply concepts that help the policy-designer initiate action. Even Mills' study of the power elite, though hardly detached in terms of values, does not enable a policy designer to come up with policies to obtain more power for his sponsor.

Impersonal Universalism

One of the correlates of detachment is "impersonal universalism," by which I mean the concern with identifying the broad impersonal causal forces that underlie events. Academic sociology developed in reaction to older personalistic theories of human behavior, for example the Great Man theory, and sought to show that individuals cannot be understood apart from society. This mode of explanation was and still is highly useful in discouraging the overly facile application of moral opprobrium to socially caused actions, and it is useful for policy design in that it tends to focus on major causes, but policy designers also need a less universal and less impersonal approach. For example, although there can be no doubt that urbanization and industrialization are responsible for many structural changes in the family, policy designers in the area of family policy cannot do anything significant about these broad forces and require analyses that deal with more manageable causes.

HERBERT J. GANS

Policy designers also need less impersonal theories for they must, after all, design policies to be implemented among persons. The policy designer works in a sociopolitical context in which moral judgments are made, praise and blame are dealt out, and hypotheses about the motivations of actors are all important. Consequently, he must be able to understand how impersonal causes are translated into — and affect — moral judgments and motives. Similarly, while it is useful for the policy designer to know that all human beings play a multiplicity of roles and that conflicts between roles can lead to social and individual strain, he must design policies for people as combinations of roles and must know how to judge the consequences of a policy for a person who is at once a worker, homeowner, landlord, father and deacon of his church.

High Levels of Generality

The universalism of academic sociology also produces levels of generality that are often too high for the needs of policy. Although many of the social problems with which the policy designer deals may well be the results of urbanization, he must have research which tells him what specific aspects of urbanization are at play and how they affect people. Urbanization can mean many things: for example, the actual move from country to city, living at higher density than in the country, having more heterogeneous neighbors, holding an industrial rather than a rural job, participating in a more complex division of labor, or encountering the life-styles and forms of social participation that are typically found in the city. A social problem resulting from rural in-migration will have to be treated quite differently than one resulting from living at high density, and what is the policy designer to do when confronted with a group which, though it holds industrial jobs and lives in tenements in a heterogenous neighborhood, still practices the peasant life-style it brought from Europe?

Similarly, the policy designer is absolutely lost when confronted with a concept like social change, for it lumps into one term all the various activities in which he is involved. Like the Eskimo who requires more than 20 different words for snow, the policy designer must have very specific concepts of social change, which spell out for individuals, groups and institutions who or what is changing from what original position to what subsequent one, in which aspects of a person's life or group's activities, and with what consequences for the rest of his life or their activities.

Conceptual Abstractness

The high levels of generality at which much of academic social science operates also breeds conceptual abstractness which results in concepts that cannot be applied to the real-life situations in which the policy designer works. Such concepts as social structure, culture and institution are helpful in the academician's task of generalizing about human behavior, but the policy designer can only work with specific human organizations that play roles in the policy he is designing. He cannot deal with political institutions; he must deal with city hall, political parties and citizen groups. He will often be helped by information about what such groups have in common as political institutions, and what roles they play in the structure of power, but his policy must eventually involve individual organizations, and he must know exactly where the power lies in a specific situation if he is to be able to act.

Perhaps one of the most important concepts in modern sociology is class, but this concept is also of little use to the policy designer. Since classes do not exist in America as concrete entities, he cannot design policy to act on them directly; he must have data which is analyzed in terms of the specific and concrete variables that he can affect. In effect, he must break down the concept into its major components: income, occupation, education, power and prestige; for he can only design policies that affect people's earnings, jobs, schooling, political position and status. Likewise, the policy designer finds little of relevance in the descriptions of the class structure and the class cultures that sociologists develop; he can do something about poverty and poor schools but not about lower-class culture, and the sociologist's careful qualification that class cultures and life styles overlap cannot help a policy designer who must know how a specific group of people will react to a policy. He wants to know what this reaction is, not whether it is lower class or working class. He needs to know how different types of poor people will feel about the choice between a poorly paying or dirty, dead-end job and being on welfare; whether these feelings are part of a larger lower- or working-class set of norms is only of parenthetical interest. Moreover, his interest in whether people can be classified as lower or working class is limited to the

HERBERT J. GANS

consequences of the hierarchical fact that working-class people are higher in the sociopolitical pecking order than lower-class people, and may express discontent if the distinctions between the strata are altered by an antipoverty program.

Another aspect of the policy designer's conceptual needs may be illustrated by the term "slum." Aside from the fact that it is a value-laden term with some questionable empirical assumptions, it is, like class, a concept that lumps many components into one often useless whole. The policy designer's problem is that until American housing policy makes some provision for low-cost housing or rent subsidies at a scale that would allow him to propose tearing down anything that is or might be a slum, he must allocate limited resources in the most beneficial manner. Thus, he must know, not whether and how an area is a slum, but the various physical and social components of the area in question and what impact they have on their residents. This will enable him to determine which of these components are harmful and not harmful, and which are more and less harmful, so that, given limited resources, he can design a policy that will get rid of the most harmful components first.

I do not want to suggest that abstract academic concepts are irrelevant to policy; often, they are crucial but not sufficiently developed for the policy designer's purposes. A good example is the sociologist's emphasis on the distinction between manifest and latent phenomena and formal and informal groups. A great deal of highly useful research has shown the impact of latent functions and informal group patterns on the goals, structure and activities of formal organizations, and the policy designer could not work effectively without knowing about the latent and informal arrangements in group life. By and large, however, he can deal only with formal groups and their manifest activities, and he must know therefore how to develop policies which affect their informal and latent components.

The final and perhaps most important drawback of conceptual abstractness is the inaccessability of the relevant data. Until there is a plethora of policy-oriented and academic research, the policy designer will have to work with the data that are available, and these are usually limited to basic and not very subtle types, for example, census statistics. Thus, the highly developed conceptual virtuosity of the academic sociologist who has studied a lower-class community or a delinquent subculture is of little relevance to the policy designer who may know no more about a poor neighborhood than is available in census tract statistics or a health and welfare council analysis, or about delinquents than he can dredge up from police records or case worker reports. This is not the fault of academic sociology, of course, but the policy designer needs to know what he can make of the data he has.

The Metaphysics of Academic Sociology

Last but hardly least, the metaphysical assumptions of much academic sociology also make it unsuitable for policy research and design. I am not concerned here with its often conservative political bias or with the fact that all kinds of political values and implications usually enter into manifestly value-free research in the selection of topics, hypotheses and concepts. These issues have received much discussion of late, and besides, policy design is not wedded to a particular political outlook. Although most social scientists currently interested in what they call policy research tend to be left-liberals, other social scientists doing a form of policy research they call systems analysis are more frequently conservative, if not in intention at least in their work.[10] Moreover, policy design can also be reactionary, radical or anarchist. It is even possible for policy designers or researchers to be politically neutral, acting as technicians who develop programs and consequences for goals determined by others. In this case, they are neutral only in intent, for they are actually adopting the political values of those who determine the goals. As Amitai Etzioni points out, "some policy research serves those in power, some—those in opposition, but it is never neutral."[11]

Whether the goals are conservative, liberal or radical, all policy designers and researchers must accept one political value, the desirability of intervention, and in so doing, they depart from the paths of academic research. Policy design and research must be concerned with *what can be* or should be, whereas academic researchers see their task as studying *what is,* or if they are predictive, what will be. This is only another way of saying that policy research must be normative, but this in turn demands a different perspective. For one thing, the policy researcher must have a thorough understanding of what is, but only for allowing him to see how the present can be changed and at what points he can help the policy designer intervene. He must develop concep-

HERBERT J. GANS

tual bridges to enable the designer to make the transition from what is to what can be, from the present to some desired future.

Academic sociology's emphasis on what is also results in what might be called a perspective of adaptation; it is mainly interested in studying how people adapt to the situations they face, and whether they are satisfied or dissatisfied with these situations, but it is not much interested in considering how people would adapt to different circumstances, or what circumstances they want. To put it another way, academic sociology has largely studied behavior, and attitudes about that behavior (how people feel about what is),[12] it has not often studied aspiration, or what people feel they should be.[13] Ironically, despite the great influence of Talcott Parsons on American sociology, most of his colleagues have ignored one of his central themes, that individuals and groups are goal-seeking, striving to achieve their aspirations. The policy researcher must of course place great emphasis on aspirations, for here is one major bridging concept between what is and can be.

Academic sociology is also especially sensitive to obstacles to change, not because researchers are conservative, but because of its emphasis on what is. Of course, the policy designer must be aware of such obstacles, but he must also have research on the readiness for change, a subject about which academic sociology has been relatively silent, except in some recent studies of black militancy. Similarly, studies of cultural factors in behavior have often defined culture as a conservative influence, partly because it has been assumed that culture is naturally persistent and hard to change. As a result, there has been little research on the "intensity" with which cultural norms are held and except in ethnic acculturation studies, on how culture changes when opportunities improve. For example, there have been many studies of the culture of poverty or lower-class culture among the poor, but none that I know of which investigated changes in culture when poor people obtained higher incomes, or what happened to behavior when people escaped from poverty.[14] These are the kinds of studies policy designers must have; they need to know what forms of situational change bring about cultural change and vice versa, and they require measures of the intensity or nonintensity and persistence or nonpersistence of all of the components of culture, social structure and personality. Instead of academic sociology's passive stance, the policy researcher must take an active one toward the subject of his study.[15]

Another unsuitable metaphysical stance of academic sociology is the systemic bias, that is, concern with the social system rather than with its parts that prevails among more traditional sociologists. For example, most functionalists study the functions and dysfunctions of social phenomena for the society as a whole, paying less attention to the functions and dysfunctions these phenomena have for individuals and groups within the society. Similarly, traditional students of deviance and social control concern themselves with the effect of deviant behavior on society, without asking who defines deviance and society or for whose benefit social control is instituted.

Likewise, when sociologists say that society defines certain activities as criminal or that it encourages deviant behavior to reinforce conformity to its norms, they reify society as a social unit that acts for its members. This reification is based on the ideas of Emile Durkheim, who developed the concept of society from his studies of small independent tribes living in a clearly bounded territory with a distinctive social structure and often without a formal government, but such an approach is not applicable to large interdependent nations.

This is clear when one looks at American society and asks not what it is but what it actually does as a society, for an identifiable unit that acts as a society does not exist. Of course, the State, that is, government, sometimes acts as a body, occasionally on the basis of considerable consensus, but more often by shoehorning a set of political minorities into a temporary majority so that a decision can be reached by majority vote. However, that decision is made by the State, not by society, and when sociologists use the term society, they really mean the State—although even it is rarely a homogeneous monolith, but rather an array of agencies which do not always act in concert. Thus it is not American society which deprives the heroin addict of easy access to his fix, and not even the State, but certain governmental agencies, who may argue and feel that they are supported by the majority of the population, but actually only speak in the name of the State and those citizens who favor taking a hard line toward the addict. This becomes evident when one looks at governmental decisions for which consensus is clearly lacking, for example, the search for victory in Vietnam or the prohibition of marijuana. In these instances, agencies of the State are pursuing actions favored by only part of the nation, and no one would suggest that these actions are approved by society.

The systemic bias encourages findings that identify the activities and interests of dominant social groups with society as a whole, and tends to underestimate the amount of dissensus and conflict. Aside from its implicit or explicit political position, however, this bias produces data that are of little help to the policy designer. Unless he is working for the federal government or for city hall and is asked to design policies that enhance control over their territories, he needs research based on a more pluralistic perspective. Most of the time, the policies he is concerned with are intended for selected clients, and the consequences of almost any program will result in benefits for some groups and costs for others. He must therefore know more about specific populations, interest groups and institutions than about society.

A final drawback of academic sociology for the policy designer is its relative inattention to theories and concepts of power. Because of the emphasis on what is and the systemic bias, sociologists in the past have not dealt sufficiently with the role that power plays—in maintaining what is, in holding the social system together, and in the life of nonpolitical institutions generally. For example, family studies have only rarely dealt with the use of power by its various members against each other—or against other families.

The policy designer who usually works in a political institution is constantly aware of the role of power in any social group, and because he is concerned with implementing as well as designing policy, he needs research on the nature and use of power, for example, by groups who would oppose a specific program. He must also know how power can be used to implement policies— and when the power of sanctions or of incentives is called for. He particularly needs data on the extent to which the use of governmental power is effective in overcoming cultural obstacles to change. Often, cultural norms, for example, in support of racial or sexual discrimination, are weaker than they seem and can be overcome by the exercise of governmental power.

Some Positive Functions of Academic Social Science

I have dwelt at length on the ways in which academic social science is unsuitable for policy design and research, but its positive role in policy must also be acknowledged, if more briefly. Indeed, policy research could not exist without academic research.

From what little is known so far of the sociology of policy design, it is clear that both policy designer and researcher frequently become so involved in the bureaucratic and political contexts in which they operate that their own perspective extends only as far as their side of the political game. Also, both are forced to pay so much attention to minor details that they lose sight of the larger picture. And when the political battles are over and their policy is implemented, both can become so enchanted with their victory that they fail to see the faults of their policy. The war on poverty is a good example, for many thoughtful researchers and policy designers became wedded to the policies they were able to get passed by Congress and soon forgot how little relevance these policies had for eliminating poverty. Moreover, because of the bureaucratic and political contexts in which they work, policy designers and researchers often find it difficult to be innovative, to scrap bad policies or to come up with ideas for new ones.

Ideally, these faults would be best dealt with if policy researchers could look at their problems with the detachment, universalism, generality and abstractness of the academic, for they would then be able to see their policies from both sides of the political fence, evaluate them coolly for their ability to achieve the intended goal, and look for innovation when it is needed. Since it is unlikely that most policy researchers can be both policy-oriented and academic in their perspective at the same time, they need to rely on academic researchers to function as outside evaluators and critics, although these academics should obviously have a general interest in policy as well as theory.

But policy research needs its academic counterpart in at least three other ways. First, one cannot design policy for intervening in society without first understanding society, and generally speaking, the better the academic research, the better the resulting policy research and design. This is particularly true at present, when policy research is an infant industry which must build on what academics have produced before, but I suspect it will always be true, for most policy research will, by definition, be specific and concrete, and must therefore look elsewhere for more general and abstract theories and generalizations.

Second, one of the major contributions of academic research, at least potentially, is its serendipity; its ability to spawn fresh ideas, unexpected findings and productive new tangents. To put it more simply, academic research will probably always be more innovative than policy research, and as such may also be a major source of innovation in policy research. This is especially true because almost all academic studies have some implications for policy, even if they are unintended, and usually unrecognized by the academic researcher. A good policy researcher should be able to spot these implications—or the leads to implications—in even the most abstract academic study.

Third, academic research is and probably always will be the methodological model for policy research, since policy researchers are typically forced to come up with quick answers and can therefore do only quick or "dirty" research. It is quite possible that they will make some significant methodological innovations for policy research, but it is also true that when it comes to rigor, reliability, validity and the like, academic researchers will provide the technical models and will themselves be the role models for their colleagues in policy research. Moreover, once the policy researcher has made the value commitments inherent in policy research, he must follow the same norms of rigor and objectivity in data collection that obtain in the academic sphere.

SOME CONCEPTUAL AND THEORETICAL REQUIREMENTS FOR A POLICY-ORIENTED SOCIAL SCIENCE

Academic research may often be unsuitable for policy purposes, but clearly, policy research cannot develop without it.[16] If policy research ever becomes a viable institutional activity, and policy-oriented social science disciplines are able to become equal in size and competence to academic disciplines, policy researchers working in government and other action agencies will satisfy many of the academic needs I have described here from academically inclined and located policy-oriented social scientists. Until this state of affairs is reached, however, they will continue to place heavy reliance on existing academic social science.

My analysis of the unsuitability of academic social science for policy has already indicated or implied most of the major requirements of a policy-oriented social science, so that it is possible to list these here in brief and summary form.

First, the purpose of policy-oriented social science is to provide the policy designer (as well as the policy implementer) with "general" and "specific" research. The former would deal with such general issues as the nature of social policy, the role of the policy designer in its various institutional contexts, the relationship between policy and the ongoing social-political process, the nature and problems of intervention in that process. General research would presumably be the distinctive task of academic policy-oriented social scientists. Specific research, done both in the academy and in action agencies, would provide detailed data on specific substantive policy fields, such as health, housing, family life and so forth, cataloguing for each issue the programs which would achieve specific goals and the resulting consequences.

Second, specific research must be based on highly specified theories and concepts which can, wherever possible, analyze the concrete groups, organizations and institutions with which the policy designer must deal. Moreover, such theories and concepts must lend themselves to maximal operationalization, so that the findings which result from them can be easily applied to the policy process.

Third, a fundamental necessity of policy-oriented social science is a model of the social-political process that is tailored to the needs of the policy designer. Such a model must have the following features:

☐ It must view the social-political process as composed of goal-seeking groups and individuals, and must therefore provide concepts about the nature of goal-formation; the relationship between goals and behavior on the one hand, and goals and underlying values on the other.

☐ It must analyze the socio-political process in terms of the specific activities (rather than abstract behavior patterns) by which goal-seeking groups and individuals proceed, and the incentives and restraints that impinge on on them and their activities.

☐ It must attempt to explain the process in terms of specific causes, particularly major and immediate ones, for the policy designer seeks to encourage or overcome these causes in the programs he proposes.

☐ It must be a normative and future-oriented theory of action, which analyzes both what is and what can be, developing concepts that allow the policy designer to develop programs that bridge the present and the desired future. In each case, the theory must spell out the obstacles to change, the agencies and norms behind these obstacles, the strength or intensity of these obstacles, and the kinds of rewards or sanctions by which they could be overcome. (The theory must also specify what cannot be, identifying those elements of the sociopolitical process which cannot be changed by policy design and political action.)
☐ One of the central concepts in the theory of the social process must be power, for the policy designer must understand how power functions in both political and nonpolitical institutions, and what kinds of power can be exerted to implement programs.

Fourth, policy-oriented social science must of course be concerned with values; it cannot delude itself that it is value free, for it must provide the policy designer with the means to achieve values stated as goals. However, the data-gathering process must follow scrupulously the dictates of rigor and objectivity prevailing in academic social science; otherwise, it is possible that the policy researcher will supply the policy designer with findings that underestimate the difficulties and the obstacles to implementing programs.

Fifth, policy-oriented research must also be particularly concerned with the values of all those participating in or affected by a specific policy, not only to discourage the policy designer from imposing his own or his sponsor's values on the beneficiaries of the policy, but also to make sure that the designed policy bears some relevance to the aspirations of those affected by it. This is not to say that policy design must honor all existing values, for policies which provide benefits to some will also create costs to others. The policy researcher must therefore collect data not only on what values are held by people affected by a specific policy, but also how intensely these are held, and what incentives or sanctions would change them if necessary.

Finally, one of the prime values underlying policy-oriented social science and its research methods must be democracy. The policy researcher, like the policy designer, must be responsive to the values and aspirations of the people for whom they are designing policy, but their relationships with people involved in both research and policy design phases must also eschew the elitism sometimes found in academic social science which treats the researched as "subjects." People who want to participate in the research itself must be allowed to do so whenever possible, and policy research and design must be predicated on the notion of planning with, not planning for people.

NOTES

I am indebted to Gary Marx for critical comments on an earlier draft of this essay.

[1] Herbert J. Gans, "From Urbanism to Policy Planning," *Journal of the American Institute of Planners*, Vol. 36, July 1970, pp. 223-225.

[2] For a more systematic analysis of the relationship between researchers and politicians, see Irving Louis Howoritz, "The Academy and the Polity: Interaction Between Social Scientists and Federal Administrators," *Journal of Applied Behavioral Science*, Vol. 5, No. 3, 1969, pp. 309-335.

[3] The model is described in more detail in my *People and Plans*, Basic Books, 1968, Chapters 6 and 7. For a more complex version of this model, see Yehezkel Dror, "A General Systems Approach to Uses of Behavioral Sciences for Better Policy-Making," Santa Monica: RAND Corporation, May 1969, paper P-4091, and his chapter in this volume.

[4] Professionals involved in designing policy have argued about the extent to which the designer should be involved in the choice of goals: some arguing that as a professional, he has the expertise to play a major role in goal choice; others arguing that in his professional role, he should serve as a technician who limits himself to program and consequence determination, taking the goal as given; while yet others have proposed various combinations of these two polar alternatives. Although this vital question is not central to the concerns of this essay, I would argue that the policy designer is justified in advocating his own goals during the political process within the sponsoring agency, and that he is equally justified in stepping out if the process is not democratic, or if working for the democratically determined goals violates the dictates of his conscience, but that he should not set himself up as an expert who has the right to impose his own goals on others.

[5] Some planners have also argued that the planner's role is to propose several alternative programs, allowing the sponsor to make the final choice. This question is also tangential here, although it may be noted that planners have been able to espouse this notion largely because they have usually paid little attention to programmatic rationality and even less to the determination of consequences. In the real world, it is likely that for most goals, there are precious few rational programs which also result in a set of optimal consequences.

[6] J. Reiner, E. Reimer and T. Reiner, "Client Analysis and the Planning of Public Programs," in Bernard Frieden and Robert Morris, eds., *Urban Planning and Social Policy*, Basic Books, 1968, pp. 377-395.

[7] I am here considering a role as a person the policy researcher could also take a part in policy design, and as Martin Rein has often suggested,

the researcher who is not part of a policy designing bureaucracy ought to use his independence to act as a policy critic.

[8] Herbert J. Gans, "From Urbanism to Policy-Planning," *op. cit.*

[9] Henry W. Riecken, "Social Sciences and Social Problems," *Social Science Information,* Vol. 8, February 1969, pp. 101-129.

[10] On the politics of the systems analysts, see Robert Boguslaw, *The New Utopians,* Prentice Hall, 1965, Chapter 8. The re-inventors of policy research of a generation ago were also conservatives, at least by today's standards. Thus, Harold Lasswell and his colleagues developed the concept of the policy sciences in the late 1940s in part as a weapon in the Cold War. Lasswell's introduction to a book on this subject begins by noting that "the continuing crisis of national security in which we live calls for the most efficient use of the manpower, facilities and resources of the American people," and in the second paragraph refers to "the problem of overcoming the divisive tendencies of modern life and of bringing into existence a more thorough integration of the goals and methods of public and private action." See Harold Lasswell, "The Policy Orientation," in D. Lerner and H. Lasswell, *et. al.,* eds., *The Policy Sciences,* Stanford University Press, 1951, p. 3.

[11] Amitai Etzioni, "Policy Research," *American Sociologist,* forthcoming.

[12] Sociologists have of course devoted much attention to values, but largely to values implicit in behavior, that is behavioral values rather than aspirational values.

[13] The behavioral perspective of academic sociology seems to be on the wane, at least in studies of the poor. Because of the large and obvious gap between their behavior and their aspirations, most sociologists of poverty, have, since Hyman Rodman's seminal paper on the "lower class value stretch," studied these aspirations.

[14] For a more detailed analysis of these points, see my "Culture, Class and the Study of Poverty," in *People and Plans, op. cit.* Chapter 22.

[15] Amitai Etzioni, *The Active Society,* Free Press, 1968.

[16] Conversely, if and when policy research becomes established, it will undoubtedly provide a fertile source for new theories and findings in basic research, for one can often understand human behavior best when it is encouraged or forced to change.

The Misallocation of
Intellectual Resources in Economics

KENNETH E. BOULDING

The problem of the misallocation of intellectual resources has the unfortunate property of being clearly important and yet extremely intractable. We have an uneasy feeling that failures today, insofar as they are avoidable at all, are always the result of misapplied intellectual resources in the past. If we had thought about things differently or thought about different things or put our energies into the discovery of knowledge that would be relevant to present problems instead of knowledge that is not, we have a strong feeling that things would have been better. It is not easy to be wise after the event and to identify exactly what misallocation in the past prevented us from solving our problems in the present. To be wise before the event is much more difficult, for the judgment as to whether intellectual resources are being misapplied today must depend on our image of the future, and our image of the future itself is subject to serious and inevitable controversy.

Unfortunately, the general theory of allocation of resources as we find it in economics is not very helpful at this point. This theory states that if we are dividing a given quantity of resources among a number of different uses, an amount should be allocated to each use such that the marginal return per unit of resource is the same in all uses. The marginal return in any use is the additional return per additional small unit of resources employed. If the marginal returns are different in different uses, then it clearly pays to transfer resources from the uses in which marginal returns are low to the uses in which the marginal returns are high. Thus, if an extra unit of resources produces eight dollars in one use and ten dollars in another use, then if we transfer a unit of resources from the first to the second, we will lose eight dollars in the first and gain ten dollars in the second. If there is some law of diminishing returns to increasing use of resources, these transfers from uses of low marginal return to uses of high marginal return will raise the returns in the one and lower the returns in the other until they are finally equalized, at which point there is no further gain from shifting resources from among the uses and presumably the allocation is the best possible.

As a purely formal theory, this is fine, but it does not help us if we cannot measure the marginal returns; and in the case of intellectual resources this is extremely difficult, partly because of the uncertainty of the future in which these returns will be manifest and partly because of the extreme difficulty of allocating any specific future product, whatever it may be, to specific intellectual operations at the present. We simply do not know the production functions of most intellectual activity, and without this the calculation of marginal returns is virtually impossible. We have an additional problem of valuation in that many of the products of intellectual activity do not receive any obvious price in the market, so that even if we could define an aggregate of physical products of a specific intellectual activity, it might be quite difficult to calculate an overall valuation of this in terms of some numeraire, such as a dollar.

Attempts have been made to calculate the dollar value of education, for instance, at different levels and in different occupations, and this perhaps is the closest we can get to specific economic evaluations in the market of intellectual activity. There does seem to be a certain long-run tendency for the rates of return on investments in education to equalize themselves among the different occupations, if allowance is made for certain nonmonetary advantages and disadvantages of the occupation itself, such as pleasantness or unpleasantness, the prestige it offers and so on. There may be considerable imperfections in this market. There is lack of knowledge and misinvestment, as for instance when people prepare themselves as obstetricians just before a sharp decline in the birth rate. While the information system in this market could certainly be improved, we do not have a feeling that it constitutes a major social problem. Somehow the educational market does allocate resources among the preparation of doctors, dentists, surveyors, pharmacists and so on, without running into extremely sharp or socially dangerous shortages or surpluses. There is, of course, a shortage of doctors among the poor, but this is because the poor are poor, and reflects the problem of distribution of income rather than the distribution of resources. There is at present a surplus of physicists, but this is because physics has become an unstable government enterprise.

It is when we get into what I have been calling the grants economy, that is, that part of the economic system in which resources are allocated by one-way transfers, that we begin to get into trouble, mainly because of the absence of feedback and the extraordinary difficulties of evaluation. The grants economy now comprises something between 15 and 20 percent of the American economy, and it organizes a much larger proportion of the distribution of intellectual resources, simply because the education and research industries are so dominated by it. Education, which is now 7 percent of the Gross National Product, is for the most part in what might be called the public grants sector, that is, it is financed by one-way transfers of funds from authorities which derive their revenues from the use of the tax power. Even private education is financed to a very large extent by grants from parents, from foundations and from endowments. The profit-making educational institution is so rare that it is regarded as positively disreputable and finds it has difficulties in becoming accredited. Research, especially pure research, likewise is heavily concentrated in the grants economy. Even in the case of industrial research the returns are so uncertain that the research budget has many aspects of a one-way transfer.

There is an allocation problem in the grants economy just as there is in the exchange economy, simply because the total of the grants is not indefinitely expandible, even though at any one time

KENNETH E. BOULDING

it may have a modest flexibility. If the total of grants is fixed, it is very clear that a grant to A means that there is going to be no grant to B. In this case, the allocation of grants, and therefore the allocation of the resources purchased by them, is very much in the control of the grantor. It is indeed a classic case of Kenneth Galbraith's "revised sequence," in which the initiative comes from the seller, and his decisions are very largely imposed on the buyers, in this case the recipients of the grants. In the exchange economy, there is more tendency to find the "accepted sequence" in which the buyer or consumer originates demands and the producer jumps to satisfy them. In the grants economy, the proposer proposes, but the Ford Foundation disposes.

There is something that begins to simulate the market in the grants economy, insofar as there are a large number of grantors and grantees, for then the grantee can shop around among the grantors and if he is turned down from one he may get accepted from another. Potentially this is a very important check on the arbitrary power of the grantors. How important it is, unfortunately, we do not know, for the one thing that does not get into the information system is failed proposals for grants. A study of these would be extremely illuminating indeed, and would not be impossible to do. It is not self-evident, of course, that the judgment of the grantees is necessarily any better than that of the grantors, and it may well be that a system of extensive interaction between grantors and grantees is most likely to give the best results, though in any system one would have to allow for a fairly large random factor.

In the absence of any accurate feedback or information about rates of return on the use of intellectual resources, one is forced back on considerations of structure; that is, is there anything in the machinery by which intellectual resources are allocated which might lead to serious biases? In the case of research we can look both on the side of the researcher himself, or the producer of knowledge, and on the side of the grantors who are in a sense the purveyors and the users of knowledge.

The main problem in pure research is the power structure within universities where most pure research goes on: old people usually have the power and young people the ideas. Of course the optimum age of creativity varies in different disciplines. It is apparently very low in mathematics and high in philosophy, and it is clearly the result of two factors operating in opposite directions. One is the sheer quantitative deterioration of the human nervous system with age: we lose about a hundred thousand neurons a day all our life. Counteracting this is the learning process which continually rearranges the declining stock of neurons into more and more elegant patterns. It is not surprising, therefore, to find that creativity in mathematics occurs at an early age, where a rich deposit of memory and experience is not so important as the ability to call on large resources in the nervous system. In philosophy and history, however, the accumulating quality of the structure is more important than the declining quantity for a longer period of time. These very physiological facts of aging make it important in all fields to avoid concentrating the granting power too much in the hands of the old and to organize the system so that there are checks and balances and that a young man with an idea who gets a rebuff at one place can find a sympathetic ear at another. It is curious how something like the simulation of the market is almost always the answer to the problem of undesirable concentrations of power.

Another structural problem that may cause misallocation is the phenomenon of fashion. This may be more important among the grantors than among the grantees. Even in the pure sciences there are fashions in research and a spectacular success in some field is likely to attract an unusually large amount of resources. Indeed it is one of the dilemmas of the dynamics of human learning, that whereas in the economics of the intellectual life nothing succeeds like success, in the total learning process what we are most likely to learn from is failure. Here again the only structural remedy for the vagaries of fashion would seem to be the atomization of the society, that is, the development of large numbers of subcultures in which different fashions may prevail in the intellectual life. Thus, the development of "competing schools" may have some effect in preventing the tyranny of fashion, for even though this tyranny may obtain in full force in one place, the person whose insights and information fall outside the rubrics of one school may find another school to go to somewhere else. The graduate student who cannot stand economics at the University of Chicago may find the University of Texas more congenial.

The danger of monopolistic power among the grantors is probably greater than that among the grantees. This is particularly

KENNETH E. BOULDING

true as national governments increase their importance in the grants economy and become the major sources of funds for research. Here, the accidents of political power or rhetoric have the potential at least of creating very serious misallocations of intellectual resources. If there is any one major source of this misallocation it is the setting up, perhaps for partly accidental reasons, of structures and organizations which then have a strong tendency to perpetuate themselves. We see this in the United States, for instance, in the great attention paid to agriculture, partly because of the structure of Congress, which in earlier days gave excessive weight to agricultural votes, and partly because of the establishment of the Department of Agriculture and of a remarkable tradition within it of the use of intellectual resources, which goes back to the establishment of land grant colleges in 1862. In the building industry, by contrast, there has been no such political pressure group, no such organization in the Executive Branch and no "university of the building trades" to correspond to the land grant colleges. It is not surprising under these circumstances that research in agriculture has been spectacularly successful and that we have had an increase in labor productivity in agriculture of almost 6 percent per year for almost 30 years, whereas the building trades have had a very low rate of development, practically none of which has come out of the building trades themselves. The deplorable condition of our cities is perhaps the main result of this particular misallocation.

One sees a similar distortion in the case of national defense. The fact that national defense is a prime expression of the national community gives it very high priority and so there has been a very serious brain drain into it which not only has very doubtful productivity but also has seriously impaired the quantity and quality of intellectual resources in civilian occupations. Perhaps the most dramatic expression of this misallocation of resources is in the fact that we have been spending yearly in preparations for chemical and bacteriological warfare almost as much as the whole budget of all the United Nations agencies. In the light of this fact, it is hard to believe that there are not strongly pathological processes at work in the structure of world society.

We may perhaps be able to take a small step towards analyzing this problem if we take a single discipline, such as economics, and try to analyze the distribution of intellectual effort within it, in the hope that this may reveal at least gross disparities between the proportion of intellectual effort devoted to a certain theme and its basic importance. In order to do this, we have to scan the *Index of Economic Journals* from 1886, classified according to subject matter; in order to get a total picture of the output of the profession, we should, of course, include books, but this task is beyond our present resources. Besides, articles give a good picture of the distribution of interests of the actively working members of the profession and tend to be more contemporaneous than books, which are often the product of work of previous years. It is reasonable to suppose, therefore, that articles give a good index of the interest of the economics profession in any one year. We have simply counted the number of articles rather than the number of pages, not only because articles tend to be approximately the same length, but also because the presence of an article may tend to be more significant than its length. By a rough check, about 10 percent of the articles are counted more than once, by being cross-classified. We assume, however, that a double or multiple classification increases the significance of the article.

The general growth of the economics profession is shown in Figure 1. The journal articles begin with the foundation of the *Quarterly Journal of Economics* in 1886. The total number of articles reached about 150 by 1892 and fluctuated around this level until about 1909, when growth began again and continued remarkably steadily at about an average of 6.8 percent per annum until the 1940s, doubling about every 11 years. It is curious that even if we take the number of articles, say, in 1886, and compound this at 6.8 percent per annum we arrive very much where we are in the sixties! This rate of growth, incidentally, is somewhat more than that of the Gross National Product, which suggests that economics is occupying a continually larger share of the product. This is not wholly surprising, as economics is, after all, what economists call a "superior good," that is, it is a luxury, the demand for which will tend to increase with increasing incomes. In the light of this consideration, the rate of growth does not seem to be excessive. A rather striking phenomenon is the quite substantial interruption of the growth of economics by the Second World War, from which the profession apparently never really recovered in the sense that, although the old rate of growth was continued, the gap made by the war was not made up. It may

Figure 1. The Total Number of Articles in the *Index of Economic Journals*, (1886-1965)

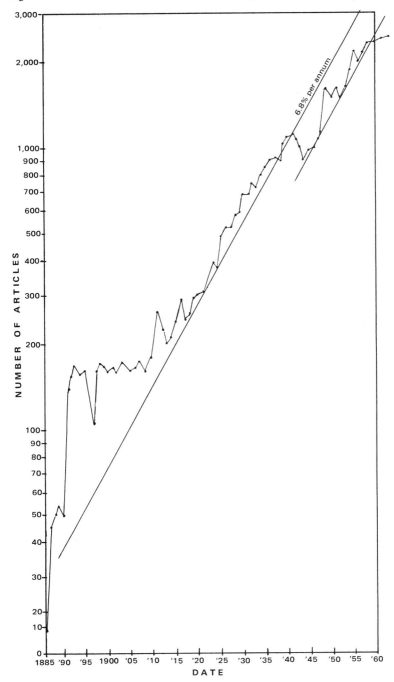

be, of course, that the rate of growth would have slackened anyhow, which would not have been surprising. But the interruption due to the war is surprisingly large and reflects the absorption of intellectuals in the war effort—and also the fact that meetings of the American Economic Association were not held during the war years.

The articles can be divided first into three categories. The first contains articles in which economists are writing to themselves, and about themselves, and about economics. This is a large category. I would put much of economic theory into it, the history of thought, and especially articles about economists, which is a large group. It is clear that economists have a fair amount of narcissism and that they like thinking about themselves and writing to each other about themselves, without a great deal of reference to the world outside. It would be interesting to know whether other scientists do as much of this. One suspects that it is particularly a habit of the social scientists and that physical and biological scientists are less given to it, but we would have to wait for a comparative analysis of other disciplines before we could confirm this hypothesis.

The second category consists of articles about the total economy, rather than about particular sectors of it. It is not always easy to distinguish these from that of the third sector, which consists of articles which refer to particular segments of the economy. The distinction, however, is necessary if we are to look at this third sector with a view to possible misallocation of intellectual resources. A very rough classification of categories gave 22 percent for the narcissistic articles, 33 percent for articles relating to the general economy, and 45 percent for articles relating to segments of the economy.

This breakdown does not seem unreasonable, though we clearly cannot impose any absolute rule on the distribution of the resources of economics among the above mentioned three sectors. We certainly expect to find all three and, while an individual may pass judgment that one of the sectors, especially the first, is excessive, it is hard to justify these judgments in any objective way. The great English economist, A.C. Pigou, is reported to have said, "We do economics because it is fun." Certainly no one would want to deprive economists or anybody else of their fun, and a great deal of the first section is fun of this kind; that is, it satisfies

KENNETH E. BOULDING

intellectual curiosity, it expresses the passion for order and consistency, and it produces at least some concepts and models that are relevant to the understanding of the economy.

Table 1 and Figure 2 show the breakdown of articles by the 23 categories of the *Index*, by ten-year periods, with the percentage of total articles in each period in each category. Considering what changes have taken place both in economics and in the world in these 80 years, the stability of these proportions is quite striking. There is a slight decline in the proportion in scope and method, a rise in theory, a decline in the history of thought, a rise (though less than might have been expected) in mathematics and statistics, a quite sharp decline in money, which is a little surprising, not much change in public finance, some rise in international economics. The proportion in economic fluctuations not surprisingly bulges in the Great Depression, although it is surprisingly high in the decade before. The proportion in war and defense economics likewise bulges in the period of the two world wars, but tails off very much in periods of peace. There is a rise in the proportion of the firm and a decline in industrial organization. The rise in the proportion in agriculture is quite striking, although it does peak in the thirties. The proportion in natural resources peaks about the same time and has been declining ever since. The proportion in labor economics has been declining and consumer economics has been fairly stationary with some ups and downs. The proportion in health, education and welfare has actually been declining until just recently, and regional planning has been increasing. The overall picture, however, is that of a very stable profession whose interests have not changed radically in 80 years. It is quite responsible to short-run changes in the economy, such as depressions and wars; it seems rather unresponsive to the long-run changes.

When we come to the distribution of effort of economists among segments of the economy, we do at least have something to compare this with in the proportion of the total economy which the particular segment occupies, as measured, for instance, by the proportion of the Gross National Product which each segment contributes. I am not suggesting, of course, that there should be a one-to-one correspondence here; some segments of the economy are intrinsically more interesting than others and have more difficult problems and one would certainly not expect to find the

Table 1
Percentage of Articles in the *Index of Economic Journals* (1886-1965), by Major Categories

	1886-1895	1896-1905	1906-1915	1916-1925	1926-1935	1936-1945	1946-1955	1956-1965	Totals	
Total no. of Articles	950	1,444	1,862	3,112	6,527	9,806	14,863	27,305	65,869	
1. Scope and Method	4.00	2.21	2.63	3.37	1.50	1.87	1.90	1.41	1.78	A
2. Economic Theory	12.21	7.76	8.81	8.26	10.39	12.56	14.45	17.49	14.40	A
3. Econ. Systems Planning	1.68	1.52	0.75	1.48	1.16	1.70	1.44	2.84	2.02	B
4. Hist. of Econ. Thought	7.26	6.03	4.56	3.18	4.19	4.36	3.66	2.99	3.64	A
5. Economic History	1.58	1.52	0.81	1.12	2.59	1.60	1.64	1.79	1.74	B
6. Contemporary Econ. Cond.	2.00	2.77	1.34	1.77	1.76	1.55	2.74	3.46	2.67	B
7. Mathematical Statistics	0.53	0.90	0.81	1.61	2.08	2.48	2.53	2.35	2.25	A
8. Social Accounting	3.26	1.04	1.61	2.60	2.38	2.03	2.78	2.99	2.64	B
9. Money, Credit & Banking	14.00	10.52	10.20	9.06	9.92	6.43	5.87	5.82	6.83	C
10. Public Finance	5.48	6.51	7.68	5.30	4.63	5.22	5.55	4.72	5.13	C
11. International Economics	7.15	8.73	6.45	8.23	8.20	6.14	9.35	9.02	8.44	C
12. Economic Fluctuations	0.21	0.21	0.32	3.21	3.27	1.88	2.20	1.92	2.06	B
13. War and Defense Econ.	0.42	1.18	2.31	7.17	0.25	9.78	2.21	0.51	2.63	C
14. Business Organizations	0.53	1.31	2.31	5.08	3.28	4.50	5.80	6.60	5.38	B
15. Industrial Organizations	13.58	20.85	21.80	14.65	17.42	13.54	11.45	11.61	13.10	B
16. Agriculture	3.37	5.67	5.64	9.54	12.73	9.54	9.91	8.72	9.32	C
17. Natural Resources	1.37	1.67	3.06	2.38	3.52	3.81	2.94	2.19	2.74	C
18. Population	1.89	1.73	1.72	1.06	1.52	0.95	0.95	0.89	1.04	B
19. Labor Economics	12.32	12.39	12.24	8.29	5.47	4.39	8.33	7.19	7.24	C
20. Consumer Economics	1.26	0.84	0.76	1.06	0.73	1.73	1.23	1.36	1.28	C
21. Health, Educ. & Welfare	4.63	2.56	2.90	0.80	1.29	1.66	1.13	1.17	1.36	C
22. Regional Planning	0.95	1.24	0.64	0.61	1.64	2.23	1.89	2.85	2.19	B
23. Unclassified	0.32	0.84	0.65	0.17	0.08	0.05	0.05	0.11	0.12	B

A = Narcissistic (22%), B = General Economics (33%), C = Segments of the Economy (45%).

distribution of intellectual resources among the segments of the economy to correspond exactly to the distribution of the Gross National Product or of National Income among the segments. Nevertheless, where there are large disproportions, questions can be raised as to why they exist. The distribution of intellectual effort, as we have seen, is a mixture of supply factors and demand factors, interest on the part of scientists constituting the demand and the interest on the part of the supporters of research constituting the supply. We can see both of these factors at work in explaining the major gaps between the proportion of resources devoted to study and the proportions of the economy.

Agriculture, as was noted earlier, is quite disproportionately studied, especially as we move towards the present. The very rapid decline in the proportion of the Gross National Product contributed by agriculture is not reflected in an equal decline in the amount of intellectual resources devoted to it. Interestingly, however, the fishing industry is much neglected (0.07 percent of total articles), especially as it presents some extremely interesting problems from the point of view of economists themselves.

At the other end of the scale from agriculture, we see things like education (0.025 percent), health (0.019 percent), and housing (0.051 percent) which have been quite scandalously neglected by economists. Education now represents more than 7 percent of the Gross National Product, by contrast with agriculture's 5 percent, and yet the output of works in the economics of education is still very small in spite of a recent upsurge. Part of the reason for this is again structural; for some reason, schools of education failed to develop departments of educational economics in the way that schools of agriculture developed departments of agricultural economics, perhaps because schools of education do not represent such an important political pressure group and also because educators themselves did not see the payoffs for latching on to the scientific revolution in the way that agriculturalists did. Whatever the reasons, the results are lamentable. One would not want to suggest, of course, that if the same intellectual resources had gone into education as have gone into agriculture in the last hundred years that education would also have developed the fantastic 6 percent per annum increase in labor productivity which we have seen in agriculture in the last 35 years. Still, it is hard to believe

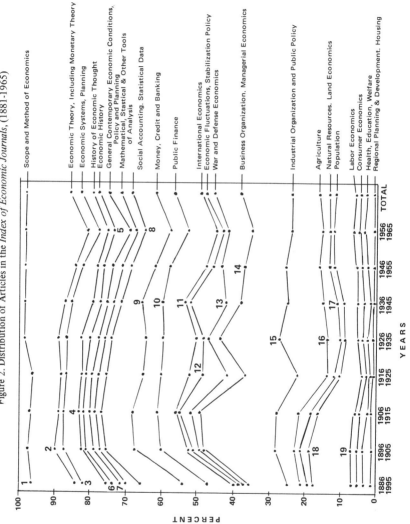

Figure 2. Distribution of Articles in the *Index of Economic Journals*, (1881-1965)

that a little more effort in the economics of education would not have had a high marginal productivity.

One sees a similar effect in medical economics. This is perhaps because these areas have been regarded as not quite worthy of the attention of economists, perhaps because they have been in the "grants sector" of the economy rather than in the market sector, and hence have been relegated to the dark underworld of doing good. Part of the difficulty here may also lie in the difficulties of measurement and the fact that the usual tools of the economists, which apply very well to the production functions of hogs, apply very poorly to the production functions of knowledge or of health.

Housing is an even more scandalous case. We might plead difficulties of measurement in the case of education and health, but housing, after all, is the production of perfectly straight-forward goods and services. Nevertheless, over 80 years there has been a mere 337 articles on housing (0.051 percent of the total) and what is worse, the interest in housing seems to have been declining ever since the 1920s. Economists were more interested in housing at the turn of the century than they are now. Here we see clear evidence of the enormous impact of demand on intellectual activity. The fact that the housing industry, by contrast with agriculture, has been anti-intellectual and anti-research, shows up dramatically in these figures.

Another much neglected area is that of war and defense economics, which rises as we might expect during the two world wars, fell to 0.51 percent of the total in the 1956-1965 decade, in spite of the fact that the war industry constitutes now about 9 percent of the GNP. The small amount of attention paid to consumer economics, only 1.36 percent of the total in 1956-65, in the light of the fact that personal consumption expenditure was 60 percent of the economy, again reflects a certain deficiency.

Table 2 shows the proportion of the total articles in a selected number of the second order classifications in which the time trend, or absence of it, is of particular interest. Thus, it is something of a shock to find that interest in the teaching of economics today is apparently less than it was in the first 50 years of the period, in spite of what seems like a good deal of current effort in the field. In economic theory, we notice the very marked increase in interest in aggregative economics and an equally

Table 2

Percentage of Articles in the *Index of Economic Journals* (1886-1965), by Selected Categories.

	1886-1895	1896-1905	1906-1915	1916-1925	1926-1935	1936-1945	1946-1955	1956-1965	Totals
1.3 Teaching of Economics	0.73	0.48	1.40	1.19	0.40	0.39	0.36	0.33	0.43
2.1 Value, Price, and Allocation Theory	2.73	2.56	3.44	3.12	4.15	4.82	5.28	5.58	4.98
2.2 Factors of Production & Distributive Shares	7.58	3.12	3.22	2.15	2.31	2.34	1.86	2.06	2.22
2.3 Aggregative & Monetary Theory, Cycles, Growth	0.85	1.25	1.13	2.09	3.68	4.85	6.32	8.93	6.38
3.2 Socialist & Communist Systems. Soviet Econ.	0.21	0.14	0.11	0.09	0.13	0.42	0.18	1.52	0.76
3.4 Cooperation. Cooperative Societies	1.26	1.04	0.27	0.77	0.14	0.18	0.17	0.19	0.24
4.8 Individuals (A-Z)	4.52	4.64	4.08	2.48	3.07	3.37	2.71	2.13	2.70
7.2 Statistical and Econometric Methods	0.21	0.90	0.75	1.55	1.88	2.18	1.78	1.55	1.67
9.2 Money. Currency. Monetary Standards	7.27	5.75	1.93	2.21	1.49	1.19	0.58	0.40	1.01
9.6 Prices. Inflation. Deflation	1.15	0.55	1.08	0.77	0.66	0.42	0.42	0.45	0.51
9.9 Monetary Policy. Central Banks	0.84	0.55	2.42	1.64	1.79	1.16	2.07	1.71	1.70
11.3 Balance of Payments. Mechanisms of Adjust.	2.10	0.97	1.18	3.79	3.82	2.95	5.71	4.17	4.09
12.2 Fluctuations. Forecasting	0.21	0.21	0.27	2.86	2.10	0.78	0.67	0.80	0.96
14.2 The Firm. The Businessman	0.43	0.55	1.18	1.45	1.06	0.72	1.21	1.12	1.07
14.5 Marketing	—	0.21	—	1.06	0.75	2.01	1.63	1.99	1.62
15.2 Market Structure and Behavior	0.84	2.14	1.34	1.09	1.10	1.38	1.20	1.66	1.42
15.6 Public Utilities. Electricity. Gas. Water	0.42	0.83	1.23	1.51	3.48	2.09	0.80	0.53	1.18
15.8 Transportation	5.37	5.96	8.54	3.79	3.69	2.13	1.73	1.76	2.43
17.2 Conservation	—	—	0.06	0.03	0.07	0.19	0.10	0.06	0.09
17.3 Land Economics	0.95	1.39	2.31	1.96	3.17	3.23	2.25	1.42	2.09
17.4 Forests	—	0.07	0.16	0.19	0.14	0.14	0.21	0.16	0.16
17.5 Fisheries	—	—	0.16	0.07	0.06	0.03	0.06	0.09	0.07
17.6 Water Resources	0.10	0.14	0.11	0.03	0.05	0.03	0.14	0.21	0.14
17.7 Minerals	0.32	0.07	0.05	0.03	0.01	0.07	0.07	0.11	0.08
20.2 Empirical Studies	1.05	0.70	0.70	1.00	0.62	1.50	1.16	1.21	1.14
21.4 Old Age Economics and Assistance	1.05	0.35	0.38	—	0.60	0.07	0.17	0.06	0.10
21.6 Unemployment Assistance	0.74	0.62	0.43	0.07	0.60	0.31	0.11	0.10	0.22
21.7 Medical Economics	0.31	0.14	0.53	0.06	0.12	0.09	0.24	0.10	0.18
21.8 Economics of Education	0.21	0.07	0.17	0.16	0.09	0.19	0.08	0.19	0.25
22.3 Urban-Metropolitan Studies	0.32	0.14	0.48	0.12	0.51	0.63	0.55	0.48	0.68
22.5 Housing	0.42	1.03	0.11	0.19	0.82	0.83	0.63	0.29	0.51

marked decline in interest in factors of production, with a slight increase, especially in recent years, in concern with socialist and communist systems and a not wholly surprising decline in concern with cooperation. The rise in studies of statistical and econometric methods is, of course, to be expected. Note, however, that these interests seem to have peaked some 30 years ago. The decline of studies of currency and monetary standards is very noticeable. The decline in interest in prices is perhaps more surprising. And it may come as a slight shock to members of the Chicago school to find that interest in monetary policy apparently peaked about 1910.

In international economics, the rise of concern with the balance of payments is rather surprising, and it is a little surprising also to find that interest in economic fluctuations peaked about 1920. We noted earlier the sharp fluctuations in interest in war and defense economics. It is curious that studies of the firm, indeed in business organization in general, which was rather low in the early years, rose sharply in the first decade of the century, and has remained fairly high ever since. It is a little sobering that the peak of interest in market structure was around 1900, long before the development of the theory of imperfect competition. The rise and decline of concern with public utilities is an odd phenomenon, reaching a sharp peak about 1930. Interest in transportation likewise has declined very sharply from its peak in the 1910 decade, which is a little surprising in the light of the fact that we feel such an acute crisis in this field at the moment.

In view of the current excitement about the environment, the very small interest in conservation, which peaked around 1940, and indeed in all the natural resource areas, is a striking comment on how ill-prepared we are to deal with the present environmental crisis. Even population studies were at their height in the first decade of this period and have declined fairly steadily ever since. It is sobering, too, to find that we were almost as much interested in empirical studies in consumer economics in the first decade as we were in the last of this whole period. We have already noted the shocking lack of interest in health, education and welfare, and what is even worse, the declining interest in this section. We were much more concerned with old age economics and unemployment insurance and even in medical economics around 1890 than we are now. The recent upsurge of studies in the economics of education has only brought it to double the minute proportion of the first decade. It is shocking to find that the interest in housing reached its peak about 1900, and that, in spite of the current to-do about urban metropolitan studies, interest has risen quite modestly since the early days.

There are many significant questions, of course, which cannot be answered by an analysis of this kind. It would require much more intricate and intensive analysis, for instance, to answer the question of the interrelation among these various parts of the structure. How far, for instance, did empirical studies modify the theories and the theories direct attention toward new empirical studies? This is perhaps one of the most interesting questions in the theory of epistemology, yet it is a question that is very hard to answer, especially with the rather superficial data of this paper.

One provocative conclusion, however tentative, is that the changes in the methodology of economics in this period did not very much affect its structure. The mathematical revolution in economics, of course, was underway even before the beginning of this period, with W.S. Jevons and Leon Walras coming in 1870, so that the period does not reflect the first transition from the more literary kind of economics and the use of mathematics grows very substantially during this whole period, something which this type of analysis underestimates. A count of the number of lines of mathematical symbols in these journals would, of course, be very interesting, but quite beyond the resources of this study. It would certainly reveal a very rapid increase, especially in the last 30 years. Refinement of mathematical techniques, however, does not seem to have changed very much the overall structure of the subject. It is perhaps too early to assess the impact of the computer, but up to now at any rate, the impact seems fairly small, again in terms of the actual structure of the subject. Up to now one would venture a guess that the impact of the computer has been in the direction of refinement rather than that of fundamental changes. This may not be true in the future.

Economics is one of the few sciences in which the structure of intellectual activity can be tested by any kind of structure in the outside world. However, an analysis of this kind could certainly be performed in the other social sciences and certainly would not be impossible in the field of medical research, where a comparison of the distribution of research effort against, say, the distribution of economic loss to disease, would be quite feasible and enormously

KENNETH E. BOULDING

interesting. There is room indeed for a large series of studies of this kind, but unfortunately there does not seem to be a great deal of motivation for such studies either on the side of supply or on the side of demand. Scientists, even social scientists, are somewhat averse to self-study, just as the universities are, perhaps because the results might be embarrassing, and these studies, at any rate up to now, have not become fashionable among the dispersers of research funds. An institute for the scientific study of science seems a long way off, yet perhaps there is hardly any other investment in which the granting agencies might indulge that would provide higher returns.

Public Policy and
the White Working Class

JOHN HOWARD

The United States lacks many types of social welfare programs taken for granted in other industrial democracies.[1] And the consequences of this are borne by broad sections of the population. Much attention in this regard has been focused on the poor, but a far larger segment of the population, including most of the white working class, feels the consequences of this lack as well, for it is at best marginal economically. Both the poor and the economically marginal would benefit enormously from social welfare programs. Paradoxically, however, the white working class, unlike nonwhites and some segments of the white intelligentsia, scarcely conceives of the need for new and more adequate social welfare programs. Consequently, as such programs come into existence they are popularly viewed as being for blacks or other minorities. This reinforces white working class resistance to them and reinforces their identification as racially-oriented programs.

In simple Marxist terms the white working class manifests "false consciousness." The political scientist Robert Lane has indicated that they moralize downward rather than upward,[2] becoming indignant about the welfare mother who receives a few dollars a year over her alloted stipend but shrugging off the price-rigging businessman who might have bilked the public of millions. This chapter discusses the foundations of this perspective, and its consequences as regards the character of social welfare policy in the United States.

Social scientists, like other Americans, have traditionally been concerned with the powerful and with social outcasts. Consequently, as Peter Schrag observed of the white worker, "there is hardly a language to describe him, or even social statistics." Poverty and affluence are the subject of endless studies and books, yet white workers are neither poor, nor, in any meaningful sense, affluent. Their life style can be conveyed in literature but social scientists have no adequate conceptual category to define their existence. Schrag attempted a summation: "between slums and suburbs, between Scarsdale and Harlem, between Shaker Heights and Hough, there are some eighty million people (depending on how you count them)". It is the world of American Legion posts, neighborhood bars, the Ukrainian club and the Holy Name Society. They live in tract homes in Daly City and south San Francisco, Bay Ridge and Canarsie, "bunting on the porch rail with the inscription 'Welcome Home Pete'. The gold star in the window."[3] This population is culturally square and traditionalist. Rock music and movies as an art form are not within their cultural purview; what the hip regard as "camp", they take seriously; what the hip take seriously they regard as boring, annoying or disgusting. It is a measure of the partial validity of the term "forgotten American" that they cannot be as precisely defined as those at the bottom or those at the top.[4]

This essay is divided into three parts, the first two of which take up the question of whether the white working class has a set of interests which might reasonably be served by changes in social welfare policy. In the first, on "comparative social welfare policy" the United States and other industrial democracies are compared. This comparison suggests that the United States lacks a number of social welfare programs commonly found in other industrial countries. In the second, the economic characteristics of the white working class are discussed, and it is indicated that they are far from being affluent. These two sections lay the foundation for the third, which identifies and analyzes those factors which generate and sustain white working class perspectives on social welfare policy and their seeming hostility despite being potential beneficiaries.

This essay rests on the assumption that public policy is formed partially in response to the constellation of pressures to which office holders are subjected. Here, the pressures to be focused on are those of the white working class as an interest group. Their attitudes and behavior cannot be accounted for in terms of any simple Marxian model. The issue is one that has agitated American radicals for decades; it is also an important question for political sociology. And, of course, it is important in grasping the tone and direction of American society.

COMPARATIVE SOCIAL WELFARE POLICY

The United States is conventionally thought of as the most advanced nation in the world. It can be plausibly argued however that in many ways the country is rather backward, for it lacks a number of social welfare programs taken for granted in western democracies. It is the thrust of my discussion that this has important consequences as regards the quality of life in the society and that it can be accounted for partially in terms of the absence of any strong sense of class interest or political consciousness on the part of white workers, those whom I have termed economically marginal.

The relative dearth of social welfare programs in this the most advanced nation in the world has been noted by several commentators. For example, Alvin Schorr has observed with regard to family allowances that "A majority of the countries of the world and all of the industrial West, except the United States, now have such programs." James Vadikan points out that family allowances " . . . constitute a means of redistributing income in such a way as to benefit the child-rearing portion of the population."[5] In most countries it is a fairly modest sum. Under the Canadian system, for example, the amount per child ranges from $6 a month to $10 a month depending on the child's age. By contrast, the French system is quite generous.[6] "The payment there varies according to region, the number of children in the family, and their ages. In Paris in 1964, for example, a family with four children received between 380 and 450 francs ($77 to $111) a month, exceeding the legal minimum wage at the time. In addition, various special payments may be made during pregnancy, at birth, (and) for improved housing."[7]

Edgar Z. Friedenberg has suggested that the United States " . . . still provides less in the way of social services, especially to the ill and aged, than an Englishman or Scandinavian would expect as a matter of right." National health insurance plans are found in one form or another in all of the industrial democracies, although the extent of benefits varies from place to place. In Great Britain complete medical, surgical, pharmaceutical and dental services are offered. In Australia, one finds restricted pharmaceutical benefits, hospital benefits, and various other kinds of services. But there are basically three types of national health programs: The government may own facilities and hire the professionals, patients may pay fees and be reimbursed, or professionals may render services under contract to the government. Most West European countries have the latter type of program. There is a good deal of nonsense talked in the United States about the British system. No doctor is forced to join the national health service but 95 percent have chosen to do so. Their income is lower than that of doctors in the United States but higher than they were before Health Service came in and higher than that of other professionals in Great Britain.

Social welfare policy extends beyond the provision of certain kinds of services and income redistribution to embrace the creation of opportunities. All developed nations have specified policies with respect to manpower and employment. These policies vary in terms of the extent to which they sustain the worker during periods of unemployment and facilitate his re-employment. Sweden has a number of sophisticated manpower programs, leading Carl Uhr to observe that "We in the United States have not yet developed as comprehensive and coordinated a set of labor policies and institutions as have evolved in Sweden." In addition to a variety of training programs for older workers whose skills have become obsolete and younger people without marketable skills, there are mechanisms for matching up workers with jobs. "Workers living in labor-surplus areas," says Uhr, "are induced by a system of allowances to move to available jobs, known to the employment service, in labor shortage areas. Unemployed persons who need and want to move great distances to job opportunities in other locations may apply for and receive travel expenses to seek new work in these areas. If they locate jobs, they may immediately receive a 'starting allowance.' This is in substance a grant which becomes repayable in part only if they do not hold the new job for at least 90 days." Other problems associated with worker mobility are anticipated: "If housing for their families is not available in their new work location, they may receive 'family allowances' for the separate maintenance of wife and children for up to 9 months in their former location. These allowances pay the rent for the family up to a maximum figure, plus a cash allowance for the maintenance of wife and children."[8]

Few of these critics argue that the United States should simply mirror other industrial democracies with regard to social welfare policy and programs. These approaches are not ends in themselves but are designed to alleviate certain kinds of mass deprivation, deprivation that is readily visible and apparently persistent in this country, which has adopted few of these policies or programs. Some scholars have pointed to what they believe to be the tangible consequences of the paucity of comprehensive social welfare measures in the United States. Daniel Patrick Moynihan has stated that "The teeming disorganized life of impoverished slums has all but disappeared among North American democracies—save only the United States. It requires some intrepidness to declare this to be a fact, as no systematic inquiry has been made which would provide completely dependable comparisons, but it can be said with fair assurance that mass poverty and squalor, of the kind that may be encountered in almost any American city, simply cannot be found in comparable cities in Europe or Canada or Japan." Robert Heilbroner echos this, "I maintain that to match the squalor of the worst of the American habitat one must descend to the middle range of the underdeveloped lands."[9]

Infant mortality rates in the United States are considerably higher than those in other industrial democracies. In 1968 with a rate of 22.1 infant deaths per 1,000 live births the country ranked above most other western, industrial democracies. It is estimated that the nation ranks eighteenth in the world, just above Hong Kong. Some might argue that this is a consequence of the extraordinarily high rate among nonwhites, but even if we consider the rate among whites only (in Mississippi, for example, 23.1 among whites; in Pennsylvania 20.3; Maine, 22.8; New Hampshire, 20.1; Vermont, 21.0; Illinois, 20.3; West Virginia,

JOHN HOWARD

24.8), the national performance is inferior to that of other western countries.[10]

Vadikan has observed that "Almost 40,000 babies die in America each year who would be saved if our infant mortality rate was as low as that in Sweden. In 1967, one million babies, one in four, [were] born to mothers receiving little or no obstetric care."[11]

To reiterate, whether the United States is the most developed nation in the world or underdeveloped depends upon the dimension one examines. If one looks at the number of automobiles per 1,000 of the population the United States leads the field. If one looks at infant mortality rates, or number of hospital beds per 1,000, or number of doctors per 1,000, or average rates of unemployment over time, the country lags, and along some dimensions lags badly.

Some might counter that the United States has programs that other democracies lack ("New Careers", Headstart, Upward Bound and so forth). It is the case, however, that these programs are directed at the poor and are not intended to meet the needs and problems of those who are marginal. Secondly, although international comparisons are difficult to make, it does appear to be true that all things taken together (save education) the United States spends relatively less on social welfare than many other countries. Bert Seidman has observed that,

It generally surprises most Americans to find out that their country, the wealthiest in the world, uses less of its natural wealth for the social welfare of its citizens than other advanced industrial nations and frequently less than many poor and developing nations which make considerable sacrifices to do so.

For example, an International Labor Organization Report published in 1964 shows that West Germany, Luxemburg, Austria, and Italy used 17 percent, 16.8 percent, 14.8 percent and 14.7 percent respectively, of their gross national product for social welfare measures. None of the 15 nations in Western Europe, except Spain and Portugal, spent less than 8.9 percent. This contrasts with 7 percent of the gross national product spent by the United States for such programs.[12]

The United States spends more on education and has a much higher proportion of its college age population in college than

West European countries. This is partially a consequence of having different channels of access to employment. However, the lower proportion of the European college age population in college does not mean that there is mass unemployment or that jobs go begging, rather the system of matching up man and job is different. There is a school of thought however which suggests that European technological development and entreprenurial efficiency may be hurt in the long run by not having a work force with as much formal education as that in the United States. If that occurs and European countries move to spend more on education, the relative position of the United States in terms of social welfare spending would remain unchanged.

Mike Harrington has indicated that "the American percentage of the gross national product devoted to direct social benefits has yet to achieve even half the typical European contribution." It is not a matter of course that the white working class with greater political consciousness would be demanding precisely these programs, but rather that they would be demanding something.

Let us now look more closely at the economic status of white workers.

THE POOR AND THE MARGINAL

It is assumed by many observers that the white working class has become conservative because it has become affluent and therefore does not need amplified social welfare legislation. Actually about 12 percent of the white population is poor while another 55 to 60 percent is economically marginal.

Like poor nonwhites, poor whites have been clearly identified by demographers, economists and sociologists. In 1967 of the 26,146,000 people in the country defined as poor, 17,764,000 were white.[13] Among the 384,000 young men in 1964, who were 20 to 24 years of age and unemployed, 310,000 were white and 74,000 were nonwhite; 450,000 or 554,000 unemployed young men 14 to 19 in 1964 were white.[14] In December, 1969, 1,137,000 white males 16 years of age and over were unemployed and 266,000 blacks. The black rate was higher, of course—5.3 to 2.5 for whites. But the figures and the rates belied the notion that unemployment was solely or primarily a black problem.

The economically marginal white is much harder to identify. His existence defines the inadequacy of the simple dichotomy between the poor and the affluent. Below, five quantitative measures are employed to define the existence of this class: income distribution, standard of living, real income, credit status and liquid assets.

As regards income distribution, in 1966, 31 percent of white families made less than $5,000; 39 percent made $5,000 to $9,999, while another 30 percent made more than $10,000 a year.[15] Seven families of ten then were poor or marginal. But income figures per se mean little unless they are related to purchasing power and standard of living. An inference with regard to the meaning of the income of white workers can be made by an analysis of reports published by the Bureau of Labor Statistics, U.S. Department of Labor. The bureau regularly devises a "standard family budget" for a four person family consisting of working husband, nonworking wife, son, age 13, and daughter, age 8. This closely approximates actual family structure. The budget is derived from "scientific and technical judgment regarding health and social well-being" and is designed to indicate the cost of a "modest but adequate" standard of living in urban areas. In 1967 the required sum ranged down from $10,092 in Honolulu to $9,744 in the San Francisco-Oakland area, $9,079 in Philadelphia and $8,641 in Durham, with a low of $7,952 in Austin, Texas. The average for 39 cities and metropolitan areas was $9,243.[16]

In the same year, production and nonsupervisory workers on nonagricultural payrolls averaged just over $5,000 a year ranging from a high of $8,060 for construction workers to a low of $4,264 for those in wholesale and retail trade. All fell well below the government's own figure of the amount needed to enjoy a moderate level of living in urban areas.[17] The mean income of craftsmen and foremen was $9,310, otherwise no workers year to year even approach the average of the Standard Family Budget.

Further the effects of inflation eroded the money gains made by the blue collar class. Between 1965 and 1969 the average wage of 47 million production and nonsupervisory workers in private industry went up $14.74 from $96.21 to $110.95 per week; at the same time, the worker with three dependents saw his tax rise by $4.80 a week. The four year increase in prices from a base of 100 in 1965 was $11.18. Adding the price rise to the tax increase and subtracting from the 1969 wage, the worker had $1.24 per week less to spend in 1969 than in 1965.[18]

None of this proves, of course, that the American blue collar and working class lives in misery and desperation. Obviously, it does not. Nonetheless, it seems undeniable that they are far from affluent, that life is probably a worrisome thing, and that the opportunity to get very far ahead seems more and more distant.

Apart from the bureau's "modest but adequate" standard, we also have to look into consumer finance to find the meaning of dollar income. The Economic Behavior Program of the Survey Research Center of the University of Michigan yearly collects detailed information on "family income, financial assets and debt, automobiles, other durable goods, and housing." Multi-stage area probability sampling is used to select a sample of dwelling units representative of the nation.

The debt status of economically marginal whites can be summed up as follows. About 55 percent of the families in the income category $5,000 to $7,449 had installment debt and 61 percent in the income category $7,500 to $9,999. Being unmarried and having no children reduced the probability of being in debt. About 65 to 70 percent of households with children were in debt. In 1967 the mean amount of debt for all families was $1,260. Payments for automobiles were most common but were closely followed by payments on other durables and for personal loans.[19]

The meaning of debt is amplified if viewed in terms of financial assets at the command of workers. About 80 percent of wage earners making $5,000 to $10,000 a year in 1967 either had no checking account or had less than $500 in an account. Sixty three percent of families making $5,000 to $7,499 either had no savings account or had less than $500 in an account; 46 percent of those families making $7,500 to $9,999 had no account or had less than $500 in an account. The amount of liquid assets then is meager and most families are a paycheck or two away from public assistance.[20]

The life style of the marginal class is suggested by other data. Less than half take vacations and those who do rarely spend much money on it. It is not the case then that there is an affluent blue collar or working class white collar class. Most white families are either poor or economically marginal. If they are marginal they have not had a rise in real income since 1965 despite a rise in paper income. Federal data suggest that they may barely make a

JOHN HOWARD

modest but adequate standard of living. They have acquired certain household goods and durables by going into debt and have the slenderest resources to sustain themselves in a crisis.

The American worker has to purchase out of his pocket services that are publicly provided in many other industrial democracies. He is taxed but there is no commensurate return as regards public services. For example, the American worker, except under highly restricted circumstances, bears out of his own pocket the cost of moving to a locale where he may find work, the cost of supporting his family while looking for work, and the cost of moving them. A whole complex of expenditures, which as we saw is a matter of public responsibility in Sweden, is paid for privately by the American worker.

Social scientists have devised a number of classificatory systems to describe the American population. To further delineate the position of economic marginals within the society I have formulated a rather gross system which does, nevertheless, make certain important distinctions.

I would, for purposes of this discussion, divide the American population into four categories.

At the bottom there are the poor (a disproportionate percentage of the black population and of Indians, Mexicans and Puerto Ricans, a disproportionate percentage of the elderly and of families headed by a female). The poor subsist on public monies, inadequate incomes or both. They are unable to make ends meet and thus may suffer from malnutrition or a wide variety of debilitating, untreated medical conditions. A segment of the black population and, increasingly, parts of the Indian, Mexican and Puerto Rican populations, show some degree of political consciousness and some conception of the need to develop national policy approaches to the problems of the deprived.

Then there are the marginals. Most of the white working class population falls into this category, and indeed most of the population. Their characteristics have already been described.[21]

Above them is a class that has substantial money income but does not own or control wealth (the distinction between income and wealth is important). They sell brain power and relatively uncommon skills and are handsomely rewarded. In this category are such persons as the upper echelon professors at the more prestigious universities, the new experts at information control, systems analysts, middle and upper echelon advertising and media men, most business management people, and the like. These people are affluent and some of them have influence with the powerful. Basically they are well-paid laborers however. The politics of this group spans the spectrum and it is difficult to tell what the factors are that account for value differences.

Last there are the true magnates, the corporate elites, the people who own or control the wealth of the country. The upper 5 percent of consumers in the country control 53 percent of the wealth. There is much greater inequality in the distribution of wealth than there is in the distribution of income, accounting for the class of income-affluent persons.

The marginals appear, for reasons we shall explore, to consider themselves closer to the top than to the bottom when in fact they are much closer to the bottom than to the top.

POLITICAL VALUES OF THE WHITE WORKING CLASS

It should be clear by now that the white working class is not affluent. Neither, of course are white workers poor. They make enough to meet daily living costs and are able to acquire appliances, durables and some other kinds of goods through installment buying. They have little in the way of liquid assets and are highly vulnerable in the event of loss of job, illness or any of a number of other kinds of misfortunes. They would benefit enormously from a wide variety of social welfare measures that are quite conventional in other industrial democracies. But they are not politically active in the pursuit of these or other social welfare measures and have left lobbying and agitation for more effective and broadly based programs up to blacks and to white liberals and radicals. They are the people whose sons get drafted and sent to Vietnam and whose children are less likely to get into college even when they are extremely capable. Inadequate opportunity for higher education is generally seen as a problem of nonwhites. The existence of inadequate educational opportunities is widespread. With regard to higher education, Project Talent, a survey funded by the United States Office of Education revealed a "marked relationship between reported family income and college entry." Data were gathered on 60,000 students. Basically, the findings were that males in the 98th to 100th percentile were likely to go to college irrespective of family income. Below that, social class became very important, with the mediocre male at the 50th percentile whose family made $12,000 a year or more being more likely to have entered college than the talented boy at the 89th percentile whose family made $3,000 a year or less. The reality behind these data are neither perceived nor translated into political reality by poor and marginal whites.

Why are economically marginal whites not further to the left politically? Why are they not active in promoting the kinds of policy approaches and programs that would appear to serve their own interests?

To be a supporter of movements to realize the kinds of social welfare policy discussed earlier in this chapter implies that one, a) recognizes the existence of certain kinds of problems, b) accounts for these problems in system terms, and therefore, c) calls for given policy approaches to cope with them. Obviously, if an individual either does not recognize the existence of particular problems, or accounts for them in personalistic terms then he does not seek system changes or new policy approaches.

Evidence on how the white worker defines his own situation is vague and inconclusive. The data provide no basis for anything other than hypothesis and speculation. Therefore let us hypothesize and speculate.[22]

The results of public opinion polls suggest that white workers have a sense of the inadequacy of their position but are at a loss to explain it. Something is wrong but they are not clear as to what. Lloyd A. Tree and Hadley Cantril, reporting on a representative national sample, indicate that personal economic conditions and employment status were cited by three out of four persons as their most pressing concerns.[23] This seems to have surprised the researchers. "Even in affluent America, the leading item mentioned under personal wishes and hopes was an 'improved or decent standard of living.' As one Arizona housewife pointed out, 'They say it's prosperous now, but I sure as heck don't notice it.' " This chapter suggests that the Arizona housewife was more nearly correct than Tree and Cantril.

Alongside an appreciation of a precarious material situation was complete confusion with regard to policy and meliorative approaches. On the one hand, the overwhelming majority of respondents making $10,000 a year or less favored government programs to accomplish social ends, but only one-third believed the government should more readily use its power. Less than one-third believed that corporate powers should be curbed while almost half favored greater government control over labor unions.

The task then is to make sense of this, to understand it, to grasp the underlying logic and rationale. If there is an underlying logic it is probably something on the following order: "Yes," the worker says, "I would benefit from various kinds of government programs; they would help me meet real and pressing material problems. Those problems, however, are caused by other segments of the population. Therefore, alternatively, the government might force these people to stop doing the kinds of things which cause problems for me."

Enlarging on this, contemporary workers who recall the desperate and hungry souls populating "Hoovervilles" during the depression, who use them as a kind of negative reference group, are likely to feel comparatively well off. Those too young to have experienced the depression undoubtedly have it recalled for them by parents. Their dollar income is substantially greater, the number of household possessions is greater, they have greater job security. This relative satisfaction with having enjoyed a certain amount of mobility probably decreases the workers' proclivity to criticize the politico-economic system or view it as inequitable and unjust. It decreases any sense of a need to agitate for new policy. It is also the case, however, that the worker still has trouble making ends meet. These difficulties, implicitly, pose a question for him. "If I'm so much better off and make so much more money than guys made before, how come I'm still having a rough time?" His belief that the system has afforded him the opportunity for a better life decreases the likelihood that he will account for his difficulties in terms of system defects. If the system were not benign he would not now be in a position where he should be enjoying a better life. In absolving the system he also absolves those who, in some sense, run it.

There are a number of ready-made scapegoats the worker can focus on in attempting to account for his difficulties (blacks, communists, hippies, liberals, "peace creeps"); of these, blacks are the most plausible and the most accessible. As blacks demand programs to deal with poverty, as they demand a guaranteed annual income, or an improved system of distribution of food to the needy and the hungry, as they demand a whole complex of

JOHN HOWARD

social welfare legislation, they must seem to the white worker to be unwilling to take advantage of the opportunities he believes exist for any person willing to work. They seem to be making vigorous raids on his pocketbook. They appear to be cheaters, people unwilling to play by the rules, people who "want something for nothing." And he believes the something comes out of his pocket.

This kind of explanation posits genuine misperception on the part of the worker. An alternative (psychologically "deeper") approach might posit displacement of frustration and hostility onto scapegoats. Roughly, the position would be phrased as follows: the worker has some glimpse of the precariousness of his position and some sense of the reasons for it. However to consciously entertain notions of system defects of that sort, would be to admit harboring ideas that are "un-American" or "communist inspired." And for the man who pastes his American flag decal on the car windshield and puts an "Honor America" sticker on his bumper, this might be no small matter. It might in the political sphere be the equivalent of a man admitting to having fleeting sexual thoughts about other men. Rather than countenance thoughts he has come to view as subversive and immoral, it is psychologically easier to displace hostility onto outgroups—blacks, hippies, "bleeding hearts", "limousine liberals" and other freaks of nature.

Additionally, there are internal differentiations in the white working class which probably act to impede the expression of a common point of view or common sentiments with regard to problems and their solutions. The 80 million or so people who comprise the marginal class are differentiated by geography, ethnicity and occupation. A number of students have discussed the persistence of ethnic identity in American communities. Michael Parenti has observed that "in a single weekend in New York separate dances for persons of Hungarian, Irish, Italian, German and Polish extractions are advertised in the neighborhood newspapers and the foreign language press.[24] Herbert Gans[25] and Gerald Suttles[26] have discussed the persistence of a tightly knit network of relationships among Italians living in Boston and in Chicago. Occupationally, the $5,000 to $10,000 category embraces secretaries and assembly line workers, senior clerks and cab drivers. Geographically workers spread out over the south with its racially dominated politics, the midwest where fear of communism is a serious sentiment, and the northeast where problems of traffic congestion and state financial support for parochial schools excite political passions.

In other words, there are a number of cross-cutting loyalties and interests that reduce any sense of common identity.

The trade unions embrace a larger portion of the American working class than any other organization. The union movement itself however is internally fragmented. Additionally (not counting about two million blacks who are trade union members) only about 14 million whites in a work force of over 70 million are union members. The American union movement very early fell into the trap of racism, excluding blacks and thereby creating a pool of strike breakers for employers and depressing the wage level of whites by insuring low wage levels for blacks. The unions neither ideologically nor organizationally are prepared to define radically progressive policy alternatives.

The muted role of the trade unions has been crucial. The political interests of most citizens are mediated through organizations. This is particularly important for populations (white workers, for example) less likely to participate electorally in the political process. Thus, for example, the underrepresentations of blacks at the ballot box is counterbalanced somewhat by the existence of a variety of politically vigorous organizations (the NAACP and The Urban League are the oldest and most resilient). Traditionally, these organizations have been the vehicles of the black bourgoisie, probably in large part because lower class people in general are less likely to belong to voluntary organizations. Recently, however, a number of groups drawing their membership from street and ghetto blacks have become prominent (the Black Panthers, the Black Muslims and DRUM, an organization of black workers in automobile plants, are the most vigorous).

Many of those who have written on the white lower class suggest that they have "a deficient sociocultural milieu," that they possess undifferentiated and unsophisticated notions with regard to the nature of the socio-politico-economic system, and that they are bigoted and suspicious.[27] The lower middle class is seen as rigidly moralistic and concerned with propriety. The self-defeating definitions of the situation entertained by these two groups go unchallenged by major alternative formulations put forth by the trade unions who have not played the educational role vis-a-vis white workers that civil rights groups have played vis-a-vis blacks. The orientation of the unions has been to conserve and preserve rather than significantly expand or explore in terms of social welfare legislation.

The white worker is not wholly unmindful of his economic interests,[28] but he doesn't translate this knowledge into any consistent conception of major programatic and policy change. This is left to a segment of the black movement, thereby decreasing further the white workers' likelihood of subscribing to such views.

One consequence of this political orientation of the white working class we have already seen in the relatively poor showing of the United States with regard to social welfare programs. Another important consequence is that the pursuit of more adequate social welfare legislation becomes equated with the pursuit of racial justice.

The black movement has focused attention on the deprived status of blacks. There has been no equivalent movement among whites to sensitize policy makers to the marginal status of most whites. While there are a variety of ethnically-based organizations—Hibernian clubs, Sons of Italy, Polish American clubs, Greek American clubs—none has a clearly formulated program with regard to the class problems of its members.[29] Many non-white groups, however, are so oriented. The black movement is too well-known to need discussion. Among Mexicans *La Huelga* has mobilized many Mexican-American agricultural workers in California and the southwest, while Rijes Tijerina and "Corky" Gonzales have rallied Mexicans in New Mexico and Colorado. Recently Indians have demanded that attention be paid to their economic and social problems.[30]

Consequently, as meliorative policy is formulated, it is done so implicitly (and sometimes explicitly) in racial terms. Seligman has observed with regard to the poverty program that "Everyone [connected with its formulation] accepted the political view that the War on Poverty was mainly for Negroes." And in fact, blacks and other nonwhites do participate more extensively than poor whites in federal programs; for example, the percentages of black and other nonwhite in the following programs is: New Careers, 67 percent; Concentrated Employment Program, 72 percent; Neighborhood Youth Corp, Summer, 56 percent; in-school, 76 percent; out-of-school, 52 percent.[31] Many colleges and universities have begun to deal with the problem of educational opportunity by recruiting more heavily from among blacks and other nonwhites, ignoring the problem of lack of opportunity among poor and marginal whites precisely because poor and marginal whites have not articulated a position reflecting any grasp of their own position in the society.

Social welfare policy in the United States is discussed with the vocabulary of race rather than that of class. In addition to posing analytic problems, the excited hostilities and passions of poor and marginal whites make it difficult for even meagerly financed and minimally intrusive programs to function successfully. In the meantime they themselves do without.

NOTES

[1] It is a measure of American thinking that the very term "welfare" is equated with husbandless mothers receiving public assistance. In the broader sense of the term it refers to policies intended to redistribute national wealth in terms of need. Pekka Kuusi, the Finnish social scientist, Gunnar Myrdal, and other European scholars have written extensively on social welfare. See, for example, Richard Titmuss, *Commitment to Welfare*, Pantheon Books, New York 1968.

[2] Robert Lane, *Political Ideology: Why the American Common Man Believes What He Does*, Free Press of Glencoe, Glencoe, Illinois, 1962, pp. 330-331.

[3] Peter Schrag, "The Forgotten American," *Harper's*, August 1969, vol. 239, No. 1431, p. 27.

[4] Christopher Jencks and David Riesman, "On Class in America," *The Public Interest*, No. 10, Winter 1968, pp. 65-86.

[5] James Vadikan, *Children, Poverty, and Family Allowances*, Basic Books, Inc., New York and London, 1968, p. 6.

[6] Some people might object to the introduction of a program of this sort into the United States on the grounds that it would have the effect of raising the birth rate. Vadikan concludes however that "Based on world wide experience over a considerable period of time, it would appear safe to conclude that a program of family allowances of modest size such as exists in Canada or such as might be considered in the United States could have no significant effects in increasing the birth rate." *Children, Poverty, and Family Allowances*, p. 101. Not even in France where family allowance benefits average one-fifth of the family budget of low-income people has it accelerated the birth rate.

[7] Alvin Schorr, *Poor Children: A Report on Children in Poverty*, Basic Books, Inc., New York and London, 1966, p. 148.

[8] Carl Uhr, "Recent Swedish Labor Market Policies," *The Manpower Revolution*, ed. Garth Mangum, Anchor Books, Doubleday and Company, Inc., Garden City, New York, 1966, p. 376.

JOHN HOWARD

[9] Robert L. Heilbroner "Benign Neglect in the United States" *trans*action, vol. 7, 12 October, 1970, p. 16.

[10] The New York Times: Encyclopedic Almanac 1970, ed. Seymour Kurtz, The New York Times, Books and Educational Division, New York, 1969, pp. 245-299; and U.S. Bureau of the Census, *Statistical Abstracts of the United States (1955 edition), Washington, D.C., 1970*, p. 5.

[11] James Vadikan, *op. cit.*, p. 24.

[12] Bert Seidman, "The Case for Higher Social Security Benefits," *The American Federationist*, vol. 74, 1, January 1967, p. 5.

[13] *New York Times: Encyclopedic Almanac*, p. 301.

[14] Arthur Ross and Herbert Hill, editors, *Employment, Race, and Poverty*, Harcourt, Brace, and World, New York, 1967, pp. 30-32.

[15] George Katond, James N. Morgan, Joy Schmiedeskamp, and John A. Sundquist, *1967 Survey of Consumer Finances*, University of Michigan, Ann Arbor, Michigan 1967, p. 11.

[16] Department of Labor, Bureau of Labor Statistics, *Monthly Labor Review*, April, 1969.

[17] Department of Labor, Bureau of Labor Statistics, *Employment and Earnings*, vol. 16, 7, January 1970, p. 67.

[18] Nathan Spero, "Notes on the Current Inflation," *Monthly Review*, vol. 21, 2, June 1969, p. 30.

[19] Katona, *op. cit.*, pp. 15-43.

[20] *Ibid.*

[21] For an excellent discussion of this population, one roughly parallel to the discussion undertaken here see "'Middle Class' Workers and the New Politics", Brendan Sexton in *Beyond the New Left*, edited by Irving Howe, McCall, New York, 1970, pp. 192-204.

[22] Among the useful works on poor and marginal whites are: *Uptown: Poor Whites in Chicago*, Todd Gitlin and Nanci Hollander, Harper & Row, New York, 1970; Eli Chinoy, *Automobile Workers and the American Dream*, Doubleday, Garden City, New York, 1955; Lee Rainwater, Richard Coleman, and Gerald Handel, *Workingman's Wife*, Oceana Publications, New York, 1956; Lee Rainwater, *And the Poor Get Children*, Quadrangle Books, New York, 1960, and William F. Whyte, *Street Corner Society*, University of Chicago Press, Chicago, Illinois, 1943.

[23] Lloyd A. Tree and Hadley Cantril, *The Political Beliefs of Americans*, Simon & Schuster, New York, 1968, pp. 9-10, 96, 99, 190, 195-196, 218.

[24] Michael Parenti, "Ethnic Politics and the Persistence of Ethnic Identification," *American Political Science Review*, LXI (September, 1967), 719m.

[25] Herbert Gans, *The Urban Villagers*, Free Press of Glencoe, New York, 1962.

[26] Gerald Suttles, *The Social Order of the Slums*, University of Chicago Press, Chicago, Illinois 1968.

[27] See, for example, Albert R. Cohen and Harold Hodges, "Lower Blue Collar Class Characteristics," *Social Problems*, Spring 1963, vol. 10, 4, pp. 303-334. Jack L. Roach, "A Theory of Lower-Class Behavior," *Sociological Theory: Inquiries and Paradigms*, Llewellyn Gross, ed. Harper and Row, New York, Evanston and London, 1967, pp. 294-315.

[28] See, S. M. Lipset, *Political Man*, Garden City, Doubleday, 1960, pp.

97-130 and A. M. Lipset and Earl Raab, "The Wallace Whitelash," *trans action*, Vol. 7, 2, December 1969, pp. 23-36.

[29]This is no longer wholly true. In both Cleveland and New York ethnically based groups have begun to stir. The major impetus has probably been the surge of the black population, but these groups may conceivably turn out to have ends and objectives which are not simply anti-black.

[30]For a discussion of protest movements by these other minorities, see John Howard, *The Awakening Minorities: American Indians, Mexican Americans, and Puerto Ricans,* Chicago, Aldine, 1970.

[31]*Handbook of Labor Statistics 1970,* U.S. Department of Labor, Bureau of Labor Statistics, Washington, D.C., 1970, p. 123.

The Management
of Federal Expenditures
for Research on Social Problems

BENJAMIN CHINITZ

The Kennedy-Johnson years were boom times for social science researchers. Federal expenditures for such research more than quadrupled in the years between 1960 and 1966, rising from $73.1 million to $325.1 million.

This enormous expansion of research budgets accompanied the proliferation of federal programs designed to deal with a long list of domestic problems: poverty, unemployment, slums, crime, inferior education and medical care, urban decay, pollution and more. The typical new program was shot through with uncertainty and ambiguity as to what its goals and objectives were, how they should be evaluated, or even what the problem was that the program was supposed to help. Therefore, even a Congress generally skeptical of the value of social science research was persuaded of the need to appropriate the funds required to clarify and test the assumptions and performance of the new programs.

Research dollars were spent in a variety of ways: to augment the research staffs of federal agencies, to finance studies by university professors and their graduate students, to augment the support of graduate education in the social sciences, to develop new centers and institutes inside and outside universities, to finance studies undertaken by commercial research corporations and independent consultants, to finance new surveys and new tabulations of existing data in the Bureau of the Census and other data-oriented agencies within the government. A variety of techniques and approaches have been pursued but the implicit, if not explicit, fundamental objective has always been to improve policies and programs, that is, to achieve a more favorable ratio of output in the form of social progress to input of financial and intellectual resources.

The notion that expenditures for research would yield positive returns was itself a hypothesis in defiance of the Biblical proverb "he who increases knowledge increases pain." But even before the pain, there were many potential slips 'twixt the cup and the lip: Would the expenditures yield new knowledge? Would the new knowledge be relevant to policy? Would the new relevant knowledge be perceived as such by policy makers? Would they act on the new relevant knowledge?

Currently there is widespread uneasiness over the Kennedy-Johnson efforts to improve the welfare of our people and the quality of the environment. There is frustration, of course, over the diversion of resources for the war in Vietnam. But there is also the nagging suspicion that we really don't know how to use what resources we have effectively, and that most new programs have fallen far short of achieving even the most modest objectives. The incumbent administration is reacting to the latter feeling with new policies and programs that are generally designed to diminish direct federal intervention, relying instead on private and local government initiative and management with federal financial support.

At the same time, there is the suspicion that the money spent on improving policy making in the domestic fields has also not produced results that justify the investment. The presumed failure of policy could be viewed as prima facie evidence of the failure of research. But while this simple deduction might be true, it is not sufficient to support the indictment against research expenditures. More direct evidence, however, is available to fortify the suspicion that the average rate of return on such expenditures is distressingly low.

Let me hasten to define what I mean by low, and to indicate the nature of the evidence. By low I mean failure to contribute adequately to *any* of the following objectives:

BENJAMIN CHINITZ

☐ The development of new capacity to service the research needs of government.

☐ The development and communication of new techniques and methodologies that are potentially useful to policy.

☐ The development and communication of new knowledge about socioeconomic phenomena that are the objects of policy.

☐ The development and communication of reliable information and unequivocal conclusions with respect to specific issues, questions and policies.

Low rates of return therefore implies that the sum of all the positive contributions under each of these categories is too small to justify the cost, and/or that an equivalent output could be achieved at much lower cost. It makes due allowances for the uncertainties inherent in the production of research. In other words, if we think of research as a fishing expedition, we are making the judgment that the probability of success is too low in relation to the expenditure of resources.

The ideal evidence for this judgment does not exist. There has been no systematic and certainly no comprehensive attempt to evaluate the results of government expenditures for research. Nevertheless, there is a disconcertingly large number of individuals on both the supply and the demand side of the research market who do not hesitate to characterize the bulk of the effort as totally unproductive. Many question the scientific quality of the work. Others are skeptical of its relevance to the needs of policy. Still others doubt whether any findings, however sound and relevant, can ultimately have an impact on policy.

I hope eventually to provide a somewhat firmer foundation for these judgments. Here I need only assert that there is considerable doubt about the effectiveness of government sponsored research. My concern is with the *process of procurement*, a term I will use to mean the way government goes about the business of managing research. To revert to my fishing analogy, a good way of finding out whether a man will have a good catch is to look at his technique.

MY STUDY IN PERSPECTIVE

Following the framework suggested by Yehezkel Dror in a recent paper,[4] we can identify three "systems": research, public policy-making, and the target systems (for example, health, education, transportation, urban renewal and the like). Roughly speaking we are (collectively) involved in trying to fashion at least two productive links: we want to make research a more effective tool in the making of policy and we want to use public policy to achieve progress in the target systems. The latter aspiration is not strictly tied to the former. Government may well achieve a very high level of effectiveness in dealing with social problems without a significant research contribution. That may be an unlikely outcome, but given the level of frustration with research, we had better hold on to such slim possibilities or yield to those who are already convinced that government cannot achieve anything in social problems. In any case, the link between policy and progress is almost entirely outside the scope of my study.

My concern is with the contribution of research to policy. Here, too, there are many large issues which I will get into only as they impinge upon my concerns. How do we produce knowledge which is useful to policy? How do we recruit talent into the relevant fields? How do we structure the disciplines at the university? What kinds of relationships do we encourage between researchers in different fields and between researchers and policy makers? And on and on. Again I refer you to Dror's work in which he has attempted to deal with many of these questions and to the large literature which he has painstakingly annotated for us in his footnotes and bibliography[5]

My point of departure is the dollars that government spends largely with the explicit purpose of developing knowledge useful to policy. Naturally, such dollars do not account for or coincide with the total effort in our society to improve the policy yield of research. The aggregate value of other sources of support, including the implicit support offered by universities in their light teaching loads and the burning of midnight oil by energetic scholars may very well exceed governmental outlays and may in fact be more effective in generating knowledge useful to policy. Whatever the case, government outlays surely loom large in the total effort and are likely to influence the total effort. Moreover, the study of the management of such outlays provides another opportunity to analyze public policy-making which is in itself a major area for research in the social sciences.

Finally, I should say that which will be painfully evident in a few moments, namely, that this essay is an attempt on my part to

Table A

Federal obligations for research in the social and
psychological sciences, by agency, 1960 and 1966[1]
(In thousands of dollars)

	1960	1966
Health, Education and Welfare	$23,411	$169,421
Defense	18,436	24,938
Agriculture	16,760	29,109
National Science Foundation	4,420	24,188
Commerce	3,042	20,469
Small Business Administration	1,990	445
Labor	1,562	8,459
Interior	1,107	3,852
Veterans' Administration	1,005	2,961
National Aeronautics Space Administration	430	6,584
Smithsonian Institution	174	2,422
Civil Service Commission	159	195
Federal Trade Commission	143	303
Office of Civil and Defense Mobilization	135	(2)
State	122	1,663
Civil Aeronautics Board	108	81
Federal Aviation Agency	54	29
Advisory Commission on Intergovernmental Relations	10	130
Office of Economic Opportunity	(2)	26,000
Arms Control and Disarmament Agency	(2)	2,000
Tennessee Valley Authority		759
Peace Corps	(2)	500
Housing and Urban Development	(2)	330
Federal Home Loan Bank Board		205
Post Office		50
Total	$73,095	$325,093

Source: National Science Foundation
[1]Fiscal years: 1960 figures are actual, while those for 1966 are estimates; both intramural and extramural obligations are included.
[2]Independent agency not then in existence.

articulate some very preliminary ideas which may or may not survive further scrutiny as my study proceeds.

SOME PRELIMINARY HYPOTHESES

What I have to offer is a series of hypotheses which emerge from what I hope is a judicious blending of a priori reasoning, introspection, observation and experience (my own and others'). In developing these hypotheses, it will be helpful on balance to have a particular domain of federal policy in mind. I say "on balance" because while there is a clear advantage in dealing with specifics, there is also the risk that the specifics may undermine the generality of the observations.

I hope I will be forgiven if I choose a domain with which I am intimately familiar both as a researcher and a policy-maker, namely, area economic development. I think it provides a fair illustration of the gap between where we are and where we would like to be in our public policy-making, a gap that the government is trying to fill partly with research.

AREA ECONOMIC DEVELOPMENT: A PROFILE

The Phenomenon (The Scientific Perspective).

There is and has been substantial variation in overall economic growth, in levels of per capita income and rates of unemployment between different sections of the country.

The Problem (The Social Perspective)

When a substantial *proportion* of the population in a local area is relatively impoverished and/or unemployed for sustained periods, the individual's disability and distress is accompanied by cumulative anemia in both the public and private local sectors. Therefore, normal ameliorative and rehabilitative measures are not likely to be adequate. How do we help these people and their descendants?

Policy Alternatives

☐ Provide artificial inducements to out-migration to augment those offered in the market place.

☐ Enlarge the flow of transfer payments and services to individuals and provide greater than normal financial and technical support to local government.

BENJAMIN CHINTZ

□ Provide artificial inducements to employers to augment the demand for labor and the wage level in the area.

The Policy Choice Reflected in Actual Legislation.

Principal reliance has been placed on the third alternative mentioned above, in the Area Redevelopment Act of 1961, the Appalachian Regional Development Act of 1965, and the Public Works and Economic Development Act of 1965, the three pieces of legislation specifically addressed to this problem. Some of the provisions in these Acts and in other federal legislation have the effect intended by the second alternative and a small pilot program not restricted to distressed areas follows the strategy suggested in alternative one.

The Procedure

□ Designation of areas as eligible for assistance.

□ Preparation of Economic Development Plans.

□ Financing of specific projects.

The Tools of Policy

□ The stimulation of an organized effort in the local area to accelerate economic development.

□ The provision of technical and financial assistance to facilitate overall planning and the identification and design of feasible projects.

□ Grants and/or loans to help finance components of the local infra-structure essential to industrial expansion.

□ Long-term low interest rate loans to enterprises locating or expanding in the local area.

Here, then, is an example of a domain of federal policy and our question is, what research capabilities need to be developed to serve the needs of the decision-maker? At the risk of not being exhaustive, I offer the following classifications.

1. The capacity to develop reliable economic indicators (for example, rate of unemployment, per capita income) for small areas on at least an annual basis.

2. The capacity to identify the critical obstacles to more rapid development in specific areas.

3. The capacity to estimate and evaluate the impacts of specific projects, after the fact.

4. The capacity to estimate and evaluate the impacts of specific projects, before the fact.

5. The capacity to measure and evaluate the marginal contribution of each of the authorized tools of policy.

6. The capacity to measure the impact of "outside" events (inclusive of other federal policies) on the economic status of distressed areas.

7. The capacity to cooperate with decision makers in the articulation of objectives and the development of decision rules.

This classification is intermediate in detail between the statement that what is needed is data and analysis, on the one hand, and on the other, a list of more specific end-uses for research, such as:

1. The efficient allocation of the present budget among competing projects.

2. The preparation of the next year's budget.

3. The preparation of longer term budgets and recommendations to the president and the Congress for modifying the basic tactics and strategy of federal policy in this field.

The administrator who sees his needs in these terms will unquestionably find the state of the research art sorely lacking on almost every count. There is economic information on small areas in government and private publications but it is far from adequate for his purposes. There is survey and data gathering capability in the research community but it is severely limited in relation to the growing demands in and outside of government. There is a modest literature and a heritage of academic research on the whys and wherefores of industrial location, population shifts and regional development but it is largely sterile in terms of concrete guidance to policy. He finds the methodology of project evaluation in a very primitive state, notwithstanding the Corps of Engineers-inspired development of cost-benefit analysis. In short, he finds that he cannot pluck the answers to his questions from existing research reports and manuals and he finds a meagre supply of competent individuals and organizations oriented to his problems. But he does have authority to spend X millions for research. His problem then is to use these resources efficiently to begin to fill the gaping holes in his knowledge. What are the elements of a good strategy to achieve that objective?

Control

If the administrator views research as critical to his decision process he will want to manage his research budget in a way that maximizes his control over the allocation of resources. Quite simply, he will want to feel confident that the allocation is guided by his objectives and needs. Since he cannot be his own research director, he will want to hire one who will act on his behalf in securing that kind of control over the research program. The research director, in turn, will want to maximize his control over the program by the careful selection of competent staff similarly oriented.

This may suggest that all research should be done in-house, to maximize control. But even assuming that the administrator could spend all his funds on staff and that the right people could be found, this might not be the optimal strategy, for there are significant economies of scale in certain kinds of research. In other words, control comes at the expense of higher average costs or lower quality for a given cost. Specialized organizations with accumulated experience can presumably provide an increment of effort on behalf of the agency at lower cost than the same effort in-house. For example, the cost of a survey conducted by Michigan's Survey Research Center ought to be less than the cost of the same survey mounted by the agency staff.

In the real world the balance between control and quality is even more heavily tipped in favor of outside procurement because of severe constraints on in-house staffing. There is first of all the overriding imperative to hold down the size of the federal payroll. There is in addition a quality constraint because the authorized grade structure precludes the hiring of more than a few top flight experienced people. Finally, a given job does not necessarily attract and hold the best candidate because, while federal salaries and working conditions are often quite competitive, there are many features of federal employment that do not appeal to professional social scientists. The result is that research staffs are typically too small and/or inferior in average quality.

I offer this as my first hypothesis: *in most federal agencies the in-house capability is much too limited to secure an acceptable measure of control.* Lack of control manifests itself in many different ways: poorly articulated research objectives, poor selection of contractor or grantee, inadequate monitoring of progress, and an inability to review reports critically, to interpret results to decision makers, and to relate results of other relevant research. The conscientious contractor or grantee is often frustrated by an unresponsive, passive and incompetent client. The incompetent or irresponsible contractor or grantee can get by with shoddy performance. At best you get a product which is of some academic value to somebody; more typically you get a product which is of no value to anybody.

A particularly vicious and wasteful form of in-house failure is high turnover of research directors and staffs. Well conceived projects launched in an atmosphere of good relations between contractor and client often degenerate because along the way the client has changed his identity and his research interests and objectives. There is typically greater stability and continuity on the supply side than there is on the demand side.

Short and Long Run Research: A Bad Mix

I asserted above that my administrator confronts a world sorely lacking in the expertise most relevant to his needs. The NASA chief who was directed to land a man on the moon before 1970 also faced an inadequate technology and personnel. But he had no alternative to investing in the development of the requisite Technology and personnel. The Great Society administrator operated in a more complicated decision-making context. His mandate was considerably less precise in the large and much more detailed in the small. He had to begin to obligate funds for specific projects in specific areas shortly after his appointment. Neither the Secretary of Defense nor the Congress could tolerate an extended gestation period. He needed research assistance to guide the allocation of resources in the short run, while the ground was being prepared for improved policies and decisions in the long run. There are, however, many factors that work against the successful reconciliation of short and long run research needs.

My second hypothesis, therefore, is this: *it is inefficient for agencies administering programs on a day-to-day basis to sponsor basic research, that is, research designed to develop fundamental capacities of the kind enumerated above.*

Why can't there be a workable division of labor within the agency? The demand for instant wisdom where there is monumental ignorance is infinitely elastic. No matter how large the staff and how generous the budget, it is still painful to engage in roundabout methods of production, to invest in people, techniques, data and other basic needs. Despite, if not because of, the fact that current consumption of research is extremely costly—supply is extremely inelastic and quality is poor—there is increasingly less sympathy for research projects that do not even offer the promise of any yield in the short run. In the extreme case, the lack of sympathy is reflected in low or zero allocations for basic research. More often, however, the result is not such a happy one. The research program goes on but it is divorced from the central concerns of the agency and is not geared to be useful even in the long run. The overwhelming pressure to seek results of immediate relevance in the short-run project leads paradoxically to a total neglect of relevance in the long-run project. "If you can't help me today, go play . . . "

Concentration versus Dispersion of Support

What is most desperately needed in research on social problems is a cumulative process of learning. As eager as we are to solve our problems in a great hurry, we are not likely to learn from a process of trial and error unless we can accumulate the experience. This argues for a reasonable concentration of effort because the communication of experience between organizations is itself a very time consuming process and one that is not generally effective in the early stages of scientific development. Yet many agencies are like the gambler who bets on many horses, fond of spreading their largesse far and wide because it increases the probability that they will win gross, if not net. There are also outside pressures that inhibit concentration such as the fear of inviting congressional investigation, the need to respond to special interests and the unrelenting pleas of contractors for a piece of the action.

My third hypothesis is therefore: *dispersion of awards inhibits the orderly development of capacity to respond effectively to the research needs of policy*. The creation of the Poverty Institute at the University of Wisconsin and the Urban Institute in Washington suggest an attempt by the federal government to achieve a greater degree of concentration of research expenditures. I shall have more to say about these institutions later.

Competitive Bidding vs. Sole Source

Research awards are made in the form of grants and contracts. In the case of a grant there is no compulsion on the part of the agency to defend the award in explicitly competitive terms. The reason for this is that a grant is explicitly not intended to yield specific outputs. Rather it is an expression of faith on the part of the agency in the research potential of a given investigator or group of investigators, a university center, or a nonprofit institute. Grants are, of course, tied to proposals that indicate specific research interests and methodologies but, after the fact, the government is in no position to withhold payment on performance criteria. Such criteria are only relevant to future decisions on new grants.

A contract, however, carries with it the implication that the government is procuring a product with specified characteristics, a concept that owes its origins to hardware procurement. The implication is reinforced by the issuance of a document by the agency known in the trade as a (RFP) Request for Proposal which describes the desired product and invites the submission of proposals. Such proposals are expected to detail how the potential contractor proposes to produce the desired product: the methodology, the resources, their costs, and the form of the output. The RFP generally provides certain guidelines as to duration and level of effort, and these, along with other aspects of the Agency's interests, are elaborated at a "bidders' conference" which is scheduled well in advance of the deadline for the submission of proposals.

This seemingly rational approach to procurement is fraught with inefficiency and is often frustrating to all parties on both sides. The inefficiency is suggested by the unfavorable relationship between the total costs of selecting a contractor in this manner and the value of the contract. These costs are borne initially in part by contractors in the preparation of proposals and in part by the agency in the review of proposals, but ultimately they are all borne by the government in the form of overhead charges against specific contracts.

I am not yet able to offer any precise statistics but I have no doubt that there are some instances in which the cost of selecting a contractor exceeds the dollar value of the contract and many instances in which the cost is a very high percentage of the value of the contract. Of course, the ratio itself is not prima facie evidence of cost-ineffectiveness. After all, if we had to spend a million dollars to discover a genius and he offered his services gratis, the ratio would be infinity, yet the process could not be deemed to be inefficient. Unfortunately, there is no genius to be discovered by competitive bidding and the process is both costly and unproductive, that is, it contributes little to the success of the project.

Where to begin? I suppose the logical starting point is the RFP itself. Very often an RFP boils down to a plea of this sort: "We're at the base of this mountain and we want to get to the top. Show us how you propose to get us up there in three (or six) months using roughly three man years of professional effort. Oh yes, and take no more than three weeks to prepare your proposal."

Examples: We wish to know how to measure and evaluate the impact of specific infrastructure investments on area development. Can you help us with that problem? How?

We have been financing a great variety of technical assistance projects. Do they serve a useful purpose? How can we tell a good project from a bad one? Can you suggest ways of solving that problem?

My point is that very often, if not in the majority of cases, an RFP is really a call for highly imaginative innovation and experimentation, but put forth as a call for a specific set of outputs. This pretense is costly for many reasons. First, it prompts the bidder to go along with it and to lay claim, via an elaborate statement with a lot of window dressing, to skills, data sources, techniques and experience which simply don't exist, and/or to greatly underestimate the difficulties of acquiring them. The resulting proposal further stimulates the expectations of the agency to the point where they begin to believe that what seems to be an impossible task can indeed be performed under severe time and resource constraints. Later, there will be the inevitable disillusion as both the contractor and the client find that it is indeed impossible to scale the peak without the proper equipment. Unfortunately, hope springs eternal, and the contractor, driven by the pressure to generate revenue, and the client, by the pressure to make or defend decisions, will repeat the same learning experience again and again.

The main point to be made here is that *when an agency is in fact looking for a contractor to explore unchartered areas of research, competitive bidding adds little to the capacity to make a rational choice among alternative bidders.* Information about the firm—its staff and track record—can be secured relatively cheaply without requiring formal proposals. The proposal, which is costly to prepare and to review, adds little to the evidence on which a choice should be made. The time of the in-house staff would better be spent reading and evaluating the firm's prior output and checking with their counterparts in other agencies who may have had prior experience with the same firm. The time of the contractor's staff would better be spent in improving the quality of their performance on existing contracts.

Sometimes, the RFP errs in the opposite direction. It describes in detail both the product and the process and leaves little or no scope to the initiative of the contractor. An honest response to such an invitation would be to describe the firm's credentials and then simply quote a price on a job which has been fully described in the RFP. But then there is the haunting suspicion that the agency will interpret this "cool" approach as indicative of a fundamental lack of interest in the project. This suspicion is fed by a teasing clause in many RFPs which invites the bidder to suggest "other" approaches to the problem. The contractor is then prompted to educate the agency in its proposal and sometimes this bold strategy pays off. More often the proposal goes over the ground covered by the RFP adding a point here and there. Again, the agency's review of the proposals adds little to its capacity to pick the right contractor.

Given the state of the art, there are very few cases in between, where the desired product has fairly well defined characteristics but there are alternative ways of producing the product. For such cases, the RFP begins to make sense, but even so it can be abused and mismanaged. There is no point in encouraging dozens of firms, as often happens, to bid for the same contract, regardless of the scope and value of the project. Preliminary screening of credentials will almost always narrow the field very considerably and when a small number of firms have been selected on this basis it *may* make sense to invite each to submit a proposal.

My fourth hypothesis is therefore: *Procurement on the basis of RFPs and proposals is generally a highly inefficient technique for selecting the appropriate organization to do research under contract. It is a poor substitute for the judicious placement of grants and sole source contracts.*

As my work proceeds I will generate additional hypotheses regarding the efficient mobilization of resources for policy-

BENJAMIN CHINITZ

oriented research. I hope eventually to be able to offer some informed judgments on the relative merits of alternative forms of organization on the supply side: university centers and institutes, independent non-profit, and commercial operations. I also intend to include in my purview the research expenditures of state and local governments. How far I can get in this effort will depend on how I go about verifying my hypotheses. This difficult problem is, however, fit subject for a whole other essay.

NOTES
[1] 90th Congress, 1st Session, House of Representatives, *The Use of Social Research in Federal Domestic Programs*, A Staff Study for The Research and Technical Programs Subcommittee of the Committee on Government Operations, April 1967.

[2] In addition to the earlier citation, there are the three volumes of hearings before the Subcommittee on Government Research of the Committee on Government Operations, U. S. Senate, on S-836, *A Bill To Provide For The Establishment Of The National Foundation For The Social Sciences*, February and June 1967 (Washington, D. C., U. S. Government Printing Office, 1967). Also, National Academy of Sciences, Advisory Committee on Government Programs in the Behavioral Sciences, National Research Council, *The Behavioral Sciences and The Federal Government* (Washington, D. C., National Academy of Sciences, 1968); and Special Commission on the Social Sciences of the National Sciences Board, National Science Foundation, *Knowledge Into Action*, 1969.

[3] Harold Orlans, *On the Quality of University Research Supported by the Government*, reprinted in The Use of Social Research in Federal Domestic Programs, Part II, Page 618.

[4] Yehezkel Dror, *A General Systems Approach to Uses of Behavioral Sciences for Better Policymaking*, RAND P-4091.

[5] Yehezkel Dror, *Public Policymaking Re-examined*. (San Francisco: Chandler, 1968).

[6] As simple as this concept may seem, I owe a debt to Worth Bateman of the Urban Institute in helping me to formulate it in these terms.

Changing Priorities in Government Investment in Technology

MURRAY L. WEIDENBAUM

The great bulk of the public discussions dealing with the role of science and technology in the United States strikes me as both discouraging and unproductive. I believe that this is so because the dialogue generally is limited to a heated exchange between two polar alternatives.

The first polar alternative I would label the "view with alarm." It has become fashionable in many quarters, particularly in the humanities, to view with alarm the extent to which "uncontrolled" science and technology are supposedly destroying our society. Almost every day I come across another denunciation of these allegedly twentieth-century Philistines and their deleterious influence on all that is noble and pure in the human condition.

The second polar alternative is somewhat harder to define. It might be said that it looks upon science and technology almost as something sacred and inviolable. Any retardation of the rate of spending for research and development is viewed as no less a sin than the suppression of truth. Or it may be that the holders of this position do not really view science and technology as being beyond criticism, but, perhaps worse yet, as ends instead of means.

Caught in the forensic crossfire touched off by these two opposing viewpoints, attempts by laymen to involve themselves in science policy often engender cries of interference, short-sightedness and worse.

The interested bystander searches for an honest and sensible position—one that tries to balance the collective benefits against the social costs of certain technological advances or proposed scientific research undertakings. Every human undertaking, including the basic research and development process, involves the utilization of certain resources. These generally include human and physical, as well as financial, resources. Obviously, there are alternative uses for such scarce economic resources, and our fundamental concern is that we allocate these resources in the most efficient and intelligent manner. Regardless of whether private or public decision-makers are responsible for these allocation choices, there is always the need for thorough analysis and justification before undertaking a major project.

However, when in the past I examined the actual justifications for undertaking many new major scientific projects, I was often struck by the absence of that objectivity and hard, factual, quantitative analysis that I associate with the core of the scientific method. I am amazed when scientists say that we must embark upon a major technological project on faith—faith that through serendipity (the invention of this all-purpose justification must rank as an important technological innovation in and by itself) it will turn out to be worthwhile after all.

Let me cite a case in point. When still in university life, I attended an important meeting of a national scientific and engineering association. The audience was assured by one very distinguished speaker that a specific current major technological undertaking would produce great benefits, of which by far the most important would be those that we cannot presently conceive of. That scientific forecaster saved his greatest contempt for what he termed the present-day doubters of the benefit of such technological undertakings. He contended that in future periods we all will look back with disdain upon these people as men of little faith.

To those who are neither scientific theologians nor wistful yearners for a simpler society, I offer a third position. It may be considered the agnostic view of the social scientist, and perhaps more particularly of the economist. To clear the air, I assume that we will not try to stifle scientific inquiry nor inhibit technological innovation. Also—and this may be the hooker—I assume that the determination of the uses to which public resources, particularly money, are put is a matter for the general public to decide.

Hence, if a professor of engineering wants to devote his leisure time to designing a commercial submarine or planning a linear accelerator, he should be entirely free to do so. However, when he asks for $100 million of taxpayers' money to start building the gadget, he should have to justify it—and not in the soft, theological terms so often used by the natural scientists in such matters, but in the hard, objective manner of the social scientist.

He should have to answer questions such as these: Are the expected benefits worth the cost? How well can he measure the benefits? Has he omitted important elements of cost to society, such as polluting the environment? Finally, and most crucial, are the returns from this use of public funds likely to be greater than from alternative uses?

I find this way of thinking about public resource allocation problems quite pertinent to the current discussion of how to utilize the technical capability being made available by reductions in defense spending. Quite a few people seem to view the problem as simply one of deciding which of the many "unmet" needs in the civilian economy are to absorb the attention—at Federal expense, of course—of the companies, facilities and people no longer working on defense programs.

I certainly share the concern over the effective use of the very valuable resources—especially people—that are becoming available, but I would stress the *effectiveness* aspect. I would return to the earlier point that scientific and engineering capabilities are means and not ends. Hence, I believe that the proper way of planning the post-Vietnam conversion is to identify the high priority civilian areas and increase the budgets for them, while cutting back the lower priority areas.

This is precisely what the Nixon administration is trying to do. Between the fiscal years 1969 and 1971, national security outlays are being reduced by $7.3 billion. Simultaneously, expenditures for human resources and other public welfare activities are being raised by $15.9 billion, expenditures for environmental improvement, education and other economic development purposes are expanding by $10.4 billion, and expenditures for crime control and other general government purposes are up $6.6 billion.

Thus, by increasing contracts and other disbursements for these key civilian areas, companies are encouraged to bid on these types of contracts and people are attracted to work in these new priority areas. Hence, resources are encouraged to be transferred from other parts of the economy. Of course, we have no guarantee that the result will be the same kinds of jobs in the same localities with the same companies.

However, change is an essential aspect of a modern society. That should not surprise us as we have seen in recent decades the tremendous expansion of the aerospace industry require attracting people and capital from other parts of the economy, often to the discomfort and displeasure of those other companies and their employees, stockholders and suppliers. Pleasant or not, we should not expect that type of movement always to be in one direction.

I would suggest that, to the extent that we can recognize the changing nature of national priorities, the better position we will be in to adjust to these changes and to take positive advantage of the new opportunities and potentials that develop.

With reference to the relationship of science and engineering to changing national priorities, I am impressed by the cogency of recent remarks by Lee DuBridge, the former science adviser to the president. As he put it, "A national policy for science should be to use our scientific talent to its maximum potential continuously and hopefully to stabilize the budget for scientific discovery as much as possible . . . In technology . . . the prime consideration is the cost/benefit analysis of what technology is essential and important to the country at this particular time."

That strikes me as a very realistic and balanced view of things. We may now expect such greatly maligned types as administrators of social welfare programs to make these benefit/cost calculations to support their budget requests for new training, health and antipoverty programs. I see great hope in extending the use of the scientific method to public resource allocation in the areas of science and, especially, technology. To the extent that this is done successfully, I would expect that we will witness increasing effectiveness in the application of the work of aerospace scientists and engineers to meeting the high priority needs of our society.

Fascist Social Policy

MICHAEL A. LEDEEN

The notion that there was such a thing as a coherent fascist approach to social problems is a highly debatable proposition. Fascism in the twenties was variously regarded as a "parenthesis" in Italian history, a sudden eruption of deviant psychological forces, and a cynical and desperate defense of the forces of monopoly capital against the threat of socialist revolution. That fascism might contain something worthy of serious consideration in and of itself seemed too far-fetched. Whatever the particular explanation, the basic theme was a constant one: that fascism was at best the last gasp of a doomed order of society, and at worst simply a passing phase or a temporary crisis, a kind of collective growing pain that would vanish once Italian society reached full maturity.

For many years, then, fascism was characterized as unworthy of serious study as social philosophy or political doctrine. The classic statement of this position was submitted by a young New York journalist, William Bolitho, who told readers of the New York *World* in 1926 that "Fascism is a social disease, a fever of the body politic, brought on by disorganized industry and general depression. There is no more a doctrine of Fascism than a doctrine of smallpox.[1]

Benito Mussolini himself encouraged this sort of interpretation by boasting of fascism's desire to remain free of ideological fetters, and by proclaiming that fascism was quintessentially pragmatic and improvisational.[2] The Italian *Duce* stressed that fascism was uniquely Italian, not "merchandise for export" and hardly a phenomenon of importance for the West as a whole.[3]

Yet this approach was appropriate only so long as fascism remained fixed in one corner of the Mediterranean, and both Mussolini and his critics quickly changed their tune when fascism became a European force in the thirties. While the Italian dictator was explaining the virtues of a universal fascism, students of the phenomenon had to account for the unsuspected strength of this political disease, and soon isolated it as a strain of that great pandemic malady of the twentieth century, totalitarianism. Instead of being treated as a momentary phenomenon, fascism was now considered to represent a potentially fatal tendency of Western politics in crisis, and the emergence of fascistic movements and regimes throughout the world, from Japan to Argentina, seemed to many to demonstrate that it was serious indeed.

Yet even in the literature of totalitarianism, there was (and is) a general unwillingness to admit the possibility that fascism was something other or something more than a technique of mass manipulation and control.[4] The analysis of fascism continued to focus upon the bizarre nature of the leaders' personalities, upon the spectacular nature of fascist politics, and upon the emptiness of fascist ideology. If this is true for fascism in general, it is especially true of Mussolini's Italy. Consider, for example, the recent judgment of A.J.P. Taylor:

Fascism never possessed the ruthless drive, let alone the moral strength, of National Socialism ... Everything about Fascism was a fraud. The social peril from which it saved Italy was a fraud. The revolution by which it seized power was a fraud; the ability and policy of Mussolini were fraudulent. Fascist rule was corrupt, incompetent, empty; Mussolini himself was a vain, blundering boaster without either ideas or aims.[5]

Yet this empty and incompetent fraud managed to stay in power for more than 20 years, a remarkable tenure in the turbulent first half of this century. It seems exaggerated, whatever one's evaluation of the force of propaganda, to assume that any government can long survive on the basis of an effective and well-produced circus; somehow bread must also be distributed. And so it would seem profitable to investigate fascism's social policies in the hope of discovering how the conflicts which had apparently brought Italy to the verge of revolution in the early 1920s were resolved within the framework of the fascist state. Whatever else one may say about Mussolini's Italy, his was a durable and for the most part a successful regime. Perhaps an analysis of fascist social policy will help us understand some of the bases for this success.

One striking characteristic of Italian fascism in the early years of the regime, from 1922 to 1925, was its lack of a formal ideology. Mussolini frequently boasted of the flexibility of fascism, of its ability to improvise solutions to problems which had baffled the doctrinaire politicians who had preceeded him. This period was one which saw Mussolini driven to the Right by a variety of forces and circumstances, not least of all by the vituperative and violent squadrist wing of his own party, which saw itself as the only "genuine" fascist force in Italy.[6]

Like Dr. Frankenstein, Mussolini found himself in danger of becoming the slave of his own creation, even to the extent of becoming mortally threatened by the *squadristi* during the Matteotti crisis of 1924.[7] The Duce of fascism was not able to deal with the squadrists from a position of relative strength until the early spring of 1925. It thus makes little sense to speak of a fascist social policy before 1925, because the direction of fascist policy and the definition of basic fascist attitudes were still at issue in the convulsions within both the Fascist party and the Fascist regime. It is only with the resolution of the crisis within fascism that the first concrete steps toward the creation of fascist society were taken. These were, at the same time, steps leading toward the creation of Mussolini's dictatorship.

FASCISM AND CLASS CONFLICT

The fundamental social problem confronting the Fascist regime was the issue of class war. For many, fascism had represented the only possible source of stability in a country which had been plagued by street violence, general strikes and attempts by radical

MICHAEL A. LEDEEN

workers' organizations to occupy the factories of the nation. One of the first actions by the Fascist government had been to create a Confederation of Fascist Trade Unions, headed by a man whose name eventually became synonymous with fascist syndicalism, Edmondo Rossoni. Rossoni's goal was a grandiose one indeed: to organize *all* the elements of Italian society involved in production into various unions, and then group these unions together into a kind of super syndicate, the *organo sindacale superiore,* which would resolve conflicts between the various elements in the interest of production itself.[8] Such actions by Rossoni's organization of fascist unions can be interpreted in a number of ways, but in terms of the eventual direction of fascist social policy the most important aspect was the drive for the unification of workers' and managers' organizations into a single structure. This organization would function beyond the boundaries of any class struggle or class conflict, and presumably would act in the interests of the nation rather than in behalf of any particular group. The Fascists increasingly employed this concept in justifying their activities, considering it to represent a "transcendence" of the class struggle.[9]

Yet such a notion had force only if the syndicalist institutions in fact represented all the interests involved, and Rossoni's confederation of fascist trade unions was hardly representative. Prior to 1925 the vast majority of Italian workers had given their allegiance to the traditional unions of the pre-fascist period, and this ran counter to the desires not only of Rossoni, who sought a more thorough control on behalf of his own organization, but also to those fascist hierarchs who would not tolerate the existence of mass organizations outside the control of the state. Therefore, the strengthening of Rossoni's confederation seemed to be in the interests of fascism; yet here again there were conflicting desires. If Rossoni succeeded in unifying Italian labor, he would become the second most powerful man in Italy. Furthermore, since so much fascist activity had been directed against socialist organizations, there was a residual suspicion of *any* kind of working-class organization, let alone one which was on the verge of becoming a massive force within the fascist state. There had been highly agitated debates on this subject from the very beginning of the Fascist regime, and the emanations from Rome had been anything but consistent. While backing Rossoni in his aim to win as many workers as possible to the side of fascist trade unionism, the Grand

Council of Fascism had proclaimed in the spring of 1923 that it was opposed to any trade union monopoly,[10] and therefore retained the option of limiting Rossoni's confederation in the future.

This would have been a very complicated situation indeed for Mussolini to resolve even in the best of circumstances, and the unstable mixture was catalyzed further by the outbreak of a series of wildcat strikes early in 1925—at the moment of fascism's momentous resurgence. In February some 60,000 workers struck in Lombardy, the Veneto, the Emilia, Liguria and Umbria, raising anew the spectre of working-class violence, and threatening fascism with the frightening prospect of a resurgence of the kind of proletarian agitation against which Mussolini had fought so vigorously in the early twenties. Yet these strikes were organized by Fascists, and actively encouraged by Rossoni himself.[11] And at the very moment when it seemed to many captains of industry that some elements of fascism had adopted the tactics of the socialist enemy, the spokesman for fascist syndicalism reinforced this frightening impression. The fascist syndicalist offensive, Rossoni announced, did not preclude "the resumption of revolutionary syndicalism."[12]

This crisis made it imperative for Mussolini to intervene forcefully, and the actions he took in 1925 laid the groundwork for the subsequent policies of the Fascist state. Mussolini's interest lay in strengthening his own hand against all opponents, both real and potential, and in bringing as many elements of the society as possible under the control of the state. He had acted in January against dissidents within party ranks. He would now, under the guise of avoiding labor violence, bring both industry and labor under a considerable degree of state control. While Rossoni's menacing actions drove the normally highly independent Industrial Confederation, the *Confindustria,* into a state of alarm, Mussolini acted first to calm the industrialists, then to bring Rossoni under control.

Before considering the particular measures Mussolini took to stabilize this perilous situation, it is important to turn for just a moment to the reactions of the Fascists to this new outbreak of proletarian activity. It must be recalled that fascism emerged from the revolutionary wing of Italian socialism during the Great War,

MICHAEL A. LEDEEN

and that this connection between fascism and socialism was of considerable importance to many leading Fascists. The agitation in early 1925 was actively encouraged by Augusto Turati,[13] soon to become the head of the Fascist party, and was viewed with considerable pleasure by Enrico Corradini, a leading nationalist and a member of the Fascist Grand Council. Corradini's reaction is of particular interest. "There is," he wrote, "an historic connection between Socialism and Fascism, dare I say an historic continuation . . . Fascism transcends socialism, but gathers the good fruits of Socialist work and according to its own law, when it is necessary, this work continues."[14]

In other words, while fascism represented a new form of politics, it also embodied much of the kind of activity which had been carried on by the radical parties of the past. This vigorous support of a dynamic proletarian movement within the ranks of fascism added to the already substantial anxiety of the Italian industrialists who had supported Mussolini hoping to block this sort of working-class agitation. With fascist syndicalism flexing its muscles, Mussolini had to act to calm the nerves of the leaders of the Confindustria.

As the strike ebbed in the spring and early summer, Mussolini made two notable changes in the Finance Ministry, appointing two men known to be favorable to the interests of the Confindustria.[15] More significantly, he issued an order to the Italian prefects which amounted to a declaration of war against those who might threaten further strikes. He proclaimed that confrontations and disputes arising from Syndicalist actions were dangerous to the body politic, and he ordered his prefects to avoid conflicts "with all energy" and to conclude any actual outbreaks of violence as quickly as possible.[16] These actions convinced the industrialists that Mussolini would not tolerate any repetition of the events of February, and it also served notice on Rossoni and his followers that the day of radical syndicalism was indeed over.

At the same time that this new code of discipline was being enforced upon Rossoni, Mussolini also made significant concessions to the syndicalist organization. Again, his motives were mixed. He was deeply concerned about the possibility of renewed proletarian action, especially from those sectors of labor not channeled through Fascist trade unions. Further, he was by no means eager to grant the industrialists sovereignty in the field of labor relations, and while Rossoni might eventually become a serious threat to Fascist supremacy, for the moment his Confederation was needed as a counterforce to the power of the Confindustria.

Consequently, Mussolini acted in the fall of 1925 to make fascism indispensable to both labor and industry, and to bring both sectors under more vigorous control. The piece of legislation that institutionalized these relations, perhaps the most important single act of social policy taken by Mussolini's regime, was the so-called Pact of the Vidoni Palace of October 2, 1925.[17]

The Pact of October 2 represented a giant step forward in Mussolini's goal of bringing the various explosive elements of Italian society under his control. It created two vast monopolies, granting Rossoni's confederation the exclusive right to represent the working class in collective bargaining, and giving the monopoly of representation of industry to the Confindustria. Further, it stipulated that all contractual arrangements between industrialists and workers' organizations had to be arrived at between dependent organizations of these two bodies.

This was an immediate triumph for Rossoni, who gained exclusive legal recognition on a national basis for the working class. A law of the following year made this monopoly even more forceful, when it made legal recognition of a Fascist union possible when 10 percent of the total workers in any given "category" belonged to the union.[18] This made it possible for the Fascists to dominate the representation of all groups of workers, even when the vast majority of the working population opposed the Fascist union, or even opposed fascism itself.

We shall return to this question of working-class representation in just a moment, but it is important to stress here the tremendous advantage which Mussolini reaped from this Pact. When the Confindustria agreed to assume exclusive representation of the industrial forces of Italy, it tacitly entered the Fascist State. By the end of the year, the process of the assimilation of industry into the structures of the government was nearly complete. The Confindustria was transformed into the General Fascist Confederation of Italian industry, the president and secretary of the confederation joined the Roman *fascio,* and the group was represented in the Fascist Grand Council. A statement of

December 16 made formal the industrialists' adhesion to fascism.[19]

The Confindustria had entered the ranks of fascism because of a provision in the pact that provided for the abolition of the so-called "internal commissions." These were workers' representatives who were consulted about various decisions affecting daily activities within the factories, and they closely approached the proletarian control of production that the Italian trade union movement had been trying to achieve. In return for his exclusive right to represent the working class, Rossoni yielded up working-class power within the factory. It seems to have been this key concession that convinced the industrialists that they should throw in their lot with Benito Mussolini.[20]

This meant, in the long run, the real end of radical syndicalism within the fascist state. And although Rossoni's critics have been quick to damn him for this abdication of proletarian strength within the industrial framework, in the context of the period the monopoly of representation he gained seemed to be more important. The internal commissions were worthless within the framework of fascism without effective political strength; given the political power he hoped to gain through the recognition of his own confederation, further concrete gains might be realized. One should not forget that Rossoni also had the older unions to contend with, and the Vidoni Pact effectively eliminated them as a threat to the Fascist Confederation. A law of April 3, 1926 made it illegal for any union outside Rossoni's Confederation to negotiate with the industrial organizations.[21] Therefore, while other unions still had the formal right to exist, all their powers were stripped from them. The greatest of the pre-fascist workers' organizations, the *Confederazione Generale di Lavoro* (CGL) vanished early in 1927.

Yet in the long run Rossoni's was a fatal error, for monopoly without freedom left him a pawn in the hands of the dictator. There was no initiative left in the Confederation; all syndicalist leaders were appointed from above, and the highest in the chain of appointers was Mussolini. In keeping with the evolution of fascism toward a personal dictatorship, the entire structure came in the end to be concentrated in the hands of the Duce.

Mussolini emerged as the real winner in this struggle, and managed to tame the syndicalists while still retaining his ability to pose as an avid trade unionist himself. Had he not created the most powerful trade union organization in Italian history? Had he not offered the workers a viable channel through which they could voice their grievances? Surprisingly, there was little working-class opposition to the Vidoni Pact, even though the old representatives of the CGL knew that their days were henceforth numbered.[22] Within two years virtually all other syndicalist organs had vanished from the Italian political scene, leaving the Fascist Confederation sole master of the working class.

It is not surprising that the leading modern historian of fascism calls the Vidoni Pact "the premise for the successive incorporation of the entire world of production in the Fascist State, and constituted a decisive event on the route of the edification of the regime."[23]

The Vidoni Pact laid the groundwork for the consolidation of the Fascist State's control over the productive forces of Italy. Within short order this was revealed to be heavily weighted in favor of the industrialists. They had already won a major round in their battle against Rossoni with the abolition of the internal commissions; by the end of the following year they had scored a virtual knockout by the legal ban on strikes and lockouts. On July 18, 1926, the Grand Council of Fascism declared that both strike and lockout were to be considered criminal offenses.[24] In place of these instruments of class war, a new Magistracy of Labor was created, to which was entrusted the adjudication of collective labor disputes. In theory, this labor tribunal was to have served labor's interests (indeed, the industrialists vigorously opposed its creation), yet in practice it remained inactive. In a period of ten years, the miserable total of 41 controversies were brought before it, 22 of these were settled out of court, three were dropped outright before adjudication, and only 16 were actually ruled upon.[25]

Yet whatever else we may want to say about the one-sided emphasis of the fascist legislation, it must be recognized that Mussolini had been strikingly successful in bringing the two opposing forces in the class struggle into a somewhat coherent framework. Above all, a new principle had been firmly established: that of the supremacy of the State's interests within the field of production. This principle was stated with unusual candor by the court philosopher of fascism, Alfredo Rocco, in a speech to

MICHAEL A. LEDEEN

the Chamber of Deputies on December 10, 1925, defending the Syndicalist legislation:

The State cannot morally or politically renounce even one thousandth of the control established by this proposed law . . . The State cannot admit, and the Fascist State less than ever, that States be constructed within the State. The organization of the syndicates must be a means to discipline the syndicates, not a means for the creation of potent and uncontrolled organisms which might threaten the State.[26]

THE FASCIST "REVOLUTION"

But, one is inclined to ask, to what end this discipline? What was the goal of this firmly established control? Such questions could only be raised once Mussolini felt confident of his own strength. With the industrialists tied closely to his own regime, and the proletarian tiger caged behind the bars of Fascist Confederation, Mussolini could turn to the justification of his new state. Indeed, such a justification was more than a simple psychological desire to give dignity to his own position. In the atmosphere of Italian politics in the middle of the 1920s it was a virtual necessity. Fascism had proclaimed itself a new form of politics; where was the evidence? What profound changes had stemmed from it? Up until the middle twenties, Mussolini was busily involved in making himself either superior or indispensable to the potent elements of Italian society. He now had to win the passions of the people.

Rocco provided the keynote in a speech late in January, 1926. He was speaking of the transformation that fascism had accomplished in Italy, and he stressed that though the form of this transformation was legal, the content was indeed revolutionary.

. . . There was, that is to say, a change in regime . . . not only in method of government, but of mentality, of political spirit, of conception of the state . . .[27]

The new mentality that fascism was attempting to institutionalize was precisely that transcendence of class struggle which Corradini had proclaimed so essential to the fascist syndicalist movement. The conception here was that society had certain interests that were more important than those of restricted sectors of that society. While liberalism had given those interests free play, fascism disciplined them, and brought them to the service of the nation. The entire direction of Fascist social policy from 1926 onward lay in an attempt to institutionalize this concept, which, as we are beginning to see, was less a concept of society than a concept of the human personality.

In the years that followed, Mussolini and his comrades attempted to create what they called a "corporate state." The key organization in this conception, the corporation, never really came into being, and an analysis of legislation dealing with it would carry us into a wonderland where, like Alice searching after the Cheshire cat, all we see of the corporation is its promising smile. We can, however, learn much for an analysis of the intent of corporate state from in a remarkably candid conversation by one of its guiding spirits, Gino Arias.[28] Arias observed that fascism retained private property, the essential element of liberalism, in its social policies. Furthermore, it took the notion of state control of the means of production from socialism. What distinguished fascism from both of these earlier systems was that fascism rejected human egotism as a point of departure for economic action. So, just as in other societies, fascism gives the individual freedom of choice, but instead of being guided by his own individual interest, the fascist citizen will be guided by the general interest—his own egotism disciplined by a "corporative conscience."

In other words, to take a memorable phrase from one of Fascism's most acute critics, Louis R. Franck, the analysis of the corporate state belongs to political theory, not to economics.[29] The corporate state involves, before all else, a notion of the malleability of human nature.

If one reads the exchanges between labor and management within the upper echelons of the fascist state, one finds this sort of language recurring over and over again. In 1926, for example, the Honorable Benni, head of the Confindustria, complained that "the workers . . . are not, and cannot yet be completely transformed at the roots . . . "[30] Bottai frequently complained about the old class-bound mentality of the industrialists, who resisted his efforts to exert greater control over their operations.[31]

Indeed, many Fascists were quite explicit in their belief that the success of the revolution awaited a change in human nature. Arnaldo Mussolini, brother of the Duce and editor of *Popolo d' Italia,* put it very well in an editorial in 1929:

MICHAEL A. LEDEEN

Fascism, rather than reduce the social problem to an algebraic question . . . has made it into a moral problem; it has affirmed before all else the nobility of work, the obligation of production, the historical necessity of the Italian people . . . [32]

The basic transformation at which fascism aimed was a change in human nature, and the creation of a new ruling class for Italy. That is why the formation of the corporations, the much-vaunted creation of fascist social theory, took so long. Indeed, it seemed at times as if the institutionalization of fascist social theory, the concrete transcendence of class-bound institutions about which fascist ideologues spoke so often and so hotly, must await the emergence of a new ruling class. The Minister of Corporations, Giuseppe Bottai, demonstrated this attitude in a report on the progress of his office to the Grand Council of Fascism in September of 1928.[33]

Bottai told the Fascist Grand Council that he was finally ready to undertake the full control of the Syndicalist organizations, the task at hand. His immediate project was to bring the Syndicalist leaders under his aegis in keeping with his instructions to give command functions exclusively to those Fascists who "give ample evidence of culture, of preparation, of a sense of responsibility, and of purity of habits." This criterion made it necessary for the Minister of Corporations to survey and discipline far more than the functioning of various institutions; it made it imperative, in Bottai's phrase, to organize "not only the formation of the ranks, but also their continuous purification."[34]

It is interesting to note that virtually the only concrete steps taken by the Ministry of Corporations from 1926 to 1934 consisted in the elimination and training of personnel while the institutions of the corporate state remained only a gleam in the eyes of the Fascist fathers. Further, typically enough, the new ruling class which the Fascists claimed to be creating was one which was to supervise syndicalist organizations; the industrialists were considered sufficiently prepared, educated and pure to tend to their own problems. The Ministry of Education created special schools to train labor leaders in 1928 and there was no corresponding instruction for industrial managers.[35]

What we are confronted with, in other words, is an attempt to bring the Italian masses under control by shifting the emphasis of governmental action from the area of social institutions to that of human attitudes and emotions. It is then, in the words of George Mosse, a great revolution of the soul.[36] Irving Horowitz has called this sort of ideology "a concept of will opposed to organization, as purity of conviction is opposed to stifling rationalism."[37] The paradigmatic statement of the nature of this fascist revolution is to be found in the "official" history of fascism written by Gioacchino Volpe:

> In the new concept that Fascism has of Italians there is outlined a new concept of man, a concept of him as he should be according to civilized ideas; as culture united with action and almost one and the same thing as action, as instruction equal to education, as science that is not lost in abstract knowledge, but as a conscious force for elucidating everything in life and everything for life; as a dynamic spirit of realization.[38]

If we come to understand that the fascist revolution is centered on the creation of new human beings, and that of necessity the creation of typically fascist institutions awaits the emergence of these new people, then the largely unstructured nature of fascist social institutions makes more sense. To put it another way, the failure of fascist social policy is rationalized by the theory of the fascist revolution, which places the fulfillment of the revolution in a future populated by fascist citizens who have sublimated their own egos on behalf of the collectivity.

FASCISM AND THE JEWS

This model for fascist social policy helps to explain, I believe, the phenomenon of fascist anti-Semitism, that curious ad hoc policy formulated by Mussolini when he moved into Hitler's fatal embrace to form the Axis. While the notion that Jews constituted a menace to society was foreign to Italian culture,[39] and while most Fascists, from Mussolini on down, reacted strongly against Hitler's anti-Semitic policies in the early thirties, the kind of discriminatory policies that Mussolini enacted in the late thirties and early forties were quite consistent with the sort of actions he had taken to bring the syndicalists under control more than a decade earlier. More important for an understanding of fascism's basic orientation, the concept of "the Jews" which Mussolini put forward, and the goal of the discrimination policies he proposed,

MICHAEL A. LEDEEN

further illuminate the basic aim of all fascist social policy: the molding of a new spirit in Italian life.

Mussolini's treatment of the Italian Jews is remarkably similar to his handling of the syndicalists. Prior to the advent of fascism, the Jews of Italy had had no coherent organization of their own, and legislation dealing with their rights varied widely from region to region. [40] This clearly would not do in the context of the Fascist State, and in 1930 and 1931 a series of laws were passed, providing for the establishment of 26 Jewish communities which would care for the liturgical and educational needs of the Jews in each zone and for the well-being of the members of the community. These in turn were each represented in a National Union of the Italian Jewish Communities, which had the sole right of representation before the government. And just as every worker was either represented by Rossoni's confederation or not represented at all, so any Jew who did not wish to join the appropriate community had to file a formal statement renouncing his Judaism. [41] Again we see the desire of the regime to maintain a rigid discipline over all sectors of the community.

Having brought the Jews under state control, Mussolini acted in his usual manner to win their allegiance. He arranged that public examinations not fall on Jewish holy days, and in his public statements he often lauded the Italian Jewish contribution to the nation.[42] Indeed, as we know, many of Mussolini's most intimate friends were Jews, and there is no reason to doubt the honesty of his mildly philo-Judaic utterances during the first decade of his rule.

A variety of circumstances combined to convince Mussolini that the Jews were not entirely sympathetic to his revolution. The large numbers of Jews involved in *Guistizia e Liberta,* the major resistance organization, and the numerous Jewish outcries against the Ethiopian invasion and the Italian adventures in the Spanish Civil War, demonstrated to him that he had not effectively assimilated the Italian Jews.[43] Yet what concerns us here is less the particular influences upon the Duce than the curious form which his anti-Semitic doctrines took in the late thirties and early forties.

Unlike the Nazi anti-Semitism he has been accused of copying, Mussolini's doctrine did not rest upon a pseudo-biological racism. Indeed, he considered Nazi racial doctrine to be unmitigated nonsense.[44] As late as 1940 we find Mussolini telling his official biographer that there was no such thing as an "Italian race," and that the Italian spiritual climate dissolved any races which might come to Italy into the melting pot of the Italian people. Should one come to Italy he suggested, it would not last long. "All races passed through the convoluted passages of the Italian distillery. None lasted long camped upon our piazzas."[45]

The distinction between Italian and Jew was not then a biological one, but, as we might have expected, a spiritual difference. For Mussolini there were various spiritual types in the world, and he believed that at certain dramatic moments in history it was possible to speak of "races" becoming coextensive with "nations." Such was the case with Fascist Italy, where the genius of the Italian race had made it possible to begin the construction of the Fascist State. Yet within that State were some recalcitrant elements that refused to be "assimilated," that did not adapt to the new spiritual climate of the period, and that insisted on clinging to the values and goals of an earlier, corrupt epoch.[46] The purpose of the anti-Semitic policies was to retrain these elements, to Italianize and "fascisticize" them, and finally to reintegrate them back into fascist society.

It is important to stress the profound difference between the nazi and the fascist conception of human nature reflected in the different versions of "racism" we find in the two countries. In an article on race that Mussolini considered very important, Mario Missiroli argued that " . . . the highest spiritual values are a conquest of conscience, the consequence of effort and perpetual choice and, as such, are not determined by natural fact . . . the ethics of fascism are founded . . . upon the absolute and incontestible supremacy of the will and moral responsibility.[47]

Here again we find the dynamic theory of human nature so central to fascist policy. Unlike the Nazis, who believed that the personality was ineluctably tied to a changeless racial principle, the Fascists insisted upon the ability to change the human spirit.

In keeping with this notion of human nature, Italian anti-Semitic policy was anything but a policy of extermination. Mussolini himself was emphatic upon this point, calling it a policy of "discrimination" not "persecution."[48] Indeed, from his own warped point of view, he was not about to embark upon a policy of mass persecution, but rather he saw himself continuing a program of disciplining Italians. One might almost say that a

MICHAEL A. LEDEEN

"Jew" for Mussolini was a recalcitrant Italian. If this seems preposterous, what are we to make of his remarks to Yvon De Begnac: "The patriotic Jew loses the polemical characteristics of the race . . . I have Arianized these men of great spirit . . . It will be a question of a generation. Mixed marriages are slowly eliminating the Jewish characteristics."[49]

Despite the biological metaphor, Mussolini's own language leaves little doubt about the nature of his concept of racism. Above all, the dictator's hatred was directed against those Italians who did not feel themselves such, who did not sense their "race." The goal of his regime was to transform the Italian people from "a race of slaves" to "a race of masters."[50] He even went so far at one point as to advocate discrimination on the grounds that it would intensify foreign antagonism toward Italy, and thus make all Italians aware of their uniqueness in the world.[51] In short, just as his antiproletarian policies had enabled Mussolini to coopt the industrialists, so his discrimination against the Jews was directed against the whole population, not just a fraction of it.

Particularly fascinating here is the conception of a temporary policy of discrimination which would produce Italians capable of returning to fascist life. It confirms the view that the basic goal of fascist action is to prepare Italians for the revolution, a revolution which is pushed constantly further into the future, and the specific nature of which remains somewhat unclear. To put it in more contemporary language, the goal of fascist social policy is to radicalize an entire population, to create that revolutionary consciousness which alone can create viable fascist institutions. It is this, I think, which accounts for the tremendous stress on the concept of youth. Since the revolution is viewed as a future one, the fulfillment of fascist promises awaits a new generation. So it is that fascists, both in theory and in practice, devoted an enormous amount of energy towards recruiting young people.[52]

The notion of youth, and the role it played in fascist ideology, would take us far afield, and it is included here only to suggest the dynamics of the Fascist regime. It should be clear that the failure of any given project within this framework can be easily rationalized, and is indeed anticipated, for those people who have been corrupted by the old order cannot be expected to conceive and execute a revolutionary program. Indeed, the failure of fascism to create a viable corporate state in the early thirties was taken to be evidence of the reactionary mentality of the Italian people, and Mussolini frequently argued that only when young Fascists came of age would the revolution reach fruition.

What is so fascinating and important about fascist social policy is that in spite of the lack of concrete achievement, the fascist regime enjoyed a remarkable success. Even by its own standards, Mussolini's Italy accomplished precious little. Yet even if we exempt the war years from consideration, fascism endured from 1922 to 1939—17 years of turmoil in European history. What can account for this durability? I think it is time we recognized that just as revolutionary movements can be based upon the creation of a revolutionary consciousness, so can regimes endure by attempting to create that same transformation of will. To be sure, the charisma of Mussolini played a profound role in this scenario, and I think it is crucial to recall that fascist movements invariably succeeded only where unusually capable and dynamic leadership existed. Yet the central notion of fascism—that the human personality can and must be changed before the revolution takes place, has proven itself to be a very powerful one in this century. Its appeal, furthermore, spreadeagles the traditional division of political movements into Left and Right wings, for whether we turn to the attempts at "radicalization of the masses" by the New Left, or to the condemnation of certain personality types by Vice President Spiro Agnew, we find increasingly that traditional appeals for institutional changes are being undermined in favor of demands that we reform people.

It may well be that Arnaldo Mussolini's belief that fascism would become a universal phenomenon was frighteningly close to the truth. His own summary is, I think, an apt one:

An unstable, unquiet Europe, disintegrated in its civil millenarian function, bound in the vague formulas of liberalism and democracy, cannot find its health, or better, its salvation, in any other way than in a new order which comprehends the necessity of the single elements in the framework of the strong state, the sensibility of the crowd in the immutable truth of an ideal politics. And it is for this reason that . . . (in all countries) we now see currents analogous to the Fascist movement.[5][3]

NOTES

[1] William Bolitho, *Mussolini's Italy* (New York, 1927), 51.
[2] Enzo Santarelli, *Storia del Movimento e del Regime Fascista* (Rome,

1967), 100-117. and Massimo Rocca, *Il Primo Fascismo* (Rome, 1964), esp. 87-116 for a contemporary analysis.

[3] When Mussolini later changed this view, he did so with typical bravado, arguing that he had never said "fascism is not merchandise for export" since it was too banal a phrase!

[4] See, for example, Hannah Arendt's *Origins of Totalitarianism*.

[5] A.J.P. Taylor, *The Origins of the Second World War* (New York, 1964), 59.

[6] Rocca, *op cit*, 95-102.

[7] Adrian Lytellton, "Fascism in Italy: The Second Wave" in *Journal of Contemporary History*. January 1966.

[8] The literature on fascist Syndicalism is quite substantial. The most acute analysis at first hand is that of Felice Guarneri, *Battaglie economiche fra le due guerre* (Milan, 1953). His analysis of Rossoni's goals is in Vol. 1, 65. In addition, cf. the famous polemic by Ernesto Rossi, *Padroni del vapore e fascismo* (Bari, 1966). The fundamental work on the edification of the fascist state is Alberto Aquarone, *L'organizzazione dello Stato totalitario* (Torino, 1965).

[9] Renzo De Felice, *Mussolini il Fascista II. L'organizzazione dello Stato fascista 1925-1929* (Torino, 1968), 246 ff.

[10] Aquarone, *op. cit.*, 114-115.

[11] De Felice, *op. cit.*, 92-94.

[12] The phrase appears in an article by Rossoni, "L'Unita del sindicalismo" in *La Stirpe*, Aprile-maggio, 1925.

[13] Aquarone, *op. cit.*, 119.

[14] Augusto Turati, "Dopo lo sciopero fascista" in *Popolo d' Italia*, 19 marzo 1925.

[15] De Stefani and Nava were replaced by Volpi and Belluzzo.

[16] De Felice, *op. cit.*, 97.

[17] The entire document is reproduced in Aquarone, *op. cit.*, 439.

[18] The law is no. 563, 3 April 1926. Cf. Aquarone, *op. cit.*, 126.

[19] Aquarone, *op. cit.*, 121.

[20] *Ibid*, 119.

[21] note 18.

[22] De Felice, *op. cit.*, 99ff.

[23] *Ibid*, 100-101.

[24] The relevant texts are reproduced and analyzed in Rossi, *op. cit.*, 154 ff.

[25] Aquarone, *op. cit.*, 133 ff.

[26] Alfredo Rocco, *Scritti e discorsi politici, III. La formazione dello Stato fascista (1925-1934)* (Milano, 1938), 979-996.

[27] *Ibid*, 905.

[28] The conversation is reported in what remains the most thorough and acute discussion of fascist economics, Louis Rosenstock Franck, *L'economie corporative fasciste en doctrine et en fait* (Paris, 1934), 400 ff.

[29] *Ibid*, 395.

[30] The document, addressed to Turati, is dated 27 December, 1926. *Archivio Centrale dello Stato (ACS), Segreteria particolare del Duce, carteggio riservato, 242/R, Gran Consiglio*, sottofascicolo 4 (1926), inserto C.

[31] See, for example, his report to the Grand Council on the "Labor Charter" in 1927. *ACS, segr. part. del Duce, cart. ris., 242/R. Gran Cons.*, sottof. 5/A (1927).

[32] *Popolo d'Italia*, 31 maggio 1929.

[33] *ACS, Segr. part. del Duce, cart. risl, 242/R, Gran Consiglio*, sottof. 6/B.

[34] *Ibid.*

[35] *Ibid.*

[36] George L. Mosse, "The Genesis of Fascism" in Mosse and Laquer, eds., *International Fascism* (New York, 1966), 19.

[37] Irving Louis Horowitz, *Radicalism and the Revolt against Reason* (Carbondale, 1968), viii.

[38] Gioacchino Volpe, *The History of the Fascist Movement* (Rome, 1936), 161.

[39] Michael A. Ledeen, "Italian Jews and Fascism" in *Judaism*, Summer, 1968, 278-281.

[40] Renzo De Felice, *Gli Ebrei Italiani sotto il fascismo* (Torino, 1961), 117-118.

[41] *Ibid*, 120-121.

[42] *Ibid*, 109-112.

[43] *Ibid*, 276 ff.

[44] *Ibid*, 147 ff.

[45] *Ibid*, 294.

[46] *Ibid, loc cit.*

[47] Quoted in A. James Gregor, *The Ideology of Fascism* (New York, 1969), 279.

[48] De Felice, *Gli Ebrei op. cit.*, 292 ff.

[49] Yvon De Begnac, *Palazzo Venezia—Storia di un Regime* (Rome, 1950), 643.

[50] Galeazzo Ciano, *Diario 1937-1938* (Rome, 1956).

[51] De Felice, *Gli Ebrei, op. cit.*, 298.

[52] Michael A. Ledeen, "Italian Fascism and Youth" in *Journal of Contemporary History*, July, 1969.

[53] *Popolo d'Italia* 28 October, 1930.

MICHAEL A. LEDEEN

Applied Social
Science and Systems Analysis

The search for social science contributions to policy making is an intensive one which has been going on for quite a long time. It well antecedes modern social science, illustrated, for instance, by the work of Jeremy Bentham in England and by the Cameralists in Europe.[1] The founders of modern sociology were strongly interested in the policy implications of their knowledge, some of them trying to combine knowledge and power through personal political activity—such as Max Weber himself. In more recent periods, the question of "knowledge for what" has been asked continuously, and efforts to apply social science knowledge to social issues have been made for many years. Even when measured by quantitative criteria, the investments in social science research—including so-called applied studies—in the United States are considerable.[2]

Despite this interest in applied social science,[3] the output of social science in terms of knowledge relevant to policy is not easy to pin down. Certainly there is knowledge significant to some problems. But a social scientist who is asked to demonstrate the possible operational significance of his discipline for the main problems facing humanity and society is quite hard put to provide illustrations.[4] This is the case also when we adopt a broad concept of "problem significant knowledge," which looks for heuristic aids and not for answers. Even when we accept as relevant, knowledge that mainly serves to educate the frames-of-appreciation[5] of policy makers in clearly policy-relevant ways, few social science theories will pass this minimal threshold.[6]

Not only is contemporary social science knowledge disappointing in policy relevance,[7] but there seem to be few promising ways to change this state of affairs through incremental adjustments. Suggestions vary from doing more of what is being done now, to setting up additional problem-oriented social research organizations. Some of the proposals are highly interesting and promise to be useful.[8] But, as I will try to show later on, most of the suggestions do not face up to the quantum jumps in knowledge necessary for developing significant policy-relevant social science knowledge.

Applied social science constitutes one of the principal rational avenues to better social policy making. A second way is the analytical decision approach, operationalized best by systems analysis; that is by improving decision making through morphological analysis, logical structuring, explication of assumptions, examination of interrelations with interconnected variables and systematic use of a variety of decision sciences techniques.[9] Based on economics, systems engineering and operations research and reinforced by significant successes when applied to certain defense decision problems, systems analysis is widely regarded as a powerful instrument for better policy making.[10]

In fact, an increasing number of efforts to apply systems analysis to social problems is underway. But, again, any summary of the policy-relevant conclusions of these efforts is disappointing. Significant findings are available when the problem is susceptible to operations research techniques (for example, transportation networks) or when the problem can be treated with methods of economics and engineering economics (such as housing). But contemporary systems analysis is not really helpful in respect to the main problems facing present and emerging society. Neither does contemporary systems analysis demonstrate any inherent capacity for growth that will make them relevant for such problems in the foreseeable future.

YEHEZKEL DROR

The independent avenues of applied social sciences research and of systems analysis both being inadequate for significant policy-making improvements, I want to explore the idea that their fusion may provide much-needed help.

In doing so, I make no claim that this is the only worthwhile search for ways to improve the contributions of social science and analytic approaches to policy making. Other effective ways may include, for instance, building up the role of social science as a social critic—with close attention to value judgments, action programs, advocacy and issues usually repressed;[11] deductive construction of models of complex social systems.[12] The scarcity of knowledge and experience about how to deal with difficult issues may well require that a number of approaches be developed and utilized concurrently. But my impression is 1) that some fusion between analytical decision approaches and applied social sciences is itself a promising approach; 2) that despite lip service, this possibility is quite neglected; 3) that some fusion between analytical decision approaches and applied social sciences is essential if other approaches are to achieve desirable results;[13] and 4) that such a fusion will interact synergetically with other approaches. Hence, the idea of some fusion between applied social science and analytic decision approaches seems to justify exploration, but without any claim of exclusivity.

To explore the possibility of fusion between analytic and applied approaches as an avenue to better policy making, let us evaluate it from the points of view of systems analysis and applied social science respectively.

THE VIEW FROM SYSTEMS ANALYSIS[14]

If systems analysis in its present state were a useful way to deal with social problems or if a more promising analytic approach were available, there would be less need to search for innovations. But in its present incrementally advanced forms, systems analysis is helpless in the face of complex social issues. In particular, systems analysis is inadequate for treating complex social issues in eight main interdependent respects:

1) Systems analysis focuses on proposing preferable policies, neglecting the institutional contexts, both of the problems and of

the policy-making and policy-implementation processes. Thus, "institution-building" is not within its domain of applicability.

2) Systems analysis does not take into account political needs, such as maintaining consensus and building coalitions.

3) Systems analysis has difficulties in dealing with irrational phenomena, such as ideologies, charisma, high-risk commitments, martyr tendencies and unconventional life-styles.

4) Systems analysis is unable to deal with basic value issues and often inadequately explicates the value assumptions of analysis.

5) Systems analysis deals with identifying preferable alternatives among available or easily synthesized ones. Invention of radically new alternatives is beyond its scope, though it can perhaps help by showing the inadequacy of available alternatives.

6) Systems analysis requires some predictability in respect to alternatives. Situations of "primary uncertainty" (when not only the probabilities of various outcomes, but the dimensions of the possible outcomes are unknown) cannot be handled by systems analysis.

7) Systems analysis requires significant quantification of relevant variables.

8) Basic strategy choices—such as attitudes toward risk and time—are not explicitly faced by systems analysis. Rather, maximin or minimax and discount of the future ("positive interest rates") are usually assumed.

These eight characteristics are not equally shared by all systems analysis studies. Indeed, the best practitioners of systems analysis will clearly label such characteristics as inadequate and diligently search for ways to overcome them. But if we look at available systems analysis studies of real issues rather than at professions of faith, introductory statements or a few outstanding studies, then my list of inadequacies of present systems analysis may justly be criticized as too mild.

Let me try and illustrate the weaknesses of contemporary systems analysis by an enumeration of some typical (though not universal) omissions in three areas of studies:

Transportation studies: Preoccupation with "mix-of-modes" issues and with satisfaction of extrapolated consumer demands, within a cost-benefit framework. Some attention to pollution effects, especially when susceptible to translation into economic values. Ignorance of changes in the values to be served by future transportation, such as transportation tastes, aesthetic feelings, new patterns of leisure use. Neglect of transportation impacts on community life and social interaction. Ignorance of possible positive functions of inadequate transportation. Ignorance of political and power implications of transportation. Inadequate treatment of interfaces between transportation and communication, housing and various aspects of the patterning of human activities in space.

Defense studies: Preoccupation with low-level aspects of defense, including equipment and tactics. Just beginning to face issues of "nonrational" adversaries. Little explication of basic value assumptions and of scenarios based on radically different assumptions. Ignorance of internal political and cultural conditions and domestic implications of external defense policies. Very weak treatment of interfaces between socio-political-cultural issues and defense issues in other countries. Very weak treatment of relations between defense activities and other external activities, especially socioeconomic ones.[15]

Public safety: Tendency to define public safety in objective rather than phenomenological terms—number of crimes, rather than feeling of safety or propensity to deviate. Concentration on efficiency of law enforcement, rather than underlying causes of problems. Short-range approach, with very little attention to longer range interfaces between public safety and, for instance, youth culture.

Were we to try and examine applications of the systems analysis to broader problem areas, such as racial discrimation, we either would not find any illustrations at all or they would be even narrower and more limited. This does not imply that systems analysis does not make important contributions to such problems by illuminating some of their components. Thus, in respect to discrimination, the finding that unemployment is less of a problem in the black community than employment in low-paying jobs is highly significant. Similarly, findings that inequities sometimes result from rent control are highly significant for social policy, and reflect systems analysis at its best. But the pride of the analytical decision approach is in its claim to provide overall penetration and "systems solutions." I think there can be no doubt that contemporary systems analysis is unable to do so in respect to main areas of social problem.

To overcome these inabilities of present systems analysis, a new basic methodology is essential. This new analytical methodology, which I call policy analysis, accepts the fundamental tenets of systems analysis, namely:

☐ Looking at problems and alternatives in a broad way, which tries to take account of many of the relevant variables and of the probable results, that is, taking a systems view.

☐ Searching for an optimal, or at least clearly preferable, solution among available alternatives within a broad cost-benefit framework, without being limited to incremental changes.

☐ Explicit and rational identification of the preferable alternative (or alternatives) through comparison of expected results in terms of operational goals; this is done with the help of a large set of techniques, ranging from mathematical models to human gaming and from sensitivity testing to canvassing of experts' opinions.

But these tenets must be supplemented, with many of the needed changes being based on applied social sciences.

To this basic framework of systems analysis, policy analysis would add the following components:

1) Penetration into underlying values, assumptions, and strategies. These include, in particular a) exploration of the basic values at which policies should be directed; b) long-range goal research; and c) explicit analysis of alternative policy strategies (such as risk choices, incrementalism vs. innovation, and goal-oriented vs. resources development-oriented policies).

2) Consideration of political variables, including a) political feasibility analysis; b) evaluation of alternative political pathways for policy approval and implementation; c) examination of social power implications of alternative policies; and d) analysis of coalition needs and political consensus implications.

3) Treatment of broader and more complex systems, involving a) lower and new scales of quantification (for example, nominal and nonmetric); b) necessity to satisfy multidimensional and diverse goals; c) far-going primary uncertainty; d) institutional change as a main mode of policy change; and e) acceptance of min-avoidances (that is, avoidance of the worst of all bad alternatives) and sensitization and long-range impacts as important goals of policy analysis, in addition to "preferization."

4) Main emphasis on policy alternative innovation, involving a) intense attention to creativity encouragement; b) much reliance on

sequential decision making, learning feedback and social experimentation, instead of models, simulation and detailed policy schemes (such as PERT); and c) much attention to new systems design, in addition to redesign of systems.

5) Much sophistication in respect to social phenomena; for instance: recognition of irrationality, ideologies, mass phenomena, depth variables and similar nonrational phenomena as main variables, both of social behavior and of legitimate goal formation, and acceptance of apperception, intuition and experience as valuable sources of knowledge and insight.

6) Institutional self-awareness, for instance in respect to a) the necessity for multiplicity and redundance of analysis and analysis units; b) early involvement of politicians, community leaders, and so forth, in the analytical activities; and c) the limits of analysis as a perceptive set for cognizing human reality and aspirations.

The social scientist will have little difficulty in recognizing many items in this list of desiderata that can be supplied by social science, either with available knowledge or by knowledge which can in principle be obtained, if suitable research efforts are made. Nevertheless, I doubt whether the social sciences, as they are today, can supply all the requisites of policy analysis. This I think becomes clear when we look at the situation from the point of view of applied social science.

THE VIEW FROM APPLIED SOCIAL SCIENCE

The issues and problems of applied social science are more difficult to discuss than those of systems analysis. This is the case because of its much more heterogeneous composition, longer history and higher state of development, and the complexity of relations between "pure social science" and "applied social science."

In fact, even the very use of the term "applied social science" may be misleading if it is assumed that there is a single referent to this verbal symbol. What we do have is a number of social sciences which in different forms are applied to a large range of heterogeneous social issues. These social sciences include, in particular sociology, social psychology and political science.

A special case not usually included in the term "applied social science" is economics, which has unique characteristics, including a good deal of overlap of pure and applied elements. The well-recognized reasons for the special nature of economics include: the different intellectual history of economics, which has been more policy oriented; the susceptibility of large parts of its subject matter to quantitative treatment; the reductionability of many of its variables to a few aggregate categories which are operational and measurable; and the relatively simple characteristics of the interrelations among some main categories which permit simulation of important aspects of economic phenomena by compact and usable models (especially simultaneous equations and, nowadays, computer programs).

Another significant characteristic of economics which makes it especially useful as advanced policy-relevant knowledge, is that it links social science knowledge and analytical approaches. Economics covers two main types of concerns: knowledge about economic institutions and behavior, and knowledge how to "economize," in the sense of optimizing the use of scarce resources. It seems to me that this dual role in economics is a main source of its strength as policy-relevant knowledge, and in this respect it is a pioneer for social science as a whole.[16]

However one explains the special aspects of economics, it clearly is in a separate category. Therefore, I am excluding it from the term "applied social science," focusing my concerns on sociology, social psychology and political science.[17]

It is difficult to generalize from the heterogeneous bundle of attempts that sociology, social psychology and political science have made to become applied. Many of them still suffer from well-recognized weaknesses.[18] These weaknesses include in particular: oscillation between idiographic micro-studies and "grand theory"; a priori commitment to equilibrium and structural-function concepts, which result in do-nothing, or, at best, incremental change recommendations; timidity in facing acute social issues and in handling taboo subjects; perfectionism, which causes withdrawal from all problems with time constraints, that is, all significant social problems; and a deep feeling of guilt about getting involved in applications which go beyond "value-free," "pure," "factual" and "behavioral" research.

But, as just mentioned, these weaknesses are recognized by a growing number of social scientists who are committed to the improvement of the human and social condition. These social scientists are supported by the growing demands of government and the various publics for social science help in facing social issues, by student pressure for "relevance," and by a number of foundations and research centers. The first fruits of a new type of applied social sciences can be detected in ideas such as social reporting and social indicators;[19] policy-oriented methodologies, such as evaluative research and social experimentation;[20] attempts to face value issues;[21] orientations toward the future;[22] broader approaches to social policy issues,[23] and, most important of all, some contributions to a few important decisions and recommendations, such as the antisegregation Supreme Court decisions and the report of the Commission on Violence, as well as specific inputs into many current decision processes.[24] Also significant are the increasing amounts of work dealing with policy making as a subject for research and improvement[25] and with the role of scientists in policy making.[26]

This list of achievements looks, prima facie, impressive. And, indeed, it reflects significant progress in applied social science. But, in order to get a more balanced view, a number of additional points must be taken into account:

First, the advances in applied social sciences are not an integrated and mutually reinforcing set of activities. Instead, different items are developed in isolation. To illustrate: Most work on substantive issues ignores the implications of studies on policy making for the political feasibility and the institutional requisites of changing discrete policies. Similarly, most studies on substantive issues do not incorporate a future dimension and neglect to adjust recommendations to alternative future possibilities. At the same time, studies on policy making are seldom related to social issues and pay little attention to the future dimensions; and alternative-future studies tend to neglect the future dimensions both of policy making and of main social issues.

Second, the various modern applied social science activities are still marginal. Only a small (though increasing) amount of research time is allocated to them. More significant is their marginal position in respect to recognition; thus, it seems that applied subjects are not acceptable as doctorate thesis subjects at the large majority of graduate social science departments.

Third, "applied social science" is just now becoming self-conscious, in the sense of developing a self-identity and building up its own frames-of-appreciation, methodology and institutions. Instead, the different social sciences tend to have their own applied corners, with significant differences, for instance, between applied political science and applied sociology. As a result, the need to reorganize the social science system itself for application are nearly completely ignored.[27] This includes such obvious needs as adjusting graduate training in social sciences so as to prepare social science professionals for policy application roles. Also neglected are the problems of organizational location of social science advisors, required interaction arrangements between them and senior policy makers, problems of training of senior policy makers to enable them to utilize social science, the novel roles of policy research organizations, and so on.

Fourth, these weaknesses of self-perception are demonstrated, for instance, by the widespread tendency to compare applied social science and its relations with pure social science to engineering and its relations with physical sciences. This comparison ignores basic differences, such as:

1) The pragmatic base of much of engineering, which anteceded physical science knowledge and in some respects still operates on an experiential basis (e.g., acoustics and metallurgy), versus the impossibility of basing applied social science on similar pragmatic sources of invention and knowledge. (In this respect, politicians and executives are more in accord with the pragmatism of engineering,)

2) The existence of a clear chain from abstract knowledge to production, moving from pure research through development, engineering and pilot-testing to production, versus the completely different nature of applied social science outputs and therefore the need for other relationships to pure knowledge.

3)The differences between physical science knowledge and social science knowledge, and therefore again the presumption that different modes of application are necessary.

4) The differences between engineering a product in the sense of a tangible, material thing and dealing with social issues, which are in part intangible, immaterial, undefined, open, dynamic, contextually shaped and value-dominated.

5) The scarcity of pure social science knowledge on which application could be based and, therefore, the fallacy of comparison with the engineering phase, which takes pure knowledge and

its development more or less for granted, or at least as something not to be planned for. The situation is different in applied social sciences, where encouragement of relevant abstract research may be a main component.[28]

Most serious of all is the absence of a methodology for prescriptive and policy-oriented social science endeavors.

Let me emphasize that I am speaking only about a methodology for prescriptive and policy-oriented research. Certainly, social science does not lack an analytic basis for its traditional main areas of concern—descriptions, analysis and understanding of behavior.[29] But the needs of prescriptive and policy-oriented research are quite different and require methodologies of their own. The absence of such methodologies is, in my opinion, among the main reasons for some of the main substantive weaknesses of much contemporary applied social sciences work, such as:

1) A tendency, when recommendations are put forth, to mix up reliable factual knowledge, implicit axiomatic assumptions, provisional theories, conceptual taxonomies, doubtful hypotheses and various types of hidden value judgments, such as on substantial goals, on willingness to take risks and on evaluation of time.

2) A tendency to neglect important special characteristics and requirements of policy-oriented research, such as the scarcity of time, the search for leverage points, the need for social invention, and the necessity for experimentation.

3) A tendency to neglect interdependencies between what is perceived as the problem and other social issues and facets, leading sometimes to quite narrow and time-bound recommendation.

4) A tendency to proceed without serious efforts to understand the relevant characteristics of politics and policy making (and, as already mentioned, without integrating studies of substantive issues with studies of policy making). As a result, there is oscillation between naivity and cynicism, and therefore between disregard for implementation and Machiavellian tactics. As a result, little attention is devoted to improvements of the policy-making system itself as a main avenue for better resolutions of social problems (with some exceptions in political science, most of them quite traditional).

5) A tendency to ignore the limitations of resources and therefore to avoid the necessity to evaluate alternatives within a cost-benefit framework.

The absence of prescriptive and policy-oriented methodology also serves to reinforce the previously mentioned weaknesses of applied social science. In the absence of such a methodology, or an awareness that such a methodology is needed, there is neither a condition of self-consciousness nor a focus for integration.

It is in the supply of a prescriptive and policy-oriented methodology that there lies the great promise of some fusion with systems analysis for applied social science.

TOWARDS A FUSION OF APPLIED SOCIAL SCIENCE AND SYSTEMS ANALYSIS

Our separate consideration of systems analysis and applied social science seem to support the conclusion that some fusion of these two may be useful, and even essential, for significantly increasing the contributions of either of them to better policy making.[30] This does not imply the disappearance of applied social science and of systems analysis in their present and emerging forms. Nor, as already stated, does it imply that such a fusion is the only effective way for improving the contributions of applied social science and of systems analysis to policy making. But it seems to me that there is a strong case for moving in the direction of some integration of applied social science and systems analysis.

The necessary integration can take different forms. As a minimum, the following specifications seem reasonable:

For systems analysis: changes in basic orientation, methodologies and concepts, so as to move from systems analysis to policy analysis, as explained above; understanding of basics of social sciences.

For applied social science: absorption of basic methodology of systems analysis, as a design for examining problems and proposing recommendations.

For both systems analysis and applied social science: a measure of shared concepts and frames-of-appreciation, sufficient to permit mutual communication, cross-stimulation and common work in interdisciplinary policy research teams.

Achievement of even such a minimum degree of fusion is hindered by many differences between the applied social sciences and systems analysis. These differences seem to include the following:

YEHEZKEL DROR

DIFFERENCES BETWEEN SYSTEMS ANALYSIS
AND APPLIED SOCIAL RESEARCH

	Systems Analysis	Applied Social Science
Differences in disciplinary bases	Economics, engineering, mathematics, operations research, decision sciences	Social sciences
Differences in main areas of application	Defense, water resources, hardware systems, transportation, some urban management	Social sub-problems related to welfare, communities, individuals
Differences in basic methodology	Prescriptive, rational, cost-benefit	Behavioral research methods
Differences in value orientations	"Efficiency," with increasing interest in "equity"	"Good Life," "social justice," "humanism," "social integration"
Differences in professional codes	Special relations with employer; often "the establishment"	Ideology of "free profession," though dependent on resources origin
Differences in reference groups	Mixed between peer-orientation and much outsider-orientation, mainly to policymaker	Much peer-orientation some orientation to action-groups
Success expectation	Low	Quite optimisitc
Differences in modes of work	Teamwork, moving from problem to problem	Individual and some teamwork; often specialization in particular problem area
Differences in organizational loci	Mainly special policy research organizations, many of them independent non-profit corporations	Mainly university departments and institutes
Career patterns	Continuous career and specific professional commitment; some exchange with teaching	Part of academic discipline; limited commitment to applied work, often auxiliary to teaching and academic research
Differences of culture	More clinical, detached, objectivizing, externalizing, "analytical"	More personally committed, emotional, attached to subjects of study

Based, as it is, on personal observation and impressions rather than on a systematic survey, this list of differences is unreliable in its particulars. But I think it is valid in pointing out overall gestalt differences between systems analysis and applied social science. Moreover, I think that the differences are closely related to the present characteristics of systems analysis and applied social science as intellectual endeavors and social activities.[3][1]

Another aggravating factor is the scarcity of scholars and researchers who, individually, have crossed the barriers between applied social science and systems analysis and who have on their own achieved some fusion between the two. This, in part, is a testimony to the strength of the differences mentioned above, especially as there are many social scientists who have the quantitative knowledge and skills necessary for the analytical decision approaches, and certainly systems analysts can easily reach social science literature. Despite this availability of nominal access, it seems that even in the policy research organizations, where social scientists and systems analysts have many opportunities to interact and engage in mutual learning, they tend to keep apart. Indeed, quite a search is made by policy research organizations and by new university policy sciences programs for persons combining social sciences knowledge with knowledge in systems analysis, suitable candidates being very hard to find. At present, the best bet to meet urgent needs at policy research organizations for such people seems to be to develop in that direction before they become fully socialized in their respective disciplines. But this is an ad hoc emergency measure, which is more of a reflection of the urgent need than a way of meeting it.

Because of such difficulties, achievement of at least some fusion between systems analysis (and analytical decision approaches as a whole) and applied social science is not an easy matter. For some progress in this direction, the following activities seem essential:

☐ New courses in policy analysis and in social science to be offered at schools and departments of social sciences and at programs in system analysis respectively, so as to prepare at least the future professionals and scholars for the necessary fusion. These courses will have to be innovative in content and method, and their preparation is a difficult task. New texts and suitable active teaching materials (cases, games, projects and so forth) are required for them.

□Teaching of applied social science and systems analysis must proceed to a significant extent through doing. This goes beyond active teaching methods in the basic courses, requiring work on real problems in workshops. For that purpose, again, new types of materials are required.

□Indeed, more than classroom teaching is necessary to permit real learning by the students of the operational contents of systems analysis and applied social science respectively. Therefore, internship in applied social science institutes and in policy analysis organizations may well be necessary. During such internship, the students should work on mixed teams, so as to be exposed to approaches and orientations different from those they are familiar with.

□In order to prepare the future applied social scientists and systems analysts for some fusion of their methods and knowledge, teachers are needed who have good experience in both areas. Such teachers are unavailable at present. Therefore, special programs must include both a period of intense study, for instance in the form of summer institutes, and a period of learning through exposure and participation—involving about a year in a social science department and research institute or in a policy analysis organization respectively. Special financing and arrangements are necessary to realize such a program.

□University programs, and preparation of teachers and material for them, deal with the future. But immediate steps are essential to achieve significant retraining of the present generation of applied social scientists and analysts, to permit the fusion essential for enabling them to make significant contributions to better policy making. This requires a different set of workshops, special training activities and internships. I think that such retraining is highly important and should receive large resources, even if there is a short-term opportunity cost in terms of time and money.

The proposed steps constitute a minimum program for achieving absolutely essential degrees of integration between systems analysis and applied social science. Various levels of more ambitious proposals can be designed and are needed and useful. But even the minimum program as proposed, will be very difficult to implement. The intellectual, organizational and cultural barriers facing attempts to move in the direction of some fusion between applied social science and systems analysis are very formidable.

But even more forbidding are the psychological barriers facing any attempt to get mature and successful scholars and professionals to engage in quasi-formal learning and to accept explicitly the need to revise parts of their professional frames of appreciation, basic methodologies and work patterns. Nevertheless, the attempt must be made; but in the longer range, much more is needed.

THE NEXT PHASE: POLICY SCIENCES

Present social issues are very urgent, and more comprehensive larger range activities depend on present availability of suitable researchers and teachers. Therefore, a crash program to build up a group of scholars and professionals who link to some extent, applied social science and analysis (in its policy analysis form) is, in my opinion, most urgent. But, in the long run, it may be preferable to engage in design of new systems rather than redesign of systems and to build up a new supradiscipline profession oriented towards the application of systematic knowledge, organized creativity and structured rationality to the human condition. This is the case, also, because of the importance of continuing and accelerating the developments of social science and analytical decision approaches in their "normal" forms, to provide parts of the basic knowledge for policy sciences, and because of the importance of other possible alternatives for the advancement of applied social science and analytical decision approaches.

Therefore, I think we should move towards the establishment of policy sciences as a new supradiscipline and profession.[32] What policy sciences should provide is a new set of paradigms which can serve as a basis for novel research, teaching and application designs, methodologies and institutions. To be quite clear, I think we need a scientific revolution[33] in order really to get the kinds of knowledge necessary to make sciences fully relevant to human and social needs.

To be specific, let me tentatively indicate some of the required unique paradigms, some of which are based on a fusion between applied social sciences and system analysis and some of which are even more far-reaching.[34]

First, breakdown of traditional boundaries between disciplines and especially between the various social sciences and decision

YEHEZKEL DROR

disciplines. Policy science must integrate knowledge from a variety of branches of knowledge into a supradiscipline focusing on public policy making. In particular, policy sciences are built upon a fusion between applied social sciences and analytical decision approaches. But they also absorb many elements from general systems theory, management sciences, conflict theory, strategic analysis, systems engineering and similar modern areas of study. Physical and life sciences are also relied upon, insofar as they are relevant.

Second, bridging of the usual dichotomy between "pure" and "applied" research. In policy sciences, integration between pure and applied research is achieved by acceptance of the improvement of public policy-making as their ultimate goal. As a result, the real world becomes a main laboratory of policy sciences, and the test of the most abstract theory is in its application (directly or indirectly) to problems of policy making.

Third, acceptance of tacit knowledge and experiences as important sources of knowledge, in addition to more conventional methods of research and study. Efforts to distill the tacit knowledge of policy practitioners and to involve high-quality policy makers as partners in the up-building of policy sciences are among the important characteristics distinguishing policy sciences from contemporary "normal" applied social science and analytic decision approaches.

Fourth, policy science shares with normal science a primary involvement with instrumental-normative knowledge, in the sense of being concerned with means and intermediate goals rather than absolute values. But policy sciences are sensitive to the difficulties of achieving "value-free" science and try to contribute to value choice by exploring value implications, value consistencies, value costs and the behavioral foundations of value commitments. Also, parts of policy sciences are involved in invention of different "alternative futures," including their value contents. Furthermore, organized creativity—including value invention—provides important inputs into parts of policy sciences (such as policy-making design and redesign of systems, policy design and policy analysis), and encouragement and stimulation of organized creativity. As a result, policy sciences should break a breach in the tight wall separating contemporary "social science" from ethics and philosophy and build up an operational theory of values (including value morphology, taxonomy, measurement, and so forth, but not the substantive absolute norms themselves) as a part of policy science.

Fifth, policy sciences should be very time-sensitive, regarding the present as a "bridge between the past and the future." Consequently, they should reject the ahistoric approach of much of contemporary social science and analytical decision approaches. Instead, it emphasizes historic developments on one hand and future dimensions on the other hand as central to improved policy making.

Sixth, policy sciences have a unique focus of interest, namely "metapolicies" (that is, policies on policies). These include, for instance, modes of policy making, policy analysis, policy-making systems, and policy strategies. While the main test of policy sciences is better achievement of considered goals through more effective and efficient policies, policy science as such is in the main not directly concerned with the substantive contents of discrete policy problems, (which should be dealt with by the relevant "normal" disciplines), but rather with improved methods, knowledge and systems for better policy-making.

Seventh, policy sciences do not accept the "take it or leave it" attitude of much of traditional social science, neither does it regard petition-signing and similar direct action involvements as a main form of policy sciences contribution (in distinction from scientists acting as citizens and from other concepts of applied social science to better policy making). Instead, they are committed to striving for increased utilization of policy science and to preparation of professionals to serve in policy science positions (without letting this sense of mission interfere with a clinical and rational orientation to policy issues).

Finally, policy sciences deal with the contribution of systematic knowledge and structured rationality to conscious human and social self-direction. But policy sciences clearly recognize the important roles both of extrarational processes (such as creativity, intuition, charisma and value judgment) and of irrational processes (such as depth motivation). The search for ways to improve these processes for better policy making is an integral part of policy sciences, including, for instance, even possible policy-making implications of altered states of consciousness. (In other words, policy sciences face the paradoxical problem of how to improve extrarational and irrational processes through rational means).

Clearly, the emergence of policy sciences as a separate inter-discipline has far-reaching implications. These implications involve the internal structure of policy sciences and its relationship to traditional disciplines (for example, special university programs in policy science[3][5] and new forms of policy research organizations), including important feedbacks to applied social science and analytic decision approaches in their various forms. More impor-tant, the emergence of policy sciences raises very difficult questions concerning the future forms of relationships between knowledge and power, such as changes required to enable politics to utilize policy sciences without being overwhelmed by them, and institutional arrangements necessary to prevent monopolization of policy sciences by the establishment and to assure utilization of policy sciences for improvement of broad democratic processes. Detailed discussion of such issues is outside the scope of this chapter.[3][6] But we should be aware that the establishment of policy sciences is a fundamental innovation, which may well result in quite novel forms of social guidance and changes in the roles of scientists and scientific knowledge.

NOTES

[1] There is an amazing scarcity of studies dealing with the history of applied knowledge and of social invention.

[2] See Gene M. Lyons, *The Uneasy Partnership: Social Science and the Federal Government in the Twentieth Century* (New York: Russell Sage Foundation, 1969).

[3] Some of the best work in applied social science is done in Europe. Thus, for instance, in the Netherlands, a special profession of "social geography" has been instrumental in applying social science knowledge to physical planning. The role of anthropologists in colonial administration provides a different set of illustrations of applied social sciences. The lack of literature in English on European experiences with applied social science is a grave omission, hindering learning and cross stimulation.

[4] As an exercise, I went through Bernard Berelson and Gary A. Steiner, *Human Behavior: An Inventory of Scientific Findings* (New York: Harcourt, Brace, 1966), trying to identify items which I would include in a "Handbook of Behavioral Sciences for Policy Making." The results are insufficient for a short article, not to speak of a "handbook." This same conclusion was reached by Alexander Syalair, who repeated my exercise. See Alexander Syalair "The United Nations and the Social and Behavioral Sciences," *The American Journal of International Law*, Vol. 64, No. 41, Sept. 1970, pp. 148-163, esp. pp. 156-157.

Similarly, an examination of the recent second edition of Gardner Lindsey and Elliott Aronson, eds., *The Handbook of Social Psychology* (Reading, Mass.: Addison-Wesley, 1968) provides very little findings which can serve as direct inputs into policy making. Volume Five is devoted to *Applied Social Psychology*, but despite the high standard of its contents, it has little direct policy implications for any major social issues.

[5] This very important concept is developed by Sir Geoffrey Vickers, *The Art of Judgment* (New York: Basic Books, 1965), Chapter 4. In contrast to the tendency in much of the United States problem-oriented literature—and especially in decision theory and systems analysis—to approach issues by decomposition and treatment of different decision components (such as goals, alternatives, and predictions), Sir Geoffrey Vickers emphasizes the need for a holistic Gestalt view of problems. See also his collection *Value Systems and Social Process* (New York: Basic Books, 1968).

[6] A good illustration is provided by the report of the Special Commission on the Social Sciences of the National Sciences Board, *Knowledge into Power: Improving the Nation's Use of the Social Sciences* (1969). The commission clearly tried hard to prove the importance of the social sciences for social problems and action. Nevertheless, the report is not at all convincing to someone who is not convinced in advance. This, I think, is a result of the real situation for which the commission is not at fault.

[7] A very good treatment of applied social science is provided in P. Lazarsfeld, W. Sewell, and H. Wilensky, eds., *The Uses of Sociology* (New York: Basic Books, 1967). Much relevant material is included in the four volumes on *The Use of Social Research in Federal Domestic Programs,* a Staff Study for the Research and Technical Programs Subcommittee of the Committee on Government Operations, House of Representatives, April 1967 (Washington, D.C.: U.S. Government Printing Office, 1967); and the three volumes of Hearings Before the Subcommittee on Government Research of the Committee on Government Operations, United States Senate, on S. 836, *A Bill to Provide for the Establishment of the National Foundation for the Social Sciences,* February and June 1967 (Washington, D.C.: U.S. Government Printing Office, 1967).

Problem-focused attempts in applied social science are illustrated, for instance, by Quincy Wright, William M. Evan, and Morton Deutsch, eds., *Preventing World War III: Some Proposals* (New York: Simon and Schuster, 1962) and by Elisabeth T. Crawford and Albert D. Biderman, eds., *Social Scientists and International Affairs: A Case for a Sociology of Social Science* (New York: John Wiley, 1969).

When we consider the growing number of books on social problems and sociology in action, the problem clearly is not one of knowledge being hidden. The severe limitations of most published material when viewed from the point of view of policy making (as distinguished from many other, not less important, criteria) must therefore be regarded as a valid and reliable reflection of the actual state of knowledge.

[8] Especially important are proposals of the Behavioral and Social Sciences Survey Committee of the United States National Academy of Sciences. See *Behavioral and Social Sciences: Outlook and Need* (Englewood Cliffs, New Jersey: Prentice-Hall, 1969).

[9] This characterization of analytical decision approaches is in no sense a definition or an exhaustive description. But it should help to clarify the meaning in which I use the terms "analytical decision approaches" and

"systems analysis." Such clarification is especially needed in this essay which is directed at a multiplicity of audiences, in the professional jargons of which these terms have different meanings.

In essence, I am using the term "systems analysis" in the sense in which it was first developed and used at The RAND Corporation. The best presentation of this view of systems analysis is provided in E. S. Quade and W. I. Bouchet, eds., *Systems Analysis and Policy Planning: Applications in Defense* (New York: American Elsevier, 1968).

This use of the term "systems analysis" must be kept clearly distinct from its uses as reference to: a) a general systems theory approach to description and analysis of behavior (e.g., as in the item "systems analysis" in the new *International Encyclopedia of Social Sciences),* and b) a computerized approach to social problem resolution and social management (as criticized, for instance, in Robert Boguslaw, *The New Utopians: A Study of System Design and Social Change,* Englewood Cliffs, New Jersey: Prentice-Hall, 1965).

The term "analytical decision approaches" covers the more general methodologies of which systems analysis is one operational expression. Other expressions of analytical decision approaches include, for instance, the classical works of Marquis de Condorcet; more modern Polish work in Praxeology (e.g., see Tadeasz Kotarbinski, *Praxeology: An Introduction to the Sciences of Efficient Action,* New York: Pergamon Press, 1965); recent work in decision analysis (e.g., see Howard Raiffa, *Decisions Analysis: Introductory Lectures on Choices under Uncertainty,* Reading, Massachusetts: Addison-Wesley, 1968); some efforts in various other areas, such as in architecture (e.g., see Christopher Alexander, *Notes on the Synthesis of Form,* Cambridge, Mass.: Harvard University Press, 1964); and the emerging, more comprehensive and inclusive "policy analysis" approach, which I will discuss later.

[10] The tendency to present systems analysis as a powerful tool for solving social problems is reflected, for instance, by Simon Ramo, *Cure for Chaos: Fresh Solutions to Social Problems Through the Systems Approach* (New York: David McKay Co., 1969).

More explicit about the limitations of system analysis in addition to Quade and Bouchet, *op. cit.,* are the works of C. West Churchman. See especially his books: *The Systems Approach* (New York: Delacorte Press, 1968) and *Challenge to Reason* (New York: McGraw-Hill, 1968).

[11] Such a conception of the characteristics and missions of useful applied social sciences is well represented, for instance, by *trans*action magazine.

[12] E.g., on the lines of the work of Jay W. Forrester, as illustrated in his book, *Urban Dynamics* (Cambridge, Mass.: MIT Press, 1969).

[13] Thus, improved governmental policy making, achieved in part through policy science based on fusion between analytical decision approaches and applied social science, is essential for effectively realizing new demands and ideas—which in turn may be developed and advanced as goals for governmental policy making with the help of other applied social science approaches.

[14] Parts of this section are based on my paper, "Policy Analysis: A Theoretic Framework and Some Basic Concepts," presented at the 65th Annual Meeting of the American Political Science Association, New York, September 2-6, 1969.

[15] The barriers to study of such issues in an appropriate way are brought

out in Irving L. Horowitz, ed., *The Rise and Fall of Project Camelot: Studies in the Relationship between Social Science and Practical Politics* (Cambridge, Massachusetts: MIT Press, 1967).

[16] At the same time, one should recognize that large parts of economics are weak in their behavioral contents. As a result, when actual behavior does not fit implicit behavioral assumptions, then contemporary economics theory provides wrong recommendations. This is the case both in respect to preindustrial countries and a growing number of situations in postindustrial societies.

[17] I include the general aspects of anthropology under sociology, and international relations under political science.

[18] See especially C. Wright Mills, *The Sociological Imagination* (New York: Oxford University Press, 1959).

[19] E.g., Raymond A. Bauer, ed., *Social Indicators* (Cambridge, Mass.: MIT Press, 1966); Eleanor Bernert Sheldon and Wilbert E. Moore, eds., *Indicators of Social Change: Concepts and Measurement* (New York: Russell Sage Foundation, 1968); and Otis D. Duncan, *Toward Social Reporting: Next Steps* (New York: Russell Sage Foundation, 1969).

[20] E.g., see Edward A. Suchman, *Evaluative Research: Principles and Practice in Public Service and Social Action Programs* (New York: Russell Sage Foundation, 1967); George W. Fairweather, *Methods for Experimental Social Innovation* (New York: John Wiley, 1967); and Elaine Cumming, *Systems of Social Regulation* (New York: Atherton Press, 1968).

[21] Recent approaches that are sensitive to the need of facing value issues but that do not adopt an extreme "advocacy" solution are well presented, for instance, by William E. Connolly, *Political Science and Ideology* (New York: Atherton Press, 1967) and by Rollo Handy, *Value Theory and the Behavioral Sciences* (Springfield, Ill.: Charles C. Thomas, 1969). See also Gideon Sjoberg, ed., *Ethics, Politics and Social Research* (Cambridge, Mass.: Schenkman, 1967).

[22] E.g., see Bertrand de Jouvenel, *The Art of Conjecture* (New York: Basic Books, 1967) and Daniel Bell, "Twelve Modes of Prediction" in Julius Gould, ed., *Penguin Survey of the Social Sciences, 1965* (Middlesex, Eng.: Penguin, 1965). Social scientists fulfilled important roles in the work of the American Academy of Arts and Sciences Commission on the Year 2000, as is reflected in the forthcoming six volumes of papers.

[23] E.g., see Howard V. Perlmutter, *Towards a Theory and Practice of Social Architecture* (London: Tavistock Pub., 1965); Leslie T. Wilkins, *Social Policy, Action, and Research: Studies in Social Deviance* (London: Associated Book Publishers, 1967); and Herbert P. Gans, *People and Plans: Essays on Urban Problems and Solutions* (New York: Basic Books, 1968).

Relevant illustrations of broad approaches to more general social issues are the contributions of social scientists to comprehensive efforts such as Bertram M. Gross, *A Great Society?* (New York: Basic Books, 1966) and Kermit Gordon, ed., *Agenda for the Nation* (Washington, D.C.: The Brookings Institution, 1968). More specific contributions are well illustrated by Daniel P. Moynihan, ed., *On Understanding Poverty* (New York: Basic Books, 1969).

[24] These inputs, which are of important aggregative impact, are well represented by the work of special social science research organizations, such as the Bureau of Social Science Research and the Center for Policy Research.

[25] E.g., see Thomas R. Dye, *Politics, Economics, and Its Public: Policy*

Outcomes in the American States (Chicago: Rand McNally, 1966); Austin Ranney, ed., *Political Science and Public Policy* (Chicago: Markham Pub., 1968); Raymond A. Bauer and Kenneth J. Gergen, *The Study of Policy Formation* (New York: The Free Press, 1968); Robert L. Crain, Elihu Katz, and Donald B. Rosenthal, *The Politics of Community Conflict: The Fluoridation Decision* (Indianapolis: Bobbs-Merrill, 1969); and Bertram M. Gross, ed., *Social Intelligence for America's Future: Explorations in Societal Problems* (Boston, Mass.: Allyn and Bacon, 1969).

[26] E.g., see Don K. Price, *The Scientific Estate* (Cambridge, Mass.: Harvard University Press, 1965); Robert Gilpin and Christopher Wright, ed., *Scientists and National Policymaking* (New York: Columbia University Press, 1964); Sanford A. Lakoff, ed., *Knowledge and Power: Essays on Science and Government* (New York: The Free Press, 1968); Donald A. Strickland, *Scientists in Politics: the Atomic Scientists Movement, 1945-46* (Purdue University Studies, 1968); and some chapters of Barnard Barber and Walter Hirsch, ed., *The Sociology of Sciences* (New York: The Free Press, 1962).

[27] But, again, there are some signs of a change. See, for instance, the proposal to set up special applied social science schools included in the report of the Behavioral and Social Sciences Survey Committee, *op. cit.*

[28] For instance, a strong argument can be made that theoretic study of macrosystems is essential for meaningful application, but is as yet neglected in sociology and handled badly in modern political science. See Amitai Etzioni, *The Active Society: A Theory of Societal and Political Processes* (New York: The Free Press, 1968).

[29] For recent work on the analytical foundations of "normal" social sciences, which builds on the strong foundations laid by persons such as Durkheim, Max Weber, Gunnar Myrdal and Merton, see, for instance, Richard S. Rudner, *Philosophy of Social Science* (Englewood Cliffs, New Jersey: Prentice Hall, 1966) and Robert Dubin, *Theory Building* (New York: The Free Press, 1969).

[30] It is important to note that such a fusion not only is one of several alternative essential conditions, but that sufficient conditions include also changes in the policy-making system (so as to permit it to better consider and absorb knowledge contributions) and in the transport channels between the knowledge system and the policymaking system. See Yehezkel Dror, "A General Systems Approach to Uses of Behavioral Sciences for Better Policymaking," in Ernest O. Attinger, ed., *Global Systems Dynamics* (New York: Karger, 1970), pp. 81-91.

[31] Systems analysis and applied social science are not the only decision-oriented disciplines and professional clusters. The legal profession, for instance, represents a quite different set of characteristics, as does also medicine and, to a lesser degree, management consultation.

[32] There are a number of precedents for emergence of new disciplines in the policy-related area, such as operations research, management sciences, administrative sciences, and, in a different way, urban studies and environmental studies. But, in my opinion, the most interesting case is that of strategic analysis, which clearly illustrates the development and significance of new policy-oriented academic and professional disciplines, with all the involved problems, potentials, and risks. This case should be carefully studied so as to permit learning for building up policy sciences. See, for instance, Bernard Brodie, "The Scientific Strategists," in Robert Gilpin and Chris-

topher Wright, *op. cit.,;* Irving L. Horowitz, *The War Game: Studies of the New Civilian Militarists* (New York: Ballantine, 1963); and Gene M. Lyons and Louis Merton, *School for Strategy* (New York: Praeger, 1965).

[33] My terminology follows Thomas S. Kuhn, *The Structure of Scientific Revolutions* (Chicago: University of Chicago Press, 1962). For a discussion of the applicability of this concept to sociology, see Robert W. Freidrichs, *A Sociology of Sociology* (New York: The Free Press, 1970) especially Chapters 1 and 2.

[34] On the characteristics of policy sciences, see my book *Design for Policy Sciences* (New York: American Elsevier, 1971). For a treatment of some of the substantive issues of policy sciences, see my book *Public Policymaking Reexamined* (San Francisco: Chandler Publishing Co., 1968).

[35] See Yehezkel Dror, "Teaching of Policy Sciences: Design for a University Doctoral Program," *Social Science Information,* Vol. 4, No. 2 (April, 1970), pp. 101-122.

[36] These issues are dealt with in the books mentioned in footnote 34.

The Social Science Study Groups

GENE M. LYONS

During the past few years three major reports have been published on the role of the social sciences in American society: *The Behavioral Sciences and the Federal Government,* published in September 1968 by an Advisory Committee of the National Academy of Sciences–National Research Council; *Knowledge into Action,* a report of the Special Commission on the Social Sciences to the National Science Board, in May 1969; and, in November 1969, *The Behavioral and Social Sciences: Outlook and Needs,* the report of the Behavioral and Social Science Survey Committee (BASS), cosponsored by the National Academy of Sciences–National Research Council and the Social Science Research Council.[1]

These three reports came at the end of a decade that had marked a formidable increase in the use and support of the social sciences by government, particularly at the federal level. For 1960, the National Science Foundation reported a total of $73 million in federal obligations for basic and applied research in the social and psychological sciences; by 1970, this total was estimated at $345 million.[2] Whatever problems of definition and comparability might be involved in interpreting these figures, they nonetheless testify to the magnitude of the increase of social science enterprise in the federal government. This growth, moreover, was accompanied by an increasingly pervasive use of social science with the advent of new social programs during the decade, particularly the antipoverty, education and training, and public health programs.

The increase in federal spending for social science was more than a technical trend in financial support, however. Indeed, by the end of the 1960s, federal programs in science, including social science, tended to reach a plateau and, in some areas, began to cut back. The increase in social science research was nonetheless now built into the system. This is not to suggest that social science research was effectively used by government. But it does suggest that the programs of the federal government were caught up in a wide variety of social processes and, for better or for worse, there was a serious interest in what social science research could offer in understanding their complexities. For some 30 years or more, there had been a general tendency to seek almost totally economic solutions to national issues—at least, so far as the federal government was involved. Now economic measures were clearly not the whole story and social research, beyond economic analysis, was required.

In many respects, the reports of the social science study groups can be seen as an attempt to develop a rational pattern of government-social science relations after a decade of pragmatic growth. But by a stroke of irony the reports were published at the beginning of a more complex period of relations characterized not only by the need for social as well as economic approaches, but also by a deep suspicion of governmental authority on the part of many academic groups, sharp divisions among social scientists about their proper role in regard to public policy, and a widespread intellectual debate over the social role of knowledge. The debate took, as its immediate foci, the war in Southeast Asia, the condition of blacks and the poor in American society, and the effects of ecological disruption (beginning with the pollution of the natural environment but soon broadening out into the more total and complex issues involving the "quality of life"). However, the implications of the debate also extended beyond immediate questions of public policy to the same overall issue the social science study groups had dealt with: the relation of social science to public policy and government authority. And in the process, the debate went even further in being part of a restructuring of government-science relations as they had evolved since World War II.

Despite their coincidence, the reports of the three study groups and the debate over the social role of knowledge were not really joined, at least immediately. The reports took shape in Washington offices and in the councils of professional associations, while the debate grew on college campuses and among dissenting groups of intellectuals. But the future is likely to be shaped by both movements, which are forced to come together in the open conventions of the professional social science associations. This confrontation has led to the rise of dissident factions challenging the authority of the established social science power structure and, in the process, its view of the proper role of social science in relation to government. This chapter is an attempt to come to grips with both movements by examining the origins and recommendations of the study group reports and analyzing their implications against some of the more searching questions raised by the critics of the social science "establishment."

THE ORIGINS OF THE REPORTS

A first observation about the three study groups is that none of them was especially initiated by social scientists. In one respect, they all have roots in the continuing efforts to find a role for social science in the federal government, efforts that have evolved through the "social trends" study published in the early 1930s, the planning agencies of the New Deal and the bevy of social science research teams that operated through the Second World War.[3] More directly, however, all three study groups were formally established through the intervention of physical and biological scientists, operating within the government structure of scientific development and utilization that had developed since that war.

For example, the first group, the National Academy Advisory Committee on Government Programs in the Behavioral Sciences, grew out of the controversy over Project Camelot, that ill-fated, army-sponsored research project on social change and internal revolution in South America. The irony of Camelot was that it was designed as a highly ambitious operation to try to get at questions of considerable interest to social scientists; but it wound up, in the eyes of many, as a catastrophe in which social science was seen as an embarrassing waste of taxpayer's money and/or as an unwitting instrument of social engineering in the hands of the military establishment.[4]

The fact is that responsible officials of the Department of Defense (DOD) were as concerned (from their own point of view) about the implications of Project Camelot as were social scientists. By then (1965) the department had a certain investment in social science that it certainly wanted to protect. It was anxious that Camelot be judged, not as typical, but in terms of the very difficult problems the military establishment faced, not by itself or for its own parochial purposes, but as one of several instruments of American foreign policy. At the same time, the subservience to dubious purposes, which Camelot seemed to represent, had to be seen against the two decades of highly professional support that the military had given to social scientists through agencies like the Office of Naval Research.

It was against this background that the Defense Department, through its Directorate for Research and Engineering, approached the National Academy of Sciences, asking for assistance in exploring the problems involved in military-supported social science research. The fact that DOD approached the academy is interesting in itself. At that time, the academy was only beginning to broaden its capacity to deal with the social sciences. From the early part of the century, the academy—and its operating arm, the National Research Council—had included within its orbit only the disciplines of anthropology and psychology from the social sciences and, within these disciplines, had generally emphasized sub-fields of interest to the dominant membership of physical and biological scientists. Not until the early 1960s did the National Research Council expand its Division of Anthropology and Psychology into a Division of Behavioral Sciences and not until the late 1960s did the National Academy of Sciences elect a small number of social scientists to join its ranks.

Certainly, the Defense Department could not, in 1965, have come to the academy with its problem because the academy represented social science. If social science was *represented* (whatever represented may mean), it was not in the academy, but

GENE M. LYONS

in the Social Science Research Council and the professional social science organizations. What the academy did represent was a key point of contact between the scientific and government communities, the kind of point of contact that, for all intents and purposes, was not available elsewhere in the social sciences. At the same time, the academy was part of an interconnected scientific establishment that had developed since World War II and that had grown in influence and in confidence by dealing with—and resolving—knotty problems in government-science relations (and Camelot was certainly knotty).

And so the academy took on the task of exploring the role of the social sciences in the federal government, but on its own broad terms and not on the more limited basis of either Project Camelot or the DOD program of social science research. It inaugurated an inquiry into the full range of federal programs involving the social sciences—their use and their support—and expanded the base of finance for the study by a grant from the Russell Sage Foundation, which supplemented the funds made available through defense agencies.

The origin of the National Science Board's Special Commission on the Social Sciences in many respects followed similar trends. Project Camelot spawned not only the National Academy Advisory Committee, but also a series of investigations in the Congress that led to the proposal for a National Social Science Foundation (NSSF). At one level, the proposal for a separate foundation was projected as a means of divorcing support for advanced research in the social sciences from the political missions of federal agencies, particularly the military departments. More broadly, it was seen as a means of expanding the total amount of federal support for social science in order to create a stronger framework and "infrastructure" of social science research that could be subsequently applied to a full range of public policy issues.[5]

It is important to remember that the idea of a separate foundation had never had great currency among social scientists. There was a curious absence of testimony about a separate social science foundation in the early debates over the National Science Foundation (NSF) and in the more recent discussions (until Project Camelot). The reason may lay in political realism—belief that the social sciences could never muster the political support that would be required to establish such an agency and then keep it funded. But at least in the early years after the Second World War, there also existed certain anxieties about government funding, a fear that the freedom of inquiry might be seriously impaired, especially in areas of political sensitivity. Then, later, as research appetites grew larger and many government agencies began to develop highly professional methods for supporting research, social scientists began to share in the increasing research budgets of agencies like the Department of Defense, the National Institutes of Health and the NSF. There really was little incentive to roil the waters.

Within NSF itself, support for the social sciences began to develop by the mid-1950s under the so-called "permissive but not mandatory" doctrine; that is, under its legislative mandate, the NSF was not required to support social science, but, as a result of its legislative history, was "permitted" to do so; By 1970, a Division of Social Science had been created under this rubric and in 1968, an amendment to the NSF Act made the whole business even more legitimate by giving the social sciences equal recognition in law. Recognition in law and recognition in fact, however, may be quite different. And so, proponents of a separate social science foundation—given its first significant political support in the post-Camelot debates—insisted that, while increased support for the social sciences from the NSF was encouraging and commendable, the Foundation would—by its nature, history and make-up—always be dominated by the priorities of the physical and biological sciences. The only way the social sciences could achieve full recognition of their problems, needs and role was therefore through a separate foundation.

The Special Commission on the Social Sciences was created by the National Science Board at the height of the debate over an NSSF in 1968. But the commission was not asked to address itself to the subject being debated, a separate foundation. Its mandate was framed in terms of the potential application of social science research to the problems of American society. The commission was in many respects the creation of a brilliant and skilled "statesman" of science, the chairman of the National Science Board, Philip Handler, who has since become the new president of the National Academy of Sciences. What the Special Commission was asked by the Board—in a period of increasing federal support for social science and in the midst of often-heated dispute over the organization of research agencies—was to provide an articulate and persuasive argument for increasing even further and strengthening even more the level of public support for social science developments. Certainly such a call—which could hardly be ignored—might also indicate that the priorities of social science could be established and championed within a broad-based scientific agency (the NSF) and did not require the creation of a separate and possibly competing agency (an NSSF).

Finally, the Behavioral and Social Science Survey (BASS) has its origins in a series of studies designed to provide guidance for federal support for science. Stimulated by physical and biological scientists, these studies, in turn, go back to the quest for new ways to formulate federal science policies in general. Under the Act of 1950 establishing the NSF, the foundation was supposed to assume responsibility for drawing up and recommending science policies to the President. In practice, the foundation has never been able to do this: the nature of "science policy" remains ill-defined; the foundation, during its early years, had to spend most of its energies surviving and developing its internal procedures, and, under these conditions, was in no position to recommend science policies that affected agencies that *competed* with it for research dollars in the federal budget.

By the early 1960s, the quest for science policy led to two movements, one inside government and the other outside. Inside government, the Office of the President's Special Assistant for Science and Technology was strengthened through the establishment of the Office of Science and Technology. But many scientists—among them, scientists who had served in top level posts in government—felt that efforts in government to develop science policies would forever be frustrated by the fragmenting tugs of competitive agencies and interests and by the demanding problems of short-range programs and budget cycles. What was required was a mechanism outside the government to examine and set out broad policy lines and alternatives on a time scale and against scientific objectives that could only gain short shrift in the overcharged environment of government bureaucracies.

In order to build such a mechanism, therefore, the National Academy of Sciences established its Committee on Science and

Public Policy (COSPUP). COSPUP, in turn, developed a work program that included a series of studies designed to set down the present state and future needs of all the sciences. Such a series of studies would then provide a blueprint for federal support of science, indicating those directions and fields that specialists within the disciplines considered to be the most important and the most ready for nurturing. Behind the venture was the assumption that, by now, federal support for science was a commitment that no longer needed debate; it now needed guidance. The BASS project is one of the latest products of this venture.

The origins of the three social science study groups show that the publication of three such reports within a short period was not entirely coincidental. By the mid 1960s, two trends had begun to take mature shape: one, the federal commitment to support science, not only as a by-product of political missions, but as an end in itself and as a concomitant to federal support for higher education. The growth of this commitment could not for long ignore the question of extension to the social sciences, whether or not Project Camelot had occurred. Camelot hastened the debate; it did not create it. For by then a second trend, of which Camelot was a symptom, had emerged: the increased role of social science research in federal programs—not just in defense, but in education, in mental health, in urban affairs, in the poverty projects—in a new period of social change in the United States.

These two trends, the federal commitment to support science and the policy demands of a new period of social change, brought to a head the need for some kind of a clarification of the social sciences in contemporary America. Whether the three study groups have provided that clarification is another matter. But the fact that they were all established through structures and procedures largely directed by physical and biological scientists is of some significance. For the substance and the style of the reports reflect the framework of analysis and a frame of reference of the "hard" sciences. The fact is that physical scientists have, since the Second World War, carried on a much more serious and systematic search for clarification of their role in government and politics than have social scientists. It is they who, like J. Robert Oppenheimer, felt they had come close, too close, to "sin" and "evil."

GENE M. LYONS

THE PROPOSALS OF THE REPORTS

The final report of the National Academy's Advisory Committee includes a range of recommendations: from measures to strengthen the internal structure of social science research programs in federal agencies to the establishment of a new National Institute for Advanced Research and Public Policy. Framed in a perspective that *accords politics its primary role in governmental decision-making* the report nonetheless emphasizes the social sciences as an important source of information, analysis and explanation about group and individual behavior and thus an important resource for policy formation.

From the experience of research in the fields of statistical services and economic analysis, the Advisory Committee draws lessons for using the knowledge and methods of the social sciences effectively in government. These lessons then lead to a series of practical suggestions, including staffing studies to identify positions for which social science training and experience should be required, in-service training programs in the scope and methods of the social sciences, and methods of organizing and reviewing social science research in any department or agency in terms of a set of strategic goals that relate agency missions to developments in the social sciences.

In the area of foreign affairs research—the area dramatized by Project Camelot—the report spells out two sets of proposals. The first was the establishment of an interagency research planning group in order to develop better balance than exists in the research effort among agencies with foreign operations and to begin to do something that has never been begun—to build cumulative bodies of knowledge on international problems. A second set of proposals, designed to contribute to international cooperation in social science research, places major responsibility on science and education agencies to support university programs for overseas research and student and faculty exchanges in the social sciences.

Beyond recommendations related to research programs in individual agencies and in special fields like foreign affairs, the report also tackles the problem of central organization for social science policies. Here, the committee opts, not for a separate social science structure, but for a serious integration of social scientists into the existing structure for formulating science policies, in the NSF, the Office of Science and Technology, and the President's Science Advisory Committee. The committee's conclusions in this regard are generally based on two broad assumptions: that major public policies in fields such as education, health and urban development, require concerted programs of research from all fields of science; at the same time, there is no less a need for coherent federal policies with respect to scientific and educational development. Two separate structures for scientific advice and programming would, in effect, weaken any effort at effective cohesion.

Finally, the Academy's Advisory Committee suggests a structural capstone to what is a kind of total "system" that it seeks to promote. The committee's recommendations are consciously interrelated, designed to produce a continual process of action and reaction through which the application of social science research would be strengthened at multiple levels of government and the financing of basic research would be sustained through pluralistic sources of support. The whole process is to be kept under surveillance by establishing central responsibility in the Office of Science and Technology. Finally, the Advisory Committee recommends the creation of a National Institute for Advanced Research and Public Policy in Washington, financed by Congress but independent in organization and operation, devoted to future-oriented studies and methodological problems that would, under the best of conditions, receive little attention in federal agencies plagued by the limits of time and jurisdictional interest.

In general, the NSB Special Commission on the Social Sciences concurs in the recommendations of the Academy's Advisory Committee. In one respect, the perspective of the commission's report is narrower; in another, it is broader. It does not deal with the field of foreign affairs; but it extends its recommendations far beyond the agencies of the federal government, into society at large. A series of proposals are thus devoted to strengthening social science research in the practicing professions, in private groups, like business and labor, in community organizations, as well as in every level of government.

A major issue in proposing so wide a program is the lack of means and organizations within the social sciences to enable the findings of social science to be effectively applied to social problems. Recognizing this, the Commission proposes the creation of new social problem research institutes through NSF grants, ultimately hoping for a network of some 25 such institutes throughout the country. Incorporating both research and action functions, the institutes are seen as organizations where social problems will be analyzed by teams of specialists and where contacts will be maintained with social action agencies so that the implication of research studies can be carried forward in terms of policy and program alternatives.

The NSB Special Commission sees as one of its major purposes, "the development of better channels for the flow of social science resources into American life." Its discussion is thus focused on existing institutions like the professions and on the creation of new institutions like the social problem research institutes. The Behavioral and Social Science Survey, however, had the task of assessing the status and future needs of the social sciences in terms of their future development as scientific disciplines. The survey has thus published a series of studies, each devoted to a separate discipline. A general report has also been published, exploring certain aspects of development that involve all the social sciences.

The recommendations of the BASS report fall into several categories. In terms of the development of the social sciences, the report recommends an annual increase of "between 12 and 18 percent" for both basic and applied research funded by the federal government in order "to sustain the normal growth of the research enterprise over the next decade." In a second category of recommendations, the report calls for substantial support for the development of "social indicators", both inside and outside the government, and for further development of the concept of a "national data center" to provide continuing and comparable information for the formulation of both theories and policies of large-scale social change. In connection with the national data center concept, as well as more generally, there is also provision for developing mechanisms to insure that social research, at all levels, protects the anonymity of individual respondents, especially as new technologies provide means of invading privacy.

One section of the general report, entitled "Institutes and University Organization for Research on Social Problems," is directly related to similar issues raised by the Academy's Advisory Committee and the National Science Board's Special Commission.

In both these latter groups' reports, there is a clear emphasis on the need for social scientists with the capacity and will to deal in applied problems. But as the Academy Committee pointed out: "The capacity for bringing knowledge to bear on practical problems has been given little attention in the education of [social] scientists. The emphasis has been on teaching and original research." This observation is reinforced in the BASS report that goes on to conclude that applied research will not be given warranted value in disciplinary departments and must be developed through a separate base in the university structure.

So far, as the BASS report shows, specialized research institutes have almost always had hard sledding in academe: they are usually orphans, do not control tenure positions, have to raise their own funds, cannot provide stability and long-term posts to young colleagues, and frequently take on doubtful assignments in order to survive. The BASS report therefore recommends a new form of organization: a graduate school of applied behavioral science. In presenting its proposal, the BASS suggests that there are several ways in which the model might be developed. In every case, however, the school should be multidisciplinary, should be engaged in continually testing the methods and findings of social science against actual social behavior, and in the process, contribute both to the development of theory and methods and to the solution of real social problems.

The BASS proposal is different from the social problem research institutes recommended by the NSB Special Commission, but it is complementary. The commission's institutes are designed as action agents to serve as transmission belts for the application of social science resources to social problems. The BASS graduate schools are research and educational programs in a university setting, organized on functional rather than disciplinary lines, but engaged in "real world" problems, both on their own terms and in terms of educational purposes.

Both the BASS report and the Special Commission—and the Academy's Advisory Committee emphasize the important connections between work in applied fields (which they all advocate) and advances in basic research. All three study groups would, I think, subscribe to these words in the BASS report in support of the graduate school notion:

... An academically sound and organizationally firm base is needed for the development of behavioral and social science applicable to the large problems of society. The attack on such problems should not wait for crises to call attention to social pathology, but should be on a continuing and long-range basis, with full attention also to the real theoretical contributions that can be made. Through research on genuine social problems, social scientists can improve the substance of their fields according to their own aspirations, while also serving society.[6]

THE IMPLICATIONS OF THE REPORTS

Within the proposals of the three study groups there persist several themes: that social science research, albeit with limitations, has a positive contribution to make to the formation of public policy and the execution of public programs; that, generally and with some exceptions, policy makers have failed to deal with social science as an important resource for policy-making; that social scientists themselves have neglected the policy implications of their work in their quest for specialized development of their individual disciplines; and that the model of government-science relations that had evolved since 1945 is appropriate for the social sciences. These themes provide the bases for general recommendations that run through all three reports: that the utility of the social sciences justifies public support for their development; that a series of interdisciplinary and policy or problem-oriented arrangements are required to bring home to both policy makers and social scientists the links between research and policies; and that the general federal system of grants, contracts and development provides a flexible framework within which social scientists can both serve society and protect their intellectual integrity.

The themes in the reports seek to consolidate and rationalize the system that had grown up during the 1960s. But they run counter to the criticism of those social scientists who are dissenting against the prevailing social science "establishment" and social science "ethos." There are, of course, varieties and contradictions among the dissenters and any generalized description bears the usual risks of being too simple and sweeping. But, by and large, the dissenters argue that social scientists may not have been too little, but too much involved in official policy-making; that too often social scientists have permitted research based on too little information and too little theory to be exploited without question by policy makers for the latter's own political purposes; that all of science, but most especially social science is inextricably wound up with social values and cannot be intellectually free under the terms of the "service" function which has priority in existing government-science relations; that the consequence of advocating a "value-disinterested" (if not "value-free") social science is to support the present political balance against pressures for change; and that, in a number of cases, social scientists share the ideological predilections reflected in the present structure of authority (which the dissenters consider biased) and deliberately use their professional capacity for its perpetuation.

The dissent, whatever its general themes, runs along a spectrum moving toward extreme radicalism. On the one hand, a member of the Caucus for a New Political Science writes that

The Caucus for a New Political Science is . . . a caucus of political scientists *within* the association of political scientists . . . Our major aim is the reformation of American political science, its revitalization and redirection . . . For too long the [American Political Science] Association sustained with little comment the values it had inherited and those of the social and political system in which it found itself. Research, together with the money which funded it, the panels which reported its results and the teaching and writing which was influenced by it, drifted away from critical areas where serious questioning would have exposed cherished views to doubt and controversy . . . The Caucus believes that the drift can be checked and that the Association, by self-conscious design can be turned from a passive, value-sustaining institution into a critical, value-examining and changing institution . . .[7]

While the attack here is on the professional association, its accusations of passivity and "value-sustaining" are flung more broadly against the academic architects of the profession, of this and several generations back. In another more radical statement of dissent there is no doubt who and what are the targets (this statement was delivered before a shocked meeting of the American Sociological Association in 1968):

. . . This assembly [of sociologists] here tonight . . . is a conclave of high and low priests, scribes, intellectual valets, and their innocent victims, engaged in the mutual affirmation of a falsehood . . . the profession is an outgrowth of nineteenth-century European traditionalism and conservatism, wedded to twentieth century American corporation liberalism . . . the professional eyes of the sociologist are on the down people, and the professional palm of the sociologist is stretched toward the up people . . . he is an Uncle Tom not only for this government and ruling class but for any.[8]

The reports of the social science study groups are a light year away from this kind of radicalism and, in many respects, seem, on first reading, to be operating on a completely different wave length than the dissenters, in general. But this is a superficial reading, even though none of the reports fully confronts the arguments of the dissenters. At the same time, all of the reports, while accepting the desirability and indeed the need for change, also accept the existing "system" as a mechanism for change. To this extent, they stand opposed to the most radical of the dissenters. But beyond this, the reports recognize, in a variety of ways, the risks of social science involvement in public policy-making, the requirements for maintaining an independent base for scientific growth, and the multiple roles that social scientists must (and will) play in a variety of institutional settings.

The National Academy's Advisory Committee, for example, was the most directly concerned with strengthening the internal research organization of federal agencies. Yet the Committee's report found "limits upon support for innovative research by operating departments and agencies . . . ":

. . . However broadly conceived and imaginatively administered department and agency programs may be, important areas may still receive inadequate attention and fields of support may be too greatly influenced by existing department and agency commitments and by the operating assumptions of existing policies . . . [9]

The immediate recommendation of the Committee was to set up a government-endowed but independently administered institute for research and public policy " . . . free from the pressures of political preoccupations and constraints . . . to examine the full range of problems the society faces, not only in the immediate future, but beyond, when new and only dimly perceived forces for change will begin to take effect."[10] The idea of such an institute was to bridge the gap between innovative research that emerged from scholarly investigation and the policy-making process. For the Committee recognized the need to develop institutional links between "free" innovative research that challenged "operating assumptions" and strategic points in the decision-making process. Thus, it placed the institute in Washington, D. C. where it could become part of a communications network involving policy makers and social scientists engaged in fundamental research.

Of the three reports, the BASS report pointed to the dual usage of social science research, to sustain or to change the existing order. In a concluding discussion, the report observed that

A good deal of attention is given, in social science, to how social order is generated and maintained, as well as to how it is changed. This emphasis on the study of normal social functions sometimes leads observers to consider the social sciences as inherently conservative and the handmaidens of establishments of various sorts . . . In fact, however, the . . . social sciences are potentially . . . revolutionary . . . This is true basically because their findings call into question traditional assumptions about the nature of human nature, about the structure of society and the unfolding of social processes . . .[11]

In all three reports, there is an underlying assertion that the social role of social knowledge is hardly a new problem. But admittedly it takes on a special intensity when government begins to employ social knowledge more deliberately than it had earlier and when, at the same time, critics of government policy call for a role for social knowledge no less political, but one that supports antigovernment movements. Between these two sets of demands any simple recourse to a "value-free" social science is meaningless. For that matter, social research is often directed as much by the subjective values of the research, in his choice of subject, methodology and conceptual framework, as by the policy interests of major patrons, government and other social agencies. The professional criteria for evaluating social research, moreover, remain limited under the fragmented and decentralized structure of the social science enterprise. By the same token, the results of social research can, through a process of popularization and even vulgarization, become a basis for political rhetoric and policy without any professional judgment on their objective validity (or, for that matter, the concurrence of the original researchers).

Both the study group reports and the criticism of the dissenters recognize the risks of being "co-opted," of being "used." At the same time, the reports all emphasize the need for developing links between research and government in order to contribute to intelligent public policy while the dissenters emphasize the need for dissociating research from public authority in order to contribute to social criticism. What both require, however, is an independent base which will permit social science, on the one hand, to contribute to public policies without being disorted and, on the other, to provide criticism of public policies without being censored. Professional ethics, rigorous methods of research, open publication, all contribute to this independence which both service and criticism demand. But research freedom also requires an institutional setting within which it is nourished for its own sake, and here the university has a vital role to play, a role that is essential to the vitality of social science as a source of both social policy and social criticism.

There is no point in trying to reconcile the themes of the study groups with the criticisms of the dissenters. For one thing, neither the themes nor the criticisms stand for single large opposing factions among social scientists. Indeed, social scientists are factionalized into many more political, methodological and ideological clusters than two broad divisions could possibly represent. For another thing, even if the functions of contributing to government policy and to social criticism were reconciled in some bland, theoretical way, those adopting one or the other route would soon fall apart when dealing with distinct policy issues or when seeking some kind of explanation for these functions. The need for the protection of free and independent universities is, however, vital for both. But is made more difficult and complex by the recommendations for a policy or problem-oriented approach to social science that runs through all three reports—and that is, for that matter, as necessary for the function of social criticism as it is for contributing to rational government.

All three reports underscore the multidisciplinary nature of social problems and the need for multidisciplinary instrumentalities to meet them. These things have to be said, but they are not new. They should awaken memories of the early urgings of

Charles Merriam and the later brilliant articulation of Harold Lasswell. Many social scientists have, at one time or another, been fascinated, instructed and stimulated by Lasswell's concept of the policy sciences. Everyone recognizes, at the same time, the obvious and inevitable multidisciplinary character of social problems. But most academic social scientists must have either experienced or witnessed continuing frustrations at launching multidisciplinary programs—especially teaching programs—in colleges and universities. Only in the "think-tanks", like the RAND Corporation, have real multidisciplinary enterprises been mounted.

There are, of course, reasons for this being so. Social scientists have, in a way, been seeking their own self-dignity and self-confidence for several decades. They have been seeking to strengthen the rigor of their methods, devising programs of quantitative analysis, exploring the possibilities of comparison, and trying to enlarge and test theoretical bases. In all these efforts, they have borrowed from colleagues in the other social sciences, so that, for example, political scientists speak of political psychology and political sociology as sub-fields and test political systems against economic models. Relations with other social sciences have largely been formed in terms of the development of one's own discipline. What the three study groups are confronting is the possibility of forming new sets of relations in terms of social problems.

Again this is not unlike the challenge raised earlier by Merriam, Lasswell and others. At earlier times, social scientists largely ignored the challenge, fearing, I would suggest, that a response would have diverted their attention and energies from the developments in their disciplines as sciences. Perhaps, a major question is to ask whether social scientists have as yet sufficient internal strength to devote more time and resources to the policy orientation—in substance as well as process—in collaboration with colleagues in other disciplines, and whether universities have the internal strength to support and protect this orientation. For the applications of social science to social problems discussed in all three reports are applications that take place in political environments or are highly related to political choices. And it is too easy to assume that the role of social science is simply to clarify the alternatives among which policy makers might choose. Clarifying political choices is, in itself, part of the political process.

In the final analysis, therefore, the reports of the three social science groups, no less than the urgings of the dissenters, move social science into the orbit of American politics. But to make this move without insuring the protection of a free university system would be a disaster. For only in the universities can the professional standards be sustained, against which the role of social scientists in politics can be rigorously evaluated. Without these standards, charlatans could flourish, partial knowledge could become frozen dogma, and sloppy research could lead to political myth. Nor, it goes without saying, would the social sciences develop in terms of adding to the store of fundamental knowledge.

The implications of the study group reports are thus two-fold: a more systematic orientation of the social sciences toward social problems and a continuing but more alert and sensitive protection of academic freedom. Both tasks have been emphasized in uncompromising terms by John Gardner:

I would not wish to see anything happen that would alter the character of the university as a haven for dissent and for creative, scholarly work. That must be preserved at all costs. But I believe that those parts of the university which are . . . involved in extensive interaction with the larger community are going to have to take that relationship more seriously than ever before . . . We need in the university community a focused, systematic, responsible, even aggressive concern for the manner in which the society is evolving—a concern for its values and the problems it faces, and the strategies appropriate to clarify those values and to solve those problems.[1,2]

NOTES

[1] *The Behavioral Sciences and the Federal Government,* NAS Publication 1680, Washington, D.C., National Academy of Sciences, 1968 ("The Academy Report"); *Knowledge into Action: Increasing the Nation's Use of the Social Sciences,* Report of the Special Commission of the Social Sciences, Washington, D.C., National Science Board—National Science Foundation, NSB 69-3, 1969 ("The National Science Board Report"); and *The Behavioral and Social Sciences: Outlook and Needs,* Washington, D.C., National Academy of Sciences, 1969 ("The BASS Report").

[2] Federal Funds for Research, Development and Other Scientific Activities, Fiscal Years 1968, 1969, and 1970, Vol. XVIII, NSF 69-31, Washington, D.C., National Science Foundation, 1969, p. 258.

[3] For earlier history, see Gene M. Lyons, *The Uneasy Partnership: Social Science and the Federal Government in the Twentieth Century,* New York, Russell Sage Foundation, 1969.

[4] For a full discussion of Project Camelot, see Irving L. Horowitz (ed.), *The Rise and Fall of Project Camelot,* Cambridge, Mass., M.I.T. Press, 1967.

[5] For the debate on the proposal to establish a National Social Science Foundation see *National Foundation for Social Sciences,* Subcommittee on Government Research, Committee on Government Operations, U.S. Senate, 90th Congress, First Session, Parts 1, 2 and 3, Washington, D.C., 1967.

[6] "The BASS Report," *op. cit.,* p. 201.

[7] H. Mark Roelofs, "Plebiscitory or Legislative Democracy," in *P.S.,* Newsletter of the American Political Science Association, Vol. II, No. 3, pp. 273-273.

[8] Statement by Martin Nicolaus, quoted in Alvin Gouldner, *The Coming Crisis of Western Sociology,* New York, Basic Books, 1970, p. 10.

[9] "The Academy Report," *op. cit.,* p. 103.

[10] *Ibid,* pp. 105-107.

[11] "The BASS Report," pp. 271-272.

[12] Quoted in Thomas E. Cronin and Sanford D. Greenberg (eds.) *The Presidential Advisory System,* New York, Harper & Row, 1969, p. 329.

Part II
THE PRACTICE OF SOCIAL POLICY

Public Policy
and Private Interest

ALVIN L. SCHORR

It was said of Samuel Johnson that he was a pessimistic man, but cheerfulness kept breaking through. This distinction should be set forth explicitly. I am a reformer by temperament, and by training disposed to believe that scientific method can show the way. This combination produces a powerful optimism that may flicker but does not die. Still, I have spent ten years observing the development of national welfare policy at close hand and must acknowledge that social science had rather little to do with it. So the optimism in this essay will be temperamental and the pessimism a reflection upon my experience—which is limited, after all. When optimism and pessimism are mixed in the open air, the result is anger; a little of that may be discerned too.

THEORY OF RANDOMNESS

My point of departure in this essay is a theory of randomness concerning the movement of social policy. This means that the nation does not move from trial and error to new trials, from experience to correcting errors, or from systematic evidence to programs based on that evidence. It means also that, although needs produce solutions, the correspondence is very far from point to point, and some needs are never noticed. I use randomness here in this narrow but, I dare say, rational sense. Of course, social policy does not develop randomly from a political point of view, but responds to the desires of the electorate as these are expressed through the political process. In effect, this is to say that, so far as welfare policy is concerned, the electorate has not been attentive to systematic evidence or even to experience. Although governments are permitted considerable flexibility within the broad issues to which electorates pay attention, they have not used this latitude to be more systematic than the electorate.

Several illustrations of the point come to mind. In welfare policy, we have for at least 15 years been behaving as if dependency were a curable handicap. Therefore, we enact programs of social services for fatherless children and their mothers, and vocational rehabilitation for unemployed men and women. Congressmen vote for these programs, in part, because they believe that they promise a reduction in the cost of public assistance. None of these programs has produced such a result and so, from time to time, officials discover that few people receiving public assistance are curable of the need for it. One such Eureka speech was delivered by then Secretary Abraham Ribicoff and another by then White House Special Assistant Joseph Califano. Each was greeted with public surprise. Yet the in some ways excellent new welfare proposals of President Richard Nixon have been wrapped in the same promise. In three or four years, no doubt, some high government official will make a speech like those of Ribicoff and Califano, which will again be greeted with surprise.

Another illustration of the point is the community action program. Probably, its central function was to act as a collaboration of social services that would bring down barriers to opportunity. If that was the intent when it was enacted, it went against the evidence that was beginning to accumulate. The so-called juvenile delinquency projects of the early 1960s were intended specifically as tests of the effectiveness of such programs in opening opportunity. The evidence was only beginning to come in when the poverty program began, and it was cloudy, but one would have had to read the findings at that point as negative.[1]

The history of the search for comprehensive urban planning offers a final illustration. For 20 years, we have moved from urban

ALVIN L. SCHORR

renewal, through comprehensive redevelopment, workable programs, community renewal plans and into model cities, not troubling to alter the slogans with each new name. We have acted each time as if the earlier conception was partial and, by directing attention to the need for comprehensiveness, we were entering a new era. Comprehension has been in shorter supply than comprehensiveness. It is dangerous to oversimplify—some changes were introduced with the new programs—but comprehensiveness was not new. And nothing was done about the central reason that comprehensiveness never took hold, namely, that the planners lacked responsibility for or control over events.[2]

(Presumably, it is not necessary to say that I support the provision of social services, and think community action and comprehensive planning good things. I simply object to justifying them on grounds we know or ought to know are unsound, or to distorting *other* programs by stuffing these good ideas down their bellies.)

Obviously, we do from time to time develop good new programs and reshape old programs in ways that evidence would suggest is sound. Community action was fine because it moved poor people toward participation—a good in itself—and because in some small way it redistributes social services. The Elementary and Secondary Education Act of 1965 has produced marginal improvements in the education of rural children and, perhaps, slowed the deterioration of central city schools; and it has fed quite a lot of children who would have gone hungry. Nixon's welfare proposals will, if enacted in the shape he offered them, raise levels of assistance in four or five states and considerably broaden eligibility in most states.

If one reflects on these or other progressive moves, however, it is evident how little they have to do with their ostensible objective or with social science. The three programs listed probably owe their genesis more to the desperate financial plight of cities and states than to any other single factor. The poverty program and the Education Act came in a time and manner dictated by more powerful developments than the need for them: the guilt of a decade of dividing affluence among the affluent (a guilt which has now, apparently, dissipated); the death of John Kennedy and the inauguration of Lyndon Johnson, with all the passion and ambition that were aroused; and the turning in frustration of the still powerful civil rights movement to goals it *could* achieve. A strong force behind the poverty program and the president's welfare proposals in middle-and working-class hatred of bureaucracy (entirely akin to the anger that leads our young people to protest). But since the real objective is war against bureaucracy, it is not necessary to test or discard ideas that are dear to us—that eating is a sign of merit, for example. And when these programs fail to wipe out poverty or hunger—because we set the programs firmly on the road to failure—it adds fuel to our anger at the bureaucrats who balked us once more, as it seems.

The point being illustrated may be clear: We get forward movement in social policy out of the resonance of developments that are quite unrelated to social science and may be unrelated to reason. Because such forward movement must satisfy its sources before anything else, the actual design of programs shows little fundamental influence of social science. Along with that, as has already been said, on some matters we get no movement at all.

If social policy moves randomly, one constructive question is why. Ideas about this will be discussed under two headings—first, public values and definitions and then, limitations in the practice of social science.

GREED

It must be self-evident that public values determine the direction of social policy. It would be difficult to argue that it should be otherwise. It is hardly novel to observe that the Protestant ethic is at the root of the problem in welfare policy. If failure and dependency are signs of God's displeasure, truly those who suffer from it need treatment more than money—and evidence to the contrary is frivolous. Quite possibly, we deal with a similar value problem in educational policy. We are generally conscious of and troubled by the fact that we do not know very much about how to improve the quality of education. But we seem to be untroubled by the fact that generally rising levels of education do not greatly affect poverty in the United States. A grade school education was once a pretty good thing. A high school education sufficed not so long ago. Very soon, a college degree will be required to assure a moderate level of income. With education as with income, apparently, the absolute level achieved matters less thar one's position relative to the average.

ALVIN L. SCHORR

The point has been made by an international comparison: The average duration of education in Great Britain is no more than the educational level our poor people achieve. The fact that our poor people would be quite adequately educated in Britain—a country widely regarded as industrial—does them no good here. In short, it is the distributional pattern in education that affects one's ability to compete for a job. Yet, with our stubborn faith in self-improvement, we provide Head Start and special funds for high schools in the ghettoes and ignore the fact that we are improving the education of the rest of the population at least as quickly. (We are running to stand still and, to be sure, few would argue that we should do less.)

One is tempted to shrug fatalistically, leaving the work ethic and Calvinist theology in undisputed possession of the field. However, when values are asserted again and again despite experience that should qualify them or where they are irrelevant, one must look for their roots. One comes to see the underlying values at play as more primitive and not so sweetly overlaid with religion. The values being asserted are greed for money and status and the right of the powerful to the spoils. Most people in the country appear to be unwilling to give up having more than someone else or feeling better than someone else, whatever peace or sense of community might be produced. (In everyday speech, this is expressed as: "Who helped us when we came!" and "I worked hard all my life and now they're giving it away!") Those are the values we are dealing with. They have made us great and powerful—I say that without irony—but we are paying a terrible price for them.

CIRCULAR DEFINITIONS

Closely (even circularly) related to public values is the public definition of issues. One understands in general that the way a problem is defined may determine the conclusions about it. For example, the fiscal problem of federal, state and local governments is in large part a result of the growing welfare burden, according to widespread public definition. Yet the figures demonstrate that in recent years welfare costs (including social security) have grown less rapidly than health costs or education costs, considered either as federal expenditures or as state and local expenditures. Indeed, federal expenditures on health have tripled and education quadrupled while welfare was growing by only half. State and local expenditures have also increased faster in health and education than in welfare.[3] An instinctive reaction, upon absorbing these figures, is to observe that the increases in health and education costs are not relevant; they are increases on a smaller base and, more important, the public is willing to bear them. Welfare increases are scandalous mainly because they are quite unwanted. That is the point, of course. Welfare costs are defined as the fiscal problem *because* welfare is disliked. So the definition of welfare as the cause of the fiscal problem is circular. Yet it fuels public resentment of the program.

Similarly, it is intriguing to observe which facts and research findings gain currency and which do not. For example, the steady, sharp increase in public assistance rates in New York City began leveling off in the fall of 1969. It was a gratifying development; the Mayor and other prominent officials took pains to speak about it in public. But the newspapers did not pick it up until it had been said quite a number of times in their presence. Again, most sociologists are aware how little research supports the view that interfaith marriage is inordinately risky. But article after article on the subject has appeared that failed to make this point, although at least some of the authors understood it. The boldest statement that is permitted—and when it came, the writer regarded it as a breakthrough—is that interfaith marriages can be successful, *if the partners are especially mature.* These examples are not cited to look for a devil in the newspapers, or to say once again that Madison Avenue can shape our minds. Rather, the newspapers are in the public grip quite as much as the other way around. If the public has seized upon rising welfare rates or the breakdown of religious barriers to account for its troubles, it is not news to cite findings to the contrary. The newspaper that insists will be thought dull and preachy.

PRAGMATISM

Apart from public definition, public values also find support or at least protection from challenge in the pragmatic nature of government. Pragmatism is not used here to mean that the government relies on no assumptions or generalizations at all. At the other extreme, one does not expect government to seek a complete set of generalizations accounting for all the behavior in some field. But even short of this, government is not hospitable to the development of plausible new generalizations, derived from social science, on which policy may or would be based. This probably is not true of economic theory, which seems to be well, if only recently, established.

It may help to illustrate the point. I have written elsewhere of the almost clinical depression, as it seemed to me, with which high government officials responded to the Detroit riots of 1967.[4] Detroit deflated the assumption on which the government was then operating, namely, that if competent men worked desperately to create visible programs for the disadvantaged, people would respond with satisfaction or at least patience. When that innocent formulation was swept away, the administration was left with nothing to put in its place. Officials might well have found themselves depressed. It would appear that the succeeding administration did not try to develop a theory, but rather shifted attention to other problems or client groups.

A few programs may seem to rest on theories—the juvenile delinquency program, the poverty program, Model Cities. On closer examination, it appears that some of the people involved in the formulation of these programs had theories, but one person's theory differed from another's. The programs that were put together compromised these differing views, and accommodated the views of others who had no theories at all but would describe themselves as pragmatists. When the programs were launched, administrators selected for application the theories or non-theory that they found congenial. That accounts, in some measure, for the difficulty in securing agreement about the theory of the poverty program. When an administration turns over, of course, there is a certain loss of interest in demonstrating the validity of a theory of the prior administration. And so the Model Cities program, which may have held a theory, was quickly converted from experimentation into a simple conduit of federal funds to cities.

In any event, the juvenile delinquency, poverty, and Model Cities program were exceptional in even dealing with theory. The bulk of federal programming in these fields—welfare, education, youth and alienation, mental health—involves very little theory at all. Why should that be so? Theories or, at any rate, theorists are resistant to compromise in an arena where compromise is an everyday necessity. Theories are natural targets for hostile Congressmen or special interest groups. For example, Secretary Robert F. Finch began his introduction of the Family Assistance Act of 1969 to the House Ways and Means Committee with the following language: "We sought, in designing the Family Assistance Plan, to identify and deal directly with the most pressing problems facing public welfare today. While it is a far-reaching and fundamental reform of public welfare, the Family Assistance Plan is a practical and pragmatic program . . . This problem solving approach, rather than a theoretical approach. . ." and so on.[5] It is a particularly interesting statement because the Family Assistance Plan was, in fact, based on a theory about the significance of work in public assistance and how it may best be maintained. But the Secretary solicited the support of Congress by opposing his pragmatism and theirs to theory.

Theories themselves can also be tools of one interest group or another, limiting the inclination of officials to deal with them academically. For example, any reasonable theory about the social impact of the distribution of income in the United States might make it difficult to justify the 1969 tax cut. At the same time, the dubious theory that inflation hurts poor people more than anyone else helped to justify a policy that created unemployment. To continue with reasons that the government may be hostile to theory, as has already been implied, the fact that the time perspective of each administration is three years or less is inimical to the testing of theories which, in these complicated days, requires a little time. A final reason for abjuring theory may be a governmental tendency to rely on incremental developments. Increments have the advantage of accommodating old interests even while attempting to develop new patterns. Yet, some theories simply cannot be tested by increments. That is the heart of the argument about the Coleman report, for example, that children who do not demonstrably respond to *somewhat* better classroom situations would respond to *much* better classroom situations. Or, as another example, it can be argued that we will not get desegregation with any program less powerful in the 1970s than FHA was in 1950s. No demonstration effort or small program can tell us what would happen in such a case, that is, if we arranged

ALVIN L. SCHORR

matters so that private enterprise profits on a large scale from desegregation.

To sum up so far: Social science has rather little relation to policy development because policies are determined by values that are often unrecognized. These values, in turn, determine the very definition of the issues, and so we get fed back to us the solution to the issues that our values demand. Then our resolutely pragmatic approach to government makes it hard from one decade to the next to know what theories, and therefore what programs, are serving us well or poorly. To be sure, pragmatism is said to keep the body politic at peace (is someone asking, "What peace?") and to help to contain a temperamentally violent people in a highly stable government. One must place considerable value on stable government. The point is merely that, despite considerable testimony to the contrary, in certain areas we have a relatively inflexible set of values. This set of values is embedded in a system that protects it from searching examination. That does not contribute to rational or social scientific policy development, which is to say that policy develops at random.

We now turn to the way social scientists operate in and in relation to government. Included in what follows are clinicians such as social workers and psychiatrists who, while working on policy development, seek guidance in systematic research. I will consider intellectual difficulties first and then self-interest.

INTELLECTUAL PROBLEMS

A worrisome intellectual problem is that social scientists take a narrow view of problems that require a broader view. That is, they approach problems by way of a single discipline. It is barely necessary to repeat what has been said so often, but it is perhaps useful to illustrate how this limitation affects policy development. For example, "culture of poverty" explanations of the behavior of poor people draw vitality from two sources that are peripheral to the evidence. One source of vitality that should bring no surprise is that this set of ideas defines the problem in a way that supports current values. The other source of vitality is that social scientists are expert in description of attitudes and status situations.[6] They are largely inexpert on such matters as nutrition and in understanding what makes social patterns change over time. So "culture of poverty" reflects the expertise of the researchers more than it explains the situation or prospects of poor people. Yet this notion is the major support for social service and educational strategies in dealing with poverty.

Economists, more than others, often offer a warning that they are about to take too narrow a view of a problem. Having come to a conclusion about some economic aspect of a question, they mutter *ceteris paribus* before making their policy recommendation. "All things being equal" ought to be treated as a proclamation of ignorance, but is more often a ritual defense against considerations that one understands not to be very important at all. An illustration of the hazards when an economist moves narrowly from his discipline occurred in the deliberations of a United Nations group concerned with social defense. They were interested in the cost-effectiveness of various approaches to crime and delinquency—that is, dollar for dollar, is prevention more effective than jails, and so forth? At one point, they found themselves discussing the most cost-effective approach to preventing juvenile delinquency in Vietnam. The war, as it did not lend itself to cost analysis in quite the same terms, was never mentioned, nor was its relationship to juvenile delinquency.[7]

Another intellectual problem in the applicability of social sciences is the value that is placed on elaboration. Our universities may be directly responsible for this. Students are taught to abandon unlearned common sense and, with it, simplicity. Somehow the necessary search for rigor in thinking is converted into overvaluing the complex and technical. Therefore, simple matters may be overlooked. For example, the significance to social behavior of nutrition and shelter were all but ignored in post-World War II research. When one seeks a policy recommendation from people so disposed, the result is either a retreat to the need for more research or a hopelessly involved recommendation. This is not to plead for reductionism but only to name the parallel error of elaborationism. People who have been trained in this manner teach or do highly technical work; they tend not to address themselves to policy development anyway. However, the pattern of thinking influences those who do set out to deal with policy matters.

ALVIN L. SCHORR

A third intellectual problem lies in the relevance to policy of the research that is done. On one hand, many of the issues that trouble sociologists and psychologists have very little consequence in the social policy world. The fact is too well known to require elaboration. On the other hand, a good deal of research is dominated by the government's needs and definitions. It is not necessary to argue that actual slanting of findings occurs very often. But the choice of research subject and the terms in which it is pursued quite often determines the outcome. As an example, it is not an accident that the negative income tax is the only substantial departure in income maintenance that has been experimented with. Staff at the Office of Economic Opportunity, The Department of Health, Education and Welfare and the President's Commission on Income Maintenance Programs decided before President Nixon assumed office that that was the program the country should have. And so an administration that came into office encouraging experimentation in various forms of income maintenance was, in less than a year, instructed by the president himself to support only income maintenance projects that had been approved in the White House. That may not be unusual behavior in a government. But how does one account for the fact that, with interest in the subject high, not a single university developed a study that broke through the government's definition or predilection?

Another intellectual issue troubles those social scientists who get directly involved with high government officials on a policy issue. They are likely to be offered friendly advice on how to shape their recommendations for maximum political effect. They may be told that a recommendation is sound, but needs to be clothed in different rhetoric. Or they may be told how large a step or what sort of strategy is likely to be effective at the moment. It is a difficult problem. One does not want to be intransigent or ingenuous nor, however, to abandon solid professional or technical ground. I offer you only my own observation. Social scientists err much more often in accommodating themselves to political advice than in intransigence.

From social scientists who are barely concerned with social policy—the elaborationists—the discussion has moved to those who are so concerned that they have to decide how purely to deal with their discipline. It is necessary to make a final point about the intellectual problem of those social scientists who try to affect social policy most broadly. Social scientists and professional organizations carrying such a role find that evidence that leads directly to policy recommendations is comparatively rare. Rather, these spokesmen are usually bringing to bear the basic values of their discipline—humanism, rationality, a therapeutic rather than a penal approach. Either that, or more explicitly, they are arguing the merits of the disciplines they know—the economist urging econometrics, the sociologist urging the importance of institutions, the social worker promoting group work and casework. The public is not really faced with social science but with contending values and interests. Decisions are not made on evidence but on who happens to have acceptance, power or the most persuasive line. The intellectual problem for these social scientists is that research and analysis is not being conducted in a manner that is useful to them. They argue from their values or intuitions, or desist.

SELF-INTEREST

We have been cataloguing intellectual difficulties in bringing social science to bear upon social policy, and perhaps it is already obvious how closely involved with these difficulties is the self-interest of social scientists. If social scientists are trained in elaborationism, it is because their professors are most secure with that. It is the surest route to academic success for faculty and students as well. The National Academy of Sciences and Social Science Research Council put the point as follows: "Many academic scientists value the prestige that their contributions to basic research and theory give them in the eyes of their peers more than whatever rewards might be obtained from clients who would find their work useful. It . . . leads not only to scientific knowledge, but also to respect and status tendered by those whose judgments they value most."[8] If universities waste no time on research that the government will not fund anyway, more students will be taught and provided stipends and more status and resources accrue to the department. If social workers promote social services and social scientists promote research, higher salaries and richer

ALVIN L. SCHORR

perquisites will be available all around. An example of the exception that proves the rule was the testimony of the National Committee for the Day Care of Children concerning the 1967 amendments to the Social Security Act. The association testified against those amendments because they would be damaging to children and their families, even though day care programs in particular were to be greatly expanded. There are not so many examples of that sort; not all the testimony on the 1967 amendments was so disinterested.

More insidious than the narrow self-interest of each discipline and more difficult to explain without being misunderstood, is the coalition of self-interests that gather around social research. Daniel Bell has made the argument that the intellectual class is now maneuvering for political power,[9] a development that facilitates and is in turn supported by building up financially secure bases of operation for intellectuals. Noam Chomsky makes a finer charge, that experts or "scholar-technicians" are maneuvering to take power from "free-floating intellectuals" who tend to be more attentive to values than techniques.[10] The two observations are not incompatible, and one may think them both right. The scholar arguing the merits of research asserts a class interest quite as much as the miner arguing the merits of coal. Certainly, excessive claims have been made for research. The point is beginning to be acknowledged retrospectively,[11] but nothing prevents social scientists from asking that funds for research be written into each new piece of legislation. There are matters we know how to study and others we do not. There are studies for which personnel is available and others for which it is not. Some research ought to be initiated by government and other research not. How is it that social scientists all together support—by silence, if not affirmatively—requests for funds for social research of any sort?

I do not, more than anyone else, want to seem impolite. One can bring to mind very fine work by social scientists, and some examples of courage and self-sacrifice. Yet it is necessary to examine the possibility that they do not represent the generality. It appears that the nation is now structured on professions and occupations as the medieval world was structured on guilds. There is no yielding of self-interest on any side, not among social scientists and not among the professions. If they believe their own

dire prophecies—those social scientists who make dire prophecies—should they not on occasion find recommendations to make
to Congress and the country that are counter to their self-interest?

CONCLUSION

The simplest conclusion is a summary that will itself seem
simple: Public policy is dominated by public values—naturally.
These values are comparatively inflexible, and are protected from
critical examination by social forces and the tendencies of
government. That is convenient, as it permits greed to operate
unimpeded and even unnamed. Social science is a mirror image of
the larger situation, despite the fact that its traditions demand that
it be quite different. Social science, too, has impediments to
substantial critical examination of major policy issues, and
tends—so the record shows—to pursue its own self-interest.
Therefore, in relationship to reason or social science, one would
expect social policy to move at random—as indeed it appears to
do.

That is how it seems to me; do I see any hope? The intellectual
tradition of social scientists provides grounds for hope. Ideologies
tend to carry on even when they are not practiced, and young
social scientists continue to be taught integrity and scientific rigor.
When they mix those ideas with the ones they are developing for
themselves—rejection of materialism and self-interest and a demand for relevance, we may see a different social science with
different effects.

As for the older social scientists, perhaps we may rely on their
sense of irony. We have already noted the cost-effectiveness
approach to juvenile delinquency in Vietnam. I have in mind also a
federal program that provides food for pregnant and nursing
mothers if their doctors will prescribe it. Jonathan Swift could
have thought of nothing finer. We might run all of public
assistance on the basis of physicians' prescriptions. One day such
black humor will be too much for social scientists, and they will
take on social policy in earnest.

NOTES
[1] Peter Marris and Martin Rein, *Dilemmas of Reform: Poverty and
Community Action in the United States,* New York, Atherton Press, 1967.

[2] For an elaboration of this argument, see "Planned Development: Vision or Fancy?" in Alvin L. Schorr, *Explorations in Social Policy*, Basic Books.

[3] U.S. Department of Health, Education, and Welfare, "Health, Education and Welfare; Accomplishments, 1963-1968, Problems and Challenges, And a Look to the Future," December 1968.

[4] *Explorations in Social Policy*, op. cit., p. 260.

[5] Statement of Honorable Robert H. Finch to the Committee on Ways and Means, U.S. House of Representatives, October 15, 1969.

[6] For example, for an exploration of the failure of sociologists to foresee the sit-in movement, see Kurt W. Back, "Sociology Encounters the Southern Protest Movement for Desegregation," presented at the International Sociological Association (Washington, D.C., September 1962); and Everett C. Hughes, "Race Relations and the Sociological Imagination," presented at the American Sociological Association (Los Angeles, August 28, 1963).

[7] United Nations, Consultative Group on the Prevention of Crime and the Treatment of Offenders, "The Economics of Training in Social Defense," Wroking Paper Prepared by the Secretariat, 8 July 1968, and Draft Report Prepared by P. J. Woodfield, 13 August 1968, Geneva.

[8] National Academy of Sciences and Social Science Research Council, *The Behavioral and Social Sciences, Outlook and Needs*, Washington, D.C. 1969, p. 193.

[9] Daniel Bell, "Notes on the Post-Industrial Society (K)," *The Public Interest*, No. 6, Winter 1967.

[10] Noam Chomsky, *American Power and the New Mandarins*, Random House, 1967.

[11] See for example Walter Williams and John W. Evans, "The Politics of Evaluation: The Case of Head Start," *The Annals of the American Academy of Political and Social Science*, v. 385, September 1969; and Thomas E. Glennan, Jr., "Evaluating Federal Manpower Programs: Notes and Observations," The RAND Corporation, September 1969.

Tax-Exempt Foundations: Their Effects on National Policy

IRVING LOUIS HOROWITZ
and
RUTH LEONORA HOROWITZ

The large tax-exempt foundation is a child of private enterprise. Nevertheless, foundations have acquired a unique role not readily describable in "private sector" terms, or in "public sector" terms either. The purpose of this chapter is to examine the impact of tax-exempt foundations upon public policy in the United States and to show that their "third sector" character makes it difficult for them to secure acceptance for their activities or form an economic base from which to chart new directions.

The term "foundations" describes those organizations that have grown during the twentieth century, most often in the form of corporations or trusts, that have broadly defined charitable purposes and substantial capital assets, and derive income from gifts, bequests and capital investments. They are granted tax-exempt status by section 501-c-3 of the Internal Revenue Code. The Internal Revenue Code also grants income, gift and estate tax deductions to persons making contributions to foundations. Organizations supported by government funds are not foundations, nor are formal educational or church institutions, organizations, "testing for the public safety" or certain non-exempt trusts which set aside some funds for charity.[1]

FOUNDATIONS AND GOVERNMENT

Large foundations became rooted in the United States at the start of this century, and are a unique product of affluent industrialism. Organizations of such size could hardly have existed without the vast surplus of wealth accumulated in the United States during the twentieth century. They grew out of the charitable organizations which flourished in earlier American history,[2] and were encouraged to an unparalleled extent by cultural influences that favored "charity" as a way of ameliorating social problems. Among these influences, one would have to count the following:

☐ Protestantism propogated the idea that men achieved salvation by good works rather than religious rituals. Money could be spent to accomplish good works, and those with sufficient funds used them to secure their afterlives and more especially, to give a higher status and meaning to the pursuit of profit.

☐ As a young nation, the United States was more or less a loose collection of diverse communities relying primarily on ethical bonds rather than on a strong national government as a source of unity. Charitable donations thus strengthened the moral firmness of individuals, and indirectly, the nation. Philanthropy was seen as encouraging the social development of the donor and improving the character of the recipient. The moral use of money enabled rich and poor to live in harmony; thus money served as a force for social cohesion.

☐ Charitable organizations were favored by a tradition of improving social conditions through voluntary associations, all the more so since it was seen as a form of moral, as distinct from interest group, pressure. The Great Fundamentalist Awakenings of the nineteenth century widely popularized this idea.

☐ In a laissez-faire culture, where government was regarded as a device for settling social disputes and not as a dispenser of welfare, charitable organizations assumed welfare-dispensing functions almost by fiat.

☐ As businessmen acquired political leadership along with vast fortunes, and as Americans identified business as the source of all good things, the populace began to look to businessmen to discharge welfare responsibilities to communities. The Federal government encouraged this by granting tax allowances for charitable contributions. And since the tax system is itself a product of this century, the special relationship between foundations and government received a basic economic impetus.

The advent of big foundations coincided with the era of muckraking, trust-busting slogans, left-wing populism and growing labor militance. This had the effect of casting deep suspicion upon business, and by association, business-originated charities or foundations. The charge that philanthropic money was "tainted" became widespread. Between 1914 and 1915 an Industrial Relations Commission set up by a number of senators to explore causes of social unrest, extended its investigation into foundation affairs.[3] The result was that the foundations were castigated for the size of their fortunes and the nature of their special privileges. They were perceived as dangerous extensions of business power, since businessmen not only endowed them, but men with business backgrounds administered them.

Investigation and suspicion notwithstanding, foundations grew as business grew. They were organized mainly as corporations and to a lesser extent as trusts.[4] The procedures for establishing a charitable trust are similar to those involving the transference of wealth from a private donor to a corporate recipient. By defining the recipient as "the public," transfer of private wealth to the community at large is possible. The trust is a device for disposing of property where legal title and managerial duties are given over to a trustee charged with overseeing the property and using it on behalf of beneficiaries specified by the donor. In the case of charitable trusts the beneficiary was "the public." The trust provided a ready form in which administration of a property or funds could be efficiently established according to existing statute and was thus applied to the establishment of foundations.

THE PRIVATE ENTERPRISE MODEL OF PUBLIC FOUNDATIONS

However, it is the corporate device that is more frequently employed. The corporate form pervades modern American business, the main source of foundation funding, and the creators of foundations are most familiar with it. It was widely adopted in this country because it provided a means to raise large amounts of capital from investors whose ownership would be separable from managerial responsibilities and from liability for debt of the business enterprise. The right to exist as a corporation is granted by each state, although state laws regarding nonprofit corporations vary so greatly that it is difficult to enumerate the rules for corporate foundation formation.[5]

The executives of a foundation trust or corporation are involved in a fiduciary relationship which legally applies where one individual is duty-bound to act for the benefit of another party according to the terms within which the relation was established. This duty involves three parts: loyalty to the beneficiaries' interest, avoidance of excessive delegation of administrative obligations, and rendering accounts to the beneficiary. Foundation administrators are vulnerable to legal sanctions if it can be demonstrated that they violated this fiduciary relationship.

The concern in this study is not with the legal bases as such for establishing foundations. Rather, our purpose is to demonstrate how the emulation of business forms for establishing foundations as *independent* entities led them to be associated with the profit-making sphere of the economy. This caused foundations public embarrassment early in the century and established a precedent for Congressional inquiry into their ethical integrity and financial affairs.[6] It was charged that if foundations serve "public welfare" while businessmen circumvent costly taxes by contributing to them, the nonprofit sector exists to serve the profit motives of businessmen and not the public commonweal. Thus, the peculiar nonprofit status of foundations, for all their privileges, lost the moral trappings of the earlier charities, and with it a certain degree of public legitimacy. This problem of the "real" purposes of foundations was further compounded when big government—especially in the New Deal period—made great incursions into their traditional activities by acquiring welfare functions and sponsoring a wide variety of civic projects, as well as research in the physical and social sciences. Although this development did not decrease foundation activities it pressed them to justify their existence. The ways in which they did so only rendered them more vulnerable to congressional suspicion.

The greatest amount of congressional inquiry into foundation affairs has occurred in the post-World War II period. One reason for this is that the years 1940-1960 were the period of greatest foundation growth in American history. Table 1, drawn from a

Table 1

Period of Establishment of 5,050 Foundations.
By Decades After 1900 and by Latest Asset Classes[1]

PERIOD	NUMBER	PERCENT	LATEST ASSET CLASSES					
			10 million or more		1 million under 10 million		Under 1 million	
			number	percent	number	percent	number	percent
TOTAL	5,050	100	175	100	800	100	4,075	100
Before 1900	18	2	1	1	9	1	8	2
1900 to 1909	18	2	8	5	5	1	5	2
1910 to 1919	76	2	14	8	36	4	26	1
1920 to 1929	173	3	27	15	65	8	81	2
1930 to 1939	288	6	45	26	100	12	143	3
1940 to 1949	1,638	32	54	31	299	38	1,285	32
1950 to 1959[3]	2,839	56	26	15	286	36	2,527	62

Source: Treasury Department Report on Private Foundations, issued on February 2, 1965, submitted to Committee on Ways and Means, 89th Congress, First Session, Vol. 1.

[1] The 5,050 foundations tabulated by the Treasury Department are these which had at least $100,000 in assets in 1962 and were thus included in the *Foundation Directory* and were also those which provided information to the Foundation Library Center as to date of organization.

[2] Less than 0.5%.

[3] Record incomplete. Also the fragmentary 1960 record (45 foundations) is not included here.

Treasury Department study conducted in 1964 and published in 1965, illustrates this growth. The foundations established since 1950 are smaller than those established before that date, but the study indicates that this is due simply to the fact that the younger foundations have not yet built up their incomes through an accumulation of gifts and investments. Not all foundations responded to the Treasury Department's questionnaire, and therefore generalizations from the Table are tentative. But no other data exist to support or refute its findings.[7]

The Treasury Report indicates that foundation growth in relation to the rest of the economy in the 1930s and 1940s can be partially associated with the "adoption of increased progressivity in estate and income taxes" during the early 1930s—this in addition to the charitable contribution deduction under each tax. Furthermore, since 1950, the total wealth of foundations has grown faster than the rest of the economy. This was considered to be due to the fact that their principle assets and corporate stocks were increasing in price more rapidly than other assets, since the value of shares owned by the foundations were quite stable. Table 2 from the Treasury Department Study offers comparisons made at the end of 1961 between the book value of foundation assets and their market value and net worth. Table 3, from the same study, gives aggregate foundation income.

We are accustomed to associating high industrialism with increases in government expenditure. Catastrophic economic events like the world depression of 1929, the devastation of World War II and the demands of the disadvantaged for improved conditions and economic support, among other events, led the public sector to increase taxation in order to assume these burdens. The consequences involved increases in government wealth, personnel and power. Moreover, advanced industrial societies sustain their high economic levels by increases in research and development activities.

One of the most important stimulants to R & D activities in the United States has been the Department of Defense, for the obvious reason that the United States assumed heavy military responsibilities as part of its postwar world leadership role. The United States, engaged in an arms race with the Soviet Union, became devoted to the idea that a dangerous and expensive weapons arsenal was essential to her security. Thus, concerns with

Table 2
Assets of foundations, beginning of tax year 1962
(Dollar amounts in millions)

	Total	Asset size				Percent of donor-related influence over investment policy				
		Very large over 10 million	Large 1 million to 10 million	Medium One hundred thousand to 1 million	Small under one hundred thousand	50% or more	Over 33% but not over 50%	Over 20% but not over 33%	Not over 20%	Un-classified
No. of foundations	14,865	175	800	4,910	8,980	11,000	810	100	2,430	525
ASSETS										
LEDGER VALUES, END OF YEAR										
1. Cash	$443	$110	$124	$166	$43	$268	$31	$21	$109	$14
2. Accounts receivable	50	12	9	25	4	32	1	1[1]	14	4
3. Notes receivable	189	118	30	35	6	117	32	18[1]	21	1
4. Mortgage loans	149	63	61	19	6	60	13	1[1]	77	1
5. Corporation stock	6,529	4,409	1,237	783	100	2,620	488	249	3,072	103
6. Other assets[2]	5,119	3,174	1,095	744	106	1,728	351	266	2,737	35
7. Total assets	11,648	7,583	2,332	1,527	206	4,348	839	515	5,809	138
LIABILITIES										
8. Accounts payable	17	8	6	3	1	8	1	1	7	1[1]
9. Grants payable	524	488	31	5	1	75	10	20	419	1
10. Bonds, etc. payable	137	73	32	27	5	101	4	11	22	
11. Other liabilities	114	53	42	15	4	44	3	2	64	1
12. Net worth (L)	10,856	6,961	2,221	1,477	197	4,120	821	481	5,297	136
MARKET VALUES, END OF YEAR										
13. Corporation Stock (M)	10,896	8,050	1,783	955	108	3,880	860	668	5,331	159
14. Total assets (M)	16,262	11,331	2,940	1,773	218	5,666	1,270	945	8,180	201
15. Net worth (M)	15,470	10,709	2,829	1,723	209	5,438	1,252	911	7,668	199

Source: 1964 Treasury Department Survey of Private Foundations.
[1] Less than $0.5 million.
[2] This is almost all bonds.

defense- and security-related research and development resulted in enlarging the operations and power of the government sector, which in turn dramatically altered the role if not the structure of American foundations.[8]

FOUNDATION LIBERALISM

Despite this customary association between an advanced public sector and an advanced industrial economy, the nonprofit sector in the United States had increased at a fast pace along with economic and industrial advances. This is striking in view of the plausible inference that increased government spending on research and civic welfare programs diminishes the areas in which foundations can operate. This has not happened for many reasons (although it contributes greatly to the unease of the foundations). First, increases in the complexity of higher education and industry have produced a great number of trained researchers and a demand for their skills. More able people are going into research. There is need for many public and private sources of support. Second, the demand for welfare and community services outran the supply made available by government, particularly because of the government's military expenditures. Foundations were able to find room to expand in this area. Third, the promotion of international contact and cooperation after World War II revealed needs and opened opportunities for travel and research in foreign countries, for the encouragement of travel and study in the United States by foreign nationals, and for expanding the charity concept to include "good works" on behalf of international cooperation. Thus, foundations expanded in this area as well.

In view of this rapid increase in the nonprofit sector we may properly conclude that one effect of the big foundations upon public policy has been to multiply its sources. The area for research which is directed toward something other than the promotion of particular industries or toward supplementing defense policy concerns is greatly enlarged. The fact that great sums are being directed toward international studies, community services and civic uses, strengthens the possibility that government may circumvent political obstacles to engage in similar activities. The increased range of these activities over time legitimizes their value and enhances the possibilities for wider public acceptance.

Table 3
Aggregate income of foundations
(Dollar amounts in millions)

		Asset size				Percent of donor-related influence over investment policy				
	Total	Very large over 10 million	Large 1 million to 10 million	Medium one hundred thousand to 1 million	Small under one hundred thousand	50% or more	Over 33% but not over 50%	Over 20% but not over 33%	Not over 20%	Un-classified
No. of foundations	14,865	175	800	4,910	8,980	11,000	810	100	2,430	525
RECEIPTS										
1. Gross profit from business activities[1]	$8	$3	$3	$1	$1.7	$1	$1	$1	$6	1
2. Interest	159	104	35	18	2.1	47	12	8	91	$1
3. Dividends	374	268	67	36	3.1	125	28	18	197	6
4. Rents	43	21	16	5	.7	18	1	9	14	1
5. Other ordinary income	57	39	5	12	1.2	30	5	3	20	1
6. Less expenses earning gross income	62	35	13	11	2.6	28	5	8	20	1
7. Net ordinary income	580	400	113	61	6.2	194	42	31	307	6
8. Gains from sales of assets, excl. inventory	484	434	33	15	1.0	45	14	3	419	2
9. Total net ordinary income plus gains	1,065	834	146	76	7.2	239	56	34	726	10
10. Contributions received	833	290	251	235	57.4	536	30	18	238	13
11. Total receipts	1,898	1,124	397	311	64.6	775	86	52	964	23
GRANTS FROM INCOME										
12. Net	693	478	139	68	8.1	233	40	30	381	8
13. Cost of distribution	64	36	16	11	.8	20	4	2	38	1
14. Gross	757	514	155	79	8.9	253	44	32	418	9
GRANTS FROM PRINCIPAL										
15. Net	239	32	68	111	28.1	174	11	6	41	8
16. Cost of distribution	16	1	5	7	2.5	4	2	3	5	5
17. Gross	255	33	73	118	30.6	178	12	8	46	13
18. Total Grants	1,012	547	228	197	39.5	431	56	40	461	21

Source: 1964 Treasury Department Survey of Private Foundations.
[1]Gross sales or receipts from related and unrelated business activities less cost of goods sold or of operations.
[2]Less than $500,000.

Indirectly, then, the foundations liberalize public policy. This effect is complex, however, and needs explanation, especially since we shall show that it is one of the main reasons foundations are criticized as well as a basis of their strength.

The liberalizing effect upon public policy is the outcome of two factors: first, the liberal outlook of the major foundations and their promotion of liberal programs; and second, government reliance (especially on the part of executive agencies) upon the experiments of liberal foundations. Thus, the federal government can promote liberal policies with minimum obstacles by virtue of the prior acceptance they may have gained under foundation sponsorship. As one foundation spokesman put it to some skeptics who questioned the value of government-foundation cooperation: "foundations can be valuable to society by probing and supporting risky or highly experimental projects in fields in which a government impact sooner or later will be necessary."[9]

In referring to the liberal outlook of the major foundations we are not denying the fact that liberalism is multifaceted and complicated by numerous historical mutations. But here it is sufficient to say that foundations are mainly associated with a liberal constituency—academic intellectuals who hold attitudes that have been opposed by political groups showing extreme right or left wing characteristics. For example, foundations favor United States involvement with foreign nations on the grounds that the world is interdependent, that wealthy nations like the United States have responsibilities to the rest of the world, and that contact between the United States and other nations is an opportunity for benevolent exchange. They disdain the nationalistic isolationism of the right, as well as left-wing suspicion of American motives and behavior abroad. Moreover, they strongly favor social science research as an approach to social problems. Research suggests to them no echoes of "socialism", as it does to the right, nor the threat of "dehumanization" by statistics and computers feared by the left.

The major foundations favor community projects that experiment with expanded citizen participation and they disdain moralizing to the poor. This means that they allocate funds to implement participation, rather than promoting the traditional notion that all citizens should be tested in the competitive processes. Nor do foundations encourage the participatory ideal through confrontations, a mode currently favored by the left. The foundations publicly commit themselves to fostering racial equality and projects encouraging such democratic goals. They have adopted an open attitude to social criticism, especially because of its present rising tide. Yet they defend their business origins and financial sources, and will not go along with critics of "big organization." To them, "big business" brings more money and although "big government" may pose problems of seeking out spheres in which to establish foundation uniqueness, it carries no dangers for the rest of the people. Their own bigness they see primarily as a consequence of surplus wealth, rising demands for responsible research, and altogether as an advantage because they can bring more resources to the investigation of problems. Moreover, that they confer with government and business personnel is for foundation executives only a natural outcome of shared concerns and experiences, not a sign, as it generally is for the left, of interlocking elite structures.

The liberalism of foundations is, however, more than a preference fostered by their associations or activities. It is a function of their precarious social and political location between government and business sectors. It enables them to idealize their third sector status as a contribution to pluralism.[10] It gives them a vocabulary for welcoming innovation into their programming, which they require in order to survive huge government incursions into their traditional areas of interest. And they must survive this without hostility, speaking the language of cooperation, for they can ill afford to tempt government into revoking their tax privileges. In short, liberalism is currently linked to foundation survival. It is the big foundation's way of steering a difficult course toward public legitimation. Some years ago a congressman apprehensively noted this liberal tendency and its sources when he said that foundations were being forced "to enter these controversial fields which many people object to as being too far to the left."[11]

The Ford Foundation occupies such a unique position in the world of foundations, that any generalizations about the liberal caste of mind based exclusively, or even primarily, on data drawn from this foundation, can easily provide a less than accurate picture of the total network. Yet, Ford does uniquely illustrate a number of the major as well as minor points presented here.[12]

Ford went into the "business" of overseas development assistance at precisely that point in history when the United States recognized that it must face up to a Third World ideology as something unique and valid, and not a subtle form of pseudocommunism. This recognition followed the internal collapse of McCarthyism in the mid-fifties; the crystallization of nationalist tendencies in the Third World only underscored the need for a liberal option. Aid to Latin America and Asia began in the early fifties, while aid to Africa began in the late fifties. Foundation studies of the benefits of such aid quickly followed.

Invariably this assistance strengthened the liberal tendencies within the Third World, just as they did these same tendencies in domestic programming. The aid to agriculture, education, economic planning and public administration, invariably followed lines that made it impossible for the American government to support the projects directly and openly, and yet the United States was anxious to support them through private or quasi-public channels.

The dramatic shift to foreign support, to the internationalization of foundations, is further reflected in the fact that what began in 1958, namely a systematic program for international grants, only ten years later, in 1968, amounted to $480 million of the $3.37 billion granted by the Ford Foundation. These grants invariably involved pivotal nations in the East-West confrontation, a confrontation that the United States could hope to win or resolve in its favor only by putting its most liberal foot forward.

POLITICAL POLICY AND FOUNDATION LIBERALISM

Under the impact of social upheavals in the United States over the last few years, foundations have shown a propensity to a more vigorous liberalism than was possible a decade ago, in the heyday of Senator Joseph McCarthy. The Council on Foundations, for example, states that:

In a year marked by dissension and violence in important areas of our society, the philanthropic scene provided several constructive developments, three of which deserve special mention: cooperation among foundations to make better use of funds and staff; increased attention to investment portfolios, including consideration of program-related investments as an adjunct to grant making; *and recognition of the need to involve citizens in decisions affecting their communities* [Italics ours].[13]

In addition to this:

The demand for more effective community participation in many areas of decision making became an increasingly important factor in foundation programs . . . in city planning, urban renewal, economic development and public education. In the last-named field, the Ford Foundation's support of the New York City Board of Education's experimental decentralization projects was sharply criticized by the president of the United Federation of Teachers, Albert Shanker, and stoutly defended by the foundation's president McGeorge Bundy, who stated his case succinctly: "A foundation should not shrink from important issues even if they become controversial, and we do not intend to back away from this one."

Another example is offered in this Council on Foundations Annual Report.

. . . the Foundation is increasingly taking the risk of providing funds and offer of expertise if asked to by community organizations within the Black Ghetto. The Foundation is disciplining itself to sit back and let Black leaders utilize the resources as they see fit . . . we see no other alternative to the Black Conditions in the Urban Crisis.

The Ford Foundation has shown a similar tendency:

In a major departure from past policy, the Foundation this year began using part of its investment portfolio directly for social purposes. In the past, the Foundation has worked mainly through outright grants to non-profit institutions. It will now also devote to part of its investment portfolio, through such devices as guarantees, profit-making as well as non-profit if necessary.[16]

On May 8, 1969, the Ford Foundation announced grants of $2.45 million to five universities for research, teaching and training in urban problems.[17] In response to the "student revolution," the foundation announced the award of funds for student-directed research on poverty in the ghettoes of New England and in the Appalachian South, on state and local tax reform, and on universities and local government.[18] Many other programs have been continued or initiated that display a strong liberal cast.[19]

The Danforth Foundation, long interested in educational affairs, has recently shown a marked concern with urban affairs.[20] It defends this concern on a basis that is strongly congenial to the liberal habit of mind.

Foundations are not properly engaged in popularity contests. At times of their tallest stature in American life they have taken stands on issues of public concern. They play the role of actor, not merely reactor . . . To oppose special privilege in any of its forms is inevitably to run the risk of controversy. But special privilege is what the urban unrest is all about. It is not just low wages, poor plumbing and no grass. It is the denial of equal status, of a voice in civic decisions, of the fullness of human dignity. We believe that all citizens must be free to participate fully in community life and in decision-making processes. Giving up privileges is hard; giving up authority is even harder. Yet these things must happen if our cities are to survive and prosper.[21]

This new awareness of the foundation as a liberal corporate conscience is also expressed by Dana S. Creed, President of the Rockefeller Brothers Fund, who defends even direct political involvement for foundations.

Minor excursions on the part of a few foundations affecting the legislature process have added considerable fuel to Congressional ire. Foundation grants to voter registration projects are the most notable example . . . This type of activity strikes a politically sensitive nerve and hits close to home for elected officials who are the lawmakers. These voter registration projects with their general objective of broadening the franchise—which is a commonly accepted objective in a democracy—have been viewed as upsetting traditional voter patterns and therefore not legitimate activities for foundations but rather political activities which, if not already prohibited under present law, should definitely be prohibited by more restrictive legislation. I am tempted to ask what might have been the outcry had the voter registration projects tended to reinforce the traditional voting patterns.[22]

Foundations also see themselves as fostering a cooperative, yet individualist liberal model for association between nations. It envisions an association between partners rather than conflict between competitors for power or a rich and benevolent patron and its dependent.

The image of foundation assistance that emerges is not simply that of a benevolent patron; ideally, it is that of a partner with resources and competences, but one who also makes exactions and is attentive to the performance of others.[23]

Foundations are in a better position than government to embrace liberal ideals, for government is often made conservative

Table 4
Reported Grants for Welfare, 1960, by Subcategories
(Dollar figures in thousands)

Category	No. of Foundations	Major Interest	$ Amount	% of social Welfare
Aged	24	0	1,273	6
Child Welfare	37	2	3,073	14
Community Funds	39	3	4,791	22
Deliquency & Crimes	19	0	806	4
Family Service	27	1	1,584	7
Handicapped	35	1	1,654	8
Housing	9	0	163	1
Industrial Relations	5	0	108	–
Intercultural Relations	12	1	1,006	5
Legal Aid	14	0	328	2
Relief	18	1	626	3
Social Research	20	1	965	4
Youth Agencies	16	3	5,345	24
Other	1	0	18	–
From a Total of	67	–	21,740	100

Source: *The Foundation Directory, Edition 1*, Foundation Library Center, Russell Sage Foundation, New York 1960.

by its constituencies and by considerations of power maintenance and economic frugality. Further, foundations are not constrained by the sharp tests of national loyalty that are required by federal funds.[24]

Statements on the liberalism of foundations parallel their allocation of funds. The two areas in which charitable "good works" have received increased support have been civic welfare and international activities. Tables 4 and 5 (arranged separately because of differences in subcategories) drawn from *The Foundation Directory,* show the increases in welfare spending by subcategory from 1960 to 1966. However, one should view the totals with reservation since in 1960 and again in 1962 family and company-sponsored foundations are underrepresented.

The $20 million in grants for varieties of civic welfare reported for 1960 and 1962 from 67 and 110 foundations respectively probably represent under half the total grants in this field, since it is to this area that frequent contributions were made by small foundations that did not report their sums to the *Directory.*

For some time, welfare, like health services, had been a declining area for foundation grants because of the expansion of social security, private health insurance, retirement plans and increased government involvement in similar fields. But in 1962, community planning innovations received one-third of the total welfare funds. This suggests that the foundations were making original contributions to civic welfare policy and striking out on new paths. This could be a major factor in the substantial increases between the 1962 figures reported in edition 2 of the *Directory* and the 1966 tabulation. The amount increased from roughly $20 million to $80.5 million.

At the same time, the number of grants increased from 268 to 1,928. One contributing factor is the increase in number of foundations reporting, from 110 in 1962 to 832 in 1966. But this does not account for the entire amount since an increased number of foundations reporting in 1964, not represented in Table 5, showed a declining rate of welfare allocation. Thus the 1966 figures do represent a genuine tendency toward growth in the welfare field. Moreover, the striking climb of allocations to "interracial relations," from about a quarter million (in 1962) to $5.8 million in 1966 (23 times greater) is no mere reflection of improved coverage. "Examination of the grants indicates many new programs on the part of foundations not previously concerned with this field."[2 5]

The largest foundations have also sought to establish more liberalizing programs in the field of international activity. For example, Ford asserts the "partnership" relation as a guide to the conduct of activity:

The International Division is the Foundation's largest. Our commitment here is deep, long-standing, and long range. We are trying to use our relatively modest resources and our relatively extensive experience to help where a private American non-profit organization can help best in the social and economic growth of societies in Latin America, Africa, the Middle East and Asia. Our primary method has been that of developing a flexible capacity to respond to the needs of responsible leaders as they perceive them; we try not to give unwanted help.[2 6]

McGeorge Bundy recently took the opportunity, in explaining Ford's international programs, to decry the insensitivity of the American Congress on foreign aid. He noted that government is obstructed by the congressional attitude.[2 7] Elsewhere he calls the United States foreign aid position a "national disgrace,"[2 8] thereby

Table 5
Reported Grants for Welfare, 1962 and 1966, by Subcategories[1]
(Dollar figures in thousands)

Category	Number of Foundations		Number of Grants		Amount		% of Welfare	
	1962	1966	1962	1966	1962	1966	1962	1966
Community Planning	23	44	34	62	$6,163	$10,800	31	13
Youth Agencies	33	266	57	373	3,651	14,019	18	17
Aged	15	57	20	65	2,513	2,454	13	3
Delinquency & Crime	6	13	10	14	1,734	351	9	1
Recreation	24	55	29	63	1,495	1,827	8	2
Children	18	82	28	117	1,426	3,100	7	4
Relief-Social Agencies	27	107	36	144	1,073	6,214	5	8
Community Funds[2]	22	610	22	838	1,044	30,795	5	38
Handicapped	17	95	21	113	589	3,749	3	5
Interracial Relations	7	40	8	94	253	5,767	1	7
Transportation & Safety	3	15	3	24	55	690	–	1
General	n.d.	15	n.d.	21	n.d.	746	n.d.	1
Total	110	832	268	1,928	$19,996	$80,512	100	100

Source: *The Foundation Directory, Edition 2 and Edition 3*, Foundation Library Center, Russell Sage Foundation, New York, 1964 and 1967.

[1] 1962 totals should be accepted with reservation since family and company-sponsored foundations are not adequately represented.

[2] This category jumped to first place because more family foundations included and these often make one grant to local community chest type organizations.

implying that foundation international programs are a liberal corrective to congressional conservatism. Moreover, the concern for "racial equality" is not to be excluded even in the international field. On April 30, 1969 Ford announced major grants for research on racial problems outside the United States. (To the Institute of Race Relations, London, concerned with race problems on an international scale, $350,000; The Minority Rights Group, London, $72,000; The South Africa Institute of Race Relations, Johannesburg was granted $200,000).[29]

The Carnegie Foundation has been oriented toward international studies, international peace and the promotion of international contact between scholars and students for so long that it shows little interest in ideological rationales for its programs. For example, in a comparison of the Carnegie Foundation's Annual Reports for 1964, 1966 and 1968 respectively, little shift in interest or political vocabulary is evident in Carnegie activities. An examination of other foundation reports shows shifting emphasis upon styles and fields of research in the international field. From 1964 to 1966, interest focused on development, trade, population and food supply problems. From 1966 to 1968 the focus was on fostering international communication between scholars, on quantitative studies in international relations, and on visiting research scholarships, "world order" studies and technical assistance to underdeveloped countries.

Table 6 indicates an overall increase in the international field, the most startling being between 1962 and 1966. In this field increased representation of the number of foundations sampled would not change our picture since it would augment only the number of small foundations and they have little interest in international activities. Two additional points should be noted: 1) the Ford, Rockefeller and Carnegie Foundations make the largest contribution, 2) yet much foundation funding does not go directly abroad, but goes, rather, to American universities for studies of foreign areas.

Other foundations have recently sought to distinguish themselves in the "life sciences" and their relation to social policy. Most notable in this regard is the Russell Sage Foundation.[30] Although it is less likely that foundation apologies for this sphere of activity will draw directly upon the liberal vocabulary, a certain bias toward "the disadvantaged" shows up in some programs of

Table 6
Reported Grants for International Affairs, 1960, 1962, and 1966
(Dollar figures in thousands)

Category	Number of Foundations			Number of Grants			$ Amount			% of International Affairs		
	1960	1962	1966	1960	1962	1966	1960	1962	1966	1960	1962	1966
Economic Aid	4	n.d.	n.d.	n.d.	n.d.	n.d.	1,496	n.d.	n.d.	8	n.d.	n.d.
Exchange of Persons	15	9	16	n.d.	21	22	4,459	1,988	2,539	24	4	2
International Studies	17	13	8	n.d.	81	47	6,632	20,308	50,800	36	39	36
Peace & International Cooperation	5	10	15	n.d.	17	33	405	1,146	4,563	2	2	3
Relief & Refugees	8	2	15	n.d.	2	16	385	30	661	2	–	–
Technical Assistance	8	7	25	61	131	5,303	8,778	26,535	28	17	19	29
Education	n.d.	13	58	n.d.	110	139	n.d.	11,520	40,513	n.d.	22	8
Health & Medicine	n.d.	15	38	n.d.	108	134	n.d.	7,240	11,280	n.d.	14	8
Cultural Relations	n.d.	6	32	n.d.	18	53	n.d.	1,288	3,069	n.d.	2	2
Other	1	n.d.	13	n.d.	n.d.	21	2	n.d.	1,272	–¹	n.d.	1
From a Total of	29	33	152	n.d.	418	596	18,682	52,298	141,232	100	100	100

Source: Foundation Directory, Editions 1, 2 and 3.
¹ Less than 0.5%

The Russell Sage Foundation and others interested in social policy.

Foundation interest in the socialization of special groups in American society has gradually been gaining momentum during the last five years. This year . . . the Foundation's efforts in this area will contribute to the understanding of the problems of such sub-groups: racial minorities, women of high ability, the blind, the aging, and professionals. Last year the Foundation announced its support of a six-month exploratory study of Negro executives in the white business world.[31]

None of the above should be construed to mean that *all* foundations reflect a liberal bias. Some speak exclusively in the hygienic terms of restricted professionalism. The Wenner-Gren Foundation for Anthropological Research, for example, is so closely oriented to professional anthropological studies that its programs seemingly bear no relationship to the American political environment. Even if one considers "professionalism" to be a special case of ideological justification, it would be difficult to relate it to the right-center-left framework we have been employing in discussing the foundations.

Indeed, just as foundations with "left-liberal" orientations exist, so too there are large foundations which overtly promote right-wing activities (the organizations funded by H.L. Hunt) or devote themselves to "traditional" charity and promotion of "conservative values." The Indiana-based Lilly Endowment reflects all the remnants of traditional philanthropy. It has a strongly religious interest, sponsors anti-communist education projects, promotes little or no social science research, and emphasizes charitable giving to foster self-reliant individuals loyal to the United States.[32] Thus the big foundations' liberal orientation to interracial equity and to increased aid to developing nations is by no means unchallenged in the foundation world. Nevertheless, the relationship with government, especially over the last two decades, has been a particularly important stimulant toward foundation liberalism. For one thing, the foundation is frequently confused by the expansion of government-sponsored research. The Danforth Foundation expresses this confusion forthrightly.

American philanthropy has never been healthier or more puzzled. This is especially true for foundations working in the field of education. On the one hand the calls for support from schools and colleges are more urgent than ever before, and the foundations are responding in ever-increasing measure. On the other hand, the complexities and uncertainties of education and the millions of new government money cause the foundations to wonder what they should do; and they seem to spend more time in pondering their role in general, and perhaps their particular grants, than was once their custom.[33]

This concern for the continuing redefinition of foundation roles is pervasive.[34] Nevertheless confusion resulted in a formula for adaptation and cooperation, well expressed in a recent Danforth report.

The Danforth Foundation has decided not to abandon those interests that touch upon the areas of Federal activity, but to adopt a policy of parallel action and, where feasible, collaboration . . . Federal money, like foundation money, is automatically neither an ogre nor an angel. We must learn to live with it creatively and to combine it with other resources to the benefit of all education.[35]

The result is that foundations have been driven into collaboration with government, or, as foundation spokesmen say, a "partnership." But a partnership still leaves the problem of what role foundations will play. They cannot duplicate government efforts; they can only complement them according to government need. There arises the self-sought and self-defined innovative role of the foundation as compared with the trepidations of their "cautious partner." The foundations are in a position to innovate. Organizational legitimacy depends on it. Moreover, complementing government research efforts means taking risks that government cannot afford politically or sometimes financially. The partnership thus involves the foundation in practical collaboration and innovative political risk-taking. A number of statements are available indicating both the fact and mutual acceptance of this collaboration. In addition to joint ventures, there are relations on the personnel level.

Foundation staff members and governmental officials do move back and forth between each other's vineyards, sometimes for a stretch of years, sometimes on *ad hoc* assignments. To those who see hobgoblins or "establishment interlock" in such arrangements, the most elementary answer is that of the patriotic obligation. Our government should get talented people where it can find them, and members of foundation staff have no less an obligation to respond than university professors or business executives. But patriotism . . . is not the only basis for the interchange. To remain alert and informed, both foundations and government need the influsion of talented and specialized outsiders.[36]

Also:

Foundations can be the source of support for disinterested evaluation of government activities. It is no reflection on the Congressional right and competence to evaluate government activity to suggest that judgments from this source are not always free of political implications. Congress itself and the Executive Branch have acknowledged the importance of independent, non-governmental appraisal of government, and where else are the evaluators of government social and economic programs to obtain non-governmental support but the foundations?[37]

Richard Magat goes on to emphasize the practical value of collaboration for foundations.

The partnership may be conducted through joint ventures with local, state, or national governments. Participation affords government direct experience in the venture, so that it does not have to rely on second-hand or after-the-fact observations and it enhances the prospects of continuing interest and financing after the foundation's role is concluded. Collaboration sometimes is also indicated for the simple reason that the undertaking may be too costly for foundations alone.[38]

Collaboration extends down to local government and on sensitive issues.[39]

So firm a trend has collaboration and foundation risk-taking become that to give it systematic attention a newly forming "Commission on Foundations and Private Philanthropy" will consider, among other things, "new roles for foundations as the government invests unprecedented amounts in traditional areas of welfare and philanthropy" as well as "guidelines to help determine the proper role of private philanthropy to controversial public policy issues and the political process."[40]

SUMMARY AND CONCLUSIONS

While the question of federal government responses to foundation activities is a subject for study in itself, it is evident that recent Patman Subcommittee investigations, and ensuing Congressional activities designed to make foundations subject to new tax reform measures, are directly aimed at the third force liberalism of foundations. A tax surcharge of 100 percent would be levied on any foundation making investments "which jeopardizes the carrying out of its exempt purposes." This seems particularly aimed to discourage foundation support for such measures as voter registration drives and black ghetto self-help programs. The section of the Bill on "Taxes and Taxable Expenditures" is particularly emphatic in using the tax rubric to penalize efforts "to carry out propaganda or otherwise influence legislation, and further "to influence the outcome of any public election."[41] Interestingly, aside from some vague references to travel and study, there is little to indicate any real concern about the overseas aspects of foundation liberalism. It is clear then, that it is in the area of domestic politics that the real thrust and real concerns exist.

The foundations have proven singularly inept at lobbying their causes. Aside from some recent action on the part of foundation officials, and aside from sporadic Congressional support—there has been remarkably little defense of the foundations from those political sources that benefit from their presence. One might argue that this situation discredits the idea of a monolithic Establishment acting as a mightly phalanx against social justice and economic change. It might be argued with equal vigor, however, that the foundations are corporate equivalents to the spies caught out in the cold. Once nailed and criticized, they perforce surrender their immunity from criticism since they forfeit their federal source of legitimation.

The main problem seems to be that the corporate model for public trusts is an unwieldy one, at least in terms of generating mass support, or even the support of selective elite groups. Cut off from a major national constituency, foundations are buffeted about by those "below" whom they seek to serve, and no less, by those "above" who determine the operational framework of foundation activities and policies. This explains the rather conventional commitment to liberal ideologies and causes, and also explains a good deal of the resentment of foundation activities from both right-wing crusaders and left-wing critics.

While foundation responses to criticism have been both cautious and vigorously self-defensive, their peculiar position between business and government has nevertheless left them vulnerable and searching for schemes to survive. Liberalism and collaboration with government agencies to liberalize policy have served these survival needs. But this only encourages more criticism from the right and the left. A major increase in the impact of either critic would precipitate a crisis in self-definition.

NOTES

[1] For the distinction between foundations and other public welfare oriented organizations, see the *Treasury Department Report on Private Foundations* submitted to the Committee on Ways and Means, 89th Congress, First Session, Washington, D.C.: USGPO February 2, 1965, Vol. 1, pp. 9-10.

[2] For an historical account see Robert H. Bremner, *American Philanthropy.* Chicago: The University of Chicago Press, 1960.

[3] See the Manly Report published in 1916: *Final Report and Testimony,* Submitted to Congress by the Commission on Industrial Relations, Senate Document No. 415, 64th Congress, First Session, Washington, D.C.: USGPO, 1916.

[4] See Marion R. Fremont-Smith, *Foundations and Government.* New York: Russell Sage Foundation, 1965, especially Chapters 1 and 2 for a discussion of the historical roots of the laws relating to charities. Other chapters in this book give an extremely clear account of the trust and corporate bases of the foundations.

[5] See M.R. Fremont-Smith, *Ibid.,* Table 2, Appendix A, pp. 479-90 for a state-by-state summary.

[6] Congressional investigation has not been directed at all philanthropic foundations. There are a number of types. See Harrison and Andrews, *American Foundations for Social Welfare,* Russell Sage Foundation, 1946, for a good description of them. Harrison and Andrews refer to four main types: (a) the name-only type, usually of a mere non-granting soliciting variety with no capital funds; (b) the "marginal type" supported by fees or foundations grants, having highly restricted purposes; (c) the "community trust type" set up to enable a number of small donors to pool their resources; (d) the big general philanthropic foundation which is the type we have been discussing and the type most subject to congressional inquiry. Within this type, the authors make a distinction between "operating" and "nonoperating" foundations, the former being those maintaining their own research staff and the latter making grants to outside researchers. A number of "general" philanthropic foundations are also a blend of both operating and nonoperating varieties.

[7] See Frank Andrews, "Introduction," *The Foundation Directory, Edition 2,* Foundation Library Center, New York: Russell Sage Foundation, 1964, pp. 15-16. It is shown here, in keeping with Treasury Department's observation that before 1900 less than 0.5 percent of the listed foundations (in the directory) were organized at that time. During the first decade of the twentieth century the growth rate was under two a year (although these included two presently worth over $25 million). The 1910-1919 rate increased to over seven a year for a total of 76, including three giants, Rockefeller Funds, the Carnegie Corporation of New York and the Commonwealth Fund. This is the time that the community trust type

becomes important. In the 1920s the rate more than doubled to 17 a year and 12 of these in the large asset range. Though the depression slows the rate of growth it still increases to nearly 30 a year. In the 1940s there are more than six times the number in the 1930s and growth reaches an all time high in the 1950s.

[8] The importance of defense rather than welfare related R & D to government sector operations is illustrated by the fact that research in the areas of health, education and welfare receives only hundreds of thousands of dollars yearly while defense related R & D is in the billions. Indeed defense R & D jumped from $1,182,944,900 in 1954 to $7,551,328,000 in 1968. See issues of *Congressional Quarterly Almanac* from 1954-1968.

[9] Richard Magat, "Foundation Reporting," Address to The *Ninth Biennial Conference on Charitable Foundations,* May 19, 1969, p. 6.

[10] Hearings Before the Committee on Ways and Means, Tax Reform, 91st Congress, First Session, Pt. 1, February 18, 1969, Washington, D.C., pp. 81-82 and 84-85.

[11] Hearings Before the Select Committee to Investigate Tax-Exempt Foundations and Comparable Organizations, House of Representatives, 82nd Congress, Second Session, Washington D.C., Nov.-Dec. 1952, p. 52.

[12] Cf. Ford Foundation in East and Central Africa. New York: Ford Foundation Office of Reports, June 1969.

[13] Council on Foundation, Annual Report 1967-1968. p. 5.

[14] *Ibid.,* p. 7.

[15] *Ibid.,* p. 7.

[16] *Ford Foundation Annual Report,* October 1, 1967 to September 30, 1968, p. 3.

[17] *News From the Ford Foundation,* May 8, 1969, p. 1.

[18] *News From the Ford Foundation,* June 19, 1969, pp. 1-2.

[19] Ford Foundation, *Annual Report, op. cit.,* pp. 3-18.

[20] See Danforth Foundation, differences in *Annual Report* for 1964 and 1967.

[21] The Danforth Foundation, *Annual Report* 1967-1968, pp. 12-13.

[22] Dana S. Creel, *Address to the Ninth Biennial Conference on Charitable Foundations,* New York University, May 20, 1969, p. 13.

[23] Francis X. Sutton, *American Foundations and U.S. Public Diplomacy,* Ford Foundation, New York 1968, p. 7 (reprint from address delivered before the "Symposium on the Future of U.S. Public Diplomacy," Subcommittee on International Organizations and Movements, House Committee on Foreign Affairs).

[24] *Ibid.,* p. 12.

[25] *The Foundation Director, Edition 3,* The Foundation Library Center, Russell Sage Foundation, N.Y. 1967, p. 50.

[26] McGeorge Bundy, Ford Foundation, *Annual Report,* October 1, 1967 to September 30, 1968, p. xvi.1, 1968, p. xvi.

[27] *Ibid.,* pp. xvii and xviii.

[28] *Foundation,* March 2, 1969, p. 1, Bundy, *News From the Ford,* p. 3.

[29] *News From the Ford Foundation,* April 30, 1969, p. 1.

[30] See the Russell Sage Foundation, *Annual Report 1967-1968,* pp. 10-20.

[31] *Ibid.,* p. 28.

[32] Lilly Endowment, Inc., *A Report for 1964,* see also *Reports* for 1965, 1966, and 1967.

[33] The Danforth Foundation, *Annual Report, 1965-1966,* p. 9.

[34] For some recent examples see McGeorge Bundy, Ford Foundation, *Annual Report, October 1, 1967 to September 30, 1968*, p. xxiii; also Dana S. Creel (President of the Rockefeller Brothers Fund), "The Role of the Foundations in Today's Society," Address to the Ninth Biennial Conference on Charitable Foundations, New York University, May 20, 1969, p. 3.

[35] The Danforth Foundation, Annual Report, 1965-66, p. 9., pp. 10-11.

[36] Richard Magat, *op. cit.*, pp. 7-8.

[37] *Ibid.*, p. 2

[38] *Ibid.*, p. 6.

[39] *Hearings Before the Committee on Ways and Means*, 1969, *op. cit.*, p. 430.

[40] Press Release made by Peter G. Peterson, Chairman of the Board and chief executive officer of the Bell and Howell Company, on April 23, 1969, p. 6.

[41] See John Walsh, "Tax Reform: House Bill Holds Penalties for Foundations," in *Science*, Vol. 165, No. 3894 (August 15, 1969), pp. 678-79.

The Policy Researcher:
His Habitat, Care and Feeding

ADAM YARMOLINSKY

Scholars have long been concerned with the subject matter that concerns the policy researcher. In fact there is an established discipline that deals in large part with this subject matter, a quite respectable discipline, with a muse all its own, many generations of graduate students, and more than its quota of university presidents drawn from its ranks. The only difference between the historian and the policy researcher is that the historian concerns himself with past policy choices, while the policy researcher concerns himself with policy choices not yet made. But the difference is a profound one, for at least two reasons.

First, the great bulk of the policy decisions that historians analyze was not influenced by policy research, because there was substantially no research input to those decisions. Policy research had not been invented, and government staffs were occupied until very recently almost entirely with implementing decisions, not with examining alternatives or evaluating results. Outside advisers were primarily personal counselors or glorified speechwriters, not systematic analysts.

And conversely, the historian has very little sense that he is, or may be affecting policy outcomes. As the policy researcher would say, the historian's computer is not operating in real time. Historians are beginning to apply the methods of policy analysis to past events. The Strategic Bombing Survey, at the end of World War II, from which so much later work on alternative military strategies developed, was in effect an historical study, using methods that should have been employed in making the basic decisions about strategic bombing, and that might have saved an enormous number of lives on both sides and spared great cities from destruction. Historical research and policy research may some day become aspects of the same general study, but that day is probably a long way off.

Meanwhile, it may be worth examining the situation of the historian today, in order to note the differences between his situation and that of the policy researcher. To define these differences may be to define the principal problems—and the principal opportunities—that face the policy researcher.

The historian belongs to a discipline that provides him with a generally accepted definition of his field and of its subspecialties. These definitions are revised from time to time, by relatively orderly processes. His primary audience is his students, and the first and last judgment on his work is the judgment of his peers, with whom he is in easy communication, within his own university department, and through journals and conferences. The tools of his trade are to be found in major libraries, although he may have difficulty getting access to particular sets of records. He may be able to use some help in gathering materials—and he can usually find it in the dependable, low cost graduate student labor market—but basically he works by himself. As an historian, he is, to a degree, a generalist, and he does not ordinarily seek a specialist's competence in other disciplines, even when they are relevant to his professional interests. True, there are overlapping specialties—history of science, economic history, legal history—but they have made their treaties with their sister disciplines, assimilating themselves, to a greater or lesser degree, to the concerns of scholars dealing with the substantive subject matter of science or economics or law.

The policy researcher, however, has essentially none of these landmarks or navigational aids to rely on. Whatever discipline he had been brought up in, it is no longer the focus of his activities and interests. Indeed, for some of the most effective policy researchers, their original disciplines served only to sharpen their minds and acquaint them with research methods generally, and they have since chosen a whole new set of navigational reference marks.

We can define policy research by an exclusionary process, as research designed to assist in the formulation or reformulation of policy, which is stretched beyond the traditional boundaries of a single discipline or a set of related disciplines by the needs of the policy maker. We can test the definition by examining limiting cases. It excludes both research which is not differentiated in character from other academic research by its policy objectives, and academic research on the nature of the policy process itself (although that research has yet to find a happy home in an established discipline). Clearly neither government-supported basic research nor government-supported applied research in particular disciplines is designed to advance the state of the art of policy research. Most of the research that goes into designing a new weapons system, or a new urban mass transit system or even a new welfare system is not policy research, but where the separate pieces of disciplinary research must be selected to meet policy needs, where new research must be undertaken that may cut across disciplinary lines, and where the product is assembled and shaped to the needs of the policy maker, the policy researcher must chart the course. By the same token, testing a new airplane design, or a new curriculum design is not of itself policy research. But choosing the criteria against which the system is to be tested necessarily involves policy research.

To elucidate further what I mean by policy research, it may be worthwhile to break it down under five headings (for which I am largely indebted to Yehezkel Dror, although I have shifted his categories somewhat): trend measurement, policy choice, program development, troubleshooting and evaluation.

When policy makers want to follow the trends in the phenomenon of poverty in the United States (or in stream pollution, or in the strategic military balance), they require a continuing research effort that necessarily transcends disciplinary limits.

Trend measurement research is nevertheless closer to traditional academic research than the research that is called for in deciding what mixture of incomes strategy and services strategy to use on

ADAM YARMOLINSKY

the poverty problem (or in designing a pollution control policy at the national, state or local level, or in shifting from massive retaliation to flexible response in strategic nuclear policy). Because a new policy is not explicitly so designated does not obviate the need for research support in developing it. Early in the Kennedy administration it was decided, after sharp debate, not to revise and reissue the bulky volume "Basic National Security Policy" promulgated by the Eisenhower Administration, but to instruct the bureaucracy to rely instead on speeches and other public statements of politically responsible officials as sources of policy guidance. This decision did not stem the flow of policy papers and government-supported research designed to elucidate general issues of national security policy.

Even more mission-oriented and less academic research is called for in developing specific programs for the various elements of an antipoverty program, welfare services, job training and placement, education, housing, health care, and so forth (or for corresponding programs in pollution control or strategic doctrine and weapons development).

When it comes to day-to-day trouble-shooting in the operations of existing programs, policy research tends to shade off into staff work, although it may be farmed out to policy researchers where the problem seems to call for more time, or concentration of resources, or imagination than the staff is able to supply.

Evaluation is a special kind of policy research, demanding a combination of hard disciplinary skills and clear focus on the policy goals of the program or project to be evaluated. It is in this area that the failures of policy research are perhaps most evident.

None of these categories is discrete from the others, and individual pieces of policy research may be difficult to classify, while individual policy researchers may be engaged in research in several of these categories simultaneously. Indeed one man may be and often is engaged in disciplinary and policy research at the same time. But here the researcher's background in his own discipline cannot by itself provide a framework for his policy research.

In the absence of a disciplinary framework, the policy re-searcher needs another set of limitations and directions to shape his inquiry. He finds these in the policy process itself, and, having chosen his subject matter, he must anticipate the locus of policy choices, and correct for errors as he goes along. This is not to say that the policy researcher becomes merely an instrument of the policy maker's will. As a scholar, he is free to pursue his own interests. As, one hopes, an original thinker, he does not simply take policy problems in the terms they are put to him by policy makers and policy advisers, and then attempt to work out solutions. If politics is the art of the possible, the true artist may be the man who can find new possibilities. There is a necessary tension in every field between its possibilities and its limitations. As F. Scott Fitzgerald said: "There is always some damn condition."

But here the broad lines of the policy researcher's useful inquiry are determined by the views of men who do not live in this world, while he does not live in theirs. His views must be communicated to these men, and are ultimately judged by their impact on policy, which is to say what the policy makers do with and about them. Since this impact is to a large extent accidental, depending on how much other advice clogs the channels of communication, and how events move in response to random influences, the policy researcher gets less feedback for his efforts than his other scholarly colleagues do, both in quantity and certainly in quality. Too many of his returns, necessarily, come from people who don't know what is good research, but do emphatically know what they like. And too often his research results never get beyond the desk of the branch chief or the section chief, so that the policy maker who could use them doesn't even know they exist. This situation contrasts sharply with the openness of channels of communication in the scholarly world.

Brilliant and profound policy research may be done by a man alone in a room with a blackboard or a scratch pad. But it is more likely to require the collection and analysis of data from a number of fields, employing techniques derived from several different disciplines. Policy problems do not turn up neatly packaged as "economics," "sociology" or even "international relations." The importance of the computer in policy research has been considerably overstated. In preparing an article on the role of the computer in Pentagon decision-making,[1] I had no difficulty finding policy decisions based on a systems analysis where a

ADAM YARMOLINSKY

computer had been unnecessary, but some difficulty finding an important case where the computer had been essential.

Yet the importance of facts and of numbers is still not fully appreciated. These are facts and numbers that must generally be derived from a wide range of sources, and subjected to critical examination in the light of several kinds of specialized knowledge, bearing in mind that most of the information that comes to the policy researcher has been gathered in an arena where objectivity is more often the exception than the rule. The researcher then generally needs to be extraordinarily tough in order to avoid becoming a prisoner of the staff, particularly where it is made up of individuals who are primarily operators rather than researchers.

Policy research in connection with a decision whether or not to proceed with the development of a new weapons system requires the collection of facts, and opinions, about United States foreign policy, the military capabilities, and, so far as it is possible to ascertain them, the intentions of potential antagonists, the effectiveness of existing weapons systems, the state of the art in a number of areas of technology, the probable shape of learning curves for production of the system, and the budgetary picture both for the Defense Department and for the federal government generally.

Policy research on a proposed income maintenance plan would involve disputed facts and issues in welfare economics, sociology, demography, budgetary pressures and the state of mind of the Congress, to name only a selection.

Policy research on automobile pollution control involves three quite separate technologies: internal combustion, external combustion and electric storage batteries, as well as the economics of the auto industry, antitrust law and urban sociology—and this is far from an exhaustive catalogue of subjects for research, in each of which there are passionately held special-interest positions, and standards of objective scholarship leave something to be desired.

In none of these cases can a single researcher hope to master all the fields of knowledge that are relevant to a policy recommendation, nor can he verify for himself more than a small fraction of the data collected. The skills that he must display are not only analytical and synthetic, but evaluative and executive as well. He must make some intuitive judgments, more so than his discipline-oriented colleagues, and he must manage and oversee the work of other professionals (and nonprofessionals), more than in most disciplinary research.

These difficulties obtain, to a greater or lesser degree, across the spectrum of policy research activities from trend measurement to evaluation, although they tend to increase as one moves across the spectrum towards the least academic and discipline-oriented kinds of policy research.

Having identified the policy researcher as a man with a lot of problems, and having defined him, by exclusion, as the scholar who has denied himself most of the benefits of the scholarly life, we can go on to try to place him in time and space. The policy researcher is, as has been suggested, a quite recent phenomenon. The National Academy of Sciences, which was created during the Civil War to put the resources of the scientific community at the disposition of the government, was seldom called on during the first three generations of its existence. The National Research Council, created for a similar purpose in World War I, played a very limited role. The development of Agricultural Experiment stations in connection with the land grant colleges and the agricultural extension system could be described as a primitive form of policy research, applying the results of experimentation in fields like plant genetics to the problems of American agriculture. Henry Wallace is more likely to be remembered for his introduction of hybrid corn than for any of the accomplishments of his later life.

The domestic economic crisis of the thirties produced a spate of legislation, most of it having its origins in academic speculation, but there were no systematic links between the research community and the economic policy makers. Wars are prime sources of innovation, and World War II saw an enormous expansion in the use of research, not only on technical questions but on issues of military and politico-military policy as well. The war's end saw the enactment of the Employment Act of 1946 and the creation of the Council of Economic Advisers to bring systematic research to bear on problems of economic policy. During the decade of the fifties, the principal subject of policy research was national security, and particularly the apocalyptic dangers of nuclear war. A number of high-level commissions studied various aspects of the problem, using many of the same people as commission members or advisers, who were also called on as consultants by the Defense Establishment. These "weaponeers" came to constitute almost a distinct class, although they tended to have academic or industrial career commitments of a more traditional character.

At the same time there began to appear a number of "think-tanks"—the RAND Corporation, the Institute for Defense Analysis, the Research Analyses Corporation and other organizations, most of them established to serve the military departments. Perhaps the most important fact about the think-tanks is that their professional staff could properly be described as full-time policy researchers. Within RAND, for example, the staff was not organized along traditional disciplinary lines. There was a department of economics, but there was also a department of logistics, and a department of social science, while particular projects could cut across departmental lines, and the most senior people in the organization were freed from departmental affiliations as members of the so-called research council.

Towards the end of the fifties, policy research was launched on a broader scale, in the Rockefeller Brothers Special Studies program, and the Eisenhower National Goals Commission, which attempted to apply the techniques of policy research to public policy issues across the board. But again they did so without making use of professional staff that was permanently oriented towards policy research. The staffs of these studies consisted primarily of people with a background in traditional disciplinary research, or of lawyers with a general background in public service—precursors, in some ways, of the full-fledged policy researcher.

With the advent of the Kennedy administration, a number of alumni of the think-tanks found their way into government, particularly in the Department of Defense, where their sympathetic presence in turn encouraged the creation of new private entities, from the Hudson Institute to the Logistics Management Institute, to special divisions of major corporations, like General Electric's Tempo. During the sixties, their influence spread to the domestic agencies of government, as exemplified in the diffusion of the planning, programming budgeting system (PPBS) throughout the federal government and into some state and local government units and the creation of quasi-public research entities like the Urban Institute, under a federal statute, and the Poverty

Research Institute at the University of Wisconsin, under an OEO grant. And on the anti-establishment side, one finds such institutions as the Institute for Policy Studies in Washington, and the Center for the Study of Democratic Institutions in Santa Barbara.

Since the Nixon Administration has taken office, new entities for policy research have been formed in and out of government, including a unit within the International Studies Division of the Brookings Institution that is prepared to do analyses of the annual defense budget and the Secretary of Defense's military posture statement, to compare with the analyses prepared within the Department of Defense. The Brookings group does not of course have access to classified material, but it is staffed to do the same kind of analytical work that was performed during the McNamara regime in the office of the Assistant Secretary for Systems Analysis—and with fewer constraints on the underlying assumptions of the research.

Plans for more elaborate use of policy research within the government have been articulated in the executive branch with the creation of the National Goals Research staff within the executive office of the president, and proposals for an organization to serve the Congress as an independent source of evaluations of executive branch proposals, even suggested by Daniel Patrick Moynihan as a fourth branch of government.

In the face of all this activity, who are the policy researchers and where are they to be found? Despite the excitement that surrounds them, they are indeed a little band of brothers. There are some 15,000 economists in the United States, and about an equal number of political scientists, but there are probably only a few thousand people who could be properly identified as policy researchers. They include no more than a few hundred people on the staffs of government-supported research institutions (since most of the staffs of these organizations are technicians concerned with the details of weapons development), a few score individuals in privately supported institutions, both profit and nonprofit, and a few hundred more university-based scholars whose primary interest is in policy-oriented rather than discipline-oriented research. These people cannot be identified in any formal fashion in the academic world, any more than within the research institutions. They recognize each other when they meet, but they tend to play down their unconventional interests, lest their discipline-oriented colleagues accuse them of lack of devotion to the "science" of economics—or sociology, or government, or whatever. They have no official learned journals—although their writing is to be found particularly in the pages of *trans*action and *The Public Interest* and in the new *Policy Sciences* and they have no regular meeting places—other than ad hoc conferences like the one at which this essay was first presented.

Because they have almost no group identity, they have yet to engage in collective bargaining on behalf of their common interests, which have thus far gone largely unrecognized. In anticipation of future bargaining sessions, it may be worth an effort of prediction as to what these demands will be. It seems likely that, at least in the university context, they will focus on three points: common funding across disciplinary lines, research staff and more integration of field work into the life of the university. The interests of policy researchers are shaped by concerns that cut across traditional disciplinary lines, and the formation of new departments or even of permanent interdepartmental committees is not an adequate answer to the problem. A shifting structure of research commitments, in which individual scholars are free to follow their interests beyond the limits of established disciplines, is essential to full participation in policy research.

This kind of structure in turn raises two problems: the relationships among research, teaching and academic advancement, which would have to be looser, in the dependence on fixed ladders of progression, than it is today; and the availability of research assistance.

There is still a good deal of resistance in the university community to bringing in as research assistants people who are not candidates for permanent teaching appointments. Yet in order to do most policy research, it is essential, as I have suggested, to be able to draw on staff resources, including people who have neither the qualifications nor the ambition for a permanent teaching position. Introduction of these people into the academic community is regarded as destructive of the collegial atmosphere, as introducing a kind of second-class citizenship, into what has been up to now a unique example of direct democracy. That it need not be seen this way is no guarantee that academic attitudes will change, but until they change, the policy researcher can only operate in the academic setting under substantial handicaps.

The need for extensive field work is perhaps a less troublesome problem. The tradition of field work on an extended schedule is well-established in anthropology and archaeology. There is no reason a priori why it cannot be established in more contemporary fields, particularly when it coincides with the expressed desire of students in professional schools for more direct and immediate contact with the problems and the people with whom they will be dealing after graduation.

It may be that policy research cannot be carried on effectively in a university context. After all, the major scientific advances of the eighteenth century took place in the scientific societies, because the universities would not afford them house room. But if the universities were to abandon the policy researcher, both parties would be the loser. The policy researcher needs exposure to scholars whose concerns are with issues that will outlast the institutions and the issues that occupy him from day to day, and he also needs exposure to students for whom the entire structure that he takes almost as a given, is an object alternatively of contempt and of all-out attack.

At the same time the university needs the presence of the policy researcher. More than 30 years ago, Robert Lynd wrote of the tendency of every social science "to shrink away from the marginal area where insistent reality grinds against the central body of theory." It is this grinding exposure to the problems of insistent reality that makes policy problems an important part of university-based research.

Perhaps the ideal arrangement would be one in which policy researchers could move freely back and forth between universities and independent research institutions, with occasional tours of service in government as well. Not all policy researchers would choose to take advantage of this freedom of movement, but for those who did, it would provide an extraordinarily broad perspective, serving research in somewhat the same fashion that government is served by persons who come and go between decision-making or high-level advisory posts in government, and careers in private life. These "in-and-outers," as Richard Neustadt and I have called them, are responsible for many of the new initiatives in any administration. For the policy researcher, the principal obstacles to this kind of lateral movement are still primarily in the university, rather than in government or in the research institutions.

There is a clear implication in the foregoing that policy researchers will not find a home in government itself. By and large, this is true. The business of government is too pressing to permit anything but the most short-range research to be carried on within the walls, and when longer range work is attempted, those who undertake it are likely to find themselves isolated from the mainstream of policy-making, as in the case of the State Department Policy Planning Council under Presidents Kennedy and Johnson. There have indeed been exceptions to this general rule, notably in the work of the Policy Planning Council during the Truman administration that resulted in the powerful national security policy document known as NSC (National Security Council) 68, but as a generality, the rule still holds.

If policy researchers have difficulty working within government, they must still learn to work with government. There is a necessary symbiotic relationship between the policy researcher, the policy adviser and the policy maker. Each one depends on the other two, and his psychic income is very much a function of the input he receives from them.

But even this happy situation does not guarantee a happy relationship between policy researchers and policy makers. If this is indeed to be a marriage of true minds, both partners have to learn to respect each other's roles, and to accommodate themselves somewhat to the limiting conditions within which the other fellow works. The policy maker has to realize that he cannot demand and obtain instant scholarship; that objectivity and reflectiveness and depth of perception can only be had at the price of some loss in immediate relevance—that word—to the policy maker's current concerns; and that a good batting average for a successful scholar is a lot lower than it is for a major league ball player.

A classic problem that policy makers have with their own bureaucracies is that bureaucrats are so much problem-oriented and so anxious to keep the machinery of government moving by solving problems, that they will not infrequently come up with a solution to a different problem than the one posed to them by the policy maker; since they can't find a solution to the problem that is put to them, they have to change the problem in order to get to a solution. This is commonly referred to in Washington as the street light syndrome, in honor of the drunk who told the policeman, puzzled by his posture on hands and knees under a street light, that he was looking for his door key. The policeman asked where he had dropped it, and the drunk replied, in his doorway. The policeman asked why he was looking under the street light, and the drunk pointed out that the light was better there.

When a policy maker refers an administrative problem to his bureaucracy with the warning that it is politically impossible to solve it by amending the legislation, he may get back a report that the best way to solve it is by amending the legislation, and here is the language proposed for the amendment.

Scholars, on the other hand—and even policy-oriented re-searchers—are by and large a good deal less problem-oriented than the policy makers who seek their advice. When asked what can be done about insurgency in Northeast Thailand, the scholar may reply with a learned dissertation on customs and folkways of Northeast Thailand, with extensive references to the customs and folkways of Southeast Thailand, which were particularly appealing to the scholar's own interests. But if the scholar is oriented to the underlying policy problem, it may turn out in the end that the key to the situation is a better understanding of the differences in ethnic patterns between the Northeast and the rest of the country. So that, as policy makers learn to be understanding of the foibles of their bureaucracies, they need to learn to be understanding of the systematic biases of scholars, and even of those enlightened scholars who are policy researchers.

But my concern here is more with the accommodations that scholars need to make in order to perform a more useful role in the process of policy-making than with the accommodations that government needs to make to scholars. And here I have to inject two caveats. Many scholars have no interest in contributing to the policy-making process in foreign affairs or elsewhere, and there is no reason why they should do so. What distinguishes the scholar from lesser mortals is that he is free to pursue his own interests, and that freedom must be preserved. The other caveat is that if the scholar ever abandons his pursuit of the truth in order to be more involved in policy-making, he destroys his own usefulness as a scholar, and his usefulness to the policy maker as well. There is no reason, as I've suggested earlier, why he shouldn't serve a term as a policy maker between periods of scholarly endeavor; but it is a positive disservice to the policy maker for the scholar to shade his conclusions in order to please his client.

Given these two caveats, there is nothing dishonorable or even inappropriate in the examination by scholars of policy problems, foreign or domestic. They can provide at least as much intrinsic interest as problems of theory or methodology. But if the scholar is to make a contribution to policy problems, he must be willing to address himself to the problems of the policy maker. He must be willing to help answer the policy maker's question, "What do you want *me* to do about it?" He may, and indeed he should try to, stretch the limitations within which the policy maker works, but he cannot ignore them.

Another way to put this requirement is to say that, if he is to be really useful to the policy maker or the policy adviser, the policy researcher must have a programmatic sense. To begin with, he must distinguish between ideas and programs. The policy researcher need not participate in this process, but he must understand its imperatives, if he is to serve the policy maker.

One way to try to clarify the relationship between the policy researcher and his clients is to look at it in a single field, and here I propose to look at the very broad field of foreign relations, where policy researchers have been involved perhaps longer than in domestic affairs.

At the outset, there is a role for the policy researcher simply in asking his client to stop and think "What difference does all my activity really make?" So much of the activity of foreign policy professionals consists of efforts to change the behavior of foreign policy professionals representing other countries, where reflection would indicate that the behavior of their foreign opposite numbers is largely determined by internal domestic politics, and that the United States has remarkably little control over such matters, beyond the reach of its sovereignty.

But if the scholar's role in foreign policy were only to ask the embarrassing questions, that would make it too easy. There is work to be done as well. And it is precisely in the area of advising the busy foreign policy professional on the nature and content of other societies that the scholar can make his greatest substantive contribution. The professional diplomat is the man who knows where, in Paris or in Phnom Penh, in Bonn or in Bujumbura, to find the door to which diplomatic notes should be delivered. He has a pretty good idea of what will happen to the note after it is slipped through the mail slot in the door. But he cannot be expected to have a really deep understanding of the internal political and economic and social lines of force that converge on the men on the other side of the door. For that understanding he must turn to the scholar who has specialized in the politics and economics and social patterns of the area.

If foreign policy is really foreign politics, and if politics is the art of the possible, a major role for the policy researcher in foreign affairs may be to advise the policy maker on what is indeed possible within the limitations of domestic politics in other continents and in other cultures. This is perhaps a reversal of the usual roles of scholar and activist. The scholar is more often thought of as the proponent of far-out ideas that the activist must scale down to what can actually be accomplished. But if we think of the truth that scholars seek as only unfamiliar reality, we see even this negative function as part of the scholar's traditional role. He can often be most useful when he is being most skeptical, when he is pointing out that the Emperor's new foreign policy scheme—as in the case of, say, massive retaliation, or the abortive proposal for a multilateral nuclear force in Europe—really does not amount to any scheme at all.

But still the scholar has some obligation to the policy maker to relate his observations to the range of alternatives available to the person he is advising, and to suggest a positive course of action that can take off from wherever the policy maker finds himself at the moment of choice. Because no policy maker worth his salt is going to accept the advice, "You can't get there from here." He may be persuaded to take a different route, or allow more time for the journey; he may even be persuaded that he is going in the wrong direction, or that he should change his ultimate objective. But if he were to find himself without any goal, even temporarily, he would lose his momentum, and this he cannot afford to do, any more than the scholar can afford to lose his objectivity.

Policy-making, like scholarship, suffers from the tendency that I referred to earlier in the words of Robert Lynd "to shrink away from the marginal area where insistent reality grinds against the

ADAM YARMOLINSKY

central body of theory." Perhaps the principal function of the policy researcher, in his relations with government as in his relations with the university, is to help keep his opposite numbers in touch with reality.

Pitfalls and Politics
in Commissioned Policy Research

KURT LANG

Subjects that arouse the curiosity of social scientists usually have to do with conditions whose remedy lies within the realm of public policy. There is a widespread belief that social science and its methods can be a source of new ideas and serve as a policy guide. Yet, up to now research efforts have not been organized along lines that encourage broad and concerted attacks on major social issues. Instead research proceeds piecemeal, taking one small problem at a time. This leads to loss not only of perspective but of data; valuable information disappears into archives.[1] Other research that is clearly crisis-oriented tends to be hurried; methods are often slipshod and reports polemical. Despite such shortcomings, the documents that result usually gain attention not only from social scientists but also from policymakers, legislators and the attentive public.

Many persons perturbed over the current state of society see one answer in allocating more resources toward the search for solutions. Surely any increased investment in the tertiary sector, of which the knowledge industry is rightly considered a part, could do no harm and would probably do good. But it does not follow that the marginal returns in terms of useful policy input would automatically justify marginal costs. Certainly those resources now available are not being put to optimum use. On the plausible assumption that anything can be had for money, there is a good deal of talk today about the prospects of solving social problems by organizational devices along the model of the Manhattan Project which developed nuclear explosives, or of the Apollo Project which put men on the moon.

But projects directed towards solving social problems would have to reflect the different nature of social science research. The Manhattan and Apollo Projects were directed toward a single clearly defined objective. The social costs hardly received consideration—at least, not as part of the programs. Such considerations are basic to the endeavors of social scientists. Their research must take account of values and priorities. That is to say, the knowledge they seek concerns not only technical feasibility but also the acceptability of programs based on their findings to those who frame policy and to those whose lives will be affected. Neither social scientists nor their sponsors can easily ignore the political implications of what they report.

With this assumption, I want to look at the ways in which research efforts of some federal advisory and policy-making bodies have been shaped by the situations and structures within which they have been conducted. I shall use illustrative examples drawn from an area broadly defined as "equal opportunity"—an area that has been central to the interests of sociologists. Sociology, after all, arose from the recognition that the incapacities of many people were not really a consequence of physical hazards or incapabilities but were caused by socially imposed risks and obstacles determined by their position within the social structure.

Three case histories—necessarily abbreviated—are used to draw some simple and tentative conclusions about issues social scientists will have to resolve if they want to assure the objectivity of their input into policy decisions. The potential effectiveness of their efforts, after all, rests ultimately on the public's belief in the objectivity of their conclusions. The case studies deal with research on civil disorder, communication gaps and educational achievement.

CIVIL DISORDER

The National Advisory Commission on Civil Disorders, generally known as the Kerner Commission, was clearly a crisis response to the long hot summer of 1967 when violence of some severity exploded in the racial ghettoes of over 200 cities. Governments typically respond to such crises by calling for investigation, but President Johnson gave this Commission a broad mandate, indeed. That is to say, the charge to the commission was not simply to investigate and recommend "methods and techniques" for averting and controlling such disorders and to define the appropriate role to be played in such efforts by local, state and federal authorities; the inquiry was clearly intended to go beyond these technical and legal requirements, as the presidential directive states, to consider the "basic causes and factors leading to [the recent] . . . disorders and the influence, if any, of organizations or individuals dedicated to the incitement or encouragement of violence."[2]

The task of the commission, as defined by this presidential charge, would seem to have provided a unique opportunity for and challenge to basic social science research. While previous governmental commissions had looked into cases of civil disorder, almost all had confined their attention to specific outbreaks. At no time since the challenge by the Confederate states to federal authority had domestic tranquility been threatened as directly as it appeared to be, given the scale of the existing disorder. It was nevertheless clear that the report the commission was expected to produce would be a political rather than a social science document. In this respect, advisory commissions dealing with broad social issues usually have had much less autonomy than such standing bodies as the Council of Economic Advisers, where economists are in firm control.

The importance of political considerations is evidenced by the persons appointed as commissioners. As is customary for such commissions, the membership was carefully balanced politically with each of certain major interest groups represented. Thus, the commission was chaired by the Republican mayor of New York City. Besides several members of Congress, equally divided among the parties, the commission included a moderate civil rights leader, a liberal police chief, an appointed state official, a businessman, a trade union leader—but not a single social scientist.

Of course, given their part-time involvement in the actual work of any commission, one would expect the commissioners to exercise less control over the final report than their formal status might allow. The Kerner Commission was no exception: the contents of its report are largely the work of a full-time paid professional staff. Direction of the commission's staff work rested almost exclusively in the hands of politically experienced lawyers, who knew their way in and out of government. Lawyers do indeed bring special qualifications to this kind of job. They are usually experienced brokers capable of soliciting cooperation needed from various groups if the task is to be completed within the prescribed time. Most important, they are habituated to working up a case under pressure, using to the fullest whatever evidence may be available. Although the commission was eager to obtain the services of a prestigious social scientist, partly to lend credibility to its report, his was not to be, so it appears, a position of major responsibility. Several who were approached turned down the offer.[3]

The final report included a good deal of historical and statistical information on Negroes and on conditions in the ghettoes, very little of which was new. The chance for the commission to use its resources to break new ground lay elsewhere, namely in the work of its field staff, but here the lack of influence of social scientists at the higher staff levels had adverse effects. The investigations headed by lawyers were apt to emphasize riot chronology, eyewitness accounts, official responses to the rioting, and an assessment of damages. Notwithstanding the importance of such information and the overall quality of many reports, they often bypassed the very questions most critical for the kind of interpretation that the social science staff was to deliver.

The potential contribution of social scientists is not only as technical analysts. Their perspectives are needed to help frame the questions and to define the terms in which these can best be answered. The nature of their expertise has sometimes been obscured by the mushrooming of social science research organizations called into existence by the growth of federally sponsored social research. Commercial enterprises seeking to profit from this demand have often been poorly staffed, with some ready to bend in any direction when there is an opportunity to reach contract. Lawyers, who lack the esoteric knowledge to judge the soundness and feasibility of various proposals, are thus dependent on social science advice. When it received several unsolicited proposals for a computerized analysis of vast masses of data, the commission rejected these on the advice of its own social scientists. It also heeded their counsel to publish—in a companion volume to its own report—three supplementary studies, conducted within an academic setting, two with the financial support of the Ford Foundation.

Not quite so sanguine was the commission's response to one specific question, included in its original charge, "What effects do the mass media have on the riots?" This is a basic sociological question, but as every experienced researcher knows, the complexity is such that hard data to answer the question are almost impossible to obtain. Yet the commission, on the hunch that a highly sensational coverage of the riots contributed to an atmosphere of tension and helped keep violence going once it had erupted, decided to sponsor a content analysis of news output of television stations and newspapers in 15 of the cities to which it had sent field teams.

I have less than full knowledge about which social scientists were consulted, but I do know that the decision, made at a higher level, to undertake this task caused dismay among the commission's own social scientists. At least one university-based institute with a staff experienced in content analysis—at least of print media—turned down the study. The commission finally turned to a commercial firm, which agreed to do the job, despite the failure of its own advisory group, hastily assembled, to validate this undertaking. The group's judgment was that the study, even if conducted in a technically impeccable fashion, would shed little light on the question it was supposed to answer.

The study, as conducted, was vulnerable from the outset. The firm to which the contract had been let lacked a sufficiently experienced staff. It assured the commission that its work would be overseen by a four-man committee, but the group never met. The chairman of that committee could not exercise effective supervision, being only a part-time consultant without authority or any clear knowledge of the terms of the contract or of the resources and time available to complete the study. Apparently lawyers on the commission staff, themselves under great pressure to deliver, did not become aware until the deadline was upon them that such an arrangement was unlikely to yield the kind of research findings needed.

The pressure of the deadline was obviously a major factor in the work of the commission. The decision by the Commissioners to skip the interim report due on March 1, 1968, and to issue, instead, a final report by that date was an accommodation to certain political facts. They had become concerned over the appearance of an increasing number of interpretations in the press that attributed the persistence of rioting to a conspiracy. Early issuance of the report, it was felt, would help counter these interpretations, especially since information so far collected permitted the conclusion that "the urban disorders of the summer of 1967 were not caused by, nor were they the consequences of, any organized plan or 'conspiracy.' "[4] It was unlikely that the report would satisfy all those ready to see a conspiracy, but given the diffuseness of the rioting, it was also unlikely that a counter-case could be easily built by fastening on to certain unexplained events (as a counter-case had been built in response to the findings of the Warren Commission). Meanwhile, the report could try to focus attention on conditions in the cities where violence had occurred.

Where research is aimed at the acquisition of knowledge, it is far more difficult to accommodate it to such stringent deadlines. The advancement of the deadline and the resultant cutbacks in staff occasioned much dismay among social scientists. Already at work under great pressure, they knew that their own efforts would be further hampered. They also resented the priority given to other investigative activities. Within this climate, as far as I have been able to gather from available accounts,[5] the cleavage based on professional orientations became superimposed on a split that had its basis in politics. The field staff of the commission included a significant proportion of young lawyers and returned Peace Corps volunteers with strong sympathies for the cause of the Negro. These people responded politically to developments within the commission. Their suspicion that more conservative staff directors might counter the younger staff's push toward reform by screening material for its political acceptability linked up with the concern of social scientists that their professional contribution would not receive due weight. Accordingly, a rough and early draft of the social science analysis, a document entitled *The*

Harvest of American Racism, began to acquire considerable importance both as a statement of faith and as a potential political weapon.

This document, which was internally circulated, apparently had some impact on the conclusions of the commission. Distrust was so great that some members deliberately spread rumors of an impending whitewash, hoping to forestall what they evidently feared; they also played with the idea of subsequently publishing the *Harvest* on their own in the event the commission ignored its basic import. Yet what impact the *Harvest* document did have on the commission's conclusions—for example, the single reference to "white racism," which appears in the summary statement—came not so much from these pressure tactics as from the use of its contents as the basis for considerable discussion *within* the commission. Very little of its original content appeared in the final report.

There is little point in reviewing here the various "findings" of the commission. They include a good bit of rhetoric. Its "basic conclusion: Our Nation is moving toward two societies, one black, one white—separate and unequal"[6] runs counter to what every student of American history has long known, namely that things have always been this way. The social scientist is normally assigned the task of producing hard facts, while the drafting of the rhetoric is left to other professionals. The point is that the social scientists working on the *Harvest,* by using riot profiles supplemented with other information, sought to formulate the latent rhetoric behind the violence the commission was appointed to investigate. This kind of analysis by present standards would be considered "soft" and likely to be ignored to the extent that it is nonstatistical. All three studies published as supplements to the report were essentially quantitative summaries: responses to survey questions and characteristics of riot arrestees. The documentation contained in the *Harvest* was not as vigorous or systematic as that in the supplementary studies. The final report did retain many of the statistics in the *Harvest* but without accompanying interpretations.

In its evaluation of the media coverage, the commission apparently felt bound by the statistics its researchers had produced but free to ignore their import. The quantitative analysis was said to indicate a media policy of deliberate caution and restraint in riot coverage, though the commission gave full play to certain errors in fact brought to its attention by local officials and media personnel. The media do not fully deserve the clean bill they received from the media study.[7] Some puzzling statistical findings have simple explanations. For example, the low proportion (4.8 percent) of TV sequences that showed people participating in "riot activity" is accounted for by the fact that, whenever police were shown, the scene was coded as "containment." I also have reservations about the significance of coding the "aftermath"—showing broken windows, burnt out buildings, and boarded stores—as "calm" and/or "normal." As regards the newspaper analysis, the work was not, as far as I know, pushed beyond the treatment of racial issues to the actual coverage of riots. Since as a rule national racial issues tend to receive more front-page space than strictly local incidents, the finding that local newspapers tended to print more stories dealing with racial disorders or troubles—read, "racial issues"—outside the strictly local context becomes plausible but not relevant to the riot coverage. It does seem clear that in the period after the Kerner Report the press gave undue prominence to unverified reports of sniping, suggesting that there had been a basic change in the nature of the violence.[8] This underlines a suspicion that interpretations drawn from the content analysis are highly questionable. No conclusions can be drawn from them, positively or negatively, about the impact on the rioting of the way the media handled their coverage.

If the use made by the Kerner Commission of its social science input is any guide at all, we may conclude that members of such commissions are likely to be bound by and to present quantitative data that, used in a report, give it the aura of objectivity. But when issues arise over how to interpret such data, the social scientist becomes involved in delicate negotiations in which he finds it hard to separate his professional role from his role as a member of the commission, involved in its internal politics.

MASS COMMUNICATION

The media of mass communication in the United States, as everyone knows, are operated as private businesses rather than as public utilities. Media performance is judged by its acceptability to an audience, most of whose members are content to choose among the available offering. Because the American mass communication system (as in most industrially advanced nations) represents a sector separate from public education and is rarely used to promote social goals, the industry has almost always been able to shield itself against even legitimate pressure by invoking the First Amendment, while most of the initiative and much of the financing for educational television has come from foundations whose officials, critical of the media performance, were eager to provide alternative services. Government carries no clear responsibility for mass communication, as it does for education. The activities of communication agencies are subject to regulation only insofar as limitation of the spectrum makes it necessary to license competitors who would otherwise crowd one another off the air. Basically federal control is confined to transmission facilities.

The Federal Communications Commission (FCC) is the agency entrusted with this regulation. Yet understaffed as it usually is and caught between competing pressures—from applicants, from the executive and legislators—the FCC is hardly the source from which to expect basic policy-oriented research. This helps explain why—at a time when all of North America was not yet within range of a clear TV-signal—no one seized the opportunity for a systematic and experimental study of the impact of a new medium. Most research then was clearly dominated by commercial interest, while government was by no means prepared to fill the gap.

The researcher, often preoccupied with suspected negative effects of the mass media, has designed much of his work to fit a quasi-medical framework with the media viewed as a possible source of contamination and some types of content as a virus responsible for certain social ills. The communication industry has used these studies to defend itself. It can cite the failure to show beyond doubt and outside the laboratory that the media are the direct cause of serious behavior or psychological problems or can persuade people to accept as true or right viewpoints or opinions they are strongly inclined to resist. There are parallels in the health field—indeed with regard to drugs and food additives, legislation calls for the producer to provide evidence of positive benefits before he can market his products. Even a far less stringent test would be unacceptable to broadcasters—they would view it as a violation of their freedom of speech.

In March 1969, under pressure from Senator Pastore, chairman of the subcommittee on communications, who appears willing to grant broadcasters a permanent franchise provided they agree to conform to his own preferred standards for program content, the Department of Health, Education and Welfare prepared to launch under its own auspices a broadly based inquiry into the subject of television and violence. It was billed as a definitive study, comparable to the major project on cigarettes and health previously conducted through the Surgeon General's office: There had been no prior investigation of program content as sweeping as this and since the findings would, presumably, be a guide for setting programming standards, it was to be supervised by an impartial advisory body made up of representatives of the various health professions.

That the broadcasting industry should exhibit concern over the outcome is only natural. Networks immediately moved to invest some of their own resources in studies of this very problem. The power of the industry is furthermore evident in some of the procedures by which the Scientific Advisory Committee on Television and Social Behavior, the name given to the advisory body, was chosen. Members of the staff of the National Institute of Mental Health drew up a comprehensive list of potential members from names solicited through a variety of sources. The list included persons from several disciplines, many of them well known for their contributions to mass communication research, not excluding some in the employ of the networks. What is significant is that, to ensure in advance the active collaboration of the television industry in the studies to be sponsored, the entire list of nominees was submitted to the networks and [according to *Science*][9] to the National Association of Educational Broadcasters, whose representatives were asked to indicate any individuals who they believed "would not be appropriate for an impartial scientific investigation of this nature." It was made clear at the same time that it would not be necessary to state the reasons for such a negative judgment.[10]

To scrutinize the credentials and objectivity of persons serving on this kind of advisory panel is an obvious and sound practice, but blackballing those who for some undetermined reason may be unpalatable to the industry most directly concerned is not, unless the other side is given the same opportunity. It should be noted that at least one network (CBS) declined to express its preferences among the names contained in the list of some 40 nominees. Nevertheless, a total of seven were rejected—undoubtedly because of views they had published or publicly expressed since they obviously did not lack scientific credentials. The scientific credentials of the individuals on the committee, as finally constituted, were similarly impeccable, but in view of the solicitous concern for the sensitivities of the networks the selection of several with close ties to the industry, by virtue of present or past employment or through their consultant capacity, while some viewpoints remained underrepresented, can hardly be taken as coincidental.

It is of course possible to argue that the degree of balance within the committee is a trivial matter. The scope of the research had been defined in advance with review by the committee largely a formality, greatly influenced by preparatory work of the NIMH staff, and confined pretty much to technical advice. True as this may be, it stands to reason nevertheless that the committee members would pass on any final report. And here one must recognize that the various attempts to establish conclusively the effects of cumulative exposure to television fare will inevitably founder on the near-impossibility of disentangling the role played by the mass media from the numerous other influences that also impinge on children's lives, including the influence of the general social climate, which the media are said to merely reflect rather than to disseminate. Any case made against television is likely to remain unproven, and extreme skepticism about anything less than an unambiguous test is generally viewed as a commendable scientific attitude.

Still another facet of the scientific attitude is a highly fragmented approach to social problems. For example, the decision to exclude from this research the violence so prominent in news reports means passing up a great opportunity to follow up some of the concerns of the Kerner Commission.[11] In this case, the framework of the study was largely defined by the Congressional Committee and, following the assumptions of that committee, was limited to an evaluation of existing commercial program content. There was no intent to chart out what the media could potentially accomplish. Most of the initiative and pressure in this direction has come from outside the industry.

The problems created by advances in communications technology do, on the other hand, force an occasional review of some of the assumptions guiding communications policy. Formulated along fairly narrow lines after radio was well established as a mass medium, this initial policy—except for reserving certain TV channel frequencies for exclusive educational use—has hardly been changed. The appointment by President Johnson on August 14, 1967, of a Task Force on Communications Policy was a response to developments in satellite technology and to the growth of cable TV. Decisions had to be made since huge investments and financial interests were involved.

Since the membership of the task force consisted of "distinguished government officials," it is not surprising that the report stresses, among other things, the positive interest of various government agencies in the use of communication facilities.[12] The director of research for the group was a RAND Corporation economist with prior experience on the project on communications satellites systems, sponsored by the Ford Foundation. Although the task force did not interpret its mandate to require a study of TV content, their report does note the lack of diversity and variety in existing programming. They also find, in several contexts, that the main obstacle to the full use of broadcasting in the public interest lies not primarily in the lack of hardware but in the difficulties encountered in the search for talent and incentives to produce the proper software. That the report was controversial is evidenced in the delay of its release and the release of the supporting research. Completed in December 1968, it was kept under wraps for a full five months. Only after its contents had been leaked to the press was it finally forwarded, without endorsement, to the House Committee and officially released.

Much of the research that went into the report sought answers to questions of technical feasibility and costs. But the work of the task force is distinguished in two respects: It represents a comprehensive approach to the dissection of a major social problem, drawing on the expertise of both engineers and social scientists. Further, in commissioning a pilot project, it departed from the usual practice of policy studies emanating at the federal level. The usual procedure has been to launch extensive surveys, the prime purpose of which is to give an "accounting" of what exists rather than to indicate the as yet nonexisting potential. The pilot project[13] specifically explores ways in which new communication facilities could make a vital contribution to various programs designed to compensate some minority groups for disabilities they face.

This pilot study was, to be sure, of modest proportions. The RAND team that conducted it interviewed only 253 Negroes in two communities. Yet in queries about where these residents learned about jobs, schools, health and welfare services, housing and so forth, the researchers were able to document the inadequacy of information sources and to indicate how the lack of communication services contributed to the isolation of the ghetto residents. A fair test of the policy implication, namely that telecommunications techniques "when properly and creatively used can be an effective means for improving urban life," they concluded, would still require a well-designed research, test and evaluation program. The task force report incorporated a proposal for an experimental program and research designed to change the quality of ghetto life.

What they are suggesting is not just an action program with evaluation built into it, as a look at the stated objectives makes clear. The research is to determine benefits and costs, test the hypotheses set forth in the pilot study, determine how long it would take to alter old viewing habits and to create credibility, and finally to identify the kinds of institutions and organizational support needed in order to make the program work. As in new nations, where talent is so precious, the idea is not to acquire new knowledge but to create experiences that will aid in putting knowledge to use. Involvement of social scientists in such programs would create new roles, both for the participating individuals and for their disciplines. Both the reward structure of a career in the social sciences and the relation of social science to administration would no doubt be affected.

EDUCATION

Most attempts to guarantee equality of opportunity have focused not on communication agencies but on the schools. The school is still perceived as the major avenue for the entry of minority group members both into jobs and into the mainstream of American life. To provide the requisite education for all has traditionally been a concern of government, but since there are disparities among the resources that different regions and communities can devote to this purpose, pressure has built to increase the federal contribution, part of this in the form of research and development that local systems cannot provide.

To be specific, the United States Office of Education, beginning in 1963, financed a network of research and development organizations and educational laboratories. In addition, Section 402 of the Civil Rights Act of 1964 specifically instructed the commissioner of education to conduct a survey "concerning the lack of availability of equal educational opportunities for individuals by reason of race, color, religion, or national origin in public educational institutions . . . " By this legislation Congress extended the techniques of social accounting to a new area. The study resulting, now called the Coleman Report,[14] was initially designed to document the existence of segregation and discrimination in American education and to trace, on the basis of nationwide information, some of their effects.

Some findings could hardly have been surprising: The great majority of American children attend schools where most of their fellow students are of the same racial background; this segregation by race is more complete in the South; achievement levels of minority group children, most of whose educational experiences are in schools largely segregated by race, are lower than those of other children; and this gap between the minority and majority groups tends to grow, rather than diminish, as children progress through the grades. Somewhat disconcerting to the liberal mentality however, was the finding that the differences in the schools attended by children of different groups with regard to such matters as plant and facilities, curriculum offerings, and quality of teaching staff was far less than the disparity of achievement might suggest. In these respects the minority groups turned out, at least on a national basis, to suffer no disadvantage at all.

Through an elaborate statistical analysis, the Coleman team attempted to account for the sources of variability in school achievement. This effort has led many people to consider the Coleman Report one of the most important social science documents of our time. Illustrative of its findings: first, that within-school variation accounted for over 70 percent of all variation in achievement and that between 30 and 50 percent of the variance (between as well as within schools) is a function of individual background and attitudes; second, that school factors accounted for only about 10 to 20 percent of the variance in achievement but that their influence was somewhat greater for minorities; and, third, that the most influential school factors contributing to student achievement were certain characteristics and attitudes of the student body, which were themselves closely related to the social environment from which students came.

These findings were hard for some people to accept—particularly the conclusion: in cases where Negroes appeared to benefit—as judged by achievement levels—from attending schools with a majority of white students, the apparent benefit was attributable less to the racial mix than to the relatively privileged educational background and higher educational aspirations of the average student in these schools.[15] Such a finding ran counter to the premise that justified pressing for immediate integration: totally segreated black schools, even with equal facilities, are ipso facto, inferior schools.

The reaction of the Civil Rights Commission to these findings is therefore of particular interest for it obviously could not ignore them. When in the following year the commission released its own report,[16] it took issue not only with the conclusions of the Coleman study but also with those of another study it directly commissioned. This second study from the University of California was, if anything, even more unequivocal in stating that the racial composition of the school has no effect on the achievement of its pupils once social class composition has been controlled.[17] This conclusion is supported by new tabulations derived from the data of the Coleman Report, data that were designed to show that the breakdown of racial segregation would have desirable consequences.

The staff of the Civil Rights Commission in its report reasoned that the potentially positive effects of desegregation were often neutralized through practices that led to at least a partial resegregation within the class room. According to its analysis the achievement of Negro children with prolonged experience in integrated class rooms was found to be slightly higher than that of others only integrated at the highest grades or with no experience in an integrated setting. This apparent effect was found to persist regardless of the racial composition of the school.

Yet the statistical controls were clearly inadequate. A careful reading of the tables selected to support the case for integration reveals that the level of parental education in the majority white classes was higher than that in the classes where all or the majority of children were Negro. What counts, given the current social class differences between Negroes and whites, is the increased opportunity for contact with classmates from a higher average social and economic background.[18] Also, Negroes in schools where they are likely to attend a majority white classroom tend to come from families that are economically better off, while those attending heavily Negro schools but classes where the majority of classmates are white are likely to have been selected because, whatever their background, they exhibited unusual ability. Sociologists have long believed that the track system tends to discriminate against Negroes; authorities are often reluctant to place middle-class white children in classes made up of "low achievers" if it puts them in a predominantly Negro class. Only recently a study of Plainfield, New Jersey, demonstrated that the average achievement of Negroes within a track was higher than that of whites in the same track.[19]

One can, of course, press for integration as a value in itself: by providing an opportunity for interracial contact and removing the stigma that so often has been attached to the segregated school, it can foster positive attitudes. The Civil Rights Commission report[20] offers evidence that an interracial school setting promotes desirable attitudes. Still by the mid-sixties the thrust of the civil rights movement in Northern cities was shifting away from integration towards other measures—community involvement and community control among others. There is little evidence in the Coleman Report to justify this shift which was mainly the product of frustration as, despite all efforts, school segregation increased rather than decreased. It was also part and parcel of the newly emerging orientation towards black power and black pride. The vast array of findings within the Coleman Report has been selectively interpreted to sustain the advocates of different conceptions and solutions.[21] The kind of multivariate analysis applied to highly variable cross-sectional data that the Coleman Report represents lends itself to this use inasmuch as statistical relationships do not suffice to establish causal responsibility.

Most important, a study meant to assess the degree of equality of opportunity differs in design and use from a study meant to set priorities for remedial intervention. Though a particular factor may account for only a small proportion of the variance (in achievement levels, for example) it may be simple to manipulate and the change can have cumulative effects. Thus, even if the racial composition of the student body has no relationship to school achievement other than that attributable to its social class composition, the shortest route to full equality of educational opportunity may still be to change the racial composition of the segregated Negro school in order to expose the students to fellow students of a different social class. One should also note that the concept of equal opportunity guiding the Coleman study was a condition in which a similar input results in similar outcomes. Yet the school cannot compensate for every inequality and, as Coleman himself has put the case since, to achieve parity the Negro needs more than equal opportunity.[22] Racial integration would raise the achievement of some black students but not without some adverse effects on others, whose social background assigns them a position of permanent inferiority vis-a-vis classmates with whom they cannot compete.

Concern over the self-concepts of Negro children—their sense of personal worth—and the feeling of many of them that they have no control over their environment has, of course, supplied some of the thrust behind the drive for community control, because it could be shown that these had a strong relationship to achievement. "As the proportion of whites in the school increases, the sense of control of environment increases, and his self-concept decreases," states the Coleman Report.[23] This apparent paradox arises from the fact that the self-concept of the Negro child is strongly related to his belief that he has or hasn't some control over his environment, whereas that of the white child reflects primarily his actual achievement in school relative to that of his peers. Thus, the black child, when placed in an integrated school, may come to recognize better than before that his own plans and efforts have consequences, but at the same time, his self-concept may come to depend less on this sense of control than on his actual performance. Those Negro children from relatively favored backgrounds, such as most of those now attending integrated schools, may be better able to handle the strain of the keener competition encountered there. To place others in a competitive situation for which their background does not prepare them can damage their self-esteem.

KURT LANG

No matter how we look at all these various findings, they point to the overriding importance for achievement of social class background and, secondarily, of social class climates. All this should not have occasioned any surprise. Only the unwillingness of many reformers to take with sufficient seriousness the reality of social class leads them to view certain social problems primarily in terms of their attitudinal and interpersonal components. In Israel, for example, where race is not a major factor, but cultural differences are, the children of fathers from industrially advanced countries acquired the basic skills far more rapidly than other children within the community attending the same grade-school classes. The difference was markedly evident by the end of their second year in school.[24] The UNESCO world mathematics survey has yielded essentially similar results. Moreover, when the leaders of the Soviet Union in the 1920s made a deliberate effort to proletarianize the universities and technical colleges by encouraging the children of the poor to enroll in secondary schools, they could not succeed. By the end of their first academic year, the majority of those from poor backgrounds had left—presumably because they lacked sufficient support from their families. The schools, in the phrase of Bukharin, became sieves retaining only the children of the better-off elements.[25]

The problem of redressing social inequalities is quite different from documenting their existence. As a first step toward remedial action, the United States Office of Education, beginning in 1963, financed a network of educational research and development organizations. The network came, ultimately, to include some 20 regional educational laboratories, whose mission unfortunately never became clearly defined. They were to conduct basic research, to create and demonstrate a rich array of tested alternatives to existing educational practices, to encourage and speed the dissemination and utilization of their research. This last mission was the real challenge.

The proposals submitted by these federally funded labs to justify their funding were full of promises bolstered by an eloquent phraseology. Each organization tried to carve out for itself an area not duplicated by any other. The point is that far from innovating, either in the area of research or imaginative new programs, many followed the political currents of the period. In 1965 and 1966, some were heavily involved in school desegregation, but three years later their emphasis had shifted. They were playing it safe. Almost all were concerned with developing curricula and teaching aids that required limited or no structural changes to implement.

It was highly dubious from the beginning that these organizations, tied as they were to the educational establishment in Washington and required, by the terms of the legislation, to serve the region in which they were located, could ever have become the agencies for more than the most minor innovation. By and large, they came to duplicate the work routinely undertaken by many ongoing agencies or tried to serve a need that commercial enterprises, eager for a share of the rapidly expanding educational market, were already prepared to serve for profit. New products, often poorly tested but incorporating new technologies, seem abundantly available but the problem of getting a school system to modify its basic practices seems nearly insurmountable and has certainly not been solved by research.

The investment in existing practices is tremendous: the share of public monies routed to the educational complex and the activities it supports is exceeded only by the proportion siphoned off to the military-industrial complex. The investment extends to research activities, many of which are dominated by professional educators for whom they provide avenues of career mobility. No matter how politically liberal the announced goals of the educational establishment, most of its members tend to be highly conservative with regard to most matters, including research, that are included within its professional sphere.

POLICY-ORIENTED RESEARCH: THE NEED FOR INDEPENDENT SYNTHESIS

The examples I have used only illustrate the range of settings in which social research is geared to policy making. In each of the three settings discussed, social research operates against a background of vested interests. Governmental commissions, such as the riot commission, are primarily political responses. The diverse interests existing within society usually receive representation on the commission itself, but the time pressure under which they must discharge their task gives the staff a not inconsiderable leeway. In the framing of policy on mass communication, private economic interests constitute the main pressure group which is forever pitted against governmental encroachment, but engineering problems force compromises that only the government can effectively enforce. Finally, in education we are witnessing the growth of a national establishment, intimately tied to research activity yet intent on keeping innovation confined to the marginal areas.

The bureaus and institutes of social research, inside and outside of universities, are another element in the newly emerging pattern. These organizations often pursue their own economic interests. Where the overhead is large, a continuing flow of government contracts and grants becomes a prerequisite for survival. Therefore, tooling up for many different types of research tends to devalue substantive expertise in favor of routines for processing data. Such research, while perhaps increasingly sophisticated in its methods, is not likely to become a source of new ideas.

It is a well-established principle that innovations typically arise from activities conducted at the periphery of organizations. Research too closely tied into existing structure is unlikely to produce major inventions even in the technical area; instead these often emanate from mavericks working independently—provided the maverick can find a sponsor to act as a broker and take over the job of promoting the new idea. In this respect, the lack of close links between academic social scientists and policy-making bodies in their area of concern may be a distinct advantage. Too close an involvement in the practical affairs of interagency rivalry can cause the social scientist to lose the detachment from which the value of advice derives. Governmental bodies eager to avail themselves of social science expertise are not always as keen in their search for fresh points of view. They may be more intent on harnessing the prestige carried in the name and title of their social science consultants.

Whatever the parochialism inherent in the agency perspective, it is sometimes surpassed by the sterile scholasticism of the academic. There is a real need for synthetic research, for working over, from a fresh perspective, materials that are routinely gathered with ever greater efficiency, though not necessarily sophistication, by the agencies themselves. Such activity basically constitutes a form of social criticism, and while some of the special studies by ad hoc advisory bodies and federally supported laboratories and institutes are supposed to perform this function, they have not always, as I have tried to show in this paper, performed in any way that even approached optimum. Hence, there is a place for the independent or university-based researcher, provided he can free himself from the hustle for support that he increasingly needs to compete in the intellectual marketplace. To perform effectively, however, such people must have access to certain information and be given the opportunity to familiarize themselves with the issues that confront the policy maker. If these academic faculty could spend their sabbaticals without other obligation in independently funded centers for policy studies and devote part of their time to examining the problems of particular agencies, a bridge might be built between two worlds without creating new pressures on the academic researcher or making it inevitable that he be so coopted as to lose his ability to play the role of critic.

NOTES

[1] It is clear, for example, that many of the social problems that reached crisis proportions in the 1960s were already on the horizon in 1933 and taken up in the President's Committee on Recent Social Trends. Yet, "the massive distortions of the depression called for crisis remedies, so that the long-term significance of 'trends' was overlooked." See *The Behavioral and Social Sciences: Outlook and Needs.* Washington, D.C.: National Academy of Science and Social Science Research Council, 1969, p. 108.

[2] *Report of the National Advisory Commission on Civil Disorders,* March 1, 1968. U.S. Government Printing Office, 1968 0-281-729.

[3] Robert Shellow, "Social Scientists and Social Action from Within the Establishment." Paper read before the 24th Conference on Public Opinion Research, May 16-19, 1969.

[4] *Report,* p. 4.

[5] See, in addition to Shellow, *op. cit.,* Michael Lipsky and David J. Olson, Riot-Commission Politics, *trans*action, 1969, V. 6 (9), 8-21.

[6] *Report,* p. 1.

[7] See *Report,* ch. 15.

[8] Terry Ann Knopf, "Sniping-A New Pattern of Violence?" *trans*action, 1969, V. 6 (9), 22-29.

[9] May 22, 1970.

[10] Correspondence on this matter was made available through the courtesy of Dr. Frank Stanton.

[11] That task has since been undertaken by the National Commission on the Causes and Prevention of Violence.

[12] President's Task Force on Communications Policy. *Final Report,* December 7, 1968. U.S. Government Printing Office: 1969 0-351-436.

[13] H.S. Dordick, L.G. Chesler, S.I. Firstman, and R. Bretz, *Telecommunications and Urban Development.* RAND Corporation Memorandum RM-6069-RC, July 1969.

[14] James S. Coleman *et al., Equality of Educational Opportunity.* U.S. Government Printing Office, 1966, FS 5-238:38001.

[15] *Ibid.,* p. 307.

[16] *Racial Isolation in the Public Schools.* A Report of the U.S. Commission on Civil Rights, 2 vols. U.S. Government Printing Office: 1967 0-243-637.

[17] A.B. Wilson, *The Consequence of Segregation: Academic Achievement in a Northern Community.* Univ. of California, Berkeley, Survey Research Center, 1969.

[18] See *The Segregated Student in Desegregated Schools,* Johns Hopkins University, Center for the Study of Social Organization of Schools, Report No. 21.

[19] See *Grouping Students for Instruction in the Plainfield, New Jersey, School System,* Teachers College, Columbia University, Institute of Field Studies, July, 1969.

[20] *Op. cit*

[21] See, for example, the symposium on Race and Equal Educational Opportunity, *Harvard Educational Review,* 1968. V. 38 (1).

[22] See the contribution of Coleman to symposium, *Ibid.*

[23] *Op. cit.,* p. 323f.

[24] Sarah Smilansky, Evaluation of Early Education, in M. Smilansky and L. Adar (Eds.), *Evaluating Educational Achievement.* UNESCO Educational Studies and Documents, No. 42. Paris, 1961.

[25] Cited in Fedotoff-White, *The Growth of the Red Army.* Princeton, N.J.: Princeton University Press, 1941, p. 293.

The Violence Commission:
Internal Politics and Public Policy

JEROME H. SKOLNICK

The 1960s are already infamous for assassinations, crime in the streets, student rebellion, black militancy, wars of liberation, law and order—and national commissions. We had the Warren Commission, the Crime Commission, the Riot Commission and the Violence Commission; and the point about them was that they were among the major responses of government to the social dislocations of the decade. Millions of people followed the work of these commissions with interest and gave at least summary attention to their reports. Social scientists were also interested in commissions, though skeptical about their value. Most would probably agree with Sidney and Beatrice Webb's description of Royal Commissions, "These bodies are seldom designed for scientific research; they are primarily political organs, with political objects."

I share this view, yet I have worked with three commissions, albeit under very special arrangements guaranteeing freedom of publication. The discussion that follows is partly analytical and partly autobiographical, especially where I discuss my work as director of the task force on "Violent Aspects of Protest and Confrontation" for the Violence Commission. If the autobiography stands out, that is because I did not participate in commissions to observe them. I studied the phenomena at issue—crime, police, protest and confrontation—not commissions. Still, my experience may be helpful in understanding commission structures, processes and dilemmas.

CONSTITUENCIES

Commissions have three functioning groups: commissioners, the executive staff, the research staff, with overlapping but distinctive interests.

Andrew Kopkind has recently written that President Lyndon B. Johnson chose the 11 commissioners for his National Advisory Commission on Civil Disorders because of their remarkable qualities of predictable moderation. The Violence Commission, chaired by Dr. Milton Eisenhower, was perhaps even more predictably "moderate" than the Riot Commission. It included a member of the southern and congressional establishment, Congressman Hale Boggs; Archbishop, now Cardinal, Terence J. Cooke, Francis Cardinal Spellman's successor; Ambassador Patricia Harris, standing for both the political woman and the Negro establishment; Senator Philip A. Hart, Democrat of Michigan, associated with the liberal establishment in the Senate; Judge A. Leon Higginbotham, a Negro and a federal judge from Philadelphia; Eric Hoffer, the president's favorite philosopher, presenting the backlash voice of the American workingman; Senator Roman Hruska, Republican of Nebraska, a leading right-wing Republican; and Albert E. Jenner, Jr., prominent in the American Bar Association and in Chicago legal affairs. In addition, there was Republican Congressman William M. McCulloch of Ohio, who had served on the Kerner Commission and was the only overlapping member of both commissions. In response to criticisms that the Riot Commission contained no social scientists, Dr. W. Walter Menninger was appointed, although he is a practicing psychiatrist and not a social scientist. Finally, there were Judge Ernest W. McFarland, the man whom Lyndon Baines Johnson had replaced in the House of Representatives, and another Texan, Leon Jaworski, a close personal adviser to the president and a prominent and conservative lawyer.

Obviously, the commissioners themselves cannot perform the investigative and analytical work of the commission. Commissioners are chosen because apparently they represent various economic and political interests, not because they have distinguished themselves as scholars or experts. In fact, they do not "represent" anyone. What they best mirror is a chief executive's conception of pluralist America.

Moreover, even if a commissioner should have the ability to do the research, he or she usually has other demands on their time. Inevitably, then, the staff of the commission does the work—all of the leg work and the research and most of the writing of the final report, with, of course, the commission's approval.

The staffs of both the Riot Commission and the Violence Commission were similar. The executive staff, working out of Washington, was charged with getting the research and writing job done and with organizing the time of the commission. In each case, the director of the executive staff was a leading Washington attorney who had ties with the Johnson administration, David Ginsburg for the Riot Commission, Lloyd Cutler for the Violence Commission. Moreover, younger attorneys were named as their closest associates.

There had been considerable friction in the Riot Commission between the research staff and the executive staff, as well as between both and the commissioners. According to Andrew Kopkind, the social scientists under Research Director Robert Shellow drafted a document called "The Harvest of American Racism" which went further than most top staff officials thought prudent in charging that racism permeated American institutions. "Harvest" characterized the riots as the first step in a developing black revolution in which Negroes will feel, as the draft put it, that "it is legitimate and necessary to use violence against the social order. A truly revolutionary spirit has begun to take hold . . . and unwillingness to compromise or wait any longer, to risk death rather than have their people continue in a subordinate status." According to Kopkind, both Ginsburg and Victor Palmieri, his deputy director, admitted that they were appalled when they read "Harvest." Shortly after its submission many of the 120 investigators and social scientists were "released" from the commission staff in December 1967 (on public grounds that money was needed to pursue the war in Vietnam). But Kopkind says that there is every reason to believe that the "releasing" was done by Palmieri (with Ginsburg's concurrence) because of the failure of

JEROME H. SKOLNICK

Shellow's group to produce an "acceptable" analytical section. The commissioners themselves are reported to have known little of the firing or of the controversy surrounding it but were persuaded by Ginsburg to go along with it.

I tell this story only because it bears on the central question of what effects, if any, informed researchers and writers can have on the final reports of commissions, the public face they turn to the world. Kopkind, for example, argues that the "Harvest" incident proves that the Kerner Report would have been "liberal" regardless of events preceding its final writing. He concludes, "The structure of the Commission and the context in which it operated suggest that its tone could have hardly been other than 'liberal.' The finished product almost exactly reproduced the ideological sense given it by President Johnson more than half a year earlier. The choice of Commissioners, staff, consultants and contractors led in the same direction." Yet that outcome is not at all evident from the rest of Kopkind's analysis, which argues, for example, that the commissioners were selected for their predictable moderation, that one commissioner, Charles Thornton, attempted to torpedo the report just before its launching and that the findings of the report were patently offensive to President Johnson. It is at least arguable that the "liberalism" of the final report was not inevitable, that it might have been far more on the conservative side of "moderate" and that the "Harvest" document had something to do with moving it to the Left.

THE EISENHOWER VIOLENCE COMMISSION

When Senator Robert F. Kennedy was assassinated and the president appointed yet another commission, many observers were suspicious. Was this the only response that Washington could give to domestic tragedy? Even the press gave the Violence Commission unfavorable publicity. The commissioners seemed even more conservative than the riot commissioners. Some considered the commission a devious plot by President Johnson to reverse or smudge the interpretation of civil disorders offered by the Riot Commission.

Furthermore, what could the Violence Commission say that hadn't already been said by the Riot Commission? The distinction between civil disorder and violence was not, and still isn't, self-evident. Moreover, because of the flap over the firing of the social scientists on the Kerner Commission, many of that community were deeply and understandably dubious about the possibility of doing an intellectually respectable job under commission auspices.

The executive staff saw this problem and coped with it, first, by establishing the position of research director, so that social scientists (James F. Short, Jr., jointly with Marvin Wolfgang, as it turned out) occupied a place in the hierarchy of the executive staff, a club usually limited to corporation lawyers. Authority still rested with the executive director, but the research directors performed four important functions; they initiated the commission policy of independent task forces with freedom of publication; they helped select the social science staff; they served as liaison between the social scientists, the executive staff and the commissioners; and they served as good critics and colleagues.

Furthermore, they promoted another departure from Kerner Commission practice, namely that social scientists and lawyers are the co-directors of task forces.

Some additional comments are warranted here because organizational structures and rules may seriously influence intellectual autonomy. University social scientists with little legal or governmental experience may assume that freedom to write and publish follows from well-intentioned assurances of future support. Yet as one experienced man with whom I shared a panel recently put it: "He who glitters may one day be hung."

The social scientist must understand the ways he can be hung and protect himself accordingly. First, his materials can be used and distorted. Second, his name can be used, but his material and advice ignored. This is particularly possible when social scientists hold highranking but relatively powerless titles on the commission. Ultimately, they are placed in the dilemma of seeming to endorse the final product. (In the Violence Commission, for example, the names of James F. Short, Jr., and Marvin Wolfgang seemingly "endorse" the scholarly merit of the final report. In addition, the presence of a recognized social science staff does the same. To this extent, we were all "co-opted," since none of us, including Short and Wolfgang, were responsible for the final report.) Third, he may experience subtle (sometimes not so subtle) pressures to shape or present his findings in favored directions. Finally, his work may be suppressed.

In general, one receives maximum protection with a *written* contract guaranteeing freedom of publication. Beyond that, however, experienced Washington hands can be quite charming—which holds its own dangers for one's intellectual independence.

From the very beginning, the executive staff expressed some doubts about the ultimate impact the commission's own report would have on public policy, or even the shape it would take. Recall that this was the summer of 1968, following the assassination of Senator Kennedy and before the national conventions of both parties. Who could foretell what future event would have what future impact on national politics? Who could, with confidence, predict the nominees for the presidency, the victor and his attitude toward the commission?

TASK FORCE REPORTS

Like the able corporation lawyers they are, the executive staff came up with a prudent primary goal, a set of books called *Task Force Reports*, which they hoped could be a solid contribution to understanding the causes and prevention of violence in America. I call this goal prudent because it set a standard that was at least possible in theory. From these studies, it was felt, the commission would write its own report; the initial idea was to have each task force report provide the materials for a summary chapter for the commission report.

Modest as this plan was, it soon ran into difficulty. Commissions are usually run at a gallop. With all the best intentions and resources in the world, it is virtually impossible to complete eight books of high quality in five months, particularly when no central vision controls the research and writing. Our own report, *The Politics of Protest*, was completed on time, but we worked under enormous pressure. Still, we had several advantages.

First, a shared perspective among key staff members contributed to a fairly consistent analysis. We shared a deep skepticism about counterinsurgency views of civil disorder as a form of "deviant" pathology that needed to be stamped out as quickly as possible. On the contrary, we assumed that insurgents might conceivably be as rational as public servants. Our approach was influenced, first, by subjectivist and naturalistic perspectives in sociology, which lead one, for instance, to take into account both the point of view of the black rioter and to assume his sanity, and to assume as well the sanity of the policeman and the white militant. Second, we were influenced by revisionist histories of America, which see her as a more tumultuous and violent nation than conventional histories have taught us to believe. Finally, we were influenced by social historical critiques of the theory of collective behavior, which interpret seemingly irrational acts on the part of rioters as forms of primitive political activity, and by an emphasis upon social history in understanding such collective behavior as student protest, rather than upon analysis of "variables."

Another advantage in favor of our task force was that our headquarters was at the Center for the Study of Law and Society at Berkeley. This kept us away from the time-consuming crises of Washington, although the tie-line kept us in daily touch with events there. In addition, the center and the Berkeley campus offered a critical mass of resources that probably could not be duplicated anywhere else. Our location, then, combined with my status as independent contractor with the commission, offered a degree of independence unavailable to the other task force directors. For example, the staff members of our task force were not required to have a White House security clearance.

Finally, the staff was far from unhappy about working for a national commission. Those involved, regardless of expressions of skepticism, were not opposed to making a contribution to a national understanding of the issues involved. My contract with the government, and its contract with me, assured the staff that its best understanding of the issues would be made public.

Given time limitations, it was impossible to undertake the original research one would need for a large-scale social science project. My inclination, shared by the research directors and the executive staff, was to recruit a staff experienced in research on the areas under study. We saw the five-month period as an opportunity to summarize findings rather than to undertake original investigation.

We did, however, conduct original interviews with black militants and with police. As can be imagined, these interviews were not easily obtained. For black militants our interviewer was a man with extensive connections, but who stipulated that he would interview only if we agreed to listen to and not transcribe the tapes and make no notations of who was being interviewed. The interviews substantiated much that we suspected and served to sharpen our analytical outlook. Similarly, the interviews we held with policemen—conducted, incidentally, by a former policeman —served to fill gaps in our thesis that the police were becoming an increasingly politicized force in the United States.

I should also add that our emphasis on social history and political analysis seemed to violate some of the expectations of some portions of our audience.

AUDIENCES AND HEARINGS

The Politics of Protest staff worked with three audiences in mind. First, we were concerned with trying to persuade the commissioners of the validity of our findings and the validity of our analysis. They were our primary audience. Our second was the general public, an audience we had little confidence in being able to influence except, perhaps, through persuading the commissioners. Most reports have a limited readership—and *The Politics of Protest* isn't exactly *The Love Machine*. So our third audience was the academic community and the media representatives. In the long run, the university had to be our major audience, since the report is scholarly and the media treated its publication as news, quickly displaced by other stories.

The audience for the hearings was both the commissioners and the general public. Several members of the executive staff believed that one reason the Kerner Commission failed to gain public acceptance was its failure to educate the public along the way. The "predictably moderate" commissioners had been emotionally moved in the hearings, especially by representatives of the black communities of America, but the public had never been allowed to hear this testimony. Consequently, the Violence Commission hearings were made public and each task force was given three days for hearings.

Hearings are a form of theater. Conclusions must be presented to evoke an emotional response in both the commissioners and the wider television audience. In this respect, the planners of the hearings can be likened to the author and director of a play with strategy substituting for plot. Yet strategies can and do go awry, and so the outcome of the play is not determined, nor can one guarantee whether the effect on the audience will be tragedic or comedic.

A staff tries to get across a point of view on the subject matter. At the same time, however, it is also expected to be "objective," that is, lacking a point of view. The expectation is that staff and commissioners will walk along fresh roads together, reaching similar conclusions. This expectation derives from the image of a trial. Such an adjudicatory model must, however, be largely fictional. The "judges," the commissioners, already have strong views and political interests, though they are supposed to be neutral. The staff, too, is supposed to lack opinions, even though it was selected because of prior knowledge.

Since strategy substitutes for plot, there really are only three possible outcomes. The play may be a flop, that is, the staff perspective is not communicated; or the perspective is communicated, but unemotionally so as to merely make a record; or emotional engagement is achieved. Here social science as theater reaches its ultimate art.

Commissioners are used to hearings, are used to testimony and probably cannot be moved in any new direction unless emotionally engaged. Commissioners are culturally deprived by the privatized life of the man of power. Whatever may have been their former backgrounds, commissioners are now the establishment. They may be driven to and from work, belong to private clubs and remain out of touch with the realities of the urban and political worlds they are assumed to understand. They are both protected and deprived by social privilege.

Moreover, their usual mode of analysis is legalistic and rationalistic. Not intellectuals, they are decision makers interested in protecting the record. Furthermore, they are committed to the prevailing social, economic and political structures, although they will consider reforms of these structures and may well be brought to see contradictions within them. In addition, they are affiliated with certain political and social interests. Consequently, there are practical limits to the possibilities of persuading any of them to a novel position.

JEROME H. SKOLNICK

The public is another audience for the hearings, but there are also constraints on teaching the public. All that "public hearings" means is that the media are present, not the mass of the public, and the media reports only the most dramatic messages. Also, commissioners themselves become part of the cast. The TV will register an exchange between a witness and a commissioner. So a strategist (director) must anticipate what that exchange might be.

Finally, the presence of the press alters the atmosphere of the hearing room. We held mostly public hearings and some hearings in executive session. With the television cameras and the radio people and the newspaper people present, the commissioners were stiff and formal. When the press left, the commissioners visibly relaxed.

Given these conditions, how does one go about casting? First, we tried to present witnesses who represented a variety of points of view. That was elementary. But within that framework we had to decide: what kinds of witnesses representing what kinds of points of view will bring the most enlightened position with the greatest effect both on the commissioners and on the general public?

There are practical limitations in hearings. Obviously, it may not be possible to get the witness you want, or to get him for a particular day. Ira Heyman, general counsel, and I were given three days for hearings to discuss the antiwar and student movements, black militancy and the responses of the social order. This was not enough time for any of these topics to be adequately discussed. The one day of hearings on black militancy was especially inadequate, although undoubtedly the most exciting. It was also the most difficult to arrange, the most trying and the most rewarding.

HOFFER VS. THE BLACKS

First, there was some question as to whether any well-known black militant would have anything to do with the Violence Commission. Even if he should want to, anybody who stepped forward to represent the militant black community could be charged with playing a "personality" game and disavowed as representing even a segment of the black community. After much thought, we decided on Huey P. Newton, minister of defense of the Black Panther party, as a widely acceptable representative of black militancy. He was willing to cooperate, politically minded and seeking an opportunity to present his point of view.

Herman Blake, an assistant professor of sociology at the University of California at Santa Cruz, joined me in interviewing Newton and was to present the interview to the commissioners. Although Blake would not officially be representing the Panthers, Newton knew him, knew of his work and trusted him to make an accurate analysis of the tape of the interview that was to be played to the commission.

As it turned out, there was no problem at all. Both Blake and I, in Charles Garry's presence, interviewed Newton in the Alameda County Courthouse Jail where he was being held while standing trial for the alleged murder of an Oakland policeman.

The Newton tape, and Blake's testimony, produced an emotionally charged confrontation between Blake and Eric Hoffer and a dignified censure of Hoffer by Judge Higginbotham, vice-chairman of the commission.

Mr. Hoffer: I tell you there is rage among the Negroes on the waterfront. It is at the meetings when they get together. Suddenly they are repeating a ritual. A text. You are repeating it. Now I have . . . I don't know of these people, where they were brought up. All my life I was poor and I didn't live better than any Negro ever lived, I can tell you. When I was out picking cotton in the valley the Negroes were eating better than I did, lived in better houses, they had more schooling than I did . . .

Mr. Blake: Have you ever been called a nigger?

Mr. Hoffer: Let me finish it. By the way, the first man in the U.S. I think who wrote about the need to create a Negro community was in 1964 when I . . .

Mr. Blake: Why do you stop calling it a community then?

Mr. Hoffer: I say that you have to build a community. You have to build a community and you are not . . .

Mr. Blake: We can't build a community with white people like you around telling us we can't be what we are.

Mr. Hoffer: You are not going to build it by rage. You are going to build it by working together.

Mr. Blake: You are defining it.

Mr. Hoffer: They haven't raised one blade of grass. They haven't raised one brick.

Mr. Blake: We have been throwing them, baby, because you been out there stopping them from laying bricks and raising grass.

Judge Higginbotham: Mr. Chairman . . .

Dr. Eisenhower: Mr. Blake . . .

Mr. Jenner: Would you do me a personal favor and stay for a moment, Mr. Blake?

Judge Higginbotham: Mr. Chairman, if I may, I feel compelled because I trust that this Commission will not let statements go in the record which are such blatant demonstrations of factual ignorance that I am obliged to note on the record how totally in error Mr. Hoffer is on the most elementary data.

The McCone Commission, headed by the former director of Central Intelligence, who I assume while he may not be the philosopher which Mr. Hoffer is, that he is at least as perceptive and more factually accurate. The McCone Commission pointed out that in Watts, California, you had unemployment which ran as high as 30 and 40 percent. Sometimes 50 percent among youth. It pointed out in great detail [that] in the Watts area you had the highest percent of substandard housing any place in L.A.

If my colleague, Mr. Hoffer, who I would like to be able to call distinguished, would take time out to read the data of the McCone Report, which is not challenged by anyone, based on government statistics, at least the first portion of his analysis would be demonstrated to be totally inaccurate, and I am willing, as a black man, to state that what I am amazed at is—that with the total bigotry, patent, extensive among men who can reach fame in this country—[not] that there has been as little unity as there has been. It is surprising that there has been as much.

I think that Mr. Hoffer's statements are indicative of the great racist pathology in our country and that his views are those which represent the mass of people in this country. I think that what Toynbee said that civilizations are destroyed from within, that his comments are classic examples of proving that.

Dr. Eisenhower: Mr. Blake, only because we have two other distinguished persons to testify this afternoon, I am going to conclude this part of our testimony. I want you to know that I personally had some questions to ask you but my good friend

Judge Higginbotham asked precisely the questions in his part that I had intended to do. So on behalf of the Commission I thank you for your willingness to come, for your candor, for being with us and I accept the sincerity and truth of what you said to us.

Mr. Blake: Thank you.

That day, I think it is fair to say, was the most emotional day of the hearings for the Violence Commission. Eric Hoffer was an exemplary witness for the depth of racism existing in this country. No wealth of statistics could have conveyed as well to the other commissioners and to the public in general what racism meant to the black man.

Yet Hoffer is also a popular public figure. Moreover, only a minute or so of the hearings was shown on national television. There, Hoffer was seen shouting at a bearded black man in a dashiki. It is doubtful that much enlightenment was achieved by the televising of that exchange. I believe that in the long run the reports themselves will have a far greater impact than the TV time allocated to the hearings.

A first draft of *The Politics of Protest* was sent off to the executive staff of the commission on December 27, 1968, approximately five months after the initial phone call from Washington. They received the report with mixed feelings. They were, I know, impressed with the magnitude and quality of the report, but it violated the kinds of expectations they had about commission reports. We were clearly less concerned about "balance" and "tempered" language than we were about analytical soundness, consistency and clarity. Some of the commissioners were described to me as "climbing the walls as they read it." And this did not make an easy situation for the executive staff. They suggested in January that it be toned down, and I did *not* tell them to go to hell. I listened carefully to their suggestions and accepted most of them concerning language and tone. But I did not alter the analysis in any of the chapters. I. F. Stone was later to call our analysis "brilliant and indispensable," and a *Chicago Tribune* editorial ranked it alongside the Walker Report as "garbage."

THE IMPACT OF COMMISSION REPORTS

Since the report was published, I have often been asked the question: Of what use is all this? Does it actually contribute to public policy? My answer is, I don't know. *The Politics of Protest* apparently made little impact on the commission itself. It was cited only once in the final report of the commission, and then out of context. But the book has been given considerable publicity, has been widely and favorably reviewed and has been widely adopted for classroom use. The major audience for *The Politics of Protest* will probably be the sociology and political science class, although more than most books on this subject it will find its way into the hands of decision makers.

The Politics of Protest will also provide an alternative analysis to the main report of the Violence Commission. Naturally, we think our analysis is more pointed, more consistent, more scholarly and more directed to the historical causes of American violence than the commission's own report, which adopts a managerial, counterinsurgency perspective that looks to symptoms rather than causes. But history will tell. Reports sponsored by commissions are ultimately intellectual documents subject to the criticism that any book or investigation might receive.

Yet they are something more as well. Despite the increasing tendency among radicals and intellectuals to challenge the usefulness and integrity of commission reports, they do tend to create an interest over and above that of similar work by individual scholars. One can even point to a series of commission reports that have had an enormous impact—those used by Karl Marx in developing his critique of capitalist production. Without the narrative provided by these commissions, Marx's *Capital* would have been a much more abstract and predictably obscure document and simply would not have attracted the readership it did. Marx himself, in his preface to *Capital*, offers an accolade to these investigative commissions.

Commission reports, whatever their analytical strictures, defects or omissions, come to have a special standing within the *political* community. If a social scientist or a journalist gathers "facts" concerning a particular institution, and these facts are presented in such a way as to offer a harshly critical appraisal of that social institution, the fathering and the analysis of such facts may be called "muckraking." But if the same or a similar set of facts is found by a commission, it may be seen as a series of startling and respectable social findings.

And herein lies the essential dilemma posed by the commission form of inquiry. On the one hand, we find a set of high-status commissioners whose name on a document will tend to legitimize the descriptions found therein; and on the other hand, precisely because of the political character of the commissioners, the report will be "balanced" or "inconsistent" depending on who is making the judgment. A commission, upon hearing one expert testify (correctly) that there is darkness outside and another testify (incorrectly) that the sun is shining will typically conclude that it is cloudy.

Nevertheless, whatever facts are gathered and are presented to the public, they are in the public domain. No set of facts is subject only to one interpretation and analysis. Surely it was not in the minds of the commissioners of inquiry in nineteenth-century England to provide the factual underpinning for a Marxist critique of capitalist production. Yet, there was no way to stop it. So my point is simply this: to the extent that a commission of inquiry develops facts, it necessarily has done something of social value. Its interpretations can be challenged. How those facts and how those interpretations will be met and used depends upon the integrity and ability of the intellectual community.

JEROME H. SKOLNICK

Television Comes
to the People of the Book

ELIHU KATZ

The decision to introduce television to Israel was taken by the government in the wake of the anguish, then the triumph, of the Six Day War. Echoes were still being heard of the decade or more of ideological debate over whether television is good or bad for the Jews; so the task was not simply to begin broadcasting as quickly as possible, but to broadcast something significant—and in two languages, Arabic and Hebrew. For, in many minds, television's primary mission was to begin a public dialogue between Arabs and Israelis.

In July 1967, I became head of the task force charged with bringing television to the people of the book. Nine months later—only four months after receiving its initial appropriation from the Finance Committee of the Knesset—Israel Television went on the air with a live broadcast of the Independence Day parade of 1968 (a show of such complexity that had we known enough about the pitfalls of television production, we might not have risked it). A few months more, and we were on the air two, then three nights a week, three to four hours per night, in the two languages, with better than a 3:2 ratio of original to acquired programs.

During the 20 months of its existence, the task force partly rebuilt an abandoned diamond factory to house the TV studios and offices; bought highly sophisticated electronic equipment; selected and trained some 300 likely-looking workers; enlisted the advice and participation of experts and nonexperts from abroad; made and unmade stars; raised political storms; and fought some very serious organizational battles in the process of moving out of the Prime Minister's Office, in which television was organized, and into the Broadcasting Authority, where we were to be a sister to radio. The tension and conflicts that climaxed at this point suggested to me that this was the time to leave. In any case, the job undertaken by the task force had been largely accomplished.

This is a personal account, and I shall leave it to the reader to do most of the generalizing. I have tried, however, to organize my story in terms of several themes which seem significant.

In the widest sense, I want to describe the structure and functions of national television broadcasting, particularly in small, new nations. The major problem is how to make good use of this extremely costly medium for providing information and shaping culture, and how to avoid succumbing to the seemingly irresistible tendency toward trivialization, Americanization and politicization. Sociological study of the mass media has lagged far behind both the study of mass media effects and the study of other social institutions. Yet the problems of the media, particularly the broadcast media, could hardly be more worthy of attention, whether in the United States, Britain, Czechoslovakia or Israel, while the ways in which broadcasting is institutionalized in new nations is surely a key to understanding their social, cultural and political development.

Most of the sociology here is retrospective, by which I mean that I did not find much time for myself the sociologist while acting as administrator and politician. As a sociologist interested in mass communications, I had relevant information and a frame of reference to bring to bear on programming policy, and I knew what kind of research to commission. But in the heat of forging intra- and inter-organizational relationships, my actions were determined by the constraints of the situation and by whatever wisdom was available in and around myself (some of which, I like to think, was the wisdom of sociology). In this kind of high-pressured context, however, I do not see how one can also play Applied Scientist; at least I couldn't.

It was only late, late at night that I turned into a real, though very tired, sociologist. I kept a diary, and when the going was really rough, the observer role sometimes saved me. It is these observations, plus latter-day reflections, on which what follows is based. Obviously, for better and for worse, they are the notes of a very participant observer.

HOW A SOCIAL SCIENTIST COMES TO BE ASKED

Several weeks before the Six Day War, Professor Louis Guttman and I proposed a series of surveys on the state of civilian morale and preparedness to Israel Galili, Minister without Portfolio, who had recently been given charge of the information activities of the government, which were formally lodged within the Prime Minister's Office. We suspected, when we began, that we might be doing survey research before and during a war. We rather hoped, but weren't sure that these surveys might give us the opportunity, if we survived, to establish the kind of continuing social survey for which we had been lobbying for some years. This was in fact what happened. What we most certainly did not suspect, however, was that the war surveys would lead to my appointment as founding director of Israel Television.

Some six months before the war, Galili had appointed a democratic young general named Elad Peled as his special assistant to launch the television project. Peled was to work formally within the framework of the Minister's Office but de facto within the Israel Broadcasting Authority (IBA), and was publicly promised Galili's support for the job of director-general of radio and television as soon as the 1965 law establishing the Broadcasting Authority could be amended to include television. In appointing Peled in this manner, Galili was trying to do two things: First, he was trying to underline the government's promise to the Knesset that, although plans for the introduction of television were indeed being made, they would not be actually implemented and certainly broadcasting would not begin without express approval of the Knesset. Peled's appointment outside of the Broadcasting Authority rather than within it thus symbolized the interpretation of the broadcasting law as having to do only with radio broadcasting, although the word broadcasting (not radio) is used in the law. Second, Galili's appointment of Peled was a public message to the then director of radio, Hanoch Givton, that he was distinctly *not* being invited to head the operation he had been hoping and planning for.

The press was critical of Galili for appointing Peled. Without knowing much about him, it was said that Peled was a general and therefore temperamentally unsuited, although the press is well aware—when it wants to be—that Israeli generals leave the army in their early forties for a second career, and thus save themselves and us from living in a garrison state. It was said that Peled was a member of Galili's political party-within-a-party. All this was, essentially, anti-Galili—whom the press was scapegoating at the time for the supposed failure of Israeli public relations. In fact, when the war was over, and Peled having returned to active duty announced his decision not to continue with TV, the same newspapers that had criticized him earlier now regretted his decision.

Peled's resignation embarrassed the Minister. He now, quickly, had to find a successor, one who could not be accused of being a political follower, was not in the army, and who would have the expertise that would counterbalance the renewed pressure to reinstate Givton. Remembering our collaboration during the war days, and noting, among other things, that I held the appropriate sounding title of Director of the Communications Institute, he offered me the job, and of course, I accepted it.

Thus does a scientist become a policy-maker: reside in a small country whose professors think they are in an ivory tower but who are, unwittingly sometimes, very much part of the elite; head an institute which has a counterpart in the real world; meet a minister during a war and volunteer your expertise; when he is in trouble and asks you to do a job, ignore the fact that your expertise is in studying, not doing, the thing he wants done. Everybody will then be pleased—for a while.

BROADCASTING POLICY

Before we did anything technological or even organizational, we began to think about broadcasting policy. A technocrat might have done otherwise. But given the background to the decision to introduce television into Israel, there were very good reasons for being concerned with content very early—reasons quite independent of my being particularly interested in the functions and effects of mass communication.

The debate over whether to bring television to Israel had arisen every few years for more than a decade. Ben Gurion had opposed it strongly, although a committee that he appointed as early as 1951, and another in 1955, had recommended favorably. Over the years at least three groups of overseas experts were consulted—UNESCO, the European Broadcasting Union and the Canadian Broadcasting Corporation—and local committees reviewed their findings. The review committees tended to hesitate on economic grounds: television was more good than bad, was the usual consensus, but it is too expensive just now. The objections among the elite went far deeper. Many influential persons opposed it for fear that television would subvert the effort to renew Hebraic culture in Israel, or more generally that television would debase (read Americanize) the culture. A closely related objection came from the religious groups—those who, later on, were so vigorously to fight television broadcasting on Friday nights. They argued that television would secularize the culture. Some political leaders feared that television would accelerate the trend towards the personalization—that is, the de-ideologization—of politics. On the positive side the arguments dealt with nation-building and integration—absorption of immigrants, maintaining better contact with distant settlements, teaching the language and so on. As in other new nations—and in the developed nations before them—each new medium is greeted by hopes and fears. What the pros and the cons have in common is an exaggerated belief in the effectiveness of the media.

When the June 1967 war came, the fears, then the hopes, were intensified. Before the war, there were some 30,000 television sets in Israel, this even though she had no broadcasting stations (except for the small experimental instructional station which until 1969 broadcast to only a few classrooms). Only about half the sets were actually plugged in. These tended to be in the hands of the more marginal members of the society, the Arabs and the Arab-speaking Jews. For several weeks before the war, a barrage of vicious propoganda from the neighboring countries invaded these Israeli homes, and caused great consternation. Why haven't we got television? was a common question. Fear of the insidious powers of the medium was very great.

When the war was over, the euphoric optimism that followed the dramatic reunion of the two populations, on the West Bank of the Jordan and in Jerusalem, gave birth to the belief that peace—at least between these two peoples—was really possible. Television might play an important part in this effort, many people felt. Television must broadcast the message of rapprochement in the Arabic language and provide a basis for mutual understanding. Such was the hope.

This was late June of 1967. Two years earlier, a Broadcasting Authority Law had been enacted whereby radio moved out of the Prime Minister's office and into a quasi-public Authority which is still tied rather closely to government. That same summer, the Government gave the IBA a go-ahead to begin planning for the introduction of television, and in December, the Columbia Broadcasting System was signed on as consultant. Givton, then Peled, drew up long-range plans with the assistance of the useful, very expensive technical advice and the very naive, overly-American programming advice of CBS. When the war came, valiant efforts were made by Givton and CBS to establish an emergency service based at the instructional studios. But the war was quickly over, and the idea was shelved, only to be born again when Peled and CBS suggested a different kind of emergency service in Arabic, to fill the new role that had been defined for television.

In choosing me, the Government could not have found a more skeptical person as far as belief in short-term mass media effects are concerned. I did not think that television could by itself cause the Arabs to like Israelis, and I said so. I did believe, and still do, that television can help, given the right kind of programming and in a situation where the content of the programs and the substance of the actions of Israelis vis-a-vis Arabs are mutually reinforcing. Specifically, I thought that, used properly, television could broaden the image of Israel beyond the highly political, highly military image that was current, and extend it into areas of mutual concern—agriculture, medicine, the family, entertainment and so forth—where Arab and Jew might find common interest. The most vivid example of this kind of programming is a weekly show for Arab children called "Sami and Susu" which is altogether apolitical and is so successful that it not only brings hundreds of letters from Arabs in Israel and the West Bank, but enough letters from Jewish children as well to have persuaded the Director-General of the new-combined radio and television service not only to withdraw his order of execution against the show but to allow it to be subtitled in Hebrew. This and the other Arabic shows were planned at a conference we called in the fall of 1967 and attended by our TV people, journalists, university people, top men in Government, and some experts—mostly Jews but also some Arabs—on Arabs and Arab affairs. It was at this meeting, and later at a Knesset discussion of our plans, that the idea of an emergency service was abandoned in favor of a two-phase plan in which the start of Arabic broadcasts would precede the start of Hebrew broadcasting but that both would be established quickly as a part of a bilingual broadcasting schedule.

I was cautiously optimistic about Arab programming, though the odds were against its succeeding because of the manpower shortage caused by the absence of an educated Arabic-speaking second-generation among Jewish migrants and the reticence to appear among the Arabs themselves. Nevertheless, it got off to a fair start. Now that the situation has deteriorated, it is more difficult to be optimistic. But I still think that programs like "Sami and Susu" do make a difference. At very least, they symbolize Israel's determination to provide normal services to Arab citizens and residents.

I was equally cautious when I spoke about the effect of television on Israeli culture generally. I warned against overstating both the hopes and the fears and tried to call attention to the possibilities of the medium if used creatively. Gradually, as I learned the business, I found myself in growing sympathy with the arguments of those who had opposed television. The opponents tended to equate medium and message. They talked about what "television" does to people, as if one has no control over what is broadcast. Surprisingly, they were righter than they knew, though for reasons they certainly did not understand. For the fact is that one *cannot* produce whatever one wants; it is simply wishful to belief that the message is totally in one's hands. First of all, talent is scarce: television devours talent, and then kills it. Like talent, money is scarce in a small country, and television is extremely expensive. It takes $10,000 to $15,000 to do a modest half-hour variety show, but—here's the rub—it takes one fiftieth of that to buy somebody else's variety show. When the temptation to buy is so enticing, it is difficult to resist. And from here, it is an easy step to the unfortunate slogan that had a short reign in the economy-conscious administration that followed mine—"If you can buy it, don't make it."

The decision to buy is not bad in itself. While it may be a departure from the original aims of nation-building and cultural renaissance, it can easily be rationalized in terms of "opening a window to the world." I suspect that the director of programs of a typical new station goes to London or New York with the best of intentions; he will buy only worthwhile programs. But soon enough he finds that worthwhile programs rarely come in series, and single programs or specials do not really solve his problem, which is to fill the half-hour from 8:30 to 9:00 PM for 26 or 52 weeks. Moreover, it is difficult for him to make contact or contracts with any but the sales organizations which market the Westerns, the crime and adventure stories and the family comedies of the major (mostly American) networks. His technical advisers from overseas will typically have given him some addresses. (In this process, some nations go so far as to enfranchise one of these sales organizations to provide all their programming other than the news.) This, in a sense, is the tragedy of television in many small nations. Broadcasters begin with the highest hopes for the nation and for the culture, and not long after, often to their own astonishment, find themselves featuring "I Love Lucy" and "Bonanza."

Israel is faring somewhat better, perhaps, but the struggle against the financial, artistic, technological, organizational and political constraints is a constant one, and there is no promise that things will necessarily get better. Often enough, they get worse, for reasons mentioned both above and below.

During my regime, broadcasting began at 7 PM with the news in Arabic, and continued in Arabic with a program which was, alternatively, either folkloristic light entertainment or a "service" show (homemaking, health, agriculture, etc.). There followed an hour of acquired material such as "The Defenders," "You Are There," or Leonard Bernstein's "Young People's Concerts" which were subtitled in both Hebrew and Arabic and intended for both audiences. Then came the Hebrew news magazine—probably the

ELIHU KATZ

most ambitious of the continuing programs—and an hour or more of programs in Hebrew such as the "Archaeological Quiz," a review of the arts, a musical review, a documentary and the like.

I insisted that the television news bulletin—the familiar 10 PM or 11 PM newscast—is trivial. I do not believe that seeing a radio announcer, even a pretty one, adds anything to a viewer's understanding of the news. Nor does the 30-second film clip help much: tonight's jungle looks no different from last night's jungle. And most of the time, the news isn't even "news," since it was 48 hours or more in transit, except for the perennial comings and goings of persons at the nearby international airport. From the beginning, then, we moved away from the traditional news program format toward the development of a news magazine based on the assumption that it was better to present a few items visually and in depth than try to keep up with radio news—which stops the country short on the hours, while people hold their breath. We began with a 45-minute show against the advice of the American experts and some of our own news people, and emphasized short documentary items of five minutes or more using archive materials, interpretative artists, commentary by guest panelists, and so forth, as well as longish items on local activities. Even at the rate of three times per week, this show proved terribly difficult to sustain, and the pacing seemed too slow for those of our news people who had spent time abroad and wanted, above all, to keep it moving. The show was cut back to half an hour and seemed to be taking shape until an edict came, just after I left, opting for the conventional quarter-hour news bulletin and still another "safe" decision. I tried to emphasize the importance of accepting the implicit division of labor among the news media, rather than undermining the assumption that people listen to the radio and read the papers, which they do. It is better to do a few items with extensive pictorial treatment, I argued, than to try to cover as much of the news (as defined by radio) as possible. It is better to present last night's story effectively than tonight's story ineffectively. While we argued endlessly about this, I think we were on the right track. And if it weren't for the pressure of even more fundamental things such as building studios, or training cameramen, we might have found even better solutions.

I felt strongly, too, that television could do a lot of pump-priming in fields such as opera, dance, drama and film. We made some early commissions to several film companies, but these proved very expensive. In the field of dance, a young Israeli director who had studied in Holland discovered a modern dance group which had never appeared before and which has now become the most sought after troupe in the country.

Then there were the specials—and these are what bring television alive. Memorable among the first year's broadcasts were the post-war parade, which I have mentioned already, a dialogue on the Arabic program between a former Minister of Defense of Jordan and the Israel Minister of Justice (something which would be quite impossible in today's changed climate of relations), the anniversary concert of the Israel Philharmonic under Bernstein, the play of Noah, the three Christmas masses from the Church of the Nativity in Bethlehem (Catholic, Orthodox and Armenian), a poetic film on Ramadan, the funeral of Levi Eshkol. Each time I think about these shows, and about the outside broadcasting unit that produced them, I become convinced again that television ought not to be on the air every day but only for special events. It is another of the tragedies of television, I believe, that it is modeled after radio and, like radio, strives to be on the air all day every day. Television anywhere would be better if it did less. I sometimes dream of the television station that would go off the air, after a special broadcast, announcing that "we have nothing more for you until our next special broadcast three days from now."

ORGANIZATION

The decision to give birth to television inside the Prime Minister's office and then to move it, after birth, to the Broadcasting Authority reminds me of the telefilm I saw recently about the kangaroo. According to Walt Disney, the kangaroo cub has a very difficult start in life. As soon as he is born, he has to crawl from the womb into his mother's pocket. Many kangaroos don't make it.

This was the first of our organizational problems. We had to create an organizational present that would have to be changed again in the near future. The present was difficult enough because the substantial capital budget we had been been awarded, and the demands we immediately began to make upon it in terms of purchases, building, salaries, expenses and the like, exceeded the capability of the administrative apparatus of the Prime Minister's office, which was its custodian. Indeed, the total budget of that office was smaller than ours, and no additional help was hired because the expectation was that we would be moving out momentarily. On the other hand, we were not granted, even temporarily, permission to hire our own administrative personnel. The first nomination I made was to the post of deputy director for administration; the man I wanted was Uzi Peled—another Peled—who was then administrative director of the Institute of Applied Social Research and lecturer in Business Administration at the University. A very large proportion of his time was spent running back and forth between our two-and-one-half finished floors (of five) in the Diamond Factory which was our headquarters, and the assorted treasurers, controllers and financial clerks in the Prime Minister's office who held the purse strings. It was an entirely unsuitable arrangement. It led to strikes over delayed salaries, court actions over delayed payment of bills, free-for-all lobbying to obtain priorities, and the like.

But the difficulties of the present were compounded by thoughts of the future. Although we were tied administratively to the Prime Minister's office, we were responsible to the IBA, from the first, for the content of broadcasts. And we knew that we would be transferring to the IBA on some not far distant date. Forecasting the future and its demands was a constant constraint on decision-making in the present. What would be the relationship of radio to television? How would grades and salaries compare with those in radio and film? Which of the 300 people we had taken on for training and temporary employment would be given permanent jobs by the Authority? When would the tenders for jobs be issued? Daily life had some of the quality of a social movement, with people giving everything they had; but underneath there was uncertainty and insecurity. Everything was too temporary. The competition to demonstrate competence was cruel both among members of the organization and on the part of the organization as a whole. The large degree of freedom available to us in the present was more than offset by the fact that our ultimate source of support was, at the moment, a kind of competitor, or, at best an irritable foster parent. All our dealings about both present and future were marked by the politics of insecurity.

The overall question was how would television fit, organizationally, into the IBA. There were those who wanted to see each department of radio give birth to a subdepartment of television such that the director of current affairs in radio, say, would direct a radio group and a television group. This was the dominant theme in the period before it was decided to organize television outside the IBA and only later to incorporate it within. Some of us thought that the media would be better off, organizationally and creatively, if they were essentially independent of each other, and even competitive. We proposed two parallel organizations, under two heads, each of whom would be directly responsible to the board of the Authority. There was even talk of a separate television Authority which would incorporate both an instructional television center and general television. Experienced television professionals abroad (the creative types, less so the executives) often responded enthusiastically to the idea that there might be an opportunity of beginning a television service unburdened by the organizational and artistic heritage of radio. Creativity is better served, they felt, if administration, engineering and production are interlocked within each medium, and if television is free from radio and closer to the other visual arts. Opposition political groups were attracted by the idea of a lesser monopoly of access to the broadcast media while others thought that greater organizational concentration—particularly, a single news operation for radio and television—would strengthen the independence of the Authority. Economically, the burden was on us to prove that parallel organizations would not be more expensive. This is what we thought, as a matter of fact, but the IBA and the Treasury thought otherwise. Alongside these extreme positions, there were a variety of compromise formulae which were constantly before us with varying degrees of integration and autonomy at the levels of overall direction, news and programs, production services, engineering and administration.

There were several major forums for these discussions: The weekly board meetings of the IBA, the meetings of the 25 member (now 31) IBA Council; a special Committee of Ministers appointed by the government; and, ultimately, a committee of the Knesset appointed to consider the proposed amendments to the Broadcasting Authority Law. Lobbying or simply being sounded out was a constant activity for everybody involved. Travel abroad or library research to study the structure of other broadcasting organizations was another favorite game, since it is not very difficult to find what one is looking for. Mobilizing the experts also was part of the fun. The CBS consultants spent a good part of their time redrawing organizational charts, and dutifully responding to the contradictory pressures put upon them from all sides. All this was incredibly time-consuming, and here—perhaps even more than in the balance of power—we were at a distinct disadvantage, since we had other things to do, like broadcasting.

The upshot of all this was the board of the IBA and ourselves could not help but become adversaries. The simple fact of being invited to appear before the ministerial committee and the Knesset committee alongside the IBA delegation is enough to account for what happened. We could have remained silent, or seconded the board on everything, and thus perhaps ensured a smooth transition from the Prime Minister's office to the IBA. But the openness of the ministers, no less than the Knesset committee, to debate and persuasion encouraged free expression. Too often, then, we found ourselves at odds with the Chairman of the Authority who could not tolerate the idea of equal time, and betrayed that more than once. In his words, he saw himself as the selfless representative of the public interest whereas we spoke for nobody but ourselves. The truth, of course, was all sides were self-interested, and all sides had arguments, as the responsiveness of those of the ministers and Knesset members who were interested (and also self-interested) will document. The dynamics of the decision-making, which tended in the direction of compromise (after the intention of delivering television to the IBA was reiterated), deserve much more than a few words, so they will be omitted here. For the present discussion, however, the organizational dilemma should be clear: every point we scored in the present was a minus for the future.

The question of merger within the IBA had bearing on two other organizational problems. One of these was the delicate problem of pacifying the occupational demands and professional aspirations of the workers in radio. During the decade of debating over whether or not television would be introduced at all, the radio people had been promised more than once that the new medium, if it came, would belong to them. In order to honor at least part of this commitment, a very elaborate set of rules had to be devised whereby radio people were given a certain priority in the competition for jobs in television, and double care was taken to make certain that those whom the director of radio could not release—his veto was part of the arrangement—would have another chance. Here, we fared rather well. Despite the intricacy of the arrangements that resulted from negotiations with the radio workers' committees, and the addition to the already debilitating temporariness and tentativeness which characterized all appointments and decisions, the radio workers generally supported us—conceivably because they were certain that they would, after all, inherit the future.

The other related organizational problem is one to which I have already alluded in outlining the debate over the structure of the Authority upon the incorporation of television. During all this debate, deluded by the interim period in which we were comparatively autonomous, we took time out to dream a thoroughly unrealistic dream. We asked ourselves, as sociologists would, What is the optimal organizational structure for maximizing creativity? Having looked at the radio, and at other organizations, it was clear that there was a great strain between the all-demanding producers and the nonunderstanding administrators. We thought we might do something about this. The research literature was not terribly helpful; the closest we could come—in our spare time—was the literature on scientific organizations and creativity. This, and more discursive writings, suggested that the organization which fosters creativity should be one in which the administration is relatively small; where resources are decentralized and easily accessible; where the administrator might even be involved in production and vice versa; where resources are relatively flexible and not committed too far in advance; where the organization provides an avenue for professional mobility and development without having to move over to the administrative ladder; where there is a tolerance of failure but a pressure to succeed. Indeed, some abortive attempts were made to rotate people in the newsrooms among the jobs of reporter, writer, presenter, editor; some efforts were made to provide producers with the whole of the capital required for the successful completion of their assignments; considerable effort was made to involve the key administrators in the most fundamental analysis of the production process. But on the whole, these efforts were partial, marginal and doomed to failure. Despite the "social movement" dimension, the jealousy over status prevented rotation, and no sooner were newly-trained workers named directors than they formed a closed shop and the Hebrew news room—which housed what was probably the largest single collection of talent in the building—literally sabotaged the Arab news and resisted all semblance of cooperation between the two staffs. The one tiny studio that was available to us for the first years created a demand for the strictest and most merciless allocation of time, and more often than not, resulted in a fight between an administrator and a production group. It didn't take long, either, for the administrators to begin to mistrust the producers, and for the producers to conspire to outwit them or to challenge their authority. The conception of decentralized authority and decentralized budgeting soon gave way to the point where one had to fill out forms to hire a taxi. The pressures of training on the job, the anxiety which characterized the interaction between inexperienced Israelis and the more experienced foreigners who had come to help, the pressure to meet overoptimistic deadlines were all so much more demanding than the problem of finding the structural key to creativity that our ringing phrase, "the creative organization," was soon dulled. Add to this the fact that we really weren't allowed to hire even the minimal administrative staff we required—for fear that we might become too autonomous by the time moving-day arrived—plus the fact that we could gain access to our own budget only through the Prime Minister's office, and the unreality of our scientific designs is apparent.

The sociology of the creative organization deserves more attention. It was another of the opportunities our group had to diagnose a problem at very close range, even if not to solve it. Of course, it may be that the solution is to leave things much as they are: perhaps bureaucracy and professional creativity *ought* to be at odds within a formal organization in order to provide checks and balances for each other. But I doubt it.

TECHNICAL ASSISTANCE

The problem of recruiting and training deserves special comment. In all of Israel, there was literally nobody with any real experience in TV except some radio people who had taken brief courses abroad, and persons from film, makeup, design and so forth who could transfer their skills. We had access to CBS' facilities for help, but time pressure did not really allow for seeing persons abroad except for the Task Force members themselves. We could not, therefore, abide by the phases of the CBS training program as originally prescribed, and had no choice but to train people on the job. This we did in two ways. We brought people from CBS, and other experts in the field of production. Secondly, we looked very quickly in New York, Los Angeles, London and Amsterdam for the experienced people we thought would both be able to teach intensively and then, as colleagues, to work alongside their tutees on the job. It was not difficult to recruit people. Hundreds of professionals indicated interest in the prospect of joining Israeli television, and several of us interviewed those who seemed promising. (This was the first time I met Americans who were as motivated by the "push" to leave the United States and/or American television as by the "pull" of Israel and the promise of what sounded like television with a purpose.) In addition, we interviewed every single Israeli in the United States or Europe who had applied; these were people without actual experience beyond the six months of a technical course or a university diploma in the field of mass communications.

When the professionals arrived in Israel, they experienced all of the traumas of new immigrants. They wanted to make a big contribution, but they were confined by different national and international styles of doing things. They wanted to be helpful, only to discover that the Israelis with whom they worked were investigating their backgrounds with the wishful expectation of finding them out as frauds (a few may have been). Some wanted to be in Israel what they weren't yet at home, and we wanted them to—so they were constantly anxious to move beyond their past achievements and live up to new expectations. They were treated to poorly kept promises about social benefits, and to long delays in payments, which only hastened their inclination to organize as foreign experts and then to be the first group to strike. This is just what the Israelis wanted—or at least those who wanted the experts to go home, for fear that they might like it and want to stay in their jobs.

THE CONTROL OF BROADCASTING

Public bureaucracies whose goal is to serve—public hospitals, for example—are characterized by a division of labor and authority among government, a board, the management, and professional workers. As a general rule, government appoints the board; the board sets policy; the management translates policy into operational practice; and the professionals exercise wide discretion within the framework of these directives. At any moment in time, in almost any such bureaucracy, there is likely to be tension among the four elements.

And so it is with broadcasting authorities. In recent years, for example, there has been tension between management and professionals in Canada; and between government and management in England. The law usually specifies the limits of authority of each, but it can never—and should never—be specific enough. The management of conflict among these four groups is the key to understanding the problems of public-national broadcasting.

In its very short life, Israel television has experienced two such major incidents. One is the recent issue between government and the board over broadcasting on the sabbath. The other involved the board and management, in my days, and I should like to tell about it.

The program that made even the skeptics and the disinterested certain that television had arrived in Israel was a "Meet the Press" type of show. As the big names began to appear, week after week, they began to make news, often front-page news. Politicians, including board members of the Broadcasting Authority (only one of whom had a TV set at home), began to think that maybe they had better watch the show than wait to read about it the next morning. But watching made them even more nervous: the rudeness of the interviewer, or the deviant opinions of an interviewee were matters of concern to the board, and legitimately so, although they were guilty of the misconception that inviting a man to be interviewed by three newspapermen is tantamount to giving half an hour of free time to his views.

One day, the board asked us to submit for approval the names of interviewees being considered for the show. They asked for ten names, of whom they proposed to approve six to eight for a like number of weeks. I protested. I tried to explain: I said that a current affairs show of this kind is done days, not weeks, in advance. I argued that it was to nobody's advantage if the board took direct control, rather than acting as overall policy-maker, critic and guardian of the public interest. The board members said that their combined political experience was exactly what was needed to get this show right, and anyway that there were too many politicians being invited, and the chairman pounded the table at me. I acquiesced, hoping that things would improve in a short time as greater mutual trust developed, and as the board realized that we realized that we now belonged to them forever. Similar control over certain radio programs had been exercised by the board in the past. The news editor and I prepared a list and I carried it to the next regular weekly meeting of the Board. The chairman, Dr. Haim Yahil, said yes or no to each of the names—despite my anguish—while the other members (five at the time; the amended law now calls for seven)—nodded approval. I gave the list to the editor of news and boarded a plane to the television festival in Monte Carlo.

The next I heard—and for reasons which I still cannot understand—the editor of news, Yoram Ronen, had invited one of the No's, no less a personage than a former chief of staff and then director of the Ports Authority. To this day, I cannot explain how it happened. Ronen is not especially noted for bravery, and all he could say when I asked was that he thought the list could be amended or changed when there was good reason, and that he was certain that the board would approve, considering the newsworthiness of the strike being threatened by port workers at Ashded. In a private meeting with Yahil, the chairman, he also seems to have said after the affair was underway that he had the feeling from me that the list was not to be taken too seriously. In any event, on the Sunday before the scheduled Monday recording of the Tuesday night broadcast, Peled, sitting in for me, informed the board that Ronen had invited General Laskov and asked for approval. The meeting exploded with anger, and Ronen was summoned. It quickly became clear that the invitation had not only been extended, but that it had been accepted, and innocently announced by IBA public relations to the press.

Members of the board admitted later that they would have done better to discipline those involved and to let the show go on. But

ELIHU KATZ

that, of course, is not what they did. They decided to stop the show. They were particularly influenced by one of their number who argued that General Laskov, the invited interviewee, was a party to a dispute which might erupt in a strike, and that if the broadcast increased the chance of a strike, even by 1 percent, it was the board's duty in the national interest to prevent his appearance. He said that Laskov's appearance would be unchallenged (thus again ignoring the fact that interviewers take the other side with vigor) and I quote, "would not contribute to calming the aroused passions" at the port.

Ronen was instructed to call General Laskov and cancel. The story immediately found its way to all the newspapers which quoted Laskov as saying that he was being censored, and that he would never again agree to appear on Israel Television (a notably short-lived oath). A great storm broke loose: the board defended itself at first by citing the threat to the public tranquility (which the press replied to by questioning whether it was the job of broadcast journalism to tranquilize the public). On day two, the board said there was no really pressing reason to put Laskov ahead of those who had already been approved, thus revealing for the first time the existence of a list. When the press attacked on grounds of censorship and blacklisting, the board issued a manifesto, on day three, saying that their job was akin to that of the editor-in-chief of a newspaper and thus they were not censoring but simply doing the job. Moreover, they insisted that nobody had been blacklisted or vetoed, but, rather, that some persons had been given priority over others for a relatively short period. And anyway—still day three—television was too new to be on its own.

Reenter myself (who should have sat it out at Monte Carlo where there were television programs and pretty girls, and very few members of Mapai). I said, in a very academic and cautious interview, that Laskov was not the issue; it simply unveiled the issue. The issue, of course, is the division of editorial responsibility among government, authority, management and the professional staff. I talked about the BBC where something similar had happened involving Rhodesian Prime Minister Ian Smith, though even there the initiative for cancelling the interview was, at least officially, that of the Acting Director General not that of the board. The point is that the board cannot allow itself to make day-to-day decisions, not only because it does not function on a day-to-day basis but because it opens itself up to the kind of criticism which should be directed at management and professional workers, not at the governing board. The board must be above it, so to speak, serving as a buffer and making long-range policy, and meting out reward and punishment to the staff over the long run, just as the board of a public hospital may decide whether heart transplants will be performed in its hospital but not whose heart will be given to whom. In short, the board cannot be editors in any serious sense of that word. If nationalized broadcasting is to flourish, there must be a consensus concerning this division of labor among the groups involved. The consensus cannot be legislated, for the legal responsibility, ultimately, must be the board's. The health of the organization requires, however, that initiative be left in the hands of the professionals who, in the course of things, will find it useful to consult the board, and to look to it for backing.

RESEARCH

One of the early appointments made to the Task Force was director of research. I was very anxious to follow the introduction of television with continuous feedback on audience expectations and reactions, and to have a good baseline for the study of effects. No other country has managed to get good "before" and "after" data on the introduction of television. So, we set aside a large sum of money for continuing survey research and channelled the money to the Israel Institute of Applied Social Research, the only professional, quality, not-for-profit survey organization in the country. Since Peled was on leave from the Institute, and I had a courtesy affiliation there, I anticipated that this contract—which was not put out for tender—would surely cause any one of the many journalists who lived at our doorstep to raise an eyebrow, and the reaction was not long in coming. A nice fat headline, one day, proclaimed that I was ensuring my academic future by investing public funds in the collection of data that would later be mine to analyze.

We followed the research results very carefully, of course, but the simple fact is that we did not put much of it to policy use. Partly this was because we had to make decisions before the data were in. Partly it was because there were policy considerations that led us to act in a certain way, even though the data seemed to argue otherwise; in such cases, of course, we had to justify our actions with specific reference to the data.

For example, one of the first jolts we experienced as a result of research was the discovery that only about 5 percent of the families in the occupied territories owned television sets. Intuitively, the policy makers had thought as we had that there were large numbers of sets, particularly on the West Bank of the Jordan, and hence the unmitigated enthusiasm for the special crash-program to get broadcasting in Arabic on the air. But this impression had been biased by the concentration of antennaes in the relatively well-to-do urban areas. Although the data surprised us, we decided to proceed nonetheless, motivated by the additional finding that the sets were concentrated in the hands of presumed influentials, and that the rate of acquisition of sets would increase rapidly if not because of us then because Jordan had just begun to broadcast. Here, then, is a case where we acted against what the data seemed to be saying, and had to do a lot of explaining to reconcile our decision with the data. A similar problem arose over the disparity between our plans for a farming show in Arabic and the discovery that very few farmers owned TV sets, partly because many of the rural areas are not electrified. Once again, a strong case was made for continuing the show by the director of Arabic programming who was convinced that the city-dwellers were still very close to the land and might even serve as intermediaries. I was very dubious about this, and tried to get the extension service of the Ministry of Agriculture to organize group listening in TV farm-forums—along the lines that have worked in Canada and India—but I did not have much success.

Others of our studies dealt with prosaic problems such as time-budgeting of the evening hours, including the time that people retired. We wanted to plan the broadcast evening so as to avoid a head-on clash with the really first-rate radio news magazine and to reach a majority of the Arab and of the Jewish population at optimal hours. This was an example of how we used research directly. An earlier study—to cite another example—showed how few Israelis could locate the occupied territories accurately on a map, even though they could name them and articulately discuss which to try to hold and which to return. We often used this finding to illustrate how easily television could contribute to the solution of a visual problem of this kind.

We commissioned what is probably the most extensive social study of the Arab populations of Israel and the occupied territories and what is probably the most ambitious study of the uses of leisure by the population of Israel. We also studied the gratifications that people get, or expect to get, from viewing. Whereas each of the other media was associated with a clearcut function—radio and newspapers with information, film with entertainment—we found that television did not initially have a well-defined image. About equal proportions of the population said that television was predominantly good for information, education and entertainment. As time goes by, the information is taking the lead. In other words, television is moving closer to the model of radio. It is too early, yet, to talk about the effects of television on other leisure pursuits.

Altogether then, there are a lot of interesting data, only a small proportion of which had any direct share in policy-making. From my point of view, the most encouraging influence of the audience response was in its continuous affirmation of its desire for home-made programs rather than imported ones, although it unquestionably likes the latter a lot, and had to suffer as the former hesitantly took shape. David Susskind once told us "to make your mistakes on the air." And that's what we did.

I have tried to tell something about the early days of national television in a small country which long hesitated to approve its establishment. I have emphasized the kinds of constraints that diverted television from nation-building and culture-stimulating missions to more standardized, trivial enterprises. I have described the challenge to social scientists and broadcasters to discover the organizational conditions most appropriate to creativity. I have tried to analyze the problems of the separation of powers in the regulation and decision-making with respect to what is broadcast; and I have analyzed some of the problems of technical assistance we faced. This case study of the transformation of a sociologist into administrator and politician has, finally, sounded the cautionary note that it is probably better to hire a sociologist than to try to do it yourself.

I might have done much more. The overnight rise of the television critic, for example, is an interesting story. Within 24 hours after the first telecast went on the air, every daily newspaper had an expert critic to say something about it. I could have dwelled at much greater length on the problems of the division of labor within the broadcast organization and the disputes over jurisdiction, over authority, and over the question of who is an artist and who is a technician. I should have gone into greater detail about the substance of audience reactions. Perhaps I will take the occasion to discuss these matters elsewhere someday.

Policy Scientists
and Nuclear Weapons

ROY E. LICKLIDER

In studying the relationships between social science and public policy, nuclear weapons policy provides a useful and informative case study for several reasons. The first is simply that it has been around for some time, at least since Hiroshima. Certainly the postwar years witnessed the mobilization of physical scientists concerned about the use of nuclear weapons.[1] Another landmark date was 1951, when the Wohlstetter bases study at RAND was initiated; this study marked the development of strategic thinking under government contract.[2] The ideas percolating among the insiders entered the public realm in the middle fifties, with the publication of pioneering books by William W. Kaufmann and Henry Kissinger in 1956 and 1957 and the subsequent concern over Sputnik and the missile gap.[3]

Second, the field has produced major intellectual developments, involving the whole complex of related concepts of deterrence, credible threats, first and second strike forces, counterforce and countervalue targeting, stable and unstable deterrents and arms control. Moreover, these ideas came from sources outside government, although many were closely connected with it. They included the private research institutes (exemplified by the RAND Corporation), university research centers, and groups of concerned intellectuals, especially the atomic scientists. Generally speaking, the research institutes started from physical science and operations research, the university research centers started from diplomatic history and traditional foreign policy (and later from social science theory), and the concerned intellectuals from particular policy and moral concerns about nuclear weapons. They came together in the area of nuclear weapons policy.[4]

The variety of institutions in the field was matched by that of the individuals within the institutions. The study of military policy by a significant group of civilians was a new phenomenon in the United States;[5] there were no accepted channels of recruitment or credentials for entrance. Moreover, the nature of the field was such that almost any substantive interest provided sufficient "handle" to justify involvement, from the geologist's work in detecting underground nuclear tests to the theologian's concern over the morality of nuclear war. Thus many people could be peripherally involved through their normal work, but for anyone to specialize in the area involved something of a break with his own profession or discipline. It therefore seems typical of many policy areas related to social science, enhancing its utility as a case study.

Moreover this body of ideas had significant effects on the policy of the United States government. In this respect, whatever one's attitude toward the results, the success of those working in nuclear weapons policy in influencing important government policy may seem a desirable model to follow. Important aspects of this included the research institute and the government research contract as links with government. In fact several of the people whom I surveyed specifically said that nuclear weapons policy had adventitiously been the first substantive area of postwar social science policy work and that other areas were developing in a similar manner.

The major data source for this paper was the material gathered in a larger study of civilians outside government who had done work in nuclear weapons policy, whom I called the "private nuclear strategists."[6] The population was composed of 491 individuals who had written one book or three articles or papers on nuclear weapons policy between 1946 and 1964 inclusively, while not directly employed full-time by the government. Employees of organizations under government contract were included. Probably the major difficulty with this criterion was lack of access to bibliographies of classified documents; therefore anyone who did only classified work in the area would not have been included. Despite some connotations of the word "strategist," publication, not policy preference, was the criterion used, and the full range of policy and methodological variety was represented.

All members of the population were sent an 11-page mail questionnaire in the middle of 1966; 191, 39 percent, eventually returned it and became our sample. Nonrespondents were studied by using standard biographical publications such as *Who's Who*. The sample seems to be representative of the population. It is somewhat slanted toward those who have written more about nuclear weapons policy and over represents political scientists. However, differences were not statistically significant[7] on the following attributes: highest academic degree, school of highest degree, sex, and ex-military status and service.[8]

This essay focuses on three particular aspects of general concern in social science policy issue-areas: distribution of ability to influence government within the field, which in turn involves its internal power structure; the importance of different types of employing institutions, particularly universities and research institutes, as barriers within the field; and the academic-policy tension inherent in any such area. In each area it is suggested that the conditions that seem to hold within nuclear weapons policy may indicate the direction in which other, more recent social science policy fields will develop.

EXTERNAL INFLUENCE AND INTERNAL POWER

The ability to influence policy, especially government policy, is a vital issue, as can be seen by monitoring the shop talk of workers in any such field. In the field of nuclear weapons policy the issue has been raised explicitly in public discussion and continues to generate a good deal of emotional heat.[9]

The issue of influence cannot be definitively settled. This study furnished no objective evidence of the influence of the private nuclear strategists upon government policy or who exercised this influence, if any. Such a study would involve studying the consumers of strategic expertise as well as its producers. However, there are several indicators of how much influence respondents *think* they have on policy. Two such questions concerned the influence of the group as a whole and of the particular respondent as an individual.

The sample had a high opinion of its influence, both individually and collectively. In response to Question 28, "How much would you say civilians not employed by the government have influenced American defense policy since World War II?" 14 percent said "not at all" or "not very much," 26 percent said "somewhat," and 57 percent said "a good deal" or "very much" (N was 177). A remarkable 41 percent of the sample said that they "as an individual [had] significantly influenced a policy of the United States government in the field of strategy and disarmament" (Question 27), while 35 percent disagreed (N was 183).

As in any social group, influence was not distributed equally. Another criterion of influence utilized the traditional academic approach, the judgment of an individual's colleagues, in Question 34:

In your opinion, what individuals have made the most significant contribution to the study of strategy and disarmament since World War II?[10]

The first five responses were coded; less than 5 percent of the sample named more than this number. Forty members of the sample were named by one or more members of the sample (self-choices were excluded); this group was called the "perceived influentials." Again there is no way of determining objectively whether these individuals have indeed had this influence.

Given that influence is distributed unequally, just how unbalanced is its distribution? Have the perceived influentials arrogated all the power to themselves, leaving the remainder of the population in frustrated impotence? Perhaps, but it does not appear so on this admittedly rather limited indicator of influence. While it is true that 50 percent of the perceived influentials claim to have significantly influenced a government policy themselves, as compared with only 39 percent of the rest of the sample, the difference is significant only at the .15 level (N's are 38 and 145). Moreover, of the respondents who said they had significantly influenced a government policy, 70 percent were *not* perceived influentials. While this does not guarantee satisfaction by the "noninfluentials" (perhaps they want to influence more than one policy), it suggests that influence is perceived to be widely distributed throughout the population. This position is buttressed by the fact that, with the exception of an academic trend (which we will discuss later) and age, the differences between the perceived influentials and the rest of the sample are unimportant; this included a battery of policy questions.

How is influence gained? Unfortunately there were no direct questions on this subject, but among the possible answers that come to mind are publications, political action, personal influence of decision-makers and government research contracts. There is evidence on the first and last possibilities.

Since the selection of our population was based upon publication criteria, data on this point was readily available. Each respondent was scored for publication points, on the basis of one article or paper (widely interpreted) as one point and a book as three points. Three points, of course, was the minimum, since it defined our population. Relating publication point scores to status as a perceived influential confirms a strong relationship between them. While 37 percent of the perceived influentials had publication point scores above 15, only 8 percent of the others did (N's were 40 and 140, and the difference was significant at the .001 level). In fact, of the 27 individuals who had scores over 15, 56 percent were perceived influentials, suggesting that if you publish a lot you have an even chance of being regarded as influential.

Similarly it was expected that perceived influentials would be more likely to have done government research. Question 21 asked "Have you ever worked on a government research contract in the area of nuclear strategy and disarmament?" 67 percent of the perceived influentials said that they had, as opposed to 41 percent of the rest of the sample (N's were 39 and 150, and the difference was significant at the .05 level).

As usual in survey research the causal implications of correlations are unclear. It may be that perceived influentials find it much easier to publish articles and receive government contracts because of their status. Alternatively their success in these areas may create their status. The former position is supported by some fragmentary data discussed later which suggests that status may come from status in the parent academic discipline. However, in a new field of study the question of where the status comes from in the first place remains a problem, especially since many of the

Table 1
Consequences of Publishing Material Disapproved by
the "Establishment"
All percentages are totaled across. *N is 144.*

	% YES	% CONDITIONAL
Not listened to by the government	33	7
Difficulty in obtaining research funds	15	9
Loss of general respect among colleagues	13	8
Difficulty in obtaining good university appointments	8	10
No effect; there is no "establishment"	17	10
No effect; the "establishment" has no real power	14	9
OTHERS:		
The "establishment" exists but judges work on its merits	10	4
The "establishment" exists but has no power over this particular respondent	9	1
Difficulty in getting published	7	2
Respondent specifically mentioned having had trouble with the "establishment" himself	3	5
There is more than one "establishment"	3	2
Other answer implying existence of the "establishment"	21	5

respondents are fairly young and have not done much work outside the field. Since there seem to be no other significant differences between the perceived influentials and the rest of the sample, it seems likely that their status is largely a product of their work rather than vice-versa.

A related indicator concerning perceived influence within the field was Question 37:

> It has been suggested that there is an "establishment" in the field of strategy and disarmament, a group which sets the limits (perhaps unconsciously) within which strategic debate and discussion is carried on. If you published material of which the "establishment" disapproved, what effects do you think this would have on you? (Check as many as you feel are appropriate.)

Aside from the six alternatives listed on the questionnaire, the five mentioned most frequently as "other" were also coded. Table 1 shows the results. There was general agreement that an "establishment" exists; 117 respondents, 81 percent of those who replied to

Table 2
Full-time employment in strategy and disarmament
"Have you ever been employed full-time *for* over four months *by any of the following types of institutions, doing work that was* directly related to nuclear strategy and disarmament? *(Check as many as are applicable.)" (emphasis in questionnaire)*

	N	%
College or university (teaching full or part time)	44	19
College or university (no teaching responsibility)	19	8
Research institute affiliated with a college or university	29	13
Private, non-profit research and/or educational institute	64	27
Private corporation (not non-profit)	16	7
Periodical (privately owned)	18	8
Federal government	36	15
Other (please specify)	7	3
	233	100

the question, checked at least one consequence. However, there was no consensus on the consequence of opposition to the "establishment," suggesting that this perception is hazy at best. None of the alternatives received the support of half of the sample; the highest was "not listened to by the government" with 33 percent agreeing and another 7 percent uncertain. Sanctions that remain this vague seem unlikely to be particularly effective, confirming the impression of a relatively loose internal power structure.

EMPLOYING INSTITUTIONS

One of the major divisions among people working on nuclear weapons policy is that different types of institutions employ them. This in turn seems likely to serve as a precedent for other policy areas. The assumption that a man's employer shapes his opinions is widely held and is often used to judge his work. In particular the distinction between the university and the research institute, especially those dependent upon government support for their funds (as most of them are), is thought to be important. It was therefore expected that there would be significant differences between respondents employed in different types of institutions, especially research institutes. Specifically I hypothesized that respondents who had been employed by research institutes would have been significantly more motivated by intellectual than policy considerations, would be more anti-communist in policy attitudes, and would read different periodicals than the rest of the sample. These hypotheses generally were not supported by the data.

The customary duality of universities and research institutes does not do justice to the proliferation of institutions in the area. Many universities, for instance, have established research institutes of their own, some of which have done work in strategy and disarmament.[10] The relationship between their personnel and the regular departments varies, but joint appointments tend to be rare and limited to senior members.[11] Faculty positions without teaching responsibilities are similarly difficult to categorize easily.

Outside the universities there have been other institutional developments. The well-known, nonprofit research institutes such as RAND have been supplemented by other corporations which are not nonprofit. These include research corporations such as Arthur D. Little, Inc., United Research Inc., and Abt Associates as well as several major corporations in aerospace and electronics which have either established research branches or done work within existing administrative structures, such as Bendix, Boeing and General Electric (which has published a journal in the area, the *General Electric Defense Quarterly*). RAND, after all, was originally a branch of Douglas Aircraft. Political action groups have also been involved, and our stress on publication criteria brought in individuals employed by periodicals, of whom the military correspondents are perhaps the most prominent.[12] Question 7 asked:

> Have you ever been employed *full-time* for *over four months* by any of the following types of institutions, doing work that was *directly related to nuclear strategy and disarmament?* (Check as many as are applicable.) [Emphasis in questionnaire.]

Table 2 lists the results on the seven types of institutional employment: college or university (teaching full or part time); college or university (no teaching responsibility); research institute affiliated with a college or university; private, nonprofit research and/or educational institute; private corporation (not nonprofit); periodical (privately owned); and federal government. A surprisingly large number had done such work; 126, 66 percent of the sample, named at least one institution. Conveniently, the sample divided almost equally between universities with and without teaching responsibilities and nonprofit research institutes.

I expected that respondents who had worked for different institutions would have had different motives for entering the

Table 3
Reasons for working in strategy and disarmament
"Opposite each of the following possible reasons for doing work in the area of strategy and disarmament, please indicate whether it had not much influence, some influence, or very much influence in your decision to enter the field."

Reason	N	% VERY MUCH	% VERY MUCH OR SOME
Concern about the threat of modern weapons to the human race	159	65	87
Intellectual interest in international security affairs	150	64	88
Desire to significantly alter American foreign policy	159	40	75
Desire to encourage world disarmament	155	34	66
Desire to teach and disseminate knowledge in this area	150	34	71
Concern about the moral problems of current American military policy	148	32	63
Desire to influence young minds	143	20	52
Experiences during World War II	142	20	41
Specific job opportunity	133	20	49
Related problem in another field	128	19	46
Desire to combat world communism	145	16	37
Influence of an individual working in the field	132	14	45
Desire to promote democracy throughout the world	137	12	44
Influence of a book or publication in the field	130	9	28
Casual exposure to the area	122	7	38
Availability of research funds in this field	128	2	23
Influence of an individual not working in the field	118	3	9
College course in the field	124	2	11
College course in another field that included a section on this area	128	2	13
Other	28	89	100

field. Kathleen Archibald, in a study using a smaller sample and more intensive interviews, found that those employed in universities said they had originally become involved because of policy interests, while those working for nonprofit research institutes had been more influenced by intellectual motives; over time the two groups became more similar in their motives.[13]

Question 32 stated:

Opposite each of the following possible reasons for doing work in the area of strategy and disarmament, please indicate whether it had not much influence, some influence, or very much influence on *your* decision to *enter* the field. [Emphasis in questionnaire]

Table 3 gives the responses of the sample to this question. The nineteen alternatives were divided into motives (internal factors) and influences (external factors). Motives in turn were divided into policy and intellectual. This gave three categories: policy motives (threat of modern weapons to the human race, altering American foreign policy, desire for world disarmament, concern about moral problems of American policy, threat of world communism and desire to promote democracy), intellectual motives (intellectual interest, teaching and disseminating knowledge and influencing young minds), and influences (World War II, a specific job opportunity, related problem in another field, a publication in the field, availability of research funds, a person or college course in or out of the field, and casual exposure to the area). Table 3 suggests that motives have been much more important than influences (implying policy and intellectual motives) and that policy motives seem equally important. The direction of the policy motives is also interesting; with the threat of modern weapons as one of the most important motives (65 percent said it had had "very much" influence) and concern about world communism second lowest of nine motives (16 percent), the sample appears to be unpromising material for an anti-communist nuclear crusade, although this as sumes a link between motives and policy positions that may be incorrect.

In line with my initial hypothesis, I expected those who had worked for universities to have been more influenced by policy motives and those in nonprofit research institutes to have been influenced by intellectual motives. Table 4 does not confirm this hypothesis. The motivations of the two groups seem to be very similar. Indeed, of the six policy motives, the research institute respondents had higher percentages on two, on three there was no difference, and only on the general motive of altering American foreign policy did the expected greater policy interest of the academics appear. There was also no significant difference on the intellectual interest motive, although the academic motives of teaching and influencing young minds were more prevalent among college teachers.

I had not expected the motives of those who had been employed by the federal government to differ significantly from the rest of the sample; while this was generally true, they had been significantly more motivated by the threat of world communism

Table 4
Factor loadings of periodicals and journals
In the first five factors, periodicals with factor scores equal to or larger than .5 are included; in the last three the cutting point is shifted to .3.

	FACTOR LOADINGS
MILITARY (17% of the variance)	
Army	.87
Journal Of The Armed Forces	.80
Air Force/Space Digest	.79
Air University Review	.79
United States Naval Institute Proceedings	.79
Aviation Week	.77
Missiles and Rockets	.76
Military Review	.75
Marine Corps Gazette	.74
Military Affairs	.66
Navy	.62
SOCIAL SCIENCE (13% of the variance)	
International Organization	.83
International Conciliation	.81
American Journal of International Law	.74
American Political Science Review	.73
World Politics	.70
Journal Of Conflict Resolution	.66
Annals Of The American Academy of Political And Social Science	.53
Daedalus	.51
Foreign Affairs	.50
Orbis	.50
ATTENTIVE PUBLIC (11% of the variance)	
Atlantic Monthly	.72
Scientific American	.71
Harper's	.70
Bulletin Of The Atomic Scientists	.67
New Republic	.62
Saturday Review	.60
Daedalus	.58
War/Peace Report	.53
PROTESTANT (7% of the variance)	
Fellowship (Fellowship of Reconciliation)	.79
Christian Century	.71
Worldview (Council on Religion and International Affairs)	.59
Intercom (Foreign Policy Association)	.56

CATHOLIC-JEWISH (6% of the variance)
America   .76
Commonweal   .64
Commentary   .57

HISTORY (5% of the variance)
American Historical Review   .69
Annals of the American Academy of Political
   and Social Science   .47
Military Affairs   .46
Virginia Quarterly Review   .43
American Political Science Review   .41
Current History   .39
Atlantic Monthly   .34

OPERATIONS RESEARCH (4% of the variance)
Operations Research   .63
Stanford Research Institute Journal   .39
Military Affairs   .31
Journal Of Conflict Resolution   .30

SURVIVAL (4% of the variance)
Survival (Institute for Strategic Studies,
   London)   .84
World Politics   .35
Orbis   .32
Reporter   .31

(30 percent said it had "very much" influenced them, while others ranged from 13 percent to 18 percent). This suggested the hypothesis that those who worked for the federal government would be more anti-communist on the questions of policy that we studied. This hypothesis was in addition to the one which predicted the employees of nonprofit research institutes to be more anti-communist than those from university positions.

Eleven policy attitude questions were included in the questionnaire. Nine of these were statements, with responses requested on a seven-point, agree-disagree scale (collapsed for analysis to three-point scales); they are listed here:

American foreign policy since World War II has not faced up to the fundamental problem of a hostile Communist foe dedicated to its destruction.

American foreign policy since World War II has placed too much emphasis on the threat of world communism and the Soviet bloc.

The aggressive tendencies of the Soviet Union have been greatly reduced since World War II.

In ten years China will be a greater threat to the United States than the Soviet Union will be.

It seems likely that, within this century, the Soviet Union and the United States will be allied against China.

The present system of deterrence seems unlikely to last until the end of the century without breaking down into a central nuclear war.

The American policy of containment of the Soviet Union has been a success.

In the nuclear age, the American government must regard itself as being responsible, not only to the American people, but also to the people of the world.

Some form of world government is the only long-term solution to the problem of destructiveness of modern weapons and opposing nationalisms.

In addition, Question 62 asked:

The major threat to American national interests abroad since World War II has been: (choose one)
Communist ideology
Russian and Chinese national power

And Question 42 asked:

Within the past five years, have you publicly disagreed with a position of the United States government in the area of strategy and disarmament?

Combining these eleven policy questions with the seven types of institutions generated 77 different relationships. Only one was significant at the .05 level; employees of private corporations are more likely to see the major threat to American interests abroad as being communist ideology rather than Russian and Chinese national power. Since a .05 significance level means one chance in 20 of happening at random, I dismissed this finding and concluded that no significant policy differences appeared in the sample. The hypothesis that employees of the nonprofit research institutes and the federal government tended to be more anti-communist in foreign policy attitudes than the rest of the sample was therefore rejected; once again the university-research institute barrier proved to be more fragile than expected.

The role of periodicals as agents of communication is obviously significant; indeed a persuasive classification of schools of thought in the field has been made in terms of "communication networks" and stressed the role of certain journals.[16] Question 30 read:

Opposite each periodical listed below, please indicate about how often you usually read its articles on the subject of strategy and disarmament.

Forty-three periodicals were listed in alphabetical order. They were chosen because they had carried significant articles in the area, and some effort was made to include as many different types of journals as possible. Newspapers were excluded. Opposite each title was a five point scale: "not familiar with periodical," "read only occasional articles," "read less than half the articles on this topic," "read more than half the articles on this topic," and "read nearly all the articles on this topic," as well as "don't know." All other journals listed by more than one individual were also coded; of the 25, only one was listed by more than ten respondents, *Survival* (the journal of the Institute for Strategic Studies, London), which had been excluded from the original list because it was British; it was added.

A factor analysis was performed on the results for the 44 periodicals.[17] Eight factors were rotated; together they accounted for 66 percent of the variance. Table 4 shows the periodicals that related closely to each of the eight factors. The names of the factors have been invented by the author on the basis of the journals loading highly on each; they have no other significance or validity.

Factor scores of respondents were used as an index of periodicals read. Of the 56 relationships generated by eight factors on seven types of institutions, only three were significant above the .05 level.[18] However, since they were all on the same factor and all well above .05, they are worth examining in more detail. Analysis was based on the percentage of respondents who had factor scores of 1.0 or above on each of the factors. This percentage varied from 0 percent in a couple of cases to 19 percent, except for the "social science" factor. Although the nonprofits actually had a slightly higher percentage here than on any other factor (16 percent), they were significantly lower than the university research institutes (38 percent), university teachers (41 percent), and university non-teachers (47 percent) (N's and significance levels were 29 and .01, 44 and .001, and 19 and .01 respectively). This may reflect the general preeminence of physical scientists at research institutes;[19] however, considering the pride of the nonprofits in their success in interdisciplinary work, it is rather surprising to see their low percentages on the factor which includes the major professional journals in political science, international relations, international law and general social science.

This is an important difference, but it should not obscure the fact that differences on the other seven factors between different types of institutions are negligible. The pattern is a single deviation from homogeneity rather than the systematic differences we had expected. With the single exception of social science periodicals, there are no important differences among employees of different types of institutions working on nuclear weapons policy in motives for entering the field, policy attitudes and periodicals read. It seems clear that a common subject matter has overcome the potentially divisive effects of different sorts of institutions. There are certainly major differences within the sample, but they do not seem to coincide with different types of institutions. Nor is there any obvious reason to suppose that this pattern will not be repeated in other policy fields of social science.

ACADEMIC-POLICY TENSIONS

This is not to say that employment is entirely unrelated to questions relating to policy. Part of the reason for the lack of difference between universities and research institutes is undoubtedly the fact that many individuals within the universities have also worked for the government on research contracts, and people who have never done such work have very different attitudes about its morality than those who have.[20]

The dichotomy between academic and policy goals is a prominent feature of every social science policy field. The rather abstract and seemingly consistent goals of knowledge for theory development and for policy guidance in practice develop into major differences in orientation, style, credentials, media, audiences and institutions. Nuclear weapons policy is an interesting example of this precisely because the tension has been so apparent. We have seen that intellectual and policy motives seem to have stimulated the sample to work in the area about equally. Indeed the division has been institutionalized with the development of the research institutes and corporations, as previously discussed, and these seem likely to remain a permanent part of the policy process in the United States. In fact, several of them have been consciously attempting to shift into other policy fields recently.

One would expect to find a strong division between respondents on various indicators relating to this distinction, and indeed upon first inspection the data seemed to support this conclusion. However, a somewhat more complex analysis indicated a different pattern. If the sample is divided by two dichotomized factors (age and status as perceived influentials) into four groups, the older noninfluentials are significantly less academically oriented than the rest of the sample in terms of the highest earned academic degree and affiliation with an academic discipline. Moreover the younger respondents seem to have been motivated by intellectual rather than policy motives. Assuming that the influentials and the younger members of the sample indicate the future development of the area, I concluded that the field of nuclear weapons policy is becoming more academic over time. Moreover it seems likely to be an indicator of future developments in other fields.

The criterion used to establish status as a perceived influential has already been discussed. The second question on the questionnaire asked for the respondent's date of birth. The answers were divided rather arbitrarily into those born before and during 1919 and after that date; this divided the sample almost equally (92 older members and 90 younger members).

Since there are no Ph.D.'s being offered in national security studies at an American university,[21] it is not intuitively obvious that possession of a doctoral degree is a useful indicator of the quality of an individual's work in nuclear weapons policy. Nevertheless among the older respondents 70 percent of the perceived influentials have this degree as compared to 35 percent of the older noninfluentials (N's were 23 and 69; the significance level was .006). At the same time, 71 percent of the younger influentials and 48 percent of the younger noninfluentials had the Ph.D.; N's were 14 and 76, and the difference was not significant. The American academic community, of course, has traditionally stressed the importance of the Ph.D.[22]

Question 16 asked: "Do you consider yourself affiliated with an academic discipline?" On the surface such identification would seem to make it more difficult to achieve eminence in an area outside the discipline (unless national security policy itself is regarded as a discipline, but it was not by our respondents). After all, identification with a discipline usually involves some consideration of one's disciplinary colleagues as a potential audience, and this may well conflict with either a client such as the government or with the audience or others working in nuclear weapons policy with different disciplinary identifications.[23] However, among older respondents 100 percent of the perceived influentials said that they were affiliated with a discipline, as compared to 50 percent of the older noninfluentials (N's were 22 and 68; the difference was significant at the .001 level). Comparable figures for younger respondents were 91 percent and 71 percent (N's of 13 and 74, with the difference not significant). The weakening of this distinction between influentials and noninfluentials among the younger group is due to the much larger percentage of younger noninfluentials who identify with a discipline as compared to their older counterparts.

The pattern on these variables is the same. Among the older age group, the perceived influentials are more "academically" oriented than the remainder of the group. Among the younger respondents, the differences are not significant. The differences between the two age groups are due to the younger noninfluentials having become more academically oriented than their older counterparts. A causal relationship should not be inferred here, although it is tempting to view this as an example of the role of the perceived influentials as a "leading group" for the rest of the sample. But this assumption is not necessary to the basic conclusion that, barring large-scale recruitment, individuals working in nuclear weapons policy are likely as a group to become more academically oriented, even though they presumably retain their interest in policy research.

If academic criteria are so important, one would expect that, despite immersion in this special area, qualifications for being perceived as influentials would continue to reflect criteria used in the parent discipline. This could be checked by seeing if perceived influentials were named on a similar list of their own disciplines, but only one such list was discovered. In a survey of political scientists, the top 19 perceived influentials were listed;[24] the only two who were in my population were also on the list of perceived influentials, suggesting that influence in one's discipline may transfer directly into a policy field.

Another supportive finding concerns motivation for doing work in the field. In this area the distinction between perceived

Table 5
Age and motives for working on nuclear weapons policy
Percentage Influenced "very much" by motive

| | BIRTH DATE | | | | |
| | 1880-1919 | | 1920-1939 | | SIGNIFICANCE |
MOTIVE	%	N	%	N	LEVEL
Desire to significantly alter American foreign policy	53	72	28	81	.008
Concern about the threat of modern weapons to the human race	73	73	58	81	.14
Desire to encourage world disarmament	47	71	24	79	.007
Concern about the moral problems of current American military policy	45	67	22	78	.009
Desire to combat world communism	20	61	13	79	N.S.
Desire to promote democracy throughout the world	15	55	10	77	N.S.
Intellectual interest in international security affairs	54	63	73	82	.01
Desire to teach and disseminate knowledge in this area	41	64	30	81	N.S.
Desire to influence young minds	27	64	15	75	.03

influentials and others drops out, but the difference between the age groups remains strong. Table 5 shows the results of combining the nine motives with an age differential. On five of the nine the difference is significant, and on a sixth it is notable. Older respondents were significantly more motivated by the policy motives of altering American policy, encouraging world disarmament, and concern about the moral problems of current American military power. They were notably more motivated by a concern about the threat of modern weapons to the human race, and they were significantly less motivated by intellectual interests. Table 5 also indicates that a significantly larger percentage of older respondents than younger were very much influenced by a desire to influence young minds, which was classified by us as an academic motive. At the risk of torturing the data, the wording of this motive, with its stress on young minds, means that it is probably inherently more attractive to older respondents. Even if taken under the original classification it weakens, but does not seriously undermine, my basic conclusion that the private nuclear strategists seem to be developing in an academic direction.

CONCLUSION

The field of nuclear weapons policy is seen by its participants as having been influential upon government policy and the sources of such influence seem fairly widely dispersed within the community. The divisions between employees of research institutes and universities do not seem to be particularly important, although the population as a whole seems to be moving toward an academic outlook as far as motivation and status qualifications are concerned. What is it that links these diverse findings together?

All three seem to indicate that the field of nuclear weapons policy has stabilized. Taking them in reverse order, the development of academic status qualifications is probably the normal process that any new field or area goes through in the process of becoming legitimate. Moreover, it allows the institutionalization of the field within the universities, freeing at least a cadre of members from the uncertainties of working for research institutes that depend upon the mood and purse of the federal government. Similarly, the fact that the divisions between research institute and university seem relatively unimportant suggests that the field has acquired legitimacy of its own, that it is relatively independent of the institutions to which its practitioners are attached.

By the same token, the fact that respondents seem to perceive influence and power as being widely dispersed within the field should reduce frustrations and help keep people within the area; indeed when respondents were asked a series of questions about how much of their professional time they spent in the field five years ago, today, and how much they expected to spend five years in the future, the results indicated relatively little decline in participation over time.[25] The fact that the sample seems little concerned about internal power problems, however, does not satisfy the frustrations that may arise from an unwillingness within the government to listen to their advice. This essay has suggested that the private nuclear strategists had significant influence upon American military policy, but it should be noted that this reached its high point in the early sixties, under the rather unusual political conditions attendant upon a new Democratic administration in office which was both sympathetic to new ideas and concerned with defense problems. The ease with which they were able to translate theory into policy may have given some of the private nuclear strategists an exaggerated view of their political prowess, which may lead to frustration in the future if this success is not repeated.

None of this, of course, answers the more basic question of why the field of study of nuclear weapons policy has become accepted, an important question when attempting to draw lessons from the experience for other fields. There seem to be two main reasons, however: the problems that gave rise to work in the field continue to demand attention, and civilians outside government seem to have found an accepted position within a division of labor among those concerned with these problems.

The first is perhaps the more obvious point. Although the field is in something of a hiatus at the moment, with the feeling that its "golden age" of the early sixties has come and gone, major problems remain in the area. Recently, even though Vietnam has continued to have a strong claim on intellectual resources, the questions of the antiballistic missile system, MIRV, the nonproliferation treaty, and the SALT talks have again brought the field into prominence. Nor is there much realistic hope that the problems of nuclear weapons will soon be solved and forgotten.

The idea of an accepted role for civilians outside government may be less obvious, but it is no less crucial for the long-term stability of the field. The strategic community, those who are concerned with nuclear weapons policy inside and outside government, can be conveniently divided into the private nuclear strategists, the professional military and civilian government employees and officials. The community seems to be developing a pattern of division of labor on issues, although whether this pattern will survive the Democratic administrations which spawned it is less clear at the moment. The private civilian strategists, who have developed practically all of the strategic concepts since World War II, carry on a continuing debate over the major issues in nuclear strategy and disarmament. This debate, which may be called the strategic debate, is carried on partly in public (increasingly so in recent years) and partly within and between government agencies. In the latter area, the government research contract is the key that brings the private strategist temporarily inside of government, although less direct means such as publication may accomplish the same ends.

From this debate, certain concepts tend to emerge as prominent solutions, to use Schelling's term. This, in turn, gives rise to a second level of debate, over the translation of these concepts into policy. In this policy debate, the other two groups within the strategic community hold dominant positions. The professional military man speaks as the practitioner who must put the ideas into operation. As such, he rightly demands and receives a major voice in the debate. The government official's role may vary with the individual personality. However, he normally represents the rest of the government within the debate; thus he is often responsible for introducing factors such as the budget or public opinion. One of the drawbacks of the system is that he often also tends, by default, to be responsible for bringing in political, as opposed to military, questions; if he does not do so, they may never be raised.

It is unlikely that this system will change radically in the forseeable future. The private strategist continues to possess both expertise and available time, making him a valuable ally in the policy debate. Nor is there any sign that other groups within the strategic community are prepared to take over the strategic debate, despite occasional exhortations for them to do so.[26] Within the policy debate, to do in-house the work now contracted out would require an immense increase in the government bureaucracy, of a kind that few are likely to advocate, at least not as long as the quality of the contract work remains reasonably high.[27]

What, then, has been the impact of the development of the private nuclear strategists upon the more general question of social science policy work? The area has developed the key institutions of the research institutes and the government research contract and has given them legitimacy. Moreover, it has established a pattern in which intellectual work has been successfully translated into government policy. Finally, it has furnished a cadre of experienced personnel who seem prepared to move from the area into other policy fields. It thus has served as an entering wedge for what may become one of the major intellectual phenomena of our time.

This paper is in part a product of my doctoral dissertation, and my debts are immense. I acknowledge with gratitude the major contributions to the larger study made by Robert Axelrod, Karl W. Deutsch, Harold D. Lasswell, J. David Singer, and H. Bradford Westerfield. It was financed by a grant from the Council on International Relations, Yale University, and by supplementary computer funds from the National Science Foundation. Stephen A. Salmore smoothed the potentially traumatic change from one computer center to another. Computations for this particular paper were supported by a grant from the Center for Computation and Information Services, Rutgers University. But my primary debts are two, one individual and one collective, to Bruce M. Russett who was a model dissertation director and to the 191 individuals who took time to answer my importunities and complete my questionnaire.

NOTES

[1] For extensive discussion of this movement, see Robert G. Gilpin, *American Scientists and Nuclear Weapons Policy* (Princeton: Princeton University Press, 1962) and Alice Kimball Smith, *A Peril And A Hope: The Scientists' Movement in America,* 1945-1974 (Chicago: University of Chicago Press, 1965).

[2] A. J. Wohlstetter, F. S. Hoffman, R. J. Lutz, and H. S. Rowan, "Selection and Use of Strategic Air Bases," R-266, RAND Corporation, Santa Monica, California, April 1, 1954 (declassified 1962), 383 pp. For discussion of this study see Bruce L. R. Smith, "Strategic Expertise and National Security Policy: A Case Study, "*Public Policy* XIII (1964), pp. 76-87, revised as Chapter VI, Smith, *The RAND Corporation: Case Study Of A Non-Profit Research Institute* (Cambridge: Harvard University Press, 1966), pp. 195-240; E. S. Quade, "The Selection and Use of Strategic Air Bases: A Case History" and Albert Wohlstetter, "Analysis and Design of Conflict Systems" in E. S. Quade (ed), *Analysis for Military Decisions* (Chicago: Rand McNally & Company, 1964), pp. 24-63 and 122-127.

[3] W. W. Kaufmann (ed), *Military Policy and National Security* (Princeton: Princeton University Press, 1956) and Henry A. Kissinger, *Nuclear Weapons And Foreign Policy* (New York: Harper & Brothers, 1957). For the missile gap, see my "The Missile Gap Controversy," *Political Science Quarterly,* LXXXV (December, 1970), pp. 600-615.

[4] The best single history of this process is Gene M. Lyons and Louis Morton, *Schools for Strategy: Education and Research in National Security Affairs* (New York: Frederick A. Praeger, 1965).

[5] For discussions of American traditions in military expertise, see *inter alia* Samuel P. Huntington, *The Soldier And The State: The Theory and Politics of Civil-Military Relations* (Cambridge: Belknap Press of Harvard University Press, 1959), pp. 143-312: Paul Y. Hammond, *Organizing For Defense: The American Military Establishment In the Twentieth Century* (Princeton: Princeton University Press, 1964), pp. 1-106; Louis Smith, *American Democracy And Military Power* (Chicago: University of Chicago Press, 1951), pp. 102-151. For an attempt to integrate the phenomenon of the private

nuclear strategists into a more general discussion of the changes in American civil-military relations since World War II, see my *The Strategic Community: Contemporary American Civil-Military Relations* (forthcoming, 1971).

[6] Roy E. Licklider, "The Private Nuclear Strategists," Ph.D. dissertation, Department of Political Science, Yale University, New Haven, Connecticut (April 1968); to be published by Ohio State University Press, 1971.

[7] "Significance level" is the probability that the relationship in question would occur by chance if there were no differences between the groups under consideration. By convention the .05, .01, and .001 levels are considered thresholds of statistical significance; however, although they are useful, they are only conventions and have no particular intrinsic significance. For the purposes of this study, significance levels over .05 were considered *significant*, those between .05 and .20 *notable*, and those under .20 *not significant*. All significance level figures in this study are based on the chi square statistic. Strictly speaking, this measure is not appropriate, since we do not have a random sample. However, the sample does appear to be fairly representative of the population, and we felt that the value of having a measure of the strength of statistical relationships justified the risks, as long as it was not interpreted too strictly.

[8] Licklider, "The Private Nuclear Strategists," pp. 15-24.

[9] Two excellent summaries of opposing points of view on this issue are Wesley W. Posvar, "The Impact Of Strategy Expertise On The National Security Policy Of The United States," *Public Policy*, XIII (1964), pp. 36-68 and Philip Green, "Science, Government, and the Case of RAND: A Singular Pluralism," *World Politics*, XX (January, 1968), pp. 301-326.

[10] Lyons and Morton, pp. 127-199; Kathleen Archibald, "The Role of Social Scientists As Outside Experts In Policy Formulation," Ph.D. dissertation, Department of Sociology and Anthropology, Washington University, St. Louis, Missouri, to be published by Basic Books, Inc., Chapter III, pp. 29-33, 51-52; Charles V. Kidd, *American Universities and Federal Research* (Cambridge: Belknap Press of Harvard University Press, 1959), pp. 175-188, cited in Archibald.

[11] Lyons and Morton, pp. 127-199; Archibald, Chapter III, pp. 30-31.

[12] For a rather inconclusive study of this group, see George V. Underwood, Jr., "The Washington Military Correspondents," unpublished M. A. thesis, School of Journalism, University of Wisconsin, Madison, Wisconsin, 1960.

[13] Archibald, Chapter III, pp. 33-34.

[14] This distinction is one of several that I owe to observations by respondents on the questionnaire.

[15] The data is given in Licklider, "The Private Nuclear Strategists," pp. 102-105.

[16] Archibald, Chapter III, pp. 43-44.

[17] Strictly speaking, factor analysis was not an appropriate statistical technique, since the data was ordinal rather than interval. However, it was felt that the benefits of reducing 44 variables to 8 factors justified the risks. The program used was Yale Computer Center's No. 6S, using the principle axis method and varimax rotation of factors with eigenvalues equal to or greater than one.

[18] The data is presented in Licklider, "The Private Nuclear Strategists," pp. 111-112.

[19] Smith, *The RAND Corporation*, pp. 60-65.

[20] Licklider, "The Private Nuclear Strategists," pp. 187-195.

[21] Such a program was considered by M.I.T. some years ago but was not adopted.

[22] Theodore Caplow and Reece J. McGee, *The Academic Marketplace* (New York: Science Editions, Inc., 1961), p. 162.

[23] For valuable further discussion of the problem of audiences, see Archibald, Chapter V, pp. 12-31 and Chapter VI, pp. 8-9, 12-13, 17-19, and 39.

[24] Albert Somit and Joseph Tannenhaus, *American Political Science: A Profile Of A Discipline* (New York: Atherton Press, 1964), p. 66.

[25] Licklider, "The Private Nuclear Strategists," pp. 156-157.

[26] An example is Colonel Robert N. Ginsburgh, "The Challenge To Military Professionalism," *Foreign Affairs*, XLII (January, 1964), pp. 255-268.

[27] For a more detailed discussion of these points, see my *The Strategic Community* (forthcoming, 1971).

Policy Initiation
in the American Political System

NELSON W. POLSBY

Optimists, it is commonly reported, contemplate the doughnut; pessimists, the hole. Attractive and plausible as this formula seems at first blush, it does not accord with my experience. Persons who are to any degree curious or reflective about the "buzzing blooming confusion" of life around them develop expectations; it is the violation of these expectations, and the consequent creation of anomalies, that quite properly draws and holds attention. Thus, for an optimist, whose world is full of doughnuts, it is holes that need explaining; a pessimist, contrariwise, grapples to understand the appearance of life's occasional doughnuts.

A study of policies that are in some meaningful sense eventually enacted is about doughnuts, and thus will probably appeal more to pessimistic than optimistic readers. Optimists who study American government have more than enough material available with which to gratify their taste for anomaly. The daily disasters of the morning newspaper aside, the literature on obdurate Congressional committees, venal or helpless regulatory agencies, slack or officious bureaucrats, autocratic judges, selfish politicians and so forth is readily to hand for the benefit of those who wish to gorge themselves on reasons why good things are done so seldom and bad things are done so often. My own ever-subtler contributions to this burgeoning art form I leave to other occasions. In these pages I hope to pursue a different tack, asking how it happens that new sets of policies are initiated in the American political system.

For the sake of simplicity I have restricted rather drastically the domain within which I have searched for answers. All the policies I will consider here have a highly visible and discrete enactment phase engaging the president and Congress. This sampling procedure has weaknesses.

First, it overrepresents the products of "events" or "happenings". Analogous to the journalist's enslavement to "news pegs", there is a systematic underrepresentation of innovations that build slowly, that accrete, for example, within the common law of administrative agencies.

Second, it artificially restricts the consideration of innovations to those kinds characteristically processed within the arenas chosen as the vantage point. It neglects innovation by state and city governments, by courts, and in the private sector.

Third, it classes as policy initiations those things that actually happened rather than those dozens or hundreds of nonevents which might have happened but did not.

There are undoubtedly other unmentioned problems, equally serious, which undermine a priori the generality one may claim for conclusions reached by careful study of the population of cases to be mentioned here. This is a serious handicap, however, only to those who feel ready to pronounce with finality upon the problem at hand. This essay is exploratory in character, and the restriction of coverage serves the function of providing a few crude controls so as to assure some sort of comparability between cases. Thus while our method forbids the formulation of universals worthy of a high degree of confidence, it does facilitate the discovery of a few low and middle-range generalizations.

Are there, to begin with, any such things as policy innovations or initiations in the American political system? It is perfectly sensible to argue, as some do, that there is nothing new under the sun. So, in a sense, a search for the genesis of policy innovations is bound to prove fruitless. We can never settle definitively the exact point in time at which any particular innovation emerged from the primordial ooze. We can, however, by tracing policy some of the way back upstream, learn something about the workings of the systems in which innovations occur. My modest purpose here is to suggest what we can learn.

I should stipulate, to begin with, that policy innovation and policy initiation are the same thing. If it isn't an innovation, it isn't an initiation. In retrospect, at least, it is clear enough what constitutes an important mutation in policy, and in reconstructing how these come about we discover policy initiations. Such initiations, of course, are different from the day to day initiatives that serve to activate the routines of government.

There is, nevertheless, ambiguity about what counts as an innovation. I do not see any clear way through this methodological, and ultimately, I suppose, theoretical thicket. There is, so far as I know, no standard that currently commands universal acceptance, by which policies can be distinguished from non-policies, or innovations from noninnovations. Nor is there an accepted method to gauge with precision the magnitude of a policy or an innovation. There is, therefore, no entirely fastidious way to circumscribe a population from which a meaningful sample of policy innovations can be drawn for inspection. I do not believe, however, that this melancholy situation should be permitted to balk empirical inquiry, or even to free theoretical rumination from empirical constraints. We can go a short way, I think, with the conventional wisdom, case evidence that comes readily to hand, and a few reasonable ground rules.

Innovation, for our purposes, will consist in the creation of a new governmental agency or mechanism which subsequently is seen to enlarge or materially affect the repertoire of responses the government makes to a given range of social problems. Alternatively, innovation consists in a policy or a set of policies that seem to have altered (or promise to alter) the lives of persons affected by them in substantial and fairly permanent ways. Thus, to begin with, I shall invite attention to summary statements describing a "sample" of policies having three characteristics in common: First, they are relatively large-scale phenomena highly visible to political actors and observers. Second, they embody from at least one point of view a break with preceding governmental responses to the range of problems to which they are addressed. Finally, unlike major "crises" with which they share the preceding traits, "innovations" have institutional or societal effects that are in a sense "lasting." No doubt the men who stood "eyeball to eyeball" with Khruschchev in the Cuban missile crisis received lasting lessons from the experience, but unless these lessons are in some way given institutional form, it is hard to see how even such a dramatic event could be classed as a policy innovation, however momentous its immediate consequences, and even though it occasioned a temporary break with past policies and past methods of making policy.

So much, at least preliminarily, for ground rules. Now for conventional wisdom. There is, I think, a fairly firm consensus on how a great deal of policy is initiated in the American political system, and this consensus will provide a final set of empirical constraints within which our own speculations may conveniently find a focus. It is, of course, commonplace to observe that a major portion of the policies that ultimately are enacted by Congress are initiated by the president.

Recently, for example, in an unusually thoughtful and rigorous presentation, Charles E. Lindblom discussed how Congressmen "depend upon 'central' executive leadership, especially in the initiation of policies . . . e.g., in the degree to which the President has taken over the task of designing a legislative program for each succeeding Congress . . . Congressional committees themselves, the chairmen themselves, have turned to the President for leadership in policy-making . . . Perhaps 80 percent of bills enacted into law originate in the executive branch."

In much the same vein James Robinson says, "Congress' influence in foreign policy is primarily (and increasingly) to legitimate and/or amend recommendations initiated by the executive to deal with situations usually identified by the executive. . .Parliaments, Congresses and legislatures react to executive initiative rather than take initiative." This observation is supported by a chapter describing 22 foreign policy decisions from the 1930s to 1961, accompanied by a table listing the executive branch as the "initiator" in 19 cases.

David Truman says: "The twentieth century, it is often noted, has been hard on legislatures. Compelled in some fashion to deal with the complexities of increasingly urbanized, rapidly industrialized, and irrevocably interdependent societies, they have found themselves alternating in varying degrees between two equally dangerous and distasteful situations; yielding the initiative as well as the implementing responsibilities to bureaucrats whose actions might be imperfectly mediated by political officials, or attempting to retain one or both of these functions at the expense of delay, indecision and instability." Samuel P. Huntington echoes the theme: "The Congressional role in legislation has largely been reduced to delay and amendment." He quotes Senator Abraham Ribicoff: "Congress has surrendered its rightful place of leadership in the lawmaking process to the White House. No longer is Congress the source of major legislation. Now it merely filters legislative proposals from the President, straining out some and reluctantly letting others pass through. These days no one expects Congress to devise the important bills." Huntington quotes a report of a Congressional committee: "More and more the role of Congress has come to be that of a sometimes querulous but essentially kindly uncle who complains while furiously puffing on his pipe but who finally, as everyone expects, gives in and hands over the allowance, grants one permission, or raises his hand in blessing, and then returns to the rocking chair for another year of somnolence . . . "

I wonder if this picture is not overdrawn. The evidence upon which such remarks are based attests to the following: that immediately preceding the enactment of most laws, the agenda of Congress has been addressed to proposals brought to it by the executive branch. Further, the resources of the executive branch have been focused upon the enactment of these proposals. This focusing process rests discretionarily and principally in the hands of modern American presidents. Thus when the president adopts a proposal as part of his legislative program, when the president sends a bill to Capitol Hill, the president mobilizes resources behind a particular policy alternative, choosing one and excluding others. Through the power and the authority of his office he makes a strong and often a successful claim on the attention of Congress. Thus, more than any other single actor, he can harness political energy and focus the political process in a meaningful and consequential way. But is he initiating policy? The conventional view is that he is.

Yet no sophisticated student of contemporary American policy-making believes that policies normally spring fully formed from the overtaxed brow of the president or even from his immediate entourage. Nor does policy appear out of the sea like

Botticelli's Venus, dimpled, rosy and complete on a clam shell. Where, then, and how, are policies initiated in American politics?

A group of students are attempting with me to study the problem empirically, by looking through the literature on American national politics in a number of discrete policy areas, and in a few selected cases—Medicare, the Peace Corps, the Truman Doctrine, the Council of Economic Advisors, the National Science Foundation, the Nuclear Test Ban Treaty, Maximum Feasible Participation in Community Action Programs, and Civilian Control of Atomic Energy—we are attempting to look upstream and spell out the ways in which these policies were initiated.

It is not feasible (nor sufficiently entertaining) to discuss here all the details of what we have been finding. What I should prefer to do in any case is sketch in a first approximation of some of the more general conclusions that our detailed observations have begun to suggest. These come under three general headings.

Our first set of conclusions has to do with types of policy initiation. As we now see it, there are two general types: acute and chronic, inside and outside, short and long.

Policy innovations generally follow upon the identification of a "need". Needs are in one sense ubiquitous: everybody needs something. So, along with a simple state of tension somewhere in society there also must exist a doctrine, or theory, or idea, or notion, or attitude or custom which legitimizes governmental activity with respect to this need. And here is the first point at which the two general types of initiation diverge. For some innovations, the need is instantaneously recognized by all parties as palpable and more or less pressing. It is, for example, relatively easy to innovate with respect to needs created by organizational opportunities or custodial difficulties within public bureaucracies, since the innovation can be rationalized as necessary to the pursuit of goals already sanctioned by the existence of machinery.

Three cases of innovation in science policy may serve to illustrate the point. Scientists who began their work before World War II are, as a matter of course, incontinently nostalgic about the era before scientific activity became a major concern of the United States Government. The critical events that form the backdrop for governmental interest in science are well-known: the scientific discovery that certain very heavy atoms could be made to release enormous amounts of energy, the apprehension in the scientific community that this knowledge was, or would shortly become, available to scientists in the Third Reich, the maneuvers by prominent scientists in the United States to inform President Roosevelt, the decision by Roosevelt to mobilize American science through a science advisory committee, the formation of the Manhattan Project, and so on.

Once the war was well on the way to being won, a new set of problems naturally arose with respect to the continuing relations between science and government. To what extent would government continue to pay for the development of science? Who would set the priorities for scientific effort? How would the technologies that wartime science had created be managed and controlled? Questions such as these forced themselves upon the attention of scientists and political leaders as World War II drew to a close. In some respects the problems they posed were unprecedented. Other heavily mobilized parts of the economy could be demobilized and remobilized as needed: manpower, steel production, fabricating plants and the like. Factories—indeed, entire cities—constructed for the purpose of making components for atomic bombs seemed, on the face of it, less amenable to easy conversion to the private sector. The stake that government now had in the skills and activities of the scientific community was far different from the days before the war—and this difference did not apply to any other comparable group in the working population. Finally, there was the acute problem of the drastic change that science had wrought in the world balance of power.

Three postwar policy innovations (among others) addressed these problems: the proposal to establish civilian control of atomic energy, the establishment of a National Science Foundation, and the proposal of a nuclear test ban treaty. Because, at the time each of these innovations was proposed, science was almost totally an activity carried on under government auspices, the identification of the need and the proposal of alternative solutions took place almost exclusively within the government itself.

Furthermore, although there was disagreement on what to do about it, there was widespread agreement that each of these needs existed. No such agreement attended the birth of Medicare. The need for public medical insurance was identified in America as early as 1915, by a group of academics, lawyers, and other professionals, organized in the American Association for Labor

Legislation. In 1934 a New Deal economist, Edwin Witte, pressed a version of Medicare on President Roosevelt, who rejected it as politically too risky. During the 1940s, Senators Robert Wagner and James Murray and Representative John Dingell used to introduce a Medicare bill in every Congress. President Truman adopted the proposal in 1949, limiting the coverage of the bill to those on old age assistance, but even in this severely limited form, it failed to pass Congress. In the Eisenhower years the idea was nursed along in the Senate by Senator Hubert Humphrey, and by 1960 it was regarded as a standard part of the Democratic party national program. As a matter of course it was advocated by President Kennedy, and after the Goldwater landslide and the redistribution of party ratios on the House Ways and Means Committee, Medicare became law in the Johnson administration.

In general, then, there is a useful distinction to be made between acute, or emergency innovations, where recognition of the need to be fulfilled is widespread and swift, and slow innovations, where there is no immediate consensus about the presence of a need, and where, in consequence, a lengthy process of incubation has to take place before the need is recognized as legitimate by the government and policy is enacted to meet it.

Differences in the ways these two types of innovation arise also lead to other characteristic differences: crisis innovations are more likely to start within government. The production of alternative solutions is juxtaposed in time to the inclination of the organization to search for innovations. This leads to jerry-building, incrementalism and satisficing under severe time constraints. Bargaining between or among affected agencies and Congressional committees may be sharp, but it is relatively unideological, and capable of settlement by side-payments, compromises, log-rolls or other standard devices for antagonistic cooperation. Innovators are bureaucrats or government experts.

Long-haul innovations are much more likely to arise as the result of outside demands on government. Innovators are typically professors or interest group experts. In the process of identifying and dramatizing the need for governmental action, opposition is created. There is a higher probability that long-haul innovations will become enmeshed in party politics and hence in ideological— or at least what passes in the United States for ideological— struggle. Alternatives are the product of research, and elaborate—

and contested—justification. There is a separation between the production of alternatives and the activation of the propensity of the system to hunt for innovation. The process of incubation becomes crucial for the survival of alternatives over the long run.

These considerations lead to the second general set of problems currently occupying our research. We have become interested in stating in terms sufficiently general so as to facilitate cross-national or other comparisons, the conditions under which 1) systems provide for the expression of "needs" and the production of "alternatives", and 2) systems actively search for policy innovations. Among the conditions turned up by our research on the American political system to date under the second rubric we have found presidents needing programs, candidates needing issues, senators needing "specialties" and bureaucrats needing work.

The first two of these hardly need elaboration. Nor, really, does the last. Recall if you will the situation of the United States Navy in the heyday of the Strategic Air Command back in the 1950s. The inducements to the Navy to search for policy innovations were immense, and with the advent of rocket-bearing submarines, ultimately successful.

The condition of the senator needing a specialty may not be immediately clear, although it has played a role of increasing importance in policy initiation at the national level. I have argued at length elsewhere that the Senate has become an important locus for the incubation of ideas and careers. Thus, "passing bills", which is central to the life of the House, is peripheral to the Senate. In the Senate the three central activities are 1) the cultivation of national constituences (that is, beyond state lines) by political leaders; 2) the formulation of questions for debate and discussion on a national scale (especially in opposition to the president); and 3) the incubation of new policy proposals that may at some future time find their way into legislation. To succeed as a senator or to enhance his political future, a senator must develop a reputation for competence, a set of policy specializations, and ties to national constituencies beyond the bounds of a single state. Yet the division of labor in the Senate is not highly structured; while it rewards specialization, it provides few cues and fewer compulsions to specialization in any particular

NELSON W. POLSBY

mode. So senators must search for ways to specialize on their own. Above all, from the standpoint of national policy-making, the Senate is a great forum. Occasionally this forum serves as the arena for the debate of grave national issues. But, more often by far, this forum is nothing more or less than a gigantic echo chamber, a publicity machine that publicizes things that individual senators want publicized. As nature abhors a vacuum, so do politicians abhor a silent echo chamber; thus the Senate has become a great incubator of policy innovation in the American system.

This is less true of the House, primarily because of its stricter division of labor, its restrictions on debate, and its greater mass of members who thus enjoy lesser notoriety. This makes the House structurally inhospitable to the hobbies and fancies of individual members, no matter how meaningful and constructive they are. Even so, from time to time, a member, or a subcommittee, finds a niche from which it can incubate policy innovation.

A characteristic pathology of this process is of course for policy incubation to degenerate into make-work, into careerism, into obsession. Some of this is, no doubt, unavoidable. It is in any case a small price to pay for the continued development of a national forum in the initiation of policy.

There is often a hiatus of years—sometimes decades—between the first proposal of a policy innovation and its appearance as a presidential "initiative"—much less a law. Commentators have greatly underestimated the role of the Senate in gestating these ideas, by providing a home for speeches, hearings and the introduction of bills going nowhere for the moment. This process of gestation accomplishes a number of things. It maintains a sense of community among far-flung interest groups that favor the innovation, by giving them occasional opportunities to come in and testify. It provides an incentive for persons favoring the innovation to keep up to date information on its prospective benefits and technical feasibility. And it accustoms the uncommitted to a new idea.

Thus the Senate is in some respects at a crucial nerve end of the polity. It articulates, formulates, shapes and publicizes demands, and can serve as a hothouse for significant policy innovation. So it has proven, at least, in a number of instances—and I think that as the Senate more and more takes on the aspect of a crowded on-deck circle for presidential election politics, policy innovations of all kinds will be nurtured and publicized and kept alive by senators seeking the favorable attention of the media.

It may be worthwhile to consider conditions under which systems are likely or unlikely to search and alternatives are likely or not to be kept floating in the air.

First, I should say, for systems to be likely to search for alternatives, they must embody a generalized cultural belief in the efficacy of rationality, a belief that there are such things as effects that are caused by causes, and capable of being altered by alterations in causes. Second, there has to be some method of explicit decision-making, or at least a method of choice among alternatives that is more explicit than the habitual repetition of inherited rituals. Finally, the existence of political competition seems essential: The piecemeal displacement of one generation's leaders by the next, the challenge of an encroaching neighbor, the need to make promises or engage the loyalties of constituents or voters. All these may impel a system to search.

Richard Scammon has recently described the process in American national politics:

> . . . There really aren't any new solutions. There are modifications, adjustments. Most good ideas have already been thought of. You don't really come in . . . with a totally new concept. You improve this, polish up that. You take a plan that was discarded four years ago, and you pull it out and look at it. And maybe you salvage Points One, Eleven, and Twenty-nine.

What puts these ideas in the air in the first place? Here it is pretty clear Lord Keynes was right: intellectuals. Or, more exactly, people who are specialized in society to the tasks of playing with ideas and putting them in the air: professors, interest group experts, government specialists. The Peace Corps idea was somebody's hobby in the United Auto Workers for years before President Kennedy happened upon it in a campaign speech he was reading out loud during the election of 1960. Brookings economist Lewis Lorwin, drawing upon analogies with similar bodies in European nations, proposed a Council of Economic Advisors years before it was slipped, almost by chance, into the House mark-up of the Full Employment Act of 1946.

The point is: Chancy as these events were, they became much

more probable by virtue of their having been explicitly invented and floated into the subculture of decision-makers.

I have no doubt that a similar fate awaits the Negative Income Tax. Already, under the guise of a "Family Assistance Program", the principle is being officially advocated by a president who needed a program. Only a short time ago a series of intensive interviews revealed that putting welfare on such a basis would command almost no support at all in Congress or among relevant interest groups. Yet the idea was taking on advocates. It was incubating in the writings of economists Milton Friedman, Robert Theobald, James Tobin and Joseph Pechman. Journals of opinion like *The New Republic* and *The Public Interest* carried articles in praise of it. Meanwhile, public and decision-maker consciousness of the "need" to do something about the administration of welfare grew apace.

The third general set of concerns being pursued by my students and myself has to do with the reevaluation of roles in the political system. "Effective" senators are for us no longer exclusively those who manage to introduce only bills that pass in the same session. Looking at the political system from the standpoint of policy initiation has induced us to rethink the role of the Senate, and, likewise, of senators. The same is true of ivory towers and their absent-minded inhabitants, who sometimes do no more than borrow creatively from a range of experience that is simply not available to ordinary politicians or bureaucrats with their own day-to-day concerns.

So far as we can judge, the American case does not present a picture of a system in perfect equilibrium, where alternatives are always ready when government decision-makers search for them. The very success, for example, of the 89th Congress in enacting programs for domestic welfare that had for the most part been in the air in one form or another since the days of the New Deal provoked a kind of crisis. By suddenly depleting the stock of ideas available for legislative enactment, the 89th Congress issued a challenge that was speedily repeated in a spate of newspaper and magazine articles bemoaning the exhaustion of ingenuity in the American political system.

President Johnson fought back by constituting anonymous task forces of experts—mostly from outside government—who were charged with coming up with new worlds to conquer. As it turned out, of course, there was still plenty of unconquered territory in the old world. The announcement of victory in the war on poverty turned out to be premature. For one thing: the Maximum Feasible Participation clause in the Community Action Program unexpectedly evened up the sides a little. But this doesn't change the main point, which is that the American political system at the national level, working at its normal rate, frequently provides opportunities for policy initiation, even when crises and emergencies of various kinds do not provoke the system to search for alternatives.

Finally, the existence of available alternatives, as I have said, seems to depend in great measure upon the ingenuity and the energy of men of ideas, who, if we look closely enough, and trace far enough back, can be observed creating the indispensable substance that the political process processes.

Government Sponsored Research
on International and Foreign Affairs

These are opportune times to reflect on the relationship of social science to the federal government and to public policy. Social scientists have been favored by official patronage on a scale unimagined only a generation ago, urged to come to grips with public problems and encouraged—although little encouragement is needed in most cases—to minister to the needs of officials in Washington who, as the collective modern prince, obviously require all the enlightenment that reason, in its modern dress, can offer.

One of the consequences of this unaccustomed affluence, honor, and (on occasion) even palpable influence has been to provoke controversy among those who hold differing and sometimes conflicting views of the social sciences and of their actual or potential relationship to the polity. There are, as there always have been, social scientists cultivating their fields, with or without governmental help, who remain indifferent to the demands of politics and public affairs and who, indeed, even scorn too conspicuous a concern with immediate relevance as itself unbecomingly worldly—although most of them, I suspect, believe or hope that in the long run what they do will prove of some practical

309

good. But many others are more passionately engaged. At one end of the spectrum, for example, Ithiel Pool, confident of the beneficent utility of social research and of the virtues of its practitioners, argues boldly for close communion with men of power as the best way of taming them into a semblance of civility: "The only hope for humane government in the future," he writes, "is through the extensive use of the social sciences by government."[1] At the opposite extreme, others see federal support for research—or at least the way in which this support has been institutionalized—as at best a mixed blessing, a golden flow of temptation; they suspect that even social scientific flesh may discover, with Oscar Wilde, that the easiest way to deal with temptation is to succumb to it, and fear that the new mandarins may be transformed into corrupt servants of power.[2]

A good deal of the debate (which often sounds like a dialogue of the deaf) has centered on the government's financial support of studies that deal more or less directly with international and foreign affairs, and much of it has been prompted by a few spectacular *causes celebres:* Camelot, after all, still serves as a classic though somewhat tiresome cautionary tale. There are several reasons for this—essentially no different from those that affect any kind of sponsored research, but "national security" and foreign affairs studies seem, somehow, to place scholar and policy-maker in particularly sharp conflictual relationships.

We must start, I think, with the fact that the "project" system is firmly entrenched as the basic device used by the government to finance social research. It is commonplace to observe that the world of scholarship and the world of politics follow different rules and that some tension is inevitable between the pursuit of "truth" which ideally inspires the social scientist and the pursuit of "power" and practical ends that presumably animates the bureaucrat and the politician and even the statesman. What is less often remarked is that the system of federal support for social research is almost deliberately designed to bring these two worlds together. We have nothing in this country resembling the British University Grants Committee, for example, which might provide federal funds for research while minimizing federal influence over their use. Instead, the American system is characterized by contracts and grants administered by government agencies for rather specific projects, which inevitably gives some voice in—and often

PIO D. ULIASSI

virtual control over—the direction of research to federal officials and bureaucracies, mostly "operating" bureaucracies in the case of research on foreign affairs.[3] The arrangement undoubtedly has its merits: For one thing, it harmonizes with an activist strain in the American academic tradition which considers the university as an institution providing "services" to the community, or at least to whatever part of the community is willing and able to pay for them. But it also tends to clash with other traditions now especially emphasized by younger social scientists—the independence of the intellectual and his critical stance toward the dominant forces and ways of his day.

Of course there is more to the matter than this. The very nature of the executive agencies that have provided most of the financial support for research on foreign affairs until recently—those with intelligence, military, diplomatic and other "missions" traditionally associated with a state's high policy—makes their relations with social scientists more strained in some ways than those of departments with primarily domestic responsibilities (scientific or other) are likely to be in the normal course of things. Agencies dealing with high policy have to function in two political systems at once, the domestic and the international,[4] and it is a fact, perhaps unpleasant but very real, that the two systems impose different and sometimes conflicting standards of conduct. Research projects that are intimately linked to such agencies through contracts and grants therefore tend to get caught up in some of the problems and dilemmas of foreign and military policy in a democratic society: the requirements of confidentiality in many of the processes of international politics, the occasional imperatives for responsible statesmen to practice the venerable diplomatic art of speaking the truth without actually revealing it, their constant and sometimes agonizing efforts to reconcile the national interest and the interest of some other or larger community come to mind immediately as examples. Thus, despite the intellectual and financial liberality that frequently has inspired the research programs of such operating agencies, there are, I think, structural tensions between their purposes and practices and the presumably more open and universal norms of the scholarly and scientific professions.

Nevertheless, social scientists and their clients and patrons in Washington for many years had a remarkably untroubled relationship, grounded on a substantial consensus regarding the main lines of American foreign policy that was created during and after the Second World War. This is not to say that all social scientists who collaborate with military and civilian operating agencies do so from the purest of motives; as a group they probably share with their now numerous critics a normal human incidence of opportunism. (Einstein once observed that if an angel of the Lord were to drive from the temple of science all those who inhabit it for reasons other than the love of truth, "it would become embarrassingly empty.") But I think most are moved by nobler sentiments, by a sincere agreement with broad national purposes that enables them to avoid ultimate value questions in justifying their conception of social research as the handmaiden of state policy. What has changed in recent years is the political climate.[5] Those who no longer are content with the fundamentals of high policy as they understand it naturally demand a more critical role for the social sciences and a stronger guarantee of professional autonomy than they perceive in existing arrangements.[6] In short, some relationships between the federal government and the social sciences that were largely taken for granted in an era of ideological good feeling are now judged as problematic.

These preliminary observations suggest what I suppose is the theme of this chapter: the difficulties of developing, with federal encouragement, a social science that is at the same time relevant to public concerns, responsive to the needs—as they seem them—of public officials, and autonomous. The argument—if an argument can be traced in such wide-ranging and frequently superficial observations—runs something like this: The net effect of federal interest in research on foreign affairs has been to create a vast and varied complex of programs, most of them at least symbolically linked to operating agencies. The linkage has created some ambiguity of purpose—it is not always clear whether a government sponsor is buying services in the academic marketplace or sustaining a socially desirable scientific activity without instrumental motives, or even doing the latter in the guise of the former—and this creates some problems for social scientists (and occasionally for their government patrons). One of the ironies in the situation, it seems to me, is that despite the considerable "politicization" of research resulting from the circumstances of sponsorship, it is not used as effectively as some advocates wish and some critics fear. In

PIO D. ULIASSI

reviewing these matters, I am led, finally, to conclude that many discussions of social research for policy purposes, especially in the area of foreign affairs, reveal a somewhat technocratic perspective which, among other things, takes a rather narrow view of what the social sciences may have to offer and, moreover, frequently ignores the fact that the use, misuse or nonuse of social research is itself part of a broader political process.

I will deal with a few of these topics empirically, drawing on whatever reliable information is available; others will necessarily call for impressionistic judgments and speculation. It goes almost without saying that as someone closely, if modestly, involved in federal research, I must cope with the bureaucrat's dilemma when he writes for a public beyond the circles of his official colleagues— either to utter platitudes or to commit indiscretions—which social scientists will quickly recognize as a clear case of role conflict.

FEDERAL SUPPORT FOR SOCIAL RESEARCH

A simple fact provides the starting point: federal programs of support for research on foreign affairs are small but important tributaries swelling the river of research gold that flows from Washington. The government has spent about $30 to $40 million annually on such studies in recent years. This is not, perhaps, an impressive amount when compared to all government outlays for the social sciences, which have grown spectacularly in the last decade, but it is still substantial enough to have considerable influence on the work of private scholars who study international politics, foreign and security policy, and the variety of topics conventionally assigned to the category of "foreign areas."[7]

However, money for such research has become much scarcer lately. Congressional and other pressures have forced a measured retrenchment in federal agencies whose bounty once seemed almost unlimited; and the International Education Act of 1966, which seemed to promise much, remains unfunded. According to preliminary estimates, federal allocations for foreign affairs research plunged to some $21 million in the 1970 fiscal year. To make matters worse, private foundations, which once supported international studies generously, increasingly have channelled their resources into domestic programs.[8] The situation has prompted a prestigious political scientist (Karl Deutsch) to warn of a "partial one-sided intellectual disarmament" in tones somewhat reminiscent of similar pronouncements that were common in the more financially austere 1950s, when respected academic leaders divined disastrous consequences if American behavioral and social researchers were overtaken by their Soviet counterparts.[9] Social scientists are perhaps as prone as other mortals to confuse their corporate misfortunes with public calamity, but there is no denying that the funding crisis is all too real and constitutes a serious depression for academic and other organizations that have experienced a revolution of rising expectations and now find themselves the victims of fluctuations in the project marketplace.

I will not try to trace here the many consequences that may follow from such erratic funding. One could assume, for example, that a reduction of about one-third in the budget from one year to the next might have some effect on the quality and direction of research on foreign affairs, on the kinds as well as number of people and institutions that may be attracted to it or repelled from it as financially or professionally unrewarding, and so on. But overall budget levels do not seem to alter drastically some basic patterns that perhaps have a more significant bearing on the present uneasy relationship between the government and the social sciences, and I want to note a few of these—covering sponsors, performers, and programs—drawing on sketchy but still useful information.[10]

Sponsors

In foreign affairs research, as in other fields of science, federal programs are the result of a great number of historical decisions, each carrying its weight of tradition and vested interest, rather than of a deliberately conceived overall policy. What we have is a polycentric system which so far, for better or worse, has defied serious coordination[11] and which few perhaps would pretend represents the most "reasonable" allocation of funds from the public purse that scholars, bureaucrats or politicians might devise. Table 1 gives an overview of sponsorship patterns through a breakdown of "obligations" for the four fiscal years for which such information is now available. The sponsors are grouped into four main categories—three which include operating agencies of various kinds and the fourth, agencies that have a more central or exclusive responsibility for research.[12] The most obvious and elementary fact to emerge from the table is that social research on international and foreign affairs is supported by many agencies and departments.[13]

The material summarized in Table 1 reveals a number of things about the role of operating agencies in the research programs of the federal government. It shows, first of all, that half of the funds dispensed from the federal treasury now come from action units of the executive—that is, from departments and independent agencies that sponsor research as an ancillary or staff function in support of their primary mission. The table reveals a second interesting although hardly startling fact: not all operating agencies have the same enthusiasm or capacity for financing research. With the exception of 1966, the Department of Defense has had a much larger budget for "external" research (studies not carried out within the government itself by regular employees) than the combined budgets of all the civilian agencies dealing mainly with foreign affairs.[14] Finally, it is also clear from the table that the budgets of these civilian agencies taken as a group are more flexible, perhaps more vulnerable, than those of the Department of Defense. Their share of the total budget dropped from a high of 39 percent in 1966 to a low of 14 percent in 1969—a precipitous decline due mainly to the shrunken coffers of the Department of State's Bureau of Educational and Cultural Affairs and of the Agency for International Development. In contrast, the Department of Defense budget has remained stable at about one-third of the federal total—indeed, it has risen a bit from 29 percent in 1966 to 33 percent in 1969. These patterns and trends account for the worries now frequently expressed in Congress and among academics about the "critical imbalance" in the research efforts of the executive units dealing with national security and foreign affairs.

There is more to the tale, however, even if one limits observations to gross trends. It is worth emphasizing that half of all government-financed research on foreign affairs is now administered by civilian agencies with educational, scientific and cultural responsibilities—the Department of Health, Education and Welfare, the National Science Foundation, the Smithsonian Institution and the National Endowment for the Humanities. Indeed, even in the short period covered by the table, such institutions have steadily increased their share of the research budget from about 30 percent in 1966 to 50 percent in 1969; and, despite

Table 1
U.S. Government Agency Obligations – Social Research on International Affairs and Foreign Areas
Fiscal Years 1966-1969*

Agencies and Departments	FY 1966 Amount	FY 1966 % of Total	FY 1967 Amount	FY 1967 % of Total	FY 1968 Amount	FY 1968 % of Total	FY 1969 Amount	FY 1969 % of Total
Educational-Cultural-Scientific								
Department of Health Education & Welfare	$6,627,554	18.55	$10,104,370	24.88	$8,952,303	26.20	$9,498,489	28.49
National Endowment for the Humanities	—		892,440	2.20	702,960	2.06	842,637	2.53
National Science Foundation	3,337,300	9.34	5,686,850	14.00	5,219,230	15.27	5,282,800	15.85
Smithsonian Institution	803,649	2.25	920,231	2.27	1,118,335	3.27	1,175,535	3.53
Total	$10,768,503	30.14	$17,603,891	43.35	$15,992,828	46.80	$16,799,461	50.40
Civilian Foreign Affairs								
Department of State	$6,450,947	18.05	$1,351,679	3.33	$992,688	2.90	$421,844	1.26
Agency for International Development	5,932,708	16.60	5,568,922	13.22	3,510,347	10.27	2,457,682	7.37
Arms Control & Disarmament Agency	828,520	2.32	985,286	2.43	558,238	1.63	678,675	2.04
Peace Corps	265,597	.74	292,829	.72	284,626	.83	639,491	1.92
U.S. Information Agency	427,621	1.20	537,887	1.32	550,268	1.61	589,226	1.77
Total	$13,905,393	38.91	$8,536,603	21.01	$5,896,167	17.24	$4,786,918	14.36
Military								
Army	$4,818,000	13.48	$4,853,005	11.95	$4,412,170	12.91	$4,992,462	14.98
Navy	405,000	1.13	331,762	.82	432,000	1.26	821,000	2.46
Air Force	1,556,000	4.35	1,946,289	4.79	1,702,713	4.98	2,236,578	6.71
Advanced Research Projects Agency	1,227,000	3.43	3,937,000	9.69	2,876,500	8.42	1,358,000	4.07
International Security Affairs	2,000,000	5.60	1,947,632	4.79	1,875,000	5.49	1,752,727	5.26
Miscellaneous	225,000	.63	90,337	.22	132,000	.39	—	—
Total	$10,231,000	28.62	$13,106,025	32.26	$11,430,383	33.45	$11,160,767	33.48
Other								
Dept. of Agriculture	$305,592	.86	$525,062	1.29	$419,868	1.23	$204,687	.61
Dept. of Commerce	—		—		—		16,450	.05
Dept. of Labor	—		—		—		162,700	.49
Exec. Office of the President	—		461,477	1.38	78,756	.23	126,300	.38
National Aeronautics and Space Administration	—		—		355,000	1.04	78,734	.24
Miscellaneous	522,326	1.46	280,892	.69	—		—	
Total	$827,918	2.32	$1,367,431	3.36	$853,624	2.50	$588,871	1.77
GRAND TOTAL	$35,732,814	99.99	$40,613,950	99.99	$34,173,002	99.99	$33,336,017	100.11

*Adapted from *FAR Horizons*, Vol. III, No. 1 January 1970. This is a bimonthly newsletter published by the Department of State's Office of External Research for the inter-agency Foreign Area Research Coordination Group (FAR), a government committee headed by the Department.

overall cuts in federal expenditures in fiscal 1970, preliminary information indicates that the proportions among the major *types* of agencies included in Table 1 remain substantially the same.

There are complex historical reasons for the picture that emerges, but I can only touch on them here. After World War II (the conventional starting point in such matters) many government administrators turned to the social sciences with hope, if not always with confidence, for help in coping with their enlarged bureaucracies and their vastly expanded and varied activities in

PIO D. ULIASSI

world affairs; and they found, among academic intellectuals, many social scientists whose wartime experiences in Washington had given them a taste for close collaboration with federal officials interested in policy-relevant studies. Sponsorship by operating agencies had several advantages in the circumstances of the early postwar years: it gave a pragmatic justification for research at a time when the government was not disposed to finance quests for pure truth; by linking the social sciences to national symbols—military power, national security, Cold War goals—it gave a measure of ideological respectability to intellectual enterprises that were suspected, in some quarters, of subversive tendencies; and it provided a modest niche for the social sciences in the federal system at a time when doubts about their scientific status (especially among natural scientists) made it impracticable to support them in any significant way through such institutions as the National Science Foundation. Since then, the dominant mood has changed considerably in Washington: in and out of Congress, people are more willing to accept a federal responsibility for the social sciences; somewhat suspicious, if anything, of too close and exclusive an affinity between social research and political authorities and interests; and more anxious to find a place for social research in institutions with presumably impeccable credentials as disinterested patrons of science and even the humanities.

A significant progression is evident: Federal support for social research begins, it seems, with narrowly instrumental objectives closely linked to governmental interests and, once legitimated, gradually is modified to serve broader intellectual and social purposes.

Research Performers

After this glance at those in the government who give, let me turn briefly to those in private life who receive—the research "performers," as federal jargon has it. Table 2 summarizes information on over 600 projects in progress or completed during one year only, but it well describes, I think, some of the overall patterns of any recent period.

It shows, for example, that a surprisingly high proportion of all projects (21 percent—141 of the 664 total) are carried out by foreign contractors or grantees, although this, as I will try to show later, probably exaggerates the actual "internationalization" of

TABLE 2

Distribution of Active Projects
(By Types of Sponsors and Researchers)
June 1968 – July 1969

Types of Agencies and Departments	Types of Contractors or Grantees				
	US Academic	US Non-academic	Foreign	Other	Total
Education Cultural Scientific	178	11	84	3	276
Civilian Foreign Affairs	96	38	28	12	174
Military	53	100	3	–	156
Other	23	9	26	–	58
Totals	350	158	141	15	664

(Compiled from various sources.)

government-fostered studies. It also reveals that among the domestic recipients of grants or (more commonly) contracts, commercial and nonprofit organizations equipped to conduct social research now compete effectively with universities—a point worth elaborating.

On the basis of the common assumption that, as a rule, the social sciences flourish best in campus soil, it is significant to find that slightly over half of all the projects included in the calculation were carried out by Americans working in universities, an indication that research on foreign affairs is still, by and large, a predominantly academic enterprise. The system, however, is not overly generous to those who toil in academia: they do, probably, a smaller proportion of all studies financed by federal agencies than their relative numbers along among all active professionals would lead one to expect.[15] This is not entirely the result of conscious design but is related to and in a sense caused by the continuing financial weight of operating agencies: Although the educational-cultural-scientific agencies included in Table 2 placed 94 percent of the domestically-based projects (178 of 189) with social scientists attached to universities, the civilian foreign affairs agencies placed 72 percent (96 of 134) and the military agencies only 35 percent (53 of 153).

Which leads to the other side of the story. Nonacademic research organizations now exist in numbers and varieties unknown in the early post-World War II years, when government sponsors of mission-oriented work relied heavily on universities, partly because institutional alternatives were not readily available. Such organizations have become extremely important performers of research directly related to federal policies and programs in national security and foreign affairs. But it is difficult to generalize about them. They include affiliates of industrial firms; free lance operations with conspicuously developed entrepreneurial skills; and nonprofit institutes in bewildering diversity—some tenuously linked to universities and others completely autonomous, some emulating academic styles of work and others scorning them, some virtually bound to a single governmental client and others more catholic in the institutions and publics they consider themselves qualified and committed to serve.

"No generalization is worth a damn," Justice Holmes once said—but he urged men to try to form "general propositions" anyway. The academic—nonacademic categories used here imply a familiar general proposition of sorts: that there are meaningful variations in the kinds of professionals typically found in such different institutional settings, in the kinds of work they prefer to do, and in the way that they characteristically define their relationships to patrons or clients. My impression—the evidence is hardly conclusive for some points—is that nonacademic researchers working in the field of foreign affairs do tend to differ from their academic colleagues in certain respects that are especially pertinent in defining the impact of the social sciences on public policy. A few tentative generalizations must serve as examples. First, they probably span a narrower ideological range than their academic peers[16] and in their particular environments they are for the most part well insulated from the winds of campus political passions. Second, they are on the whole more favorably disposed toward applied research, which after all has a certain cachet for practical administrators who are one of their primary reference groups; indeed, nonacademic social scientists can become highly sensitized to the "needs" of their clients, undistracted by ancillary functions such as teaching and unencumbered by pressures to do academically more prestigious types of research.[17] Finally, nonacademic social scientists are more prone than their university colleagues to accept contractual relationships involving considerable deference to their clients' formulations of research problems and a measure of tolerance for the proprietary demands of sponsors.[18]

Nonacademic research organizations have, in any event, established themselves as a new institution displaying some of the characteristics associated with its middle position between the intramural intelligence and research organizations of the government and the completely autonomous academy.[19]

Characteristics of Programs

Even the most cursory survey of government-sponsored work would not be complete without some discussion of the kinds of work that federal agencies support. Although there is no single listing of studies, the available information provides ample evidence of the scope and variety of programs. An inventory of research on foreign affairs recently published by the Department of State, for example, while incomplete, includes more than 500 projects carried out under the auspices of 13 major agencies during a single year.[20] Yet not too long ago, Herbert Kelman, a friendly critic, could say that there was a distressing dearth of federal support for basic research on foreign policy and foreign areas that could meet the "criteria of true independence and international conception."[21] How accurate is Kelman's observation?

In truth, basic research has not been a dominant feature of federal programs, most of which have been inspired by more immediately practical objectives than the advancement of social science. Most of the international and foreign area studies financed by the government have been justified by being linked to the missions of operating units of the executive branch and any program that has strayed too conspicuously from applied studies of almost self-evidence short-run utility the possible accusation of "irrelevance" from within the bureaucracy and the always present danger of political suspicion or attack from without. All of which has not prevented some operating agencies, particularly the Department of Defense, from nourishing, over the years, a considerable body of research in psychology and the social sciences of more than transient intellectual interest. But even now, despite the soundly established position of programs not linked to executive units engaged in foreign policy and operations, only about one-third of the federal budget is allocated for what the sponsors themselves will publicly describe as "basic" research.[22]

PIO D. ULIASSI

To take one of Kelman's other points, it is difficult to say how "independent" research funded by Washington—basic or other—is or should be. Ideally, one could hope for some balance between commissioned research responding to the practical concerns of administrators—and reflecting their views and policies to some extent—and more autonomous research uncolored by official interests and unfettered by political considerations. A tendency toward this ideal can be sensed in two characteristics of the present situation. One is pluralism: The federal government provides many alternative sources of support for research on foreign affairs within and among agencies and even among different kinds of agencies and thus provides some protection from complete dependence on a single client or patron. But pluralism is more limited than it seems. Most studies in agricultural economics, for example, are naturally financed by the Department of Agriculture and it is no revelation that most studies of education abroad are financed by the Office of Education; but even in a broader subject area such as "political processes" most studies are financed by a relatively small number of agencies. The other characteristic is the growing role of grant-giving educational, scientific and cultural institutions with programs that are more responsive to academic interests than those of operating agencies often can be. But here again there are limits: Such institutions do not administer, as a rule, major programs dealing with the more central problems and issues of contemporary foreign policy. In short, the more specific a research topic, the more likely it is to depend for financial support on a single or on a few potential sponsors; and the more central a project is to contemporary political issues the more likely it is to be financed by operating agencies which themselves are prominent actors in foreign affairs. But on balance, the conclusions reached by a committee of sociologists are, I believe, no more than just: "Government research support is now more often given for purposes and through mechanisms that are consistent with scholarly autonomy than ever before . . . " [23]

Kelman points to another aspect of government-financed research—the extent and nature of participation by foreign scholars. Two-thirds or more of all projects carried out with federal money involve some travel or research abroad, although the proportions vary among agencies. Most of these projects require only informal or casual encounters with foreign scholars. But a far from negligible number call for international collaboration of some sort, with foreign specialists providing technical services, engaging in their own locally conceived studies, or even occasionally joining American colleagues in genuinely collaborative cross-cultural research. Nevertheless, despite the good intentions of many federal administrators, relatively few projects financed by the federal government provide for a degree of foreign participation that constitutes, as one official document puts it, a "truly symmetrical relationship between American and foreign specialists." [24] Whatever the intellectual consequences of this exclusion may be (presumably foreign scholars might occasionally have significantly different perspectives on research problems), it helps to fire the suspicions of "scientific colonialism" that have been aired so frequently in recent years.

Obviously commissioned research still dominates federal programs. But it would be rash to conclude that commissioned research is always narrowly subservient to the interests of its putative sponsors. The research needs of operating agencies seldom emerge spontaneously within bureaucracies but are often articulated for or with them by private consultants and therefore reflect the intellectual and political outlooks of some sectors, at least, of the highly diverse communities of social scientists. Moreover, mission-related government requirements occasionally have served as a rationale to support basic work under contractual conditions that respected the favored researchers' freedom of inquiry. Under the circumstances, it is understandable that many social scientists have considered the "impurity" of funds from operating agencies of only slight importance and in any case a minor price to pay—so long as private or governmental alternatives were not readily available—for the public benefits (and no doubt the private pleasures) of scientific affluence. One could make the best of an imperfect world and prudently echo St. Augustine's cry: "Make me chaste, O Lord—but not yet."

The aforementioned facts about government-sponsored studies on foreign affairs are easy to establish and, I think, beyond serious controversy. Government help has made possible a vast amount of work that probably would not have been done, or not done so thoroughly, without federal aid and the help has been channeled through an increasing variety of agencies, mechanisms and programs. Moreover, government support has prompted or strengthened a number of institutional developments of considerable significance. For example, it has enshrined the project system as the normal research arrangement and of course has encouraged the evolution and proliferation of nonacademic organizations, the "think tanks" and their commercial imitators and competitors. Even social scientists themselves have been affected. Once virtual strangers to the inner ways of government, they are now—as someone once said of RAND men—almost as thick in Washington as Jesuits were in the seventeenth century courts of Vienna and Madrid.

What such facts may imply for the social sciences and, for that matter, the government is something else again, and is far more difficult a matter to deal with objectively.

SOME CONSEQUENCES OF SPONSORSHIP

Even such a rapid survey of the patterns of international and foreign area studies favored by governmental agencies suggests a number of problems and issues. As Albert Biderman among others has remarked, the dominant note of public debate changed in the sixties "from concern with achieving greater acceptance and support for social science to apprehensions regarding the corrupting influence of dependence on government financing." [25] But "corruption" is far too strong a word and hardly does justice to the range of opinions, which cover a wide spectrum from those of "establishment" social scientists who look upon the government experience and find it at least passingly good to those of radical critics who indiscriminately condemn all who accept federal monies as a "willing stable of intellectual mercenaries convinced that their work is independently conceived and in the national interest." [26] I know of no fully satisfactory way of categorizing the types of concerns that are expressed in this debate, but it seems to me that for international studies, at least, arguments tend to cluster around three topics—the intellectual, political and ethical consequences or implications of government sponsorship. All three kinds of arguments are closely linked to the uses, or alleged uses, of research by government bureaucracies and perhaps this will excuse my venturing into observations that normally are reserved to those close to the academic scene.

Social arrangements, fortunately, are for the most part too messy to encourage us to reduce all intellectual work to the presumed interests of its patrons, but it is only common sense to assume that the problems that are selected for study and the ways they are formulated are influenced if not mechanically determined by government interest and support. Let me try to identify some of these influences.

The selection of topics, which is affected both by negative and by positive factors, poses the easiest problem. On the negative side there are, at any given time, powerful conventions regarding what it is inappropriate for *any* organ of the government to sponsor in the social sciences. The most conspicuous and significant case is the treatment of American society itself. Except as incidental inputs into planning and evaluation studies, it is difficult to find, among the thousands of government financed projects of the last two decades, any significant body of work on intrasocietal topics: the characteristics of American elites, bureaucratic and political processes, the underlying attitudes, interests and institutions that may affect United States foreign relations. The operating agencies are "other" rather than "self" oriented when it comes to foreign affairs as an area of research, more inclined to think in terms of the international environments in which they must act than in terms of the domestic system in which they are imbedded. And both they and the federal agencies with more purely scientific responsibilities are wary of probing into contemporary national affairs that have not, as yet, been sanctioned as proper subjects for government-financed studies.[27] Cynics may consider this only a case of political discretion as the better part of scientific valor, but there is more to it than that.[28]

On the positive side, agency budgets loom as the controlling factor. Apart from areas that are politically taboo, the focus of research reflects the relative distribution of funds among units of the executive branch. No agencies are completely free to act as patrons for all kinds of research—certainly not the operating ones, although some have enjoyed a remarkable latitude in developing their programs. The Department of State, United States Information Agency (USIA), Arms Control and Disarmament Agency (ACDA), Agency for International Development (AID), the Peace

PIO D. ULIASSI

Corps and the many units of the Department of Defense—all have their particular interests as well as their common concerns in research and their particular interests naturally tend to dominate their programs. What and how much is done, then, on economic or political development, social change, insurgency or counterinsurgency, "psychological warfare," arms control and so on depends largely not on whether such topics titillate scientific curiosity, or respond to some abstract notion of the public good, but on the financial resources of particular bureaucracies committed, by the nature of their functions, to pay some attention to them: an elementary but hardly a trivial observation.[29] Funding variations among the executive departments have an especially marked impact on research patterns because of the already noted absence of any effective mechanism for establishing government-wide goals and priorities in foreign affairs research even for the operating agencies.

It is more difficult to demonstrate that sponsorship seriously affects the way in which research problems, once selected, are formulated. This is not an overresearched subject and the evidence I can muster is, for the most part, anecdotal and impressionistic. However, operating agencies do often claim a share in the shaping of research, at least to the extent of insisting on "relevance" to their perceived needs, with some interesting consequences.[30] It is also clear that occasionally even "undirected" research may be subtly affected by sponsorship: Camelot, to take an overworked but usefully familiar case, bore the intellectual marks of its gestation in an environment sensitive to the counterinsurgency interests of its remarkably tolerant Army sponsors, according to some commentators.[31] But what is probably as important as the flow of influence in individual cases is the apparent statistical tendency for government sponsors to seek out or to attract social scientists whose general outlook is congenial to them: "A hundred flowers have no doubt bloomed," a reviewer of American political-military literature once observed, "but they have almost without exception been tactical flowers on a single strategic stem."[32]

This is not the occasion to pursue this subject. My objective is simply to note what should be obvious, that government sponsorship is not indiscriminate or "neutral" and that it affects what is done and how. This is a matter of some importance both to those who have an academic interest in the advancement of knowledge and to those who are concerned about the distinctive strengths and weaknesses of sponsored research as an imput into the policy process.

Politicization of Research

But for the moment, I want to discuss a second aspect of the linkage that has been established between many social scientists interested in foreign affairs and the government: the "politicization" of research, or what may be described as the transformation of scholarly activities into political acts. All social research admittedly is political in some sense: the most cloistered scholars, comfortable in their once-secure retreats, act politically as they probe into the nature of society, help to define social problems and issues, and influence, however indirectly, public decisions on the allocation of values. But social science financed by operating agencies is political in a special way: it is connected to the nonscientific purposes of its sponsors, governmental organizations which themselves have, as a rule, jurisdictional responsibilities in the area of inquiry and known or suspected policy preferences in it. The association affects both the way in which research is administered and the way in which it is perceived by attentive publics here and abroad. Let me be a bit more specific.

Whatever social scientists may think, most government administrators have no doubt that when they finance mission-related research in foreign affairs they are doing something "for which the government must bear a degree of political or diplomatic responsibility that is not usually associated with federal research support motivated largely or exclusively by an interest in the advancement of science," as one official put it candidly. [33] In plain language, this means that the government claims in principle, if not always in practice: first, a considerable share in defining the scope and objectives of research; second, some control over research activities, especially over field work abroad that may prove politically or diplomatically sensitive; and finally, some control over the dissemination of research information and results—all of this justified by policy considerations which "sometimes require a degree of confidentiality even in the posing of research questions closely related to foreign policy and operations" and by respect for foreign publics who may not always be edified by the candor of science in the service of policy: [34] "The good ambassador," goes

PIO D. ULIASSI

an ancient diplomatic injunction, "will watch over his words, never deride the country he is in, nor disparage the prince to whom he is accredited." The point here is not the legitimacy of such claims—although I think them reasonable—but the fact that politicization prompts political authorities (including those strongly committed to freedom of inquiry) to demand a voice in research decisions that traditionally have been reserved to social scientists and their professional peers.

There is another aspect to politicization that has been made familiar by the difficulties of many American social scientists attempting to work in developing countries. The association of research with actors in controversial areas of public affairs also inevitably colors the way in which people here and abroad perceive it. It is difficult in practice, however admirable in theory, to compartmentalize attitudes toward social scientific work—even basic work—from its sponsors and what they may symbolize at a particular time and place. Thus the financial nexus between social research and operating agencies makes it, to some extent, hostage to political fortune. There is something ironic, for example, in the fact that much of the social scientific work financed by the federal government was once legitimized by being related to the practical concerns of operating agencies and is now sometimes stigmatized for the same reason.[35] And I need hardly elaborate the fact that the linking of research to operating sponsors has sometimes proved detrimental both to United States foreign relations and to the interests of private scholars in maintaining a favorable climate for research abroad. Foreign publics, intellectuals, and leaders are understandably inclined to see such research as serving political rather than disinterested scientific purposes and to react to it on the basis of their own calculations and ideological dispositions—sometimes favorably and sometimes not.[36]

Robert Nisbet once put it tartly: "When a major Federal department—be it Defense, State, or Commerce—sponsors a scientific project, even one composed of dues-paying psychologists and sociologists, it is elementary that not even the elixir of scientific method is sufficient—to wipe away the fact of sponsorship."[37]

The Moral Dimension

It is impossible to discuss the politics of research without at some point drifting into a discussion of professional ethics. One other consequence of the federal government's heavy investment in national security and foreign area research has been an increased concern for the moral dimensions of the social sciences. Not so long ago, Edward Shils put his hope for protection against the potential abuses of research in the academic community itself: "The social sciences," he wrote, "are conducted within and under the auspices of the great universities, which nearly everywhere in the West are the Gibraltars of genuine humanism."[38] Whether or not the universities were or remain such bastions of humane learning, individual scholars, professional associations, and the government itself have, in the last half dozen years especially, argued the need for more explicit and perhaps more formal standards of professional conduct.

The fundamental reason for this, I suppose, is to be found in the increasing involvement of social scientists with the rest of society. Part of the new involvement is of course due to changes in the social sciences themselves—their quantitative expansion, their greater precision, their "intrusiveness" into once confidential spheres of private or public life, their greater relevance for detailed application and their potentially greater effectiveness as instruments of manipulation or control. Part of it is also due to the shift in the institutional setting of social scientific work; the proliferation of nonacademic centers of applied research raises such questions, for example, as whether the people working in such institutions are or should be bound by precisely the same codes as those that may apply to the academy.[39] And, finally, part of the involvement results from the enormously expanded influence of exogenous forces, mainly governmental, on the work being done in many fields of social research. It is this last development that has provided the occasion for a great deal of personal and professional soul searching among social scientists.

At the personal level, the problem usually comes down to the question of what political or moral responsibilities the social scientist incurs in the choice or acceptance of financial patrons, especially when his sponsors or clients are public agencies with operational missions. If his research is "applied" he is linked unambiguously with the uses to which his professional skills and knowledge may be put. If his work is "basic" there is frequently a reasonable presumption that, given a sponsor's interests, some applications of his findings (among many conceivably possible ones) are more likely than others.[40] But even if his work bears no relationship to the political actions of a sponsor, the social scientist who accepts funds gives his benefactor, in return, a measure of legitimation—to the institution if not to a particular policy or set of policies. Under such circumstances, a social scientist can hardly be morally indifferent as citizen if not as scientist, to the source of funds, even if he retains full freedom to pursue his intellectual interests.

At a more clearly professional level, the problem has been to identify significant problems of ethics, to clarify what are complex issues in which the "facts" themselves are sometimes elusive, and to prescribe normative rules that are, it seems, extremely difficult to operationalize. It is impressive to see how many professional associations, other private groups, and components of the federal government itself have launched studies, issued reports and sketched guidelines dealing with standards of professional conduct—and how many of these deal with the troublesome issues associated with international and foreign area studies financed by operating agencies—especially such matters as the acknowledgement or nonacknowledgement of financial support, classification or open publication, and the obligations of social scientists and their patrons or clients to foreign publics, colleagues and authorities. [41]

In short, the more extensive and intimate involvement of social scientists with other institutions, especially governmental ones in the field of foreign affairs, has created difficult and sometimes novel problems of personal moral choice and honorable professional conduct for which the inherited canons of academic scholarship provide neither clear guidelines nor firmly institutionalized rules.

Almost 20 years ago, Robert Merton and Daniel Lerner pointed to what they considered "a central problem confronting the policy-oriented social scientist today, as he faces the choice of affiliations with the academic, business or government communities. If he is to play an effective role in putting his knowledge to work, it is increasingly necessary that he affiliate with a bureaucratic power-structure in business or government. This, however, often requires him to abdicate the academic privilege of exploring policy possibilities which he regards as significant. If, on the other hand, he remains unaffiliated to a power structure in order to preserve fuller freedom of choice, he usually loses the resources to carry through his investigations on an appropriate scale and the opportunities of getting his findings accepted by policy makers as a basis for actions." [42] Since then, social scientists have indeed affiliated with the government on a scale that Merton and Lerner probably did not anticipate and the problems for social scientists resulting from the affiliation have been considerable, as I have tried to suggest here. But has the linkage really led to more and better use of social scientific knowledge in public policy? This is a difficult and perhaps an impossible question to answer with any assurance.

THE USES, OR NONUSES, OF SOCIAL SCIENCE

In theory, all the social research financed by the operating agencies of the federal government is supposed to be useful to them. In practice, the situation is quite different and many people in Washington, as well as many social scientists, are all too well aware of the discrepancy between the government's investment in research and its actual use of the product.

This, of course, is an impressionistic observation and one, more-over, that has to be qualified. In the first place, private social scientists routinely provide officials with a vast amount of descriptive information which the government, like any sophisticated bureaucracy, absorbs in vast amounts, however selectively, and probably applies in some way. There are also areas in which the more direct and specific impact of research on policy is fairly evident. Perhaps the most conspicuous example is provided by the work of RAND and similar organizations, which has had a significant influence on strategic doctrine and defense management techniques. And of course there is always the climate of opinion in which official policy is made and which social scientists perhaps help to mold more than most intellectuals.

Nevertheless, there are limits, however vaguely defined, to what can be claimed. It would be hard to say, for example, that the Department of Defense, which has fostered so much social science, has really applied all its studies. The Agency for International Development has for years struggled with the problem of communicating research findings convincingly to those charged with policy and operations. The Department of State has had, on the whole, mixed results even with its modest contract program. On balance, it is hardly an exaggeration to say that the utilization of extramural research leaves a great deal to be desired from the point of view of those who do not share the extreme skeptic's opinion that the relevance of social science to public policy, at least to foreign policy, is largely a figment of the academic imagination.

There is, no doubt, "an irreducible gap between research and action which, no matter how much we may narrow it, and how frequently we may bridge it, will never be closed," as a high federal research administrator has observed.[43] There are any number of useful ways of trying to understand the reasons for this gap; I find it convenient, in a brief survey such as this, to see it in terms of relevance, communication and bureaucratic processes.

What Is Relevant?

One of the more common complaints voiced by people in Washington is that a great deal of work in the social sciences seems meaningless to those who have to get on with the practical business of governing. For example, E. Raymond Platig of the State Department, though a firm advocate for the social sciences, has some harsh words on the subject: "The policy and program implications of much private research are either so irrelevant to the world view of the policy-action officer or so implicit that a major and often unrewarding intellectual effort is required to extract them."[44]

It should hardly be necessary to insist that behavioral and social scientists do some things that are quite unrelated to public policy in any immediately practical sense, but it *is* necessary because it has become fashionable, in some quarters, to justify practically every scientific activity in utilitarian terms. Some of this, I suspect, is probably no more than the expression of a mild form of anti-intellectualism which is uncomfortable with science for its own sake as an intrinsically satisfying play of human curiosity. But I also suspect that the sometimes heavy dependence of social scientists on operating agencies has encouraged them to make, more or less consciously, premature or extravagant claims for the utility of their wares, with the result that they frequently sound, to government officials, like the deaf men of literature muttering answers to questions that no one has asked.

The search for relevance sometimes can be frustrating to the social scientist and disillusioning to his client. Most people in policy or operational positions are inclined to look to research (as they do to its intramural version, "intelligence") for "facts"—only to find, all too often, that the facts of the social scientist may not be any fuller or better than those provided by common sense and their own resources. They look for studies with definite "findings"—and discover that there are rarely definitive answers to complex policy problems. They are encouraged, especially by more scientifically-oriented researchers, to expect predictions—only to discover that the predictive powers of social scientists are usually little more than an aspiration when applied to the concrete and often unique cases with which they have to cope.

I am exaggerating, of course, but one essential condition for winning acceptance for the social sciences in the policy process is to do work that is both meaningful to the man of action *and* distinctively "social scientific"—that is, that appears to him as something different from and superior to, folk knowledge, high journalism, or the wisdom of any politically seasoned sage. This is seldom easy.

Problems of Communication

However we define relevance, the application of social research to policy matters involves communication. The social scientist is not usually himself the policy-maker (although a growing number of people in Washington have some training in the social sciences) and ways must be found to bring the two together. Social scientists, accustomed to the conventions of the academy, tend to ignore this problem, or at least to assume that the communications model that serves to bind a community of professional intellectuals, with its formal emphasis on scholarly publication in a common technical language, is roughly transferable to the political realm. This is questionable.

The first difficulty in communication is, as everyone knows, getting attention. Most bureaucrats and higher officials simply do not have the time, even if they have the inclination and preparation, to peruse the scholarly literature that may have some bearing on their work. Something probably could be done to improve communications through the use of "middlemen" and "translations." But the value of such devices is limited by the nature of social science itself. If, except in the most narrowly technical fields, what the social sciences have to offer are new perspectives, new interpretations, rather than conclusive findings and firm policy recommendations, then the communication that is required must be something more than a condensed and mechanical transmission of "findings." What is called for is something akin to a dialogue—a difficult and time-consuming process.

Even this may imply an overly rational model of communication. As we move from more technical areas to more complex problems of social and political analysis, prediction and prescription, research itself becomes more difficult, more infused with values, more tentative in its results. At the same time, the policymakers to whom it is addressed are themselves men and women of flesh and blood who cannot be expected to respond to research, in all cases, with dispassionate intellectuality. It is remarkable, I think, how little attention has been paid to this aspect of the communication process. We would never expect to change attitudes, for example, without understanding something about the functions they serve in the psychic economy of an individual; and we rarely assume that they can be changed by the gentle persuasiveness of reason alone. Yet this is precisely what we do assume most of the time and almost casually when we talk about the communicating research that is relevant to policy matters.

The Bureaucratic Context

This rather pessimistic observation leads me to a final point on research utilization. Policy-making, we all too easily forget, is a social process—as Raymond Bauer put it, "a social process with intellectual elements contained within it rather than an intellectual process" alone.[45] To illustrate, let me show how one senior RAND analyst, James Schlesinger, once described this social process in a bureaucratic organization: "Whatever their disciplinary background," he notes, analysts tend to treat policymaking "as if it were governed by a rational and unified deciding unit." But

The reality is quite different. Decisions are nominally made by senior political figures who are harried, have insufficient time to study problems in detail, who are gripped by emotions of their youth or by prior experiences, and who are susceptible to claims made by subordinate groups which are couched in a way to appeal to their prejudices. Below them are a set of mutually jealous and warring bureaucratic groups, clamoring for resources and anxious to protect established preserves. To the extent that they are not closely watched, the subordinate bureaucratic groups will attempt to achieve their objectives quietly or even surreptitiously. Moreover, their capacity for resistance to high-level objectives enunciated from above, but to which they take exception, is breathtaking. Actual programs and allocative decisions will consequently diverge quite sharply from those that would be predicted on the assumption of a national intelligence. Instead they will be strongly influenced by prejudice, incompetency, and by infighting, deviousness, and bootlegging within the bureaucracies. Changes which appeal rational and desirable will be compromised half to death, and the compromises themselves will be slow in coming. [46]

Those who have worked in bureaucratic organizations or have studied them can judge for themselves whether Schesinger exaggerates, but I doubt that anyone would consider him completely off the mark. But very little serious research has been done on the bureaucratic aspects of decision-making, or for that matter on the way in which bureaucratic conflicts and choices themselves are constrained by the larger political system. And, consequently, very little is known about the role of knowledge in such a process.

CONCLUDING OBSERVATIONS

Let me round out this essay by recapitulating some themes.

The social sciences and the federal government need each other and whatever the strains in their relationship, the relationship itself is now firmly established. Social research has become, in considerable measure, "big" science, dependent for its continued vigor on the kind of financial assistance that only the federal government can provide, even if private sponsors help to ensure pluralism and to encourage innovation. In international and foreign area studies, the federal government itself now provides support in forms that are more consonant with traditional images of what the scholar-scientist ought to be than was the case in the years immediately following World War II, even with the continued predominance in many sectors, of operating agencies and their interest in policy-relevant studies tailored to their largely self-defined requirements.

Yet, despite the utilitarian emphasis in government sponsorship, we know very little about how the social sciences are used by public agencies. We can see that much research is simply ignored even by its sponsors, that some may be used for special pleading before the political act and for legitimation after, and that some of it may actually have some independent effect on policy decisions. But there is little empirical evidence of a systematic kind about such things. And there is no really satisfactory model of the uses of social sciences in public policy. The expert-client (or patient) relationship established in such areas as law, applied psychology and medicine, for example, does not seem to fit the realities of bureaucratic and political processes.

Which brings me to the final and most tentative observations. To the extent that there is a model implicit in current practices, it seems to be a rather technocratic one. One manifestation of this technocratic orientation is, I believe, the striking emphasis that is placed on sponsored research as the most direct and reliable way of influencing public policy—when sponsored work can be, in most instances, only a small and partial selection of scientific material that is in some way relevant to public debate and choice. To the extent that sponsored work must be roughly consonant with the basic values and outlooks of its sponsors, it seems most likely to be used for the implementation rather than the formulation of policy and thus the social scientist who commits himself largely to sponsored work tends toward an "engineering" conception of his role. Another aspect of the technocratic orientation is the almost exclusive commitment of policy-oriented social scientists to the executive branch of the government. The interest of many operating agencies in research is, I am convinced, an excellent thing in its own terms, whatever the problems it leads to. Few, I think, could seriously argue that modern government would be more efficient, more responsive to public need, more humane even, if it were cut off even more than it is from social research and social scientists. Nevertheless, it is curious that so little thought has been given to the implications, for a democratic polity, of the cult of social science expertise and the conspicuously uneven distribution of intellectual resources among the various components of the political system.

The views expressed in this paper are strictly those of the author and do not in any sense reflect the official position of, or even the informal consensus within, the Department of State.

NOTES

[1] Ithiel de Sola Pool, "The Necessity for Social Scientists Doing Research for Governments," in Irving Louis Horowitz (ed.). *The Rise and Fall of Project Camelot* (Cambridge and London: M.I.T. Press, 1967), p. 268. At his pugnacious best, Pool is well worth reading as one of the most informed and candid academic paladins of social research sponsored by operating agencies of all kinds.

[2] The recent literature reflecting such views or anxieties is so vast that I can only mention a few examples that I have found particularly helpful or provocative, in addition to some of the papers in the just-cited Horowitz volume. Among the more polemical works are two that deal with sponsored research incidentally as part of a broader critique of liberal scholarship: Theodore Roszak (ed.), *The Dissenting Academy* (New York: Vintage, 1968) and Noam Chomsky, *American Power and the New Mandarins* (New York: Pantheon, 1969). A review article by Philip Green, "Science, Government, and the Case of RAND—A Singular Pluralism" *World Politics*, Vol. XX, No. 2, January 1968, pp. 301-26) is a rare and controversial example of a thoughtful examination of government-sponsored work in a nonprofit setting seen as part of a larger bureaucratic-political process. Perhaps the single most useful collection is Elizabeth T. Crawford and Albert D. Biderman (eds.), *Social Scientists and International Affairs* (New York: John Wiley, 1969). The value of the reprinted articles, which themselves cover a number of issues from a variety of perspectives, is augmented by the editors' commentaries and by their conscious effort to deal with the subject in terms of a "sociology of social science." I should add that concern about the impact of government funding on research is not limited to radical criticis. For example, a pillar of the academic and Washington Establishment, while an Under Secretary of State, told members of the International Studies Association: " . . . I am not one who views the development of large programs of Government research financing happily, especially in the social sciences. I rejoice that so many people still do their research alone, with relatively small budgets obtained from their universities or from a scattering or private foundations, and write their books without the benefit of expensive apparatus which in the end can only be provided by Government." Eugene V. Rostow, "Safeguarding Academic Freedom," reprinted in *Far Horizons,* Vol. 1, No. 3, May 1968, p. 2.

[3] Here I am glossing over important differences in the mechanisms devised by various Washington agencies to administer research. The role of central bureaucracies is modified, in many instances, by the use of professional advisory groups even in operating agencies and, in the more scientifically-oriented institutions, by panels of private behavioral and social scientists with virtual decision-making power over grants.

[4] Of course almost all government departments are now involved in foreign affairs and it is difficult to make a clear distinction between domestic and foreign policy. Still, when the primary object of official attention and operations are political entities outside the state's jurisdiction we may reasonably

PIO D. ULIASSI

talk about "foreign" policy, with "high policy" defined as those elements of policy that are, in the eyes of political authorities, most closely related to national welfare, prestige and security.

[5] Anyone familiar with the content of government-sponsored programs over the past two decades would question, I believe, the assumption that there has been a change in these programs sufficient to explain recent hostility toward them. If anything, I would say on the basis of very rough impressions, most government projects are now more congruent with dominant academic values than those of ten or twenty years ago. It is interesting to note, for example, that hardly anyone seems to have questioned the propriety of Air Force funding, in the early 1950s, of work on a World Urban Resources Index by a university-affiliated institute, with the expectation that the project would "enable analysts to make comparative studies of urban and regional complexes and develop more dependable methods for the selection of air targets," according to an account of the military applications of sociology. See Raymond V. Bowers, "The Military Establishment," in Paul F. Lazarsfeld, William H. Sewell and Harold L. Wilensky (eds.), *The Uses of Sociology* (New York: Basic Books, 1967), pp. 241-42.

[6] This is not to say that ideological peace reigned supreme in the forties and fifties. But radical dissidents—and even not-so-radical ones—were evidently fewer, quieter and in any case less concerned about the impact of government funding on the social sciences since government programs did not loom very large.

[7] Funds for research on foreign affairs have ranged from about 15 percent of total federal expenditures on the behavioral and social sciences in the mid-sixties to about 10 percent in more recent years. Apart from publications of the National Science Foundation, the most convenient sources of information on funding are: *Far Horizons,* a bimonthly newsletter issued by the Office of External Research of the Department of State, which covers programs in foreign affairs; and *The Behavioral and Social Sciences: Outlook and Needs,* a report by The Behavioral and Social Sciences Survey Committee created under the auspices of the Social Science Research Council and the National Academy of Sciences (Englewood Cliffs, New Jersey: Prentice Hall, 1969), which includes a chapter on federal financing of the behavioral and social sciences.

[8] See Education and World Affairs, *A Crisis of Dollars: The Funding Threat to International Affairs in U.S. Higher Education.* (New York: Education and World Affairs, 1968).

[9] Deutsch's statement appeared in what I believe was a fugitive memorandum several years ago that I have not been able to retrace. The earlier prophets were a committee formed at the initiative of then Vice President Richard Nixon and their views may be found in a phamphlet, *National Support for Behavioral Sciences* (Washington, D. C., February 1958). According to Harold Orlans, a master at deflating scientific pretensions, although Mr. Nixon's "subsequent recollection of the group was courteous, rumor has it that officials were so appalled at the sums requested that the group's final report . . . had even less influence than its contents merited." See Orlans, "Social Science Research in U.S. National Science Policies," unpublished remarks prepared for the UNESCO Round Table on Social Research Policy and Organization, Copenhagen, 1969, pp. 17-17.

[10] For two other analyses based on the records of the Department of State and covering substantially the subjects of this section, see: Department of State, Foreign Affairs Research Council, *A Report on the First Three Years,* August 1968 (Xeroxed; available from the Department's Office of External Research); and Cyril E. Black, "Government-Sponsored Research in International Studies" *World Politics,* Vol. XXII, No. 4, July 1970, pp. 582-96). In 1964, the Department of State took the initiative in creating a voluntary interagency Foreign Area Research Coordination Group (known as FAR) as a means of encouraging consultation among federal organizations financing research on foreign affairs and as a medium for discussing common interests and problems. FAR serves as a useful function, but its most ardent defenders would, I believe, make modest claims about its effectiveness in "coordinating" the research satrapies of Washington.

[11] In 1964, the Department of State took the initiative in creating a voluntary interagency Foreign Area Research Coordination Group (known as FAR) as a means of encouraging consultation among federal organizations financing research on foreign affairs and as a medium for discussing common interests and problems. FAR serves a useful function, but its most ardent defenders would, I believe, make modest claims about its effectiveness in "coordinating" the research satrapies of Washington.

[12] Nothing in life is simple. The Department of Health, Education and Welfare is an "operating" agency too, but I still think it appropriate to link it with Washington's culturally and scientifically oriented institution.

[13] If administratively distinct programs, rather than departments and agencies, are counted, there are more than 30 sponsors of foreign affairs research in the executive branch of government.

[14] But we must be wary of statistics. The 1966 figures for the Department of State included more than $5,000,000 allocated by the Bureau of Educational and Cultural Affairs for institutional grants which the Department decided, upon reflection, did not strictly qualify for inclusion in a survey of research financing. They were not included in later years.

[15] This is an informed guess based on crude comparisons of professional employment. For patterns of employment of economists, psychologists, sociologists and political scientists in the National Scientific Register, see talbe in Neil J. Smelser and James A. Davis, *Sociology* (Englewood Cliffs, N.J.: Prentice-Hall, 1969), p. 130. Without pursuing the complications of this problem here, there is presumptive evidence for the statement in the text.

[16] This appears to conflict with Roy Licklider's finding that among specialists on nuclear weapons policy the locus of employment is not correlated with significant intellectual or political differences. See pp. 000-000. There are other ways of looking at the problem, however, even if limited to weapons policy matters. For example, in Robert Levine's *The Arms Debate* (Cambridge: Harvard University Press, 1963), *passim* those social scientists he classifies as "anti-Communist marginalists" and "middle marginalists"—the two categories that I know contain the largest number of people who have worked with government funds-are found in *both* academic and non-academic settings. The "antiwar marginalists" and the "antiwar systemists,"

PIO D. ULIASSI

however, include numerous academics but practically no social scientists identified with a nonprofit or commercial research institute actively engaged in doing contract work for clients. See also below, f.n. 32.

[17]It is interesting to note, for example, in view of the pattern of government funding, that every one of 18 "most influential" scholars in the field of international relations named in a recent study works on campus. See Bruce M. Russett, "Methodological and Theoretical Schools in International Relations" in Norman D. Palmer (ed.), *A Design for International Relations Research: Scope, Theory, Methods, and Relevance* (Monograph 10, The American Academy of Political and Social Science, Philadelphia, October 1970) p. 101. Most of the 18 have worked with government support at some time. Presumably the far more numerous nonacademic social scientists who work with government support must, by necessity or choice, get their satisfactions elsewhere, probably through a stronger commitment to client acceptance rather than to broader peer recognition.

[18]See Harold Orlans' remarks in the introduction to a Congressional report on the administration of federal social research: the reduction or elimination of"government control over the release of information gathered in the course of research *on campus* . . . has led to a lack of information (or even of that vital precursor to information, questions) about controls on the release of research information. For the problem has now, in large measure, been moved to a new institutional sector—that of the independent nonprofit or profit-making organization which subsists in good part by *doing* proprietary work for private and governmental clients. With a few notable exceptions . . . [such organizations] are accustomed to offering proprietary services, and are unlikely to complain about them." U.S. Congress, House of Representatives, Research and Technical Programs Subcommittee of the Committee on Government Operations, "The Use of Social Research in Federal Domestic Programs— Part IV, Current Issues in the Administration of Federal Social Research," p. 18. The same volume includes responses from numerous federal officials to a committee request for information on the kinds of controls maintained over the dissmeination of research products and the rationales for them.

[19]A study of the best-known member of the species is Bruce L. R. Smith, *The Rand Corporation: Case Study of a Nonprofit Advisory Corporation* (Cambridge: Harvard University Press, 1966). The Green article cited earlier is a review of this book.

[20]*Government-Supported Research—International Affairs, Research Completed and In Progress, July 1968-June 1969,* a report prepared for the Foreign Area Research Coordination Group by the Office of External Research, Department of State, November 1969. The next few pages draw largely on this document and the two reports cited in f.n. 10.

[21]Herbert C. Kelman, "The Use of University Resources in Foreign Policy Research," *International Studis Quarterly,* Vol. 12, No. 1, March 1968, p. 24).

[22]This is an estimate based on preliminary unpublished figures, prepared by executive agencies, for fiscal year 1970. Definitions of "basic" and "applied" research are of course notoriously variable.

[23]Report of the Committee on Government Sponsorship and Freedom of

Research, American Sociological Association, published in *The American Sociologist,* Vol. 3, November 1968, pp. 39-41.

[24] Department of State, Foreign Affairs Research Council, *Report,* p. 17.

[25] Albert D. Biderman and Elisabeth T. Crawford, "Paper Money: Trends of Research Sponsorship in American Sociology Journals," in *Social Science Information,* Paris, Vol. 9, No. 1, February 1970, p. 51.

[26] Africa Research Group, "African Studies in America: The Extended Family," (Cambridge, Mass., 1969), p. 2. (Pamphlet).

[27] In the late 1950s, for example, a congressional committee criticized the Department of State for commissioning domestic opinion polls. But the polling was stopped, mainly for economy reasons, even before the congressional action.

[28] The reluctance of the National Science Foundation, for example, to incorporate political science in its programs may have been due, according to some commentators, as much to political as to scientific reasons—unless political science is, indeed, less "scientific" than (say) anthropology.

[29] Paul F. Lazarsfeld once put it succinctly: "The main danger of commissioned research arises from the fact that for some practical problems there is more money available than for others." Lazarsfeld (in collaboration with Sydney S. Spivack), "Observations on Organized Social Research in the United States," A Report to the International Social Science Council (New York, August 1961), p. 37. Xeroxed.

[30] One consequence is of course to push research toward the "applied" end of the "basic-applied" spectrum. Applied research may, also, take on a somewhat conservative cast if the terms of reference discourage innovative work that may be too risky or too far removed from the short-term concerns of its sponsors.

[31] See, for example, Horowitz, "The Rise and Fall of Project Camelot," in Horowitz (ed.), *op. cit.,* especially pp. 30-34.

[32] The quotation is from T. V. Sathyamurthy, "From Containment to Interdependence," *World Politics,* Vol. XX, No. 1, October 1967, p. 147. The author seems to refer to "establishment" authors in general, not all of them necessarily financially linked to government patrons. But of the five "schools" identified by Levine in *The Arms Debate,* the three "marginalist" ones dominate "the councils of government, particularly of the executive branch," he says (p. 280). It seems likely that two of the three—the "anti-communist marginalists" and the "middle marginalists"—dominate among government counselors. On a somewhat different subject, Donald L. M. Blackmer deals with some aspects of the "unusually" close communication and rapport between academic specialists on the Soviet Union and their government counterparts in "Scholars and Policymakers: Perceptions of Soviet Policy" (a paper prepared for the 1968 Annual Meeting of the American Political Science Association). Crawford and Biderman (*op. cit.,* pp. 156-58) deal more generally and impressionistically with "political affinity and disaffection" in the relations of social scientists and the government and emphasize the great variety of considerations that have colored the attitudes of social scientists toward contractual arrangements.

[33] Letter from Thomas L. Hughes, Chairman of the State Department's

Foreign Affairs Research Council, published in the *American Anthropological Association Fellow Newsletter*, June 1968, p. 9.

[34] *Ibid.*

[35] Domestic political concern about the role of *operating* agencies in foreign affairs research is perhaps best reflected in the Senate's efforts to restrict the activities of the Department of Defense. Section 203 of the Military Procurement Authorization Act for Fiscal Year 1970 establishes that "none of the funds authorized to be appropriated by this Act may be used to carry out any research project or study, unless the project or study has a direct and apparent relationship to a specific military function or operation." In practice it is very difficult, however, to establish firm boundaries to the research interests of *any* agency.

[36] Many observers have rightly pointed out that government sponsorship is only one aspect of foreign sensitivity in research matters. See, for example: Klaus and Knorr, "Social Science Research Abroad, Problems and Remedies," *World Politics*, April 1967, Vol. XIX, No. 3, pp. 465-85.

[37] Robert A. Nisbet, "Project Camelot: an Autopsy," in *The Public Interest*, No. 5, Fall 1966, p. 59.

[38] Edward A. Shils, "Social Inquiry and the Autonomy of the Individual," in Daniel Lerner (ed.) *The Human Meaning of the Social Sciences* (New York: Meridian Books, 1959), p. 153.

[39] Gunnar Myrdal dealt with this problem almost 20 years ago: "The employment to an ever-increasing extent of social scientists in all sorts of practical tasks and, particularly, the coming into existence of a commercialized branch of social science raise, as I see it, the demand for a code of professional ethics for the guidance of social science practitioners." "The Relation Between Social Theory and Social Policy," in *The British Journal of Sociology*, Vol. IV, September 1953, p. 230. Many government agencies distinguish between nonacademic and academic contractors in their research programs, on the principle that the latter should be exempt from certain restrictions that may properly be imposed on the former.

[40] See Kelman, "The Use of University Resources," *loc. cit.*, p. 25: "When the sponsor has a visible interest in the outcome and a significant likelihood of acting on the findings, any one of us takes on a measure of responsibility by accepting his support."

[41] From the government side, two important recent statements are: "Privacy and Behavioral Research," issued by the Executive Office of the President, Office of Science and Technology, Washington, February 1967; and "Government Guidelines for Foreign Area Research," issued by the member agencies of the Foreign Area Research Coordination Group and published in *Far Horizons*, Vol. I, No. 1, January 1968. Among the more comprehensive documents issued by professional associations are: "Background Information on Problems of Anthropological Research and Ethics," prepared by Ralph L. Beals and the Executive Board of the American Anthropological Association, published in the *American Anthropological Association Newsletter*, Vol. 8, No. 1, January 1967; and "Ethical Problems of Academic Political Scientists," Final Report of the American Political Science Association Committee on Professional Standards and Responsibilities, published in

P.S., Newsletter of the American Political Science Association, Summer 1968, Vol. I, No. 3.

[42] Robert K. Merton and Daniel Lerner, "Social Scientists and Research Policy," in Lerner, Harold D. Lasswell and others, *The Policy Sciences, Recent Developments in Scope and Methods* (Stanford: Stanford University Press, 1951), pp. 29293.

[43] Raymond Platig, "Research and Analysis," in *Annals of the American Academy of Political and Social Science,* Vol. 380, November 1968, p. 53.

[44] *Ibid.*

[45] Raymond A. Bauer, "Social Psychology and the Study of Policy Formation," in *American Psychologist,* Vol. 21, No. 10, October 1966, p. 935.

[46] James R. Schlesinger, "The 'Soft' Factors in Systems Studies," in *Bulletin of the Atomic Scientists,* November 1968, pp. 14-15.

Name and Title Index

Agnew, Spiro, 106
Archibald, Kathleen, 280
Arias, Gino, 100

Bauer, Raymond A., 333
*Behavioral and Social Sciences:
Outlook and Needs, The* (National Research Council and Social Science Research Council),
133
*Behavioral Sciences and the Federal
Government, The* (Advisory Committee of the National Academy of Sciences—National Research Council), 133
Bell, Daniel, 167
Ben Gurion, David, 253
Bentham, Jeremy, 109
Bernstein, Leonard, 256, 258
Biderman, Albert, 323
Blake, Herman, 244-6
Boggs, Hale, 235
Bolitho, William, 90

Bottai, Giuseppe, 100-1
Botticelli, Sandro, 301
Boulding, Kenneth E., 34
Bukharin, Nicolai, 229
Bundy, McGeorge, 182, 185

Califano, Joseph, 156
Cantril, Hadley, 63
Capital (Marx), 247
Chicago Tribune, 246
Chinitz, Benjamin, 71
Chomsky, Noam, 167
Cooke, Terence J., 235
Corradini, Enrico, 95, 99
Creed, Dana S., 183
Cutler, Lloyd, 236

De Begnac, Ivon, 105
Deutsch, Karl W., 313
Dingell, John, 303
Disney, Walt, 258
Dror, Yehezkel, 73-4, 109, 198
DuBridge, Lee, 89

345

Durkheim, Emile, 26

Eayrs, James, 8
Einstein, Albert, 312
Eisenhower, Dwight D., 199, 303
Eisenhower, Milton, 235, 245
Eshkol, Levi, 258
Etzioni, Amitai, 24

Finch, Robert F., 162
Fitzgerald, F. Scott, 200
Foundation Directory, The (Russell
  Sage), 184-5
Franck, Louis R., 100
Friedenberg, Edgar Z., 55
Friedman, Milton, 307

Galbraith, John Kenneth, 7, 37
Galili, Israel, 251-2
Gans, Herbert J., 13, 65
Gardner, John, 151
Garry, Charles, 244
General Electric Defense Quarterly,
  279
Ginsburg, David, 236-7
Givton, Hanoch, 252, 254
Goldwater, Barry, 303
Gonzales, "Corky," 67
Guttman, Louis, 251

Handler, Philip, 138
Harrington, Michael, 58
Harris, Patricia, 235
Hart, Philip A., 235
Harvest of American Racism, The
  (Shellow et al.), 218
Heilbroner, Robert L., 56
Heyman, Ira, 243
Higginbotham, A. Leon, 235, 244-6
Hitler, Adolph, 102
Hoffer, Eric, 235, 244-6
Holmes, Oliver Wendell, 319
Horowitz, Irving Louis, 1, 102, 170
Horowitz, Ruth Leonora, 170
Howard, John, 52
Hruska, Roman, 235
Humphrey, Hubert H., 303
Hunt, H.L., 189
Huntington, Samuel P., 300

Index of Economic Journals, 40-1,
  43-4, 46, 48

Jaworski, Leon, 235
Jenner, Albert E., Jr., 235, 245
Jevons, W.S., 50
Johnson, Lyndon B., 71-2, 157,
  207, 214, 223, 235-7, 303, 307
Johnson, Samuel, 155

Katz, Elihu, 249
Kaufmann, William W., 272
Kelman, Herbert, 320-1
Kennedy, John F., 71-2, 157, 199,
  203, 207, 303, 306
Kennedy, Robert F., 237, 239
Keynes, John Maynard, 7, 306
Khruschchev, Nikita S., 299
Kissinger, Henry, 272
Knowledge into Action (Special
  Commission on the Social Sci-
  ences to the National Science
  Board), 133
Kopkind, Andrew, 235-7

La Huelga, 67
Lane, Robert, 52
Lang, Kurt, 212
Lasswell, Harold, 15, 150
Ledeen, Michael A., 90
Lerner, Daniel, 329-30
Licklider, Roy E., 272
Lindblom, Charles E., 299
Lorwin, Lewis, 306
Love Machine, The (Susann), 241
Lynd, Robert, 206, 210
Lyons, Gene M., 133

McCarthy, Joseph, 181
McCulloch, William M., 235
McFarland, Ernest W., 235
McNamara, Robert S., 204

Magat, Richard, 191
Marx, Karl, 247
Menninger, W. Walter, 235
Merriam, Charles, 150
Merton, Robert K., 329-30
Mills, C. Wright, 7, 20

Missiroli, Mario, 104
Mosse, George, 102
Moynihan, Daniel Patrick, 56, 204
Murray, James, 303
Mussolini, Arnaldo, 100, 106
Mussolini, Benito, 91-2, 94-7, 102-6

Neustadt, Richard, 206
New Republic, The, 307
Newton, Huey P. 244
Nisbet, Robert, 327
Nixon, Richard M., 88, 156-7, 165, 204

Oppenheimer, J. Robert, 140

Palmieri, Victor, 236
Parenti, Michael, 65
Parsons, Talcott, 25
Pastore, A., 221
Pechman, Joseph, 307
Peled, Elad, 251-2, 254
Peled, Uzi, 259, 266, 268
Pigou, A.C., 42
Platig, E. Raymond, 331
Policy Sciences, 205
Politics of Protest, The (Skolnick), 239, 241, 246-7
Polsby, Nelson W., 296
Pool, Ithiel de Sola, 310
Popolo d'Italia, 100
Public Interest, The, 205, 307

Quarterly Journal of Economics, 40

Ribicoff, Abraham, 156, 300
Robinson, James, 299
Rocco, Alfredo, 98-9
Ronen, Yoram, 266-7
Roosevelt, Franklin D., 302-3
Rossoni, Edmondo, 93-100, 103

St. Augustine, 322
Scammon, Richard, 306
Schelling, Thomas, 292
Schlesinger, James R., 333
Schorr, Alvin, 54, 155
Schrag, Peter, 53

Science, 221
Seidman, Bert, 57
Seligman, Ben B., 67
Shanker, Albert, 182
Shellow, Robert, 236-7
Shils, Edward, 328
Short, James F., Jr., 238
Skolnick, Jerome H., 234
Smith, Ian, 267
Spellman, Francis, 235
Stone, I.F., 246
Survival (Institute for Strategic Studies, London), 285
Susskind, David, 270
Suttles, Gerald, 65
Swift, Jonathan, 168

Taylor, A.J.P., 91
Theobald, Robert, 307
Thornton, Charles, 237
Tijerina, Rijes, 67
Tobin, James, 307
*trans*action, 205
Tree, Lloyd A., 63
Truman, David, 299
Truman, Harry S., 207, 303
Turati, Augusto, 95

Uhr, Carl, 55
Uliassi, Pio D., 309

Vadikan, James, 54, 57
Volpe, Gioacchino, 102

Wagner, Robert, 303
Wallace, Henry, 202
Walras, Leon, 50
Weber, Max, 109
Weidenbaum, Murray L., 86
Wilde, Oscar, 310
Witte, Edwin, 303
Wohlstetter, Albert, 272
Wolfgang, Marvin, 238
World (New York), 90

Yahil, Haim, 266
Yarmolinsky, Adam, 196

CONTRIBUTORS

Kenneth E. Boulding

Professor of economics at the University of Colorado and program director of the Program of Research on General Social and Economic Dynamics at the Institute of Behavioral Science. His books include: *The Meaning of the Twentieth Century, The Impact of the Social Sciences,* and most recently, *Economics as a Science.*

Benjamin Chinitz

Professor of economics at Brown University. During 1965-66 he served as Deputy Assistant Secretary of Commerce for Economic Development. His research is supported by the Ford Foundation.

Yehezkel Dror

Professor of political science at the Hebrew University of Jerusalem and the World Institute, Jerusalem. He is the author, with Benjamin Aiken of *High Pressure Planning,* and most recently, of *Public Policy-making Reexamined.*

Herbert J. Gans

Professor of sociology and planning, Massachusetts Institute of Technology and MIT-Harvard Joint Center for Urban Studies. Among his books are *The Urban Villagers, The Levittowners,* and *People and Plans.*

Irving Louis Horowitz

Professor of sociology and chairman of the department of sociology at Livingston College, Rutgers University. He is the editor of Studies in Comparative International Development, and editor-in-chief of *trans*action magazine. He is the author of numerous books on policy-making, international affairs, and political sociology.

Ruth Leonora Horowitz

Teaches in the political science department at the University of Washington, Seattle. She is completing her doctorate at Washington University on the policies of organized labor toward social reform in the New Deal period.

John Howard

Associate professor of sociology at Livingston College, Rutgers University. He is the co-author of *Life Styles in the Black Ghetto,* coeditor of *Where It's At: Radical Perspectives in Sociology,* and editor of *Awakening Minorities.* In September, 1971 he will become Dean of the social science division of the State University of New York at Purchase, New York.

Elihu Katz

Director of the Communications Institute of the Hebrew University of Jerusalem and a member of the Department of Sociology at the Israel Institute for Applied Social Research, Jerusalem. Among the books he has authored or co-authored are *Personal Influence, The Politics of Community Conflict,* and *Medical Innovation.*

Kurt Lang

Professor of sociology at the department of sociology, State University of New York at Stony Brook. He is the author, with Gladys E. Lang, of *Politics and Television, Voting and Non-Voting,* and *Collective Dynamics.*

Michael A. Ledeen

Assistant professor of history at Washington University, St. Louis, Missouri. He is the author of a forthcoming book *Universal Fascism, The Theory and Practice of the Fascist International.*

Roy E. Licklider

Assistant professor of political science at Douglass College, Rutgers University. He formerly taught at Tougaloo College. He is the author of the forthcoming *The Strategic Community.*

Gene M. Lyons

Professor of government, Dartmouth College. He is presently on leave to serve as director of the Department of Social Sciences at Unesco. His most recent book is *The Uneasy Partnership: Social Science and the Federal Government in the Twentieth Century.*

Nelson W. Polsby

Professor of political science, University of California at Berkeley. Among his books are *Congress and the Presidency,* and most recently, *Presidential Politics* with Aaron Wildavsky.

Alvin L. Schorr

Associated with the Florence Heller Center for Advanced Studies in Social Welfare, Brandeis University. He is the author of *Poor Kids: A Report on Children in Poverty* and *Explorations in Social Policy.*

Jerome H. Skolnick

Professor at the University of California at Berkeley School of Criminology and research sociologist at the Center for the Study of Law and Society there. He was director of the Task Force on Violent Aspects of Protest and

Confrontation of the National Commission on the Causes and Prevention of Violence. He is the author of *Justice Without Trial.*

Murray L. Weidenbaum

Assistant Secretary of the Treasury for Economic Policy. He is on leave from Washington University, St. Louis, where he is professor of economics. His most recent book is *The Modern Public Sector.*

Adam Yarmolinsky

Professor of law at Harvard and a member of the Institute of Politics of the JFK School at Harvard. He is currently on leave from Harvard as Chief Executive Officer of the Welfare Island Development Corporation. He served in the Kennedy-Johnson administrations as special assistant to the Secretary of Defense and Deputy Director of the President's Anti-Poverty Task Force.

Pio D. Uliassi

Chief of the Academic Relations Division of the Office of External Research, Department of State, Washington, D.C.